Louisiana Politics

Louisiana Politics

FESTIVAL IN A LABYRINTH

Edited by James Bolner

Louisiana State University Press
Baton Rouge and London

Copyright © 1982 by Louisiana State University Press
All rights reserved
Manufactured in the United States of America

Designer: Joanna Hill
Typeface: Primer
Typesetter: G & S Typesetters, Inc.
Printer: Thomson-Shore, Inc.
Binder: John H. Dekker and Sons

Mark T. Carleton's essay, "The Louisiana Constitution of 1974," was originally
published, in slightly different form, in the *Tulane Law Review*.

LIBRARY OF CONGRESS CATALOGING IN PUBLICATION DATA

Main entry under title:
Louisiana politics.
Includes index.
Contents: Louisiana political culture / David M.
Landry and Joseph B. Parker—The Louisiana
Constitution of 1974 / Mark T. Carleton—The
Legislature / Patrick O'Connor—[etc.]
1. Louisiana—Politics and government—
1951– —Addresses, essays, lectures.
I. Bolner, James.
JK4719.L68   320.9763   81-15593
ISBN 0-8071-0983-5   AACR2
ISBN 0-8071-0984-3 (pbk.)

Contents

Maps   vii

Figures   ix

Tables   xi

Preface   xv

1. The Louisiana Political Culture
   DAVID M. LANDRY AND JOSEPH B. PARKER   1

2. The Louisiana Constitution of 1974
   MARK T. CARLETON   15

3. The Legislature
   PATRICK F. O'CONNOR   43

4. The Governor
   ED RENWICK   75

5. The Judiciary
   RONALD M. LABBÉ   89

6. The Bureaucracy
   CHARLES HOLBROOK AND MARK T. CARLETON   123

7. Parish Government
   JUNE SAVOY ROWELL   143

8. Municipal Government
   RICHARD L. ENGSTROM   181

9. Intergovernmental Relations
   RILEY BAKER   221

10. Political Parties
    PAUL GROSSER   255

11. Blacks in Louisiana Politics
     JEWEL L. PRESTAGE AND CAROLYN SUE WILLIAMS   285
12. Voting Behavior in Gubernatorial Elections
     JOHN WILDGEN   319
     Appendix: Louisiana Statistical Data   345
     Notes on Contributors   363
     Index   367

Maps

1-1   Cultural Regions in Louisiana   3
1-2   Nonwhite Population of Louisiana Parishes   6
5-1   Louisiana Courts of Appeal Circuits   108
5-2   Louisiana Supreme Court Districts   111
12-1   Percentage Voting for Huey Long, 1928   321
12-2   Population Distribution, 1970   322
12-3   Percentage of Blacks in the Population, 1970   323
12-4   Percentage Voting for Earl Long, 1956   324
12-5   Percentage of Population Illiterate, 1970   332
12-6   Median Family Income, 1970   333
12-7   Percentage Voting for Davis, 1959   334
12-8   Percentage of the Population Roman Catholic, 1970   335
12-9   Percentage Voting for Edwards, 1971   337
12-10 Percentage Voting for Treen, 1979   338

Figures

5-1	Louisiana State Court System	102
6-1	Growth in the Number of Classified Employees in Louisiana	129
6-2	Departments Under Statewide Elected Officials and the Department of Public Service	137
6-3	Departments Under the Direct Control of the Governor and the Department of Civil Service	138
7-1	Organization of Louisiana Parish Government	146
7-2	Police Jury Organizational Plan	149
7-3	Baton Rouge City-Parish Government	153
7-4	New Orleans City-Parish Government	154
7-5	Proposed Reorganization of Parish Government	178
12-1	Bifactionalism, 1944–1948: Davis and Long	325
12-2	Bifactionalism, 1948–1952: Long and Kennon	326
12-3	Bifactionalism, 1952–1956: Kennon and Long	327
12-4	Ticketing in 1952: Kennon and Moore	329
12-5	Income Disparity in Louisiana, 1970	331
12-6	Major Realignment, 1956–1960: Long and Davis	335
12-7	Neo-Bourbon Succession, 1960–1964: Davis and McKeithen	336
12-8	Gubernatorial Alignments, 1896–1979	336
12-9	Ticketing in 1971: Edwards and Bernard	340
12-10	Insulation of Presidential and Gubernatorial Voting	341

Tables

3-1	Republicans in the Louisiana Legislature	48
3-2	Competition in Legislative Primaries in Louisiana and Other Southern States	51
3-3	Membership Stability in the Louisiana Legislature	53
3-4	Occupations of Louisiana Legislators	55
3-5	Legislative Committees and Bill Assignments, 1978	61
3-6	Number and Sizes of Standing Committees, 1952–1976	62
3-7	Turnover of Committee Chairmen, 1956–1976	64
3-8	Continuity of Committee Assignments	66
5-1	Cases Filed and Opinions Rendered in the Louisiana Supreme Court	113
5-2	Civil and Criminal Appeals Affirmed and Reversed, 1976	115
6-1	Race and Sex of Classified Employees and General Population	127
6-2	Age of Classified Employees and General Population	127
6-3	State Employment Turnover	130
7-1	Socioeconomic Statistics for Louisiana Parishes	147
7-2	State Tax Allocated to Local Governmental Units, 1972–1973	157
7-3	Parishes and Judges Within Louisiana Judicial Districts	164
7-4	Selected Powers of Parish Governing Bodies over Special Districts	170
8-1	Municipalities Incorporated, 1969–1978	185

8-2 Municipalities by Type of Charter and Population
      as of May 13, 1978   186
8-3 Municipalities with Special Legislative Charters, 1978   187
8-4 Municipalities Adopting Commission Plan of
      Government, 1910–1919   192
8-5 Municipalities with Commission Form of Government
      in 1969   194
8-6 Municipalities with Home Rule Charters Under the
      General Provision of the 1921 Constitution   206
8-7 New Home Rule Municipalities, 1974–1978   208
8-8 Numbers of Local Governments Within Louisiana
      SMSAs   214
9-1 Percentages of Louisiana General Revenue Derived
      from Federal Aid, 1940–1979   232
9-2 State Payments to Local Governments in Selected
      Years by Type of Government   246
10-1 Dimensions of Political Cleavages in Louisiana Politics   270
10-2 Louisiana Social and Economic Development,
      1950–1970   271
10-3 Changes in Selected Louisiana Social and Economic
      Dimensions, 1950–1970   273
10-4 Republican Party Registration, 1975–1980   277
10-5 1980 Presidential Election in Louisiana   280
11-1 Slaveholding Among Louisiana Families, 1840   287
11-2 Black Voter Registration in Louisiana, 1910–1964 299
11-3 Black Percentage of Population as Related to
      Other Political Factors, 1959–1964   303
11-4 Black Voter Registration in Louisiana, 1965–1979 305
11-5 Black Elected Officials, 1968–1979   306
11-6 Voter Registration in Urban Areas   312

Appendix
  1 Louisiana Parish Population and Social Statistics, 1970   347
  2 Louisiana Standard Metropolitan Statistical Area
      Population and Social Statistics, 1970   349
  3 1975 and 1976 Louisiana Parish Election Data   350
  4 1975 and 1976 Louisiana Standard Metropolitan
      Statistical Area Election Data   353

5 1979 Louisiana Parish Gubernatorial and Lieutenant
Gubernatorial Election Data   354
6 1980 Louisiana Parish Presidential Election Data   356
7 1980 Louisiana Standard Metropolitan Statistical Area
Presidential Election Data   358
8 1980 Louisiana Population by Race and Spanish
Origin and Housing Counts   359

Preface

All institutions of higher learning in Louisiana offer one or more courses dealing with the state's political life; yet, for many years teachers of these courses have complained about the lack of materials on Louisiana government and politics suitable for use in college-level courses. Teachers have been forced to rely on the works of sociologists and historians, the bare text of the state constitution, journalists' commentary, and the publications of such organizations as the Public Affairs Research Council and the League of Women Voters.[1] No current work examines the state's political processes—clearly among the most exciting and provocative in the nation—from the perspective of modern political science. The present work is the response of the political science profession in Louisiana to this need. The initial suggestion that the book be written was made at a conference on teaching political science sponsored by the Louisiana Political Science Association at Louisiana State University in 1976.

Each of the twelve chapters in the book deals with a major aspect of Louisiana government and politics. All except those dealing with local

1. Louisiana Legislative Council, *The History and Government of Louisiana*, updated by Riley E. Baker (Baton Rouge: Claitor's, 1975), is primarily a descriptive guide to the state's history and governmental agencies. William C. Havard's somewhat more critical *Government of Louisiana* (Baton Rouge: Louisiana State University, Bureau of Public Administration, 1958) has long been out of print. The collection of materials by Mark T. Carleton, Perry H. Howard, and Joseph B. Parker (eds.), *Readings in Louisiana Politics* (Baton Rouge: Claitor's, 1975) is a helpful historical collection but suffers from a lack of contemporary material. Other works of special relevance to an understanding of the state's political life include: Perry H. Howard, *Political Tendencies in Louisiana, 1912–1952* (rev. ed.; Baton Rouge: Louisiana State University Press, 1971); Perry H. Howard, "Louisiana: Resistance and Change," in William C. Havard (ed.), *The Chang-*

government and intergovernmental relations focus on government at the state level. While the chapters may be read independently and out of the order in which they appear, the chapter topics themselves suggest a general ordering. The chapters on the state's political culture and the 1974 constitution are introductory. The next three chapters treat the three major branches of the state government and the state bureaucracy. The remaining chapters discuss various facets of local government and politics and the interaction of these local units with the state and national political institutions and processes.

Readers will note that the book lacks a "unifying theme." The authors and the editor agreed at the outset that it would be best to approach each topic independently and that to attempt to pursue a "theme" would give the work a stilted quality. It has been my task to minimize duplication; I readily concede that on occasion an item—say, the governor's legislative role—has been treated more than once; however, the treatments have sufficiently differing points of view to justify their inclusion. The appendix is intended to enhance the volume's value as an instructional and reference resource.

While the authors have used the most recent information available to them, complete 1980 census data were unavailable. Preliminary 1980 population data by parish and parish subdivision are included in the appendix.

During the time that this book was being prepared for publication the title it carried was simply *Louisiana Politics*. As the project neared completion, it occurred to me that this was too plain a title for so colorful a subject. I considered a number of likely candidates: "Louisiana Politics: The Pelican's Maw," "Come to the Political Crawfish Boil," "A Recipe for Political Jambalaya," and others. While toying with the con-

---

ing Politics of the South (Baton Rouge: Louisiana State University Press, 1972); William C. Havard, Rudolf Heberle, and Perry H. Howard, *The Louisiana Elections of 1960* (Baton Rouge: Louisiana State University Press, 1963); Perry H. Howard, Maxwell E. McCombs, and David M. Kovenock, "Louisiana," in David M. Kovenock, James W. Prothro, *et al.* (eds.), *Explaining the Vote: Presidential Choices in the Nation and the States, 1968* (Chapel Hill: Institute for Research in Social Science, 1973), ch. 15; Allan P. Sindler, *Huey Long's Louisiana: State Politics, 1920–1952* (Baltimore: Johns Hopkins University Press, 1956); T. Harry Williams, *Huey Long* (New York: Knopf, 1969); William I. Hair, *Bourbonism and Agrarian Protest: Louisiana Politics, 1877–1900* (Baton Rouge: Louisiana State University Press, 1969); and Joe Gray Taylor, *Louisiana: A Bicentennial History* (New York: Norton, 1976).

cept of festival—virtually every Louisiana hamlet has one—I hit upon
the combination of "festival" in a "labyrinth." Many of the definitions
of *labyrinth* provided in *Webster's Third New International Dictionary*
suit our subject extraordinarily well. Consider how richly these apply
to Louisiana's festal politics: "a structure full of intricate passageways
that make it difficult to find the way from the interior to the entrance
or from the entrance to the center"; "a maze in a park or garden
formed by paths separated by high thick hedges"; "something often
bewilderingly involved or tortuous in structure, arrangement or character: a complex that baffles exploration (as of mind) from which it
is difficult to extricate oneself"; "an intricate sometimes symbolic
pattern; *specif*: such a pattern inlaid in the pavement of a medieval
church"; "a device consisting of an arrangement (as a succession of
grooves and rings; tortuous passageways) usu. for the purpose of offering resistance to fluid flow (as to prevent leakage . . .)"; and even this
one, "an enclosure consisting of an undulatory passage connected
to the rear of a loudspeaker and providing improved low frequency
response."

This book tells of the festivals through which Louisianians celebrate
their political life and heritage. It does not demolish the labyrinth, but
it describes its layout so that those who read here will learn something
about hedges designed to block political views and about "tortuous
passageways" that offer "resistance to the fluid flow" of the public will.
It is my hope that those who use this book will be enlightened as to the
darker intricacies of the labyrinth, that the festivals will one day celebrate the eradication of ignorance and corruption in this beautiful
place.

Many persons contributed much to the editing of this book. Donn
Kurtz, professor of political science at the University of Southwestern
Louisiana, contributed the majority of the tables in the Appendix. I
wish to thank my colleagues, Cecil V. Crabb, Jr., and Ellis Sandoz, for
supporting the project while serving their respective terms as chairman of Louisiana State University's Department of Political Science;
Josephine Scurria, Angela Dupont, and Linda Cook for helping with
the typing; Beverly Jarrett, Martha Hall, Joanna Hill, and Judith Bailey
of the LSU Press for their editorial assistance and encouragement;
Carol Shivers, my dedicated student worker, whose patience and dili-

gence have been truly outstanding; Janet Montelaro and Dick Hoff-
man for their generous assistance in preparing the charts and graphs;
my former graduate assistant John Gates for his time and talents; and
my wife for her innumerable suggestions and her unfailing support
and understanding.

Louisiana Politics

1.

The Louisiana Political Culture

DAVID M. LANDRY AND JOSEPH B. PARKER

Gabriel A. Almond and Sidney Verba define political culture as "the specifically political orientations—attitudes toward the political system and its various parts, and attitudes toward the role of the self in the system."[1] To understand the attitudes of Louisianians toward their political system, one must first examine the ethnic heterogeneity, the economic tensions, and the political expectations of the citizens. With these factors in mind, we can better determine how Louisianians see their role within their political system and what expectations they have of their government.

Ethnic and Geographic Diversity

The political culture of Louisiana derives from a unique mixture of Mediterranean, Anglo-Saxon, and Afro-American values. The state's present ethnic distribution reflects the various colonial settlements in Louisiana's colorful history. The French were the first to settle in New Orleans, followed by the Spanish. These groups, together with a large population of Italians, make New Orleans a predominantly Catholic city and give it a distinctly Mediterranean character. The Acadiana region, which comprises twenty-two parishes in southern Louisiana, was also settled by French Catholics, exiles from Acadia (Nova Scotia) after the French ceded Canada to Britain. The number of Acadians, or Cajuns, as they have come to be called, has swelled from fifteen thou-

1. Gabriel A. Almond and Sidney Verba, *The Civic Culture: Political Attitudes and Democracy in Five Nations* (Princeton: Princeton University Press, 1963), 12.

sand in the 1760s to over one million today. In fact, about 40 percent of the state's present population can claim French ancestry. Like the New Orleanians, the people of Acadiana are Mediterranean in their outlook. They are known for their friendliness, frankness, and zest for life. Cajuns are quick to point out that they differ from their neighbors in the northern part of the state, and they are proud of their resistance to assimilation into Anglo-Saxon culture.

Largely because of the Latin tradition of tolerance, racism was rarely as intense or, one might argue, was never as institutionalized in South Louisiana as it was in other parts of the South. In the French parishes, for example, a higher percentage of blacks were registered to vote prior to the 1965 Voting Rights Act than in any other area of the South. Nor did the Ku Klux Klan find much support in South Louisiana primarily because the Klan is anti-Catholic as well as antiblack.[2]

A generally more tolerant attitude prevails throughout South Louisiana. The sale of alcoholic beverages on Sundays has never been an issue there, and gambling is a widespread pastime among Cajuns, although it is illegal by state statute. According to Marc R. Gore, senior intelligence analyst with the Louisiana State Police, Criminal Intelligence Section, illegal gambling is the state's third largest industry, with a value of $244,695,000.[3] Most South Louisianians also tend to support public financial assistance to parochial schools and to oppose legalized abortion, reflecting their Catholicism.

The thirty parishes of North Louisiana have more in common with neighboring Texas, Arkansas, and Mississippi in terms of political culture than with the southern part of the state. The Anglo-Saxon Protestants who settled the area during the nineteenth century have always been suspicious of the Cajun life-style and the uninhibited activities in New Orleans, "the city that care forgot." The more conservative North Louisianians generally support antigambling proposals, Sunday blue laws, and restrictions or bans on the sale of alcoholic beverages. Many of these voters oppose public aid for parochial schools.

The contrast between North and South Louisiana was recently demonstrated by the referendum on the 1974 state constitution. The

2. John H. Fenton and Kenneth N. Vines, "Negro Registration in Louisiana," *American Political Science Review*, LI (September, 1957), 713; Joe Gray Taylor, *Louisiana* (New York: Norton, 1977), 159.

3. Marc R. Gore, "Illegal Gambling in Louisiana," *Louisiana Business Survey*, VII (October, 1977), 3.

Map 1-1
Cultural Regions in Louisiana

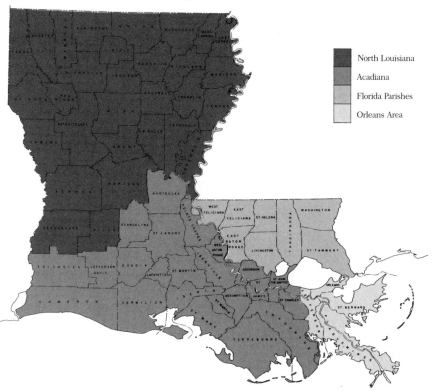

North Louisiana

Acadiana

Florida Parishes

Orleans Area

Outline map compiled and drawn by Louisiana State Department of Highways, Traffic and Planning Section

constitution lacked a prohibition against state support for parochial schools, and it contained a strongly worded provision on equal rights. It was opposed by the Republican Central Committee, the Louisiana Association of Manufacturers, and a number of fundamentalist clergy-men.[4] A majority of North Louisiana's voters, 60.8 percent, voted against the constitution. On the other hand, the AFL-CIO, the NAACP, the Catholic bishops, and the political allies of Governor Edwin Ed-

4. Public Affairs Research Council, "Special Election on the Constitution, April 20, 1974," *Analysis* (April, 1974), 2–15.

wards, the first French-speaking governor of the state in the twentieth century, supported the constitution. As expected, Acadiana and metropolitan New Orleans supported it, too. It was a clear demonstration of the state's cultural cleavages.

Religious differences explain some of the divergences between North and South Louisiana, but in the last twenty years, the most dramatic change in the regional balance of power has been South Louisiana's growth in population and in economic power. The northern section of the state, until recently, generally dominated both the state legislature and the governor's office. Now, however, only 32 percent of the state's population resides in the thirty northern parishes. The region's political influence is in decline. While many northern parishes have been losing population, the parishes of the South have been gaining in population. Reapportionment has given the Acadiana and New Orleans areas 64 of the 105 representatives in the house of representatives. There are only 29 from North Louisiana, and 12 from the Florida parishes. In the senate 23 of the 39 senators are from either Acadiana or the Orleans area.[5]

South Louisiana has also thrived economically in comparison to the North. In 1975 the median family income in Acadiana was $6,787 and in the Orleans area was $8,979, but in the North Louisiana parishes the median income was only $5,634.[6] As the petrochemical industries and the exploration for oil and gas have expanded in South Louisiana, the population has grown, and the nature of politics has changed from rural populism to urban populism and from rural Bourbon-like conservatism to *nouveau riche* suburban conservatism. The once dominant populism of the rural dirt farmer in the hill country of North Louisiana is now being replaced by the liberal forces of blacks in the larger metropolitan areas and the labor unions located mostly in the river parishes. The old planter conservatives of the delta have now been replaced by a growing class of entrepreneurs and managers throughout the state.

A. J. Liebling in his book *The Earl of Louisiana* found the balance between the Catholics in southern Louisiana and the Protestants in

5. Public Affairs Research Council, *Citizens' Guide to the 1976 Louisiana Legislature* (Baton Rouge: Public Affairs Research Council, 1976), 19–22.
6. Compiled from *Statistical Abstract of Louisiana* (n.p., n.d.), Table VII–13, pp. 218–20.

the North to be as delicate as the balance between the Moslems and the Christians in Lebanon. In Louisiana, however, there is a third group, as well, to complicate matters even further. After a long period of disfranchisement, blacks have made important political inroads in recent years. Large numbers of blacks were registered to vote in the late nineteenth century before the Bourbon-planter elite manipulated state laws to keep them from the polls. The 1898 constitutional convention adopted numerous provisions that reduced the number of registered black voters from 130,444 in 1896 to 5,320 in 1900. Following the Voting Rights Act of 1965, black registration soared again. By 1976, 22.6 percent of the people registered to vote in Louisiana were black. This figure is quite close to the percentage of blacks in the general population—27 percent. In addition, federally mandated reapportionment has given blacks more clout at the polls. Their influence extends over the entire state but is most pronounced in the metropolitan areas and in East Feliciana, West Feliciana, Tensas, St. Helena, Madison, and East Carroll parishes, where blacks make up over 50 percent of the registered voters. In New Orleans, where one-fourth of all the blacks in the state reside, 44 percent of all registrants are black.[7]

Blacks in the core city areas and the river parishes have been an important source of support for the more liberal populist candidates in recent elections. New black political organizations have been very effective in increasing voter turnout. The Southern Organization for Unified Leadership (SOUL) and the Community Organization for Urban Politics (COUP) are two of the largest black groups in New Orleans.[8] In 1977 black voting strength in New Orleans resulted in the election of that city's first black mayor. Ernest "Dutch" Morial achieved victory by garnering 94 percent of the votes cast by blacks.

In statewide races the black vote is considered critical, and if it is combined with a majority of the blue-collar vote in Acadiana and North Louisiana, it can constitute a winning combination for the more liberal candidate. Both Edwin Edwards and Jimmy Carter capitalized on this coalition, as did the proconstitution forces in 1974. Any fairly

7. A. J. Liebling, *The Earl of Louisiana* (New York: Simon and Schuster, 1961), 15; Perry H. Howard, *Political Tendencies in Louisiana, 1912–1952* (rev. ed.; Baton Rouge: Louisiana State University Press, 1971), 170; Jack Bass and Walter DeVries, *The Transformation of Southern Politics* (New York: Basic Books, 1976), 179; James Calhoun (ed.), *Louisiana Almanac, 1975–76* (Gretna, La.: Pelican Press, 1977), 345.
8. Bass and DeVries, *The Transformation of Southern Politics,* 179.

Map 1-2
Nonwhite Population of Louisiana Parishes

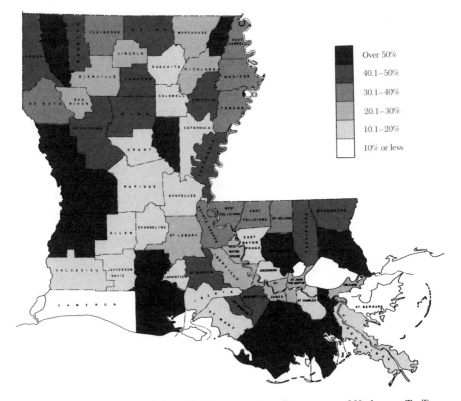

■	Over 50%
■	40.1–50%
■	30.1–40%
■	20.1–30%
■	10.1–20%
□	10% or less

Outline map compiled and drawn by Louisiana State Department of Highways, Traffic and Planning Section

liberal or populist candidate will have to mobilize this coalition to win a statewide election. Louis Lambert put this coalition together in his unsuccessful bid for governor in 1979. Under very adverse conditions, he received 49.7 percent of the vote (96 percent of the black vote). He lost badly only in the more affluent conservative suburban parishes such as Jefferson, Lafayette, Terrebonne, and Caddo. Neo-Bourbons and Republicans ruled the day again in 1980 when Jimmy Carter failed to put together a winning coalition.

Neo-Bourbons and Neo-Populists

The ethnic and regional differences, although they are the roots of much controversy, are not the only sources of political conflict in the state. The classic southern struggle between the economically conservative Bourbons and the more liberal Populists continues to be a major influence on Louisiana's political culture. The poor Baptist dirt farmer in the hills of North Louisiana tends now to unite with the blue-collar Cajuns of Acadiana and the blacks of New Orleans against the more affluent business and professional groups of suburbia on the "bread and butter" economic issues. The presidential race in 1976 and the gubernatorial contest in 1979 illustrated this trend well. In both elections blacks, workers, and the poorer citizens in Acadiana and the North supported the more liberal candidate, while suburban and wealthier voters backed the more conservative candidate.

Louisiana has been able to juggle the Bourbon-like fiscal conservatism and the more liberal Populist philosophy of taxing and spending. The two philosophies enjoy an uneasy coexistence. The Bourbons prevailed during the nineteenth and early twentieth centuries, but since the days of Huey P. Long, public policy has been strongly influenced by Populist demands. The Populists have traditionally supported the expansion of government services of the sort first provided by the New Deal and greatly expanded by the Great Society on the federal level. They have favored the redistribution of wealth—taking from the rich to give to the poor—and they have had considerable success in placing the financial burden for government services on the business community, particularly the big corporations. The state relies heavily on oil and gas severance taxes, whose impact is felt mainly by consumers outside of Louisiana. Most middle- to low-income Louisiana families face very little taxation. Property taxes are particularly low; there is no state sales tax on food or drugs; and state income tax is also quite low. The average citizen has benefited from generous government services without the heavy tax burden usually required to pay for them, and he expects this state of affairs to continue.[9]

The neo-Bourbons have controlled the governor's mansion only

9. Howard, *Political Tendencies in Louisiana*, 155–294; Public Affairs Research Council, "Resolving Louisiana's Financial Dilemma," *Analysis* (March, 1977), 4.

three times since the election of Huey Long, Louisiana's premier Populist: during the administrations of Sam Jones, 1940–1944; Robert Kennon, 1952–1956; and most recently, David Treen, 1980–present. The business community and the oil and gas companies are, of course, neo-Bourbons, and one of their primary spokesmen is the Louisiana Association of Business and Industry (LABI). This group wants government programs curtailed and private enterprise unhindered. It favors businesslike efficiency in government, a balanced state budget, and the lowest possible taxes, especially on corporate income and property. If new revenues are needed and increased taxes are unavoidable, the neo-Bourbons prefer the sales tax since it is a consumer's tax whose largest burden falls on middle- or lower-income groups. The neo-Bourbons generally stand for what they call "good government," which translates to the Populist as less government and thus less revenue for state programs.

Neo-Bourbons find their support in the more affluent suburban parishes of Jefferson, St. Tammany, Terrebonne, East Baton Rouge, Lafayette, and Caddo. They were chiefly responsible for the election of David Treen, Louisiana's first Republican governor in over one hundred years, and they supported Gerald Ford in 1976. For example, Jefferson Parish, with the highest per capita income in the state, gave 57 percent of its vote to Ford in 1976—the highest percentage of any parish in the state—and 64 percent to Treen in 1979. Both of Louisiana's Republican congressmen have also had their political base of support in suburbia—one in New Orleans' suburbs and one in Baton Rouge's suburbs. The neo-Bourbon vote follows the Republican party and also tends to support the conservative faction within Louisiana's Democratic party. Prior to the rise of the Republican party in Louisiana, the conservatives voted with the Anti-Longs against the Longs (Populists). This split along economic lines within the Democratic party is still present.

One area of conflict between Bourbons and Populists is the property tax. The constitutionally mandated assessment for business property is 15 percent of fair market value; business property in Louisiana goes largely underassessed.[10] But the Populist also finds underassessment of his home a blessing. In addition, the Populists succeeded in enact-

10. *Wall Street Journal*, May 9, 1978, Sec. 1, p. 1.

ing a $7,500 homestead exemption, which places homes valued at $75,000 or less beyond the reach of parish property taxes. Ninety percent of all homeowners pay no property tax at all.

Whenever property taxes are extraordinarily low, as they are in Louisiana, sales taxes will usually play a more important role in supplying government its needed revenues. The regressive character of the sales tax is dramatically illustrated by the findings of a study of New Orleans families. Families with annual incomes in the $5,000 to $15,000 bracket paid a higher percentage of their incomes in state and local taxes than those in the $30,000 to $40,000 income brackets.[11] The influence of the conservative business elite in the political process is evident. On the other hand, the Populists have not been unsuccessful. They won a state sales tax exemption on food and prescription drugs.

In fact, although Louisiana's upper-income families remain relatively undertaxed compared to those of other states, all income groups are afforded the luxury of undertaxation because of the revenues received from gas, oil, and other mineral resources.[12] These nonrenewable resources have constituted a declining share of state funds. According to Charles Roemer, who served as commissioner of administration under Governor Edwin Edwards, severance and royalty taxes constituted only 23 percent of the 1979 state revenues. This was a decline of 37 percent over a five-year period. Sales taxes in 1979 constituted a larger percentage of the state budget than severance taxes for the first time in recent years according to the Public Affairs Research Council. The deregulation of oil and gas, however, is expected to bring a new bonanza to the state treasury.[13] The state in fiscal year 1980 received over $1 billion in severance taxes and royalties. This may double or triple by 1984 at the present rate of increase in the price of crude oil.

While the Populists argue that the wealthy are undertaxed, their philosophy of heavy spending on government services, which dates

11. "Surge in Incomes—Which States Do Best," *U.S. News and World Report,* May 23, 1977, p. 179.
12. National Advisory Commission on Intergovernmental Relations, *Significant Features of Fiscal Federalism, 1979–80 Edition* (Washington, D.C.: National Advisory Commission on Intergovernmental Relations, 1980), 48.
13. Public Affairs Research Council, "The Proposed State Budget: A Look Forward and Backward," *Legislative Bulletin,* XXVI (May 5, 1978), 1.

back to Huey Long, is still alive and well in Louisiana. In 1975 Louisiana spent $30.00 more than the national average of state spending per citizen. Of the $681.91 spent per resident, $49.54 went to health care, for which the national average was only $33.40. The Populists contend that Louisiana's social statistics justify heavy expenditures in the area of human services. In 1969 the percentage of families below the poverty level was the third highest in the nation, and adult educational attainment was the lowest in the nation. Nationally, 5.5 percent of persons over twenty-five years of age had less than five years of formal education, but in Louisiana it was 13.1 percent. Clearly, the poor quality of the public education system has been detrimental to the economic growth of the state.[14]

Louisianians' expectations of high government expenditure on services without burdensome taxes, especially on the higher-income groups, has posed an interesting dilemma. The state's per capita income is increasing at a faster rate than the national average, but the state's tax base is not increasing at the same rate because it is regressively structured.[15] Eventually, the state's treasure chest of severance tax revenues will be empty, but for now, neither the Bourbons nor the Populists must shoulder the burden of governmental generosity.

Tolerance and Frivolity

Louisiana's citizenry has an unusual attitude toward politics that is perhaps the crowning feature of the state's political culture. By and large, Louisianians tolerate and even expect political inefficiency and corruption. They look upon politics as entertainment, and they want their politicians to amuse them. Of course, every state political system has its share of venality, but in Louisiana much of the public tends to accept cronyism, favoritism, frivolity, and nepotism as normal rather than exceptional. Historian T. Harry Williams pointed out that "people in Louisiana have an ambivalent attitude about corruption. On the one

14. State Planning Office, "The State of the State, 1977: An Economic and Social Report to the Governor," quoted in New Orleans *Times-Picayune*, June 5, 1977, Sec. 1, p. 37; Public Affairs Research Council, *Statistical Profile of Louisiana* (Baton Rouge: Public Affairs Research Council, 1973), 3; Public Affairs Research Council, "The Impact of Illiteracy in Louisiana," *Analysis* (February, 1978), 3.

15. "Surge in Incomes," 79.

hand, we deplore it. On the other hand, we brag about it." Some argue that, as long as it does not come directly from public funds, a little "legal graft" is acceptable, but outright fraud of public money is not.[16]

Even when scandals are reported, they cause little public excitement. Basically, the political culture of Louisiana is highly tolerant of political irregularities or stories about such irregularities. Mere revelations of misconduct in office will not produce indignation from the public since the citizenry has been conditioned to expect such behavior. During the past decade, ethics in government was not a major issue in Louisiana politics, and it is unlikely to be very important during this decade.

Politics in Louisiana is looked upon as an entertainment outlet. People play politics for fun, and some even bet on their favorite politician, spotting so many votes to his opponent. Political pranks are common in Louisiana, and storytelling is a way of life. One of the most popular governors in recent years, despite numerous scandals in his administration, was the gregarious Cajun, Edwin Edwards. He was proud of his ability to tell a joke, as well as his ability to catch the eye of the ladies. He made no bones about flying off to Las Vegas for an occasional gambling spree.

Louisiana's prosperous economy, especially in the oil-rich south, has also allowed Louisianians to be more tolerant of waste and inefficiency than they might be if the state were in a situation of revenue scarcity. Louisiana can afford government waste because the oil and gas companies, utilities, and other corporations pay a significant part of the tax burden. In addition, the lack of two-party competition has turned elections into personality contests, rather than serious debates on the issues.

From 1928 to 1964 the Long/Anti-Long bifactionalism offered a reasonable substitute for two-party competition since the two factions had quite distinct political philosophies and programs. Since 1964, however, there has been an absence of clear distinctions as to who stands for what. Instead, there has been a confusing multifactional array of candidates who avoid issues or at best take obfuscated stands on the major issues. In 1949 V. O. Key, Jr., pointed out that multifactionalism in a one-party state makes rational choice extremely difficult for

16. Gore, "Illegal Gambling in Louisiana," 3–4; T. Harry Williams, interview, January 10, 1974, quoted in Bass and DeVries, *The Transformation of Southern Politics*, 158.

the voter, for he finds it difficult to separate the candidates' stands on
the issues. Voters in such a situation tend to be influenced by slick,
professional, media-oriented campaigns with an excess of political
gimmickery. Key also pointed out that without political party organizations to raise funds and supply volunteers, candidates become more
vulnerable to the special-interest groups who can supply the candidates the necessary support. Such a system grants interest groups an
extraordinary amount of political power and leads to a political system
favoring more powerful groups.[17]

Louisiana elections, like elections throughout the nation, have increasingly become contests between campaign management experts
rather than political contests based upon issues.[18] In addition, without
a party platform to follow, the elected officials have no general goals to
seek while in office, and the voters have no yardstick by which to measure their performance. Although a second political party—the Republican—has entered the scene in Louisiana politics, the situation remains essentially the same because the Democratic party of Louisiana
does not have a single outlook on issues and retains significant conservative elements. In essence, this makes Louisiana still a one-party
state, but one that is multifactional, with a separate conservative faction known as Republicans. The result is a government dominated
by Bourbon-oriented industrial groups such as LABI and Populist-
oriented union influence. This was clearly evidenced when LABI's favorite candidate, David Treen, and the AFL-CIO's favorite, Louis Lambert, both made the gubernatorial runoff in 1979. The election of the
Republican governor may help solidify the state Democratic party and
thus help to end the confusion. However, political parties are generally
declining rather than gaining in influence.

Conclusion

The three underlying themes of ethnic variety, economic conflict, and
tolerant attitudes help to explain the political culture of Louisiana.
These three influences intertwine in complex ways; they are not mu-

17. Dan Nimmo, *The Political Persuaders* (Englewood Cliffs, N.J.: Prentice-Hall,
1970).
18. V. O. Key, *Southern Politics in State and Nation* (New York: Knopf, 1949),
302–310. See Nimmo, *The Political Persuaders.*

tually exclusive. Together they lead the average citizen to expect adequate government services despite low taxes and a high degree of governmental inefficiency. Since the 1930s, Louisiana government has
provided extensive public services to its people. The people expect
these services to be continued and new programs to be added. However, the tolerance of governmental inefficiency undercuts efforts to
improve services without raising taxes. Thus, we have the contradic-
tion of high expectations for services but not for performance. It is a
state of affairs permitted by one of the lowest rates of individual taxation in the United States.

As Louisiana's sources of revenue—oil, gas, and minerals—are depleted, this situation is likely to change. But one thing is certain about
politics in Louisiana—it will remain intense and colorful. The state's
rich cultural heritage and diversity separate it from the rest of the nation and give it a flavor all its own.

2.

The Louisiana Constitution of 1974

MARK T. CARLETON

It is much too early for any definitive studies of the Louisiana constitution of 1974 or of the convention that wrote it, especially in so brief a treatment as this.[1] But something can be said about Louisiana's elitist tradition of constitutional revision, of which the 1974 document is the prevailing example. Why the constitution was written when it was can be explained, and its significant provisions summarized. Finally, we can recall how the 1974 constitution was ratified and draw some instructive conclusions about that event within the continuum of Louisiana politics.

Constitutional revision in Louisiana, whether in conventions or by amendment, has been sufficiently continuous to justify including it with Mardi Gras, football, and corruption as the premier components of state culture. No other state has had as many constitutions (eleven) as Louisiana, and probably no other state has amended its recent constitutions as often as Louisiana—the 1921 constitution alone, for example, was amended 536 times within fifty-one years.

Historically, the initiators and principal practitioners of constitutional revision have been the state's public elite—governors, legislators, and other officeholders, together with lobbyists for various local and special interests. These educated, articulate, powerful, and relatively affluent Louisianians have used the process of constitutional revision to construct or maintain a governmental apparatus conforming to their own specifications. Only twice in modern times have the peo-

---

1. But see Richard L. Engstrom and Patrick F. O'Connor, "Restructuring the Regime: Support for Change Within the Louisiana Constitutional Convention," *Polity*, XI (Spring, 1979), 440.

ple of Louisiana played a decisive role in constitutional revision—in 1896 and again in 1972. Otherwise, most Louisiana voters have played either a passive role in the revision process or no role at all.

Eight of Louisiana's constitutions were written during the nineteenth century. All but the first climaxed major political struggles and embodied the principles and objectives of the victorious party, faction, or race. While constitutions were still being employed as political weapons, another use for Louisiana's fundamental law had begun to emerge. From 1852 on, the constitution was increasingly viewed as a statutory bank vault within which the favored schemes, phobias, and interests of the prevailing elite could be secured "beyond the reach of fickle legislatures and ungrateful governors" in the future.[2] Among the statutory items that have inflated successive Louisiana constitutions are a concession to a private lottery company (followed in a later constitution by a prohibition of lotteries), limitations on and exemptions from various kinds of taxation, measures designed to protect New Orleans, authorization for building and financing the Superdome, and a chemical formula for tractor fuel. Indeed, the call to arms of almost every special interest during the past century has been "put it in the constitution." Thus, each constitutional convention after 1845 surpassed its predecessor as a "super legislature" in which competing special interests secured a "patchwork of 'deals and dickers' containing endless statutory trivia."[3]

By the 1890s the elite preferred to revise the constitution by amending it, a process less costly and troublesome than staging constitutional conventions. But revision by amendment required voter approval after a proposal had first been endorsed by two-thirds of the legislators in each house, and in 1896 voters stunned the elite by rejecting all proposals on the ballot. One of them would have disfranchised over half the electorate in poor and illiterate Louisiana by requiring ownership of property or proof of literacy as qualifications for suffrage. And because disfranchisement of black Republicans and white Populists (most of whom were coincidentally poor and ignorant) was the highest priority of Louisiana's Democratic elite in 1896, there

2. C. Vann Woodward, *Origins of the New South, 1877–1913* (Baton Rouge: Louisiana State University Press, 1951), 12.

3. Alden L. Powell, "A History of Louisiana Constitutions," in Louisiana State Law Institute, *Project of a Constitution for the State of Louisiana with Notes and Studies* (Baton Rouge: Louisiana State University Press, 1954), Vol. I, Pt. 1, p. 503.

was no alternative but to assemble a rigged convention two years later to constitutionalize what the voters—including many of the designated victims—had rejected.[4] Failure of constitutional revision by amendment in 1896 neither discredited nor terminated the process. Disfranchisement of most Republicans and Populists two years later reduced and homogenized the electorate and stifled two-party politics in Louisiana for almost six decades. Political contests in the interim usually involved only Democratic factions who often disagreed completely on substantive matters but united on the usefulness of constitutional revision by amendment. Progressives, Longites, Anti-Longites, and McKeithenites all found the process equally satisfactory when their particular interests had to be protected. The ready accessibility of the amending process, together with its usually successful results, made constitutional conventions unnecessary and were the foremost reasons why none were held in Louisiana between 1921 and 1973.

A lesser though still important deterrent to holding conventions was the nearly equal balance of power and influence between factions, especially from 1940 to 1964. A call for a convention by one faction could be negated by screams of indignation and public-spirited outrage from the other, as Governor Earl K. Long discovered to his annoyance in 1951. As long as enough voters kept rubber-stamping the priority constitutional proposals, successive Democratic administrations and local interests in Louisiana continued to make good use of the amending process. Within a political generation or two—while republicanism remained in hibernation, blacks in political limbo, and most white voters suitably compliant or apathetic—the lesson of 1896 was completely forgotten.

Between 1921 and 1972 the Louisiana legislature approved 802 constitutional proposals, an average of almost 16 per year. In many cases, however, the number placed on a single ballot for ratification greatly exceeded the average; in 1960 voters were asked to endorse 55 proposals, an all-time high. By 1972 the voters had ratified 536 of the proposals, or 67 percent of the total approved by the legislature since

4. For more extensive analyses of the Populist crisis in Louisiana and of the constitutional shenanigans that finally terminated it, see William I. Hair, *Bourbonism and Agrarian Protest: Louisiana Politics, 1877–1900* (Baton Rouge: Louisiana State University Press, 1969), 170–279, and Mark T. Carleton, *Politics and Punishment: The History of the Louisiana State Penal System* (Baton Rouge: Louisiana State University Press, 1971), 59–84.

1921.[5] Most of these amendments were not whimsical or esoteric, as, for example, the three-dollar automobile license fee was, but embodied dedicated tax revenues, port commission operations, state civil service, and a myriad of local and parochial matters, many pertaining only to New Orleans. With the incorporation into the constitution of so much statutory material, it first became necessary to amend some of the original articles or add new ones. As conditions changed, many amendments had to be amended again, and so on, until at last the 1921 constitution became so lengthy, annotated, and confusing that it was incomprehensible to all but a handful of legal authorities and government researchers. Specialists in state government and constitutional revision nationwide came to regard the Louisiana constitution as a perfect example of what a state constitution should *not* be. Within Louisiana the 1921 constitution in its last years could have meant no less to the average citizen had it been written in Bulgarian or Parsi.

Constitutional revision by amendment, which by 1970 had become *government* by constitutional amendment in effect, would have probably gone on indefinitely in Louisiana if the process had involved only its instigators and chief beneficiaries, the state's public elite. As we have seen, however, constitutional revision by amendment has an inherent self-destructing agent—disinclination of the voters to play their necessary roles in the process. Just as they had done in 1896, Louisiana's voters in 1970 again dismayed and shocked the elite by rejecting *all* constitutional proposals on the ballot, fifty-three in number that year. Nineteen of the proposals concerned only New Orleans, and nine of those in turn involved only the New Orleans Sewage and Water Board, an agency that had been constitutionalized for protection near the turn of the century.

In two subsequent elections held during 1972, voters again rebelled by turning down thirty-six of forty-two proposed amendments, many of which also affected New Orleans only. Proposal 26 on the November ballot exemplified the level to which government by constitutional amendment had fallen: it would have enabled New Orleans City Park employees to transfer from the state civil service system to the city civil service system. Assuming that the employees themselves desired the

---

5. James I. Barnidge, "The Louisiana Constitutional Convention of 1973: The Road to Revision," *Louisiana History*, XV (1974), 40–43.

change, the final decision should have been made locally, either by the mayor, the head of city civil service, or the New Orleans voters. But because the employees were under state civil service, which was in the constitution, authority for the transfer had to come from the voters statewide, and the proposal was rejected. As a spokesman for "good government" observed shortly afterward, "the people of the state became fed up with amendments and killed them all. Now the Sewerage and Water Board can't change because it's in the constitution. . . . New Orleans sought protection and now it's a straitjacket."[6]

In 1950, twenty-two years before government by constitutional amendment was frustrated for the second time in Louisiana, Alden L. Powell had complained that the "chief criticism" of the amending process was that it allowed "hundreds of amendments" to be approved "by a minority of interested voters who had taken advantage of the general lethargy of a disinterested and uninformed electorate to amend the Constitution almost at will." Before 1879, popular ratification of a proposed amendment had required a majority of those *voting in the election*, but since that date, only a majority of the voters *voting on the amendment* was necessary for ratification. The "minority of interested voters" necessary to ratify an amendment had been as small as 6 percent of the registered voters statewide. By 1970–1972, however, many voters in Louisiana were no longer lethargic or disinterested. Of approximately one million Louisianians who cast presidential ballots in November, 1972, for example, over half also voted one way or the other on thirty proposed constitutional amendments. Most of the twenty-six defeated proposals fell far short of ratification; in one case, the margin of defeat was 275,000 votes.[7]

Did responsible and informed Louisianians who evaluated each proposal on its merits derail government by constitutional amendment? Probably not. While these events were taking place, the median school year reached by Louisiana adults was only 10.8 and the state led the

6. Baton Rouge *State Times*, November 21, 1972, Sec. A, p. 1; Edward J. Steimel, "Interest Representation in the Constitution," in Louis E. Newman (ed.), *Focus on CC-73: Discussion Series, April–July, 1973* (Baton Rouge: Institute of Government Research, 1973), 98–99.

7. Powell, "History of Louisiana Constitutions," 508; Mark T. Carleton, "History of Louisiana's Constitution," in Louis E. Newman (ed.), *Focus on CC-73: Discussion Series, April–July, 1973* (Baton Rouge: Institute of Government Research, 1973), 6; Baton Rouge *State Times*, November 21, 1972, Sec. A, p. 1.

nation in percentage of adults who were either functionally or totally illiterate.[8] Illiteracy had been much more prevalent in 1896 when Louisiana voters caused the similar constitutional crisis discussed earlier.

United States Supreme Court Justice Potter Stewart once stated that, while he could not define hard-core pornography, "I know it when I see it."[9] In like manner, Louisiana voters—in many cases short on formal education and lacking a sophisticated perception of governmental complexity—could nonetheless recognize what was opposed or clearly irrelevant to their own immediate interests. As Louisiana's public elite continued to bombard the voters with increasing amounts of statutory trivia, which was remote and narrow in application or vague and confusing, the disruption of government by constitutional amendment became inevitable.

By 1972, therefore, the need for major constitutional revision in Louisiana had become, again, a political necessity. With no realistic prospect for continued use of the amending process, the alternatives were either a constitutional revision commission or a constitutional convention, the latter of which might more readily secure public confidence and support. But obtaining popular ratification of a constitution from any source by a sullen and fed-up electorate during the Watergate era could not be taken for granted.

Under the newly inaugurated administration of Governor Edwin W. Edwards, the 1972 legislature enacted a measure providing for the selection of delegates to a constitutional convention, the scheduling of convention sessions, the hiring of research personnel, and related matters. There were to be 132 delegates in all, 105 of whom would be elected from the corresponding number of single-member house districts, together with 27 delegates appointed by the governor. (Of the 146 delegates to the 1921 convention, only 12 had been gubernatorial appointees.) Governor Edwards was directed to appoint 15 delegates to represent "the public at large" and one delegate to represent each of the following: industry, labor, education, civil service, wildlife and conservation, law enforcement, the judiciary, the professions, consumers, agriculture, youth, and racial minorities. Even though government by

8. Public Affairs Research Council, "The Impact of Illiteracy in Louisiana," *Analysis* (February, 1978), 3.
9. *Jacobellis* v. *Ohio*, 378 U.S. 197 (1964).

constitutional amendment had been brought down by an electorate fed up with special-interest amendments, it was considered necessary to include comprehensive special-interest representation in the constitutional convention. But then, by 1972, a constitutional convention in Louisiana without representation of special interests would have been as unthinkable as a legislature without lobbyists. The delegates, once appointed or elected, were instructed to convene in Baton Rouge, organize into committees, and elect officers on January 5, 1973, after which they were to adjourn until July 5. In the meantime, the research staff, the first ever authorized to assist a Louisiana constitutional convention, was "to prepare a preliminary draft of a new constitution." After reconvening on July 5, the delegates would receive the staff report, "hold some public hearings," and prepare the finished draft of a constitution by January 4, 1974. Finally, the statute required that the document be submitted for popular ratification no later than November, 1974.[10] On the surface, this provision suggested a marked democratization of constitutional revision in Louisiana since no constitution had been popularly ratified for almost a century, the documents of 1898, 1913, and 1921 having been promulgated over the voters' heads by suspicious legislatures.

The overly optimistic hopes of some civic-minded groups and individuals were that the constitutional convention of 1973, or CC-73, as it was soon labeled, would be an assembly open to the people and receptive to popular views and that it would write a people's constitution that the people could understand. Unfortunately, these hopes derived not only from ignorance of past Louisiana conventions and how they had performed, but from two false assumptions: (1) that the people would recognize the significance of CC-73 and become actively involved in its deliberations, and (2) that the convention itself would write a basic, fundamental document, free of technicalities, that could (and would) be read, understood, and endorsed by the average citizen.

In an address delivered on the Baton Rouge campus of Louisiana State University between convention sessions, Governor Edwards himself admitted that the need for constitutional revision had not intruded upon the thoughts of most Louisianians. Edwards, who had

10. Powell, "History of Louisiana Constitutions," 467; State of Louisiana, *Acts of the Legislature: Regular Session of 1972* (Baton Rouge: State of Louisiana, 1972), I, 4–9.

stated the need for a new constitution during his gubernatorial campaign, disclosed that he "was told, rightly so, by many people that nobody in Louisiana of sufficient numbers [was] concerned about a new constitution. You cannot run a campaign for governor on the issue. Polls showed . . . that [in 1971] less than two percent of the people in the state were concerned about a new constitution." Those who did care added up to "a very small minority" of the total population and were to be found among "knowledgeable, concerned people in the professions, judges, professors, law students, and . . . people like PAR [Public Affairs Research Council] and CABL (Council for a Better Louisiana], and others who had studied state government."[11]

Possibly because the proponents of constitutional revision shared the governor's awareness that popular indifference would create grave difficulties, those able to arouse and inform the public actively sought to do so. Organizations such as the League of Women Voters held symposia throughout the state to acquaint citizens with the whys and wherefores of CC-73; the press (newspapers, radio, and television) maintained a running commentary on convention debates and decisions; the Public Affairs Research Council of Louisiana, a respected nonpartisan governmental research agency, issued numerous critiques and other reports of matters before the convention; finally, many of the delegates themselves spoke at informational meetings in various parts of the state. No previous Louisiana constitutional convention had received a fraction of the sustained and in-depth coverage lavished upon CC-73. Perhaps no other event in the entire history of the state had been so widely publicized. For those who wanted to know about CC-73 and what it was doing, sources of information were numerous, comprehensive, generally reliable, and accessible.

It soon became apparent, however, that these informational efforts had largely been in vain, for evidence indicated that few Louisianians cared to know anything about the significance or the proceedings of CC-73. A well-advertised lecture series held on the Baton Rouge campus of LSU, for example, was consistently outdrawn by whatever rock group was performing simultaneously in the student union. It was as a participant in the same series that Governor Edwards stated that inter-

11. Edwin W. Edwards, "The Roles of the Governor and the Legislature in the Constitution," in Louis E. Newman (ed.), *Focus on CC-73: Discussion Series, April–July, 1973* (Baton Rouge: Institute of Government Research, 1973), 76.

est in constitutional revision was limited to such people as law students and professors. His audience, almost predictably, consisted of about thirty law students and professors! Attendance at similar meetings throughout the state, several of which I visited, was similarly and disappointingly low.

If the people were not interested in CC-73, then who was? Midway in the sessions, a delegate expressed to me her dismay that no one had testified before or had communicated with her committee except "lobbyists for the special interests." When I testified before one of the convention committees as a technician rather than a lobbyist, I was preceded by the director of corrections and followed by the president of the District Attorneys' Association. Examination of committee documents will confirm these individual experiences on a broad scale. The reader will soon discover a heavy preponderance of testimony and written communication from persons representing oil companies, chambers of commerce, labor organizations, taxpayer groups, parish school boards, and police juries.[12]

A possible reason for both the sustained public indifference to CC-73 and the aggressive lobbying to which the convention was subjected was the composition of the convention itself. That is to say, CC-73 was no more a people's convention than any of its predecessors had been. It was, instead, a cross section of the current Louisiana public elite, composed of persons with whom, although they had elected 105 of the delegates, the people as a group found it difficult to identify. Not only were the delegates seasoned lobbyists themselves in many cases but they expected and wanted to be lobbied.

It has been noted earlier that the median grade level achieved by adult Louisianians in the 1970s was 10.8. A way of embellishing this fact would be to say that adult Louisianians, in the main, had no more than an eleventh grade, or at best, a high school education. Only 3 of the 132 convention delegates possessed a level of formal education roughly equivalent to the state average, that is, had gone no further than high school. On the other hand, 93 delegates had graduated from college, and many of these had gone on to acquire graduate or professional degrees. Thirty other delegates had attended college. The point

12. *Records of the Louisiana Constitutional Convention of 1973: Committee Documents* (Baton Rouge: Louisiana Constitutional Convention Records Commission, 1977), X–XIII, especially "Committee on Revenue, Finance, and Taxation," XII, 295–718.

is not that a majority of delegates should have received only a high school education; it is that a vast gap in educational background existed between the delegates and the people they represented. Leaders in any society are usually better educated than the masses, and a great disparity between the two has been a deeply entrenched characteristic of Louisiana politics. In the case of CC-73, the great difference in educational attainment between the delegates and the people furthered the tendencies of each to think, act, and live in different worlds.

The elitist composition of CC-73 is even more strikingly demonstrated by the delegates' occupations and by their accumulated experience in public affairs or public employment. Lawyers were the most common in terms of occupation; forty-seven of the delegates, more than a third of the total, were of that profession. Public employees were next, with seventeen delegates, followed by educators with twelve. Forty delegates, many of them lawyers, were current or former legislators; thirty-six had served on various public boards or commissions; and forty-nine had experience in public service or employment on the local level. Among the last were four parish tax assessors and one deputy assessor. (All five of these delegates, as could be expected, wound up on the Revenue, Finance, and Taxation Committee.) The presence in CC-73 of so many current or former government officials ensured that much of the thinking, talking, and writing done within the convention would be conducted in "governmentese," an ersatz and dehumanized language of legal, quantitative, managerial, and budgetary jargon. While it may be increasingly convenient for government personnel to communicate with each other in "governmentese," it becomes equally difficult for those who comprehend the language to communicate with those who do not, which includes almost everyone else.

Among the appointed delegates to CC-73 were the executive vice-president of the Louisiana AFL-CIO, a state supreme court justice, and a future executive counsel to the governor. There was even a geographical element of elitism present in CC-73—all 27 appointed delegates were residents of South Louisiana.[13] This fact becomes more understandable, if not less irksome to North Louisianians, when it is recalled that the governor himself was a South Louisianian, and that

13. Public Affairs Research Council, *Citizens' Guide to the 1973 Constitutional Convention* (Baton Rouge: Public Affairs Research Council, April, 1979), *passim.*

Louisiana's population, industries, and interest groups—to say nothing of the governor's own political base—were all concentrated in the southern part of the state. Perhaps as a concession to North Louisiana, the delegates elected the young and exceptionally able speaker of the house, E. L. "Bubba" Henry of Jackson Parish, chairman of the convention.

Membership in the convention also reflected, to some degree, the changes that had overtaken Louisiana in the wake of the "civil rights revolution," the movement toward equality between the sexes, and the gradual reemergence of two-party politics. There were twelve black delegates, the first since 1879; six Republican delegates, the first since 1898; and ten female delegates, four of whom were also black.[14] In 1921 three delegates were white women.

Thus, by the time CC-73 had convened, three important facts were perceptible or would soon become perceptible: (1) there was minimal correlation in the public consciousness between popular rejection of government by constitutional amendment and the existence of CC-73 as the direct consequence of that rejection; (2) as a result of the foregoing, the public at large viewed the deliberations of CC-73 either with indifference or hostility as another "ripoff" by those politicians in Baton Rouge; and (3) like its forerunners in the Louisiana constitutional tradition, CC-73 was an essentially elitist gathering transacting business in an essentially elitist manner.

Consequently, the first assumption of the civic-minded—that the people of Louisiana would become interested and involved in CC-73— had failed to materialize. But what of the second assumption—that the delegates (perhaps in spite of themselves) might still write a constitution sufficiently basic and simple for average Louisianians to understand and to ratify. Could that not be achieved? As events developed, the more appropriate question was not whether average Louisianians *could* read and understand what the convention was preparing, but rather *would* they.

However their personal interests, biases, loyalties, and levels of ability or performance may have varied, the delegates to CC-73 worked diligently at their task and ultimately produced a constitution for Louisiana which, although imperfect, was nonetheless much shorter, sim-

14. *Ibid.*

pler, and considerably better than the bloated and crippled old document of 1921. Its faults, not surprisingly, were traditional and were squarely labeled as such by Governor Edwards when he addressed the convention on January 10, 1974:

> Now I must suggest to you . . . that what criticisms I have of the document, and what problems have arisen in the feelings and the hustlings and bustlings of our state, arise, very candidly, from your failure to recognize that you were here to write a constitution, rather than to serve as legislators. . . . Had you stopped your work after completion of the Bill of Rights and the three Articles on the Executive, the Legislative, and the Judiciary, a beautiful, fantastically well-engineered and prepared document would have been your work product. Practical aspects of your job, however, required you to go further; and it is when you got into those provisions which are really legislative, and not constitutional matters that the problems began to develop.[15]

Louisiana's constitutional tradition, in short, had not been broken. Even in the computerized late twentieth century "the efforts of certain special interest people to get in or out of [the] document" (as the governor put it) had met with considerable success, and the proposed eleventh constitution of the State of Louisiana would contain at the outset its share of statutory trivia.

As instruments of basic or fundamental law, state constitutions should: (1) specify and guarantee individual rights, (2) provide for separation of powers between the branches and levels of state and local government, and (3) define the duties, powers, and responsibilities of each governmental branch or level. Providing that "no person shall be denied the equal protection of the laws," for example, or that "the governor shall be the chief executive officer of the state" adheres to the legitimate and enduring content of a state constitution.

On the other hand, a state constitution should not limit tax rates or license fees, grant exemptions or concessions to any group or individual, or become involved with the details of administration. These and other statutory matters should be enacted, amended, or repealed by

---

15. *Records of the Louisiana Constitutional Convention of 1973: Journal and Calendar* (Baton Rouge: Louisiana Constitutional Convention Records Commission, 1977), II, 1157.

the legislature as changing circumstances may require. As pointed out earlier, however, most of Louisiana's constitutions have been packed with statutory content.

To those familiar with its bulky, multivolume predecessor, brevity is the most noticeable and commendable feature of the 1974 constitution.[16] An extensive reduction in constitutional verbiage was accomplished in CC-73 by continuing portions of fifteen articles of the 1921 constitution as statutes (Article XIV, Part II, Section 17). No longer, for example, will employees of City Park or the Sewerage and Water Board in New Orleans be within the constitutional amending process unless someone puts their agencies back into the constitution. The realization that statutory matters properly belong in the statutes was long in coming to Louisiana, and even then it came with qualifications and exceptions.

Remembering that slavery existed in Louisiana for 150 years, and that blacks continued to be victimized by legally sanctioned discrimination until quite recently, the most progressive, refreshing, and laudable provision of the 1974 constitution is Article I, Section 3, "Right to Individual Dignity," which provides that "no person shall be denied the equal protection of the laws. No law shall discriminate against a person because of race or religious ideas, beliefs, or affiliations." Even though legal discrimination against racial minorities had already been eradicated by the federal courts and Congress, the inclusion of this passage in a Louisiana constitution is noteworthy. Equally significant is a further provision of the same section, "No law shall arbitrarily, capriciously, or unreasonably discriminate against a person because of birth, age, sex, culture, physical condition or political ideas or affiliations." While proponents of sexual equality might consider all discrimination as arbitrary, capricious, or unreasonable, until and unless ratification of the proposed Equal Rights Amendment to the federal constitution is achieved, Louisiana's constitution provides more explicit protection against sexual discrimination than does the federal constitution.

Under the 1921 constitution, as amended, the legislature convened

16. The Claitor's edition, published on 5½- by 8¼-inch paper, comprises 141 pages of text, while a replica of the original, published as Volume III in *Records of the Louisiana Constitutional Convention of 1973* on 8½- by 11-inch paper, has only 42 pages of text.

for sixty-day regular sessions in even-numbered years and for thirty-day fiscal sessions in odd-numbered years. The distinction soon became meaningless because members eagerly made exceptions for measures not fiscal in sessions restricted to fiscal matters. The 1974 constitution provides for annual legislative sessions of sixty days within eighty-five calendar days but also requires that "no measure levying a new tax or increasing an existing tax shall be introduced or enacted during a regular session in an odd-numbered year." In a similar vein, and preserving the essence of a 1956 amendment to the former constitution, the 1974 document additionally requires that "the levy of a new tax, or increase in an existing tax, or the repeal of an existing tax exemption shall require . . . enactment . . . by two-thirds of the elected members of each house of the legislature."[17] The original two-thirds rule, as it was commonly known, was proposed by a conservative legislature to contain the "tax-happy" tendencies of Earl K. Long, whose return to the governorship was correctly anticipated in 1955. While some have always criticized it as an excessive restraint, others came to cherish the two-thirds rule as a weapon of good government, and thus it was preserved by CC-73.

Under all constitutions since 1845, the lieutenant governor had served as *ex officio* president of the senate. The 1974 constitution relieved him of that burden (and left him with little else to do) by providing that "each house shall choose its officers, including a permanent presiding officer selected from its own membership."[18] Support for this provision came from those who believed that a member of the executive branch should not exercise power in the legislative branch.

By 1973 the executive branch had grown to include 267 agencies, boards, commissions, and offices, possibly the largest of all state bureaucracies. The principal entities were headed by statewide elected officials such as the attorney general or the treasurer. But most of them were run by gubernatorial appointees, and the responsibility of directly supervising all these agencies and their personnel became too much for one person. Governor Edwards had suggested a cabinet-style reorganization of executive agencies during his campaign, and CC-73 adopted his idea by mandating reorganization of all executive agencies into "not more than twenty departments," nine headed by statewide

17. Louisiana Constitution, Art. III, Sec. 2A; Art. VII, Pt. I, Sec. 2.
18. *Ibid.*, Art. III, Sec. 7C.

elected officials, one by the director of state civil service, and ten by gubernatorial appointees.[19] (By 1978, the legislature had enacted the structural requirements of this mandate.) Another potentially significant provision relating to the executive branch was Article IV, Section 20, which authorized the legislature after 1976 to make the positions of commissioner of agriculture, commissioner of insurance, commissioner of elections, and superintendent of education appointive rather than elective. In 1981, however, all of them remained elective.

In 1966 voters had ratified a proposal to enable the governor to succeed himself. No governor had done so since Murphy J. Foster, the "disenfranchising" governor, in 1896. As a concession to his enemies, delegates to the 1898 convention prohibited gubernatorial succession, and the provision was retained in two successive constitutions. Serving nonsuccessive terms was not prohibited, however. Earl K. Long served two terms, 1948–1952 and 1956–1960; and Jimmie Davis was also governor twice, 1944–1948 and 1960–1964. John McKeithen, an extremely popular governor in 1966, was the first beneficiary of the succession amendment, and Edwin Edwards, easily reelected in 1975, also benefited from a provision of the new constitution, which states: "A person who has served as governor for more than one and one-half terms in two consecutive terms shall not be elected governor for the succeeding term."[20] Once again, it should be noted, the constitution does not forbid such a person from repeating the process after sitting out a term.

Article VI dealing with local government may prove to be the most beneficial segment of the 1974 constitution. Much of the statutory trivia in recent constitutions had to do with local and parochial affairs. In Louisiana, as elsewhere, this situation arose from the application of Dillon's Rule, which held all local governments to be creatures and dependencies of the state. As Richard Engstrom and Patrick O'Connor observe, the 1921 constitution "had several 'home rule' provisions," but "in operation they did not result in an escape from Dillon's Rule and local officials continued to trek to the state capital in pursuit of specific statutory authorizations"—which, as we have seen, were frequently planted in the constitution. But "the 1974 constitution . . . contains self-executing initiative provisions for both home rule and statutorily

19. *Ibid.*, Art. IV, Sec. 1B.
20. *Ibid.*, Art. IV, Sec. 3B.

chartered municipalities and parishes (counties), and has in contrast been described as the 'emancipator' of local government within the state."[21] Having been thus emancipated, local and parochial governments can presumably go about their business with the hoped-for result of a shorter Louisiana constitution in the future.

Such are the more germane, or at least more responsibly drafted provisions of the 1974 constitution. The article on the judiciary might also be among them, but its fundamental purity is somewhat tarnished by a provision guaranteeing retirement benefits to judges and their widows, a provision more appropriately established by the legislature than by the constitution.[22]

While the 1974 constitution prescribes the structure of state and local government with relative clarity and brevity, other provisions were obviously included at the behest of special interests. Among them are a freeze on state income tax rates (Article VII, Part I, Section 4, A); a prohibition against local and parochial severance, income, or motor fuel taxes (Article VII, Part I, Section 4, C); allocations of severance taxes and mineral royalties to certain parishes (Article VII, Part I, Sections 4, D and E); the venerable three-dollar license fee for private motor vehicles (Article VII, Part I, Section 5); and two dozen exemptions from property taxation—including "boats using gasoline as motor fuel," but not boats using diesel fuel (Article VII, Part II, Section 21). A moralistic legacy from the nineteenth century, and the most hilarious statement in the constitution, especially to Louisiana racing fans, is contained in Article XIII (General Provisions), Section 6: "Gambling shall be defined by and suppressed by the legislature."

Although these provisions had both defenders and detractors, none aroused heated controversy within or beyond the convention. As for the auto license fee, most delegates and many concerned observers knew that failure to include it could doom the proposed constitution. Governor Edwards believed that inclusion of the three-dollar license fee was "absurd" and "absolutely stupid," but necessary "because we need the votes of people who have automobiles."[23] The most controver-

21. Richard L. Engstrom and Patrick F. O'Connor, "State Centralization Versus Home Rule: A Note on Ambition Theory's Powers Proposition," *Western Political Quarterly*, XXX (June, 1977), 290–91.

22. Louisiana Constitution, Art. V, Sec. 23.

23. Edwards, "The Roles of the Governor and the Legislature," 78–79.

sial provisions had to do with state civil service, public education, and the misunderstood and ill-administered field of property taxation.

Article X, Section 3 re-created the State Civil Service Commission and provided that six members be appointed by the governor from nominations submitted by Louisiana's six private university presidents. An additional seventh member was to be "elected by the classified employees of the state from their number as provided by law." Because there was to be no added member representing "management," PAR, which speaks for management, charged that the independence and impartiality of the commission could be destroyed. PAR also criticized the revised criteria for promotions within civil service—the proposed constitution added length of service to the traditional requirements of merit, efficiency, and fitness.[24] There would seem to have been little cause for alarm concerning the civil service provisions. One representative of forty-nine thousand classified employees on a seven-member civil service commission is not excessive, especially when none of the other six members would likely be a Communist, a Teamster, or even a member of the International Ladies' Garment Workers' Union. And if the criteria of merit, efficiency, and fitness must still be considered for promotions within the civil service, more good than harm could result from considering length of service as well, especially when it is in the state's interest to recognize and retain its more experienced and productive employees.

While the civil service provisions may have provoked some grumbling in boardrooms and around Rotary luncheon tables, an argument over the kind and number of public education boards became so divisive that convention delegates were persuaded to offer the voters two alternative proposals for consideration at the same referendum with the rest of the constitution. Alternate A provided for five constitutional boards: a board of regents to oversee and determine programs in higher education; three separate management boards for LSU, Southern University, and the rest of the state's colleges and universities; and a policy board for elementary and secondary education. Under Alternate A the superintendent of education would serve as administrative officer only for elementary and secondary education. Alternate B provided for two constitutional policy boards, one each for higher educa-

24. Shreveport *Times*, April 7, 1974, Sec. 1, p. 1; Louisiana Constitution, Art. X, Sec. 7.

tion and for elementary and secondary education. Under Alternate B the state superintendent would become an education czar as the administrative head of all public educational institutions and activities in the state.

Even though Alternate A was opposed by the governor, the superintendent of education (who obviously preferred Alternate B), and many Louisianians, it won handily over Alternate B on referendum day, 331,339 to 199,085. The principal reason for this victory was the determined and well-organized support of Alternate A by the LSU system and its alumni in league with similar support from Southern University. Under the system prevailing in 1974, LSU had had a separate board and would retain it under Alternate A; Southern did not have a separate board but would acquire one under Alternate A. With Louisiana's two oldest and largest public universities united in mutual self-interest, the opposition had no chance.

It is important to recall that ninety-three thousand fewer votes were cast on the education alternatives than on the constitution itself.[25] Although there is no way of proving it, the added and unseemly power struggle within public education may have alienated, or further alienated, a number of voters. Many who expressed no preference on the alternates could simply have chosen to repudiate the proposed constitution in toto for all the squabbling and uncertainties it represented to them.

"Property taxes: Oh, how happy I am to publicly state my position on property taxes. How popular it is going to make me with everybody. How anxious I was to get here and let you know what I think should be done about property taxes."[26] Thus spoke Governor Edwards to the delegates in reference to the most technical, controversial, and publicized issue before the convention. Property taxation in Louisiana has been a labyrinthine no-man's-land of misrepresentation, misinformation, and irrepressible disagreement, even among those who make their living administering it. One would almost rather defend capitalism before the Supreme Soviet than have to resolve property taxation in Louisiana into something comprehensible to the nonspecialist. I am

25. Public Affairs Research Council, "Special Election on the Constitution, April 20, 1974," *Analysis* (April, 1974), 10.
26. *Records of the Constitutional Convention: Journal and Calendar*, II, 1,160.

as happy with this portion of my assignment as Governor Edwards was with his, and therefore, I am grateful that the space remaining permits only the briefest discussion of the crucial relationship between property taxation and the Louisiana constitution of 1974.

Property taxes are by definition *ad valorem* taxes, and *ad valorem* in Latin means according to value. Therefore, a tax levied on property must correspond in some rational manner to the value of the property. But how does one determine the value of property for purposes of taxation? Should the value be what the property sold for—thirty years ago—or should it be what the property may be worth today? What is the value of a small "Mom-and-Pop" grocery store? Of the immense Exxon refinery in Baton Rouge? Even after one has reached a fair appraisal of the true value, actual value, or fair market value of a piece of property, what should the assessed value be—90 percent? Sixty-five percent? Three percent? The *assessed value* of property is the portion of its full value on which taxes are levied. Rarely is property taxed at 100 percent of full value, or actual cash value. Instead, an *assessment ratio*, or percentage of full value, is established to determine the assessed value. Should the assessment ratio be higher on revenue-producing property (the "Mom-and-Pop" grocery store, the Exxon refinery) than on residential property? If so, how much higher? Should residential property be taxed at all?

These are only basic examples of the complex and technical judgments that must be made in the administration of property taxation. There is certainly more to it than meets the layman's eye, even within a jurisdiction where property taxation is administered on the basis of well-known and commonly accepted criteria that are professional, uniform, impartial, and equitable. If, on the other hand, property taxation is administered according to obscure and perennially contested criteria that are political, widely differentiated, negotiable, and inequitable, there one finds the fast and loose under-the-table operations that have long characterized property tax administration in Louisiana. With them one finds the always confused, defensive, and gullible taxpayer who instinctively assumes that he is being skinned. In addition, when politics overwhelms professionalism in property tax administration and the cure for systemic ailments is sought in more politics, the field for demagoguery becomes boundless. The hoopla that inflicted Proposition 13 on California is one recent example; ratification of the 1974 constitution in Louisiana was an earlier one.

The property tax "tar baby" that eventually fell into the lap of CC-73 need not have developed. Under the 1921 constitution and according to statutory law as well, a state agency of three gubernatorial appointees, the Louisiana Tax Commission, was charged with the triple responsibilities of (1) assessing the properties of railroads, pipelines, and utilities; (2) establishing the actual cash value of other taxable property on lists submitted annually by the seventy elected parish assessors of Louisiana; and (3) insuring uniformity of taxation by fixing the percentage of the actual cash value upon which taxes were to be collected and by changing or otherwise correcting any assessments before returning the lists to the assessors. Had the commission faithfully and consistently carried out their legal responsibilities, subsequent events in Louisiana would have been quite different.

But the commission performed only their own assessing functions and "almost completely abdicated their functions in telling the assessors what to do."[27] Failure of the commission to supervise the assessors and to insure uniformity of property taxation, as required by law, left each assessor essentially free to value and assess property as he or she pleased.

The results by 1971 were blatantly inequitable. A comprehensive survey by PAR revealed that in Caddo Parish, for example, "a $30,000 house was assessed at $21,000 while a $32,000 house was assessed at $3,000 and a $62,000 house was assessed at $11,300." In Jefferson Parish, PAR discovered "a $12,500 house . . . assessed at $2,100 and a $12,300 house at $400. An assessment of $4,500 was put on houses sold for $125,000, $75,000, and $45,200. Of two houses sold for $75,000 each, one was assessed at $4,500 and the other at $6,000."[28]

Even if there had been general uniformity of assessment within parishes—and there was not—differences between parishes were equally unreasonable. The average assessment ratio in Caddo Parish, for example, was 24.5 percent of actual cash value, one of the state's high-

27. Frank Simoneaux, "The Law and the Practice," in Public Affairs Research Council, "Property Tax Seminar," *Analysis* (December 1972), 14.

28. Public Affairs Research Council, "Property Tax Inequities," *Analysis* (October, 1971), 4–5.

est. A home appraised at $50,000 would thus be assessed, on the average, at $12,250. But Louisiana's homestead exemption of $2,000 in 1971 ($5,000 for veterans) would have lowered the assessed value of the property even further—to $10,250. Caddo's average millage was then 41.6, or $41.60 per $1,000 of assessed value. Hence, our homeowner in Caddo, if he were not a veteran, would have owed $426.40 in parish property taxes in 1971. As a veteran, his parish property tax bill would have been only $301.60. In Jefferson Parish, on the other hand, where the average assessment ratio was only 7.5 percent (although the average millage was a substantially higher 108.7 mills per $1,000 of assessed value), a $50,000 home owned by a nonveteran would be assessed, on the average, at $1,750 and taxed only $190.23. (Millages may legitimately vary from parish to parish even if assessment ratios are uniform statewide.) A veteran owning a $50,000 home in Jefferson Parish would have owed no parish property taxes at all in 1971. ($50,000 × .075 = $3,750 − $5,000 = 0.)[29]

The PAR survey analyzed discrepancies in the assessment of residential property only. Louisiana offered in 1971, as it does today, a five-year exemption from property taxation to new business and industry. The exemption is renewable for an additional five years under certain conditions. Business and industrial property may represent millions, or even billions of dollars, but it represents relatively few votes. Hence, the parishwide and/or statewide discrepancies in assessment of business and industrial properties whose exemptions had expired can be readily imagined.

The actual dollar amounts paid in property taxes in Louisiana, whether by homeowners or others, were among the nation's lowest. Nevertheless, the inequities of assessment within the state resulting from failure of the Tax Commission to execute its responsibilities were legally vulnerable and not destined to last. On March 22, 1973, the property tax "tar baby" fully emerged as a state district court decision in the case of *Bussie* v. *Long*. In simple terms, the court held that inequities in property tax assessment clearly existed in Louisiana, contrary

29. *Ibid.*, 10. The state collected an additional 5.75 mill property tax in 1971, but it is omitted from our example because it was repealed shortly afterward. Considerations of scope and emphasis also preclude discussion here of the Property Tax Relief Fund and its successor in the 1974 constitution, the Revenue Sharing Fund.

to law, and that they not only violated the state constitution but denied the "equal protection of the laws" guaranteed by the Fourteenth Amendment to the United States Constitution. The State of Louisiana, through the Tax Commission, was given until July 1, 1975 (subsequently extended to January 1, 1976, by the Court of Appeal) to implement uniformity of property tax assessment. Failure of the state to comply could have resulted, finally, in court-imposed statewide assessment of taxable property using actual cash value as the basis for assessment.[30]

Although a court order had been issued and a deadline set, there was no cause for the immediate panic stirred up shortly afterward by cynical and opportunistic officials. In the first place, the state had almost three years in which to implement uniformity of property tax assessment. The obvious remedy was for the Tax Commission, under threat of fine or imprisonment, to obey the law and the court order by establishing the actual cash value of taxable property in the state and to fix the percentage of the actual cash value upon which property taxes would be assessed. In the second place, whether this percentage (*i.e.*, the assessment ratio) was 100 percent, 40 percent, or 1 percent of actual cash value was immaterial to the court so long as the percentage set was applied uniformly throughout the state by January 1, 1976. Only if nothing had been done by that date would the court impose uniform assessment at actual cash value. Finally, however, *actual cash value* did not mean what some people said it meant. State Senator J. D. DeBlieux, an attorney for the plaintiffs in *Bussie* v. *Long* and himself a convention delegate, clarified the matter before the convention subcommittee on ad valorem taxation on March 30, 1973: "I know Mr. Chehardy [Jefferson Parish tax assessor] and those who have been taking his side have always tried to confuse the public by saying actual cash value is one hundred percent of value. . . . The [assessed value] is the percentage of that valuation which would take [*sic*] to apply to the millage. There is nothing in Judge Doherty's decision that said that property had to be listed and assessed . . . at one hundred percent of its value or its actual cash value."[31]

30. *Victor Bussie et al.* v. *Mrs. Blanche Revere Long et al.*, 257 La. 629 (1971); *Bussie* v. *Long*, 286 So.2d 689 (1973).

31. *Records of the Louisiana Constitutional Convention of 1973: Committee Documents*, XII, 302–303.

Thus, the idea that 100 percent assessment or assessment at actual cash value was inevitable, which was so freely bandied about during CC-73, was incorrect from the beginning. The most vital point to keep in mind is that CC-73 need not have concerned itself with property taxation at all. The order of the court could have been easily complied with by the Tax Commission prior to the deadline. Consequently, even if the proposed constitution had been rejected by the voters on April 20, 1974, more than two years would have remained during which 100 percent assessment could have been avoided by other means.

Nevertheless, CC-73 did take up the matter of property taxation and the ensuing uproar between conflicting special interests generated considerably more heat than light. The assessors labored to devise a means of assessment that would satisfy the court yet preserve their own popularity by insuring that property, especially residential property, could continue to be lightly taxed. Business and industrial spokesmen, who claimed they were already paying 76 percent of all property taxes collected in the state, endeavored to defeat any schemes that might result in greater tax burdens being placed upon them. Assessor Chehardy defended the principle of homestead exemptions and attacked the industrial exemption, considered by many to be a major inducement in bringing new industry and additional jobs to relatively underdeveloped Louisiana. PAR Executive Director Edward J. Steimel countered by reminding the delegates that property tax reform was "an exceedingly complex issue" that could not be understood "so long as many highly placed political leaders continue to appeal to the basest of all human instincts—greed. For nothing anyone else says seems to be sufficient when certain men will yell 'they're going to raise your taxes.'"[32] But that is precisely what certain men did continue to yell, during and after the convention right up to referendum day.

By the time Governor Edwards appeared before the convention in its waning moments on January 10, 1974, the property tax provisions submitted by the Committee on Revenue, Finance, and Taxation had been reported to the whole convention. Among the members of this committee, it will be recalled, were the five assessor-delegates. The

---

32. *Ibid.*, 317. See the comprehensive, accurate, and rational presentations before the Committee on Revenue, Finance, and Taxation of Senator J. D. DeBlieux (quoted in part above) and Representative Frank Simoneaux, *ibid.*, 434–37, 442–49. PAR's position on what the property tax provision should have contained is in Public Affairs Re-

committee proposal created a legal system of classification to encompass the de facto classification already in existence. Land was to be assessed statewide at 10 percent of fair market value, as were "improvements for residential purposes" (homes). Other property (*i.e.,* business-industrial properties and apartment houses) was to be assessed at 15 percent of fair market value. Governor Edwards urged the convention to assess each category at 12.5 percent, so that "no one can then say that we've been unfair, or that we're jeopardizing anybody's right to own and hold a piece of property or to own and hold any home."[33] The convention rejected his suggestion.

The proposal also raised the homestead exemption to $3,000 and provided for a further increase to $5,000 for all homeowners, not only veterans, should the legislature subsequently enact the provision by a two-thirds vote. (In 1976 the legislature did just that, to the predictable anguish of those on whose nonexempt property millages might rise sharply, and in 1980 the exemption was raised once again, by constitutional amendment, to $7,500.) Henceforth, assessors themselves, rather than the Tax Commission, would "determine the fair market value of all property" within their districts, another instance of legalizing the way things had been done in fact for years. Railroad, pipeline, and utility properties, however, would continue to be assessed by the Tax Commission. Finally, all property in the state was to be assessed by December, 1978, and reassessed every four years thereafter.[34]

During the two months between adjournment of the convention and referendum day (set by the governor for April 20, 1974), Louisianians took one side or the other. Among the organizations supporting ratification were the NAACP, League of Women Voters, Louisiana AFL-CIO, Louisiana Education Association, and a number of local officials' organizations: the sheriffs', school boards', district attorneys', police jurors', municipal associations', and assessors'.[35] Among the organizations opposed to ratification were the Louisiana Teachers' As-

---

search Council, "The Property Tax," in *Convention Commentary* (Baton Rouge: Public Affairs Research Council, August 3, 1973), No. 3.

33. *Records of the Louisiana Constitutional Convention: Journal and Calendar,* II, 1,161–162.

34. Louisiana Constitution, Art. VII, Pt. II, Secs. 18, 20, 23.

35. Public Affairs Research Council, "Special Election on the Constitution," 2.

sociation, Republican State Central Committee, Louisiana State Chamber of Commerce, Louisiana Manufacturers' Association, Public Service Commission, and, for what it was worth, the Ku Klux Klan.

Also, and ominously, opposed to ratification were the majority of metropolitan, large-circulation newspapers; they contended that the document was "brazenly political," as if any other kind of constitution could be written in Louisiana. PAR, the influential government research organization, took no specified stand for or against the entire document, but "its director . . . [had] been highly critical of the taxation, civil service, and education provisions."[36] Joining with influential forces in opposition to the proposed constitution were many voters, who, as indicated by scattered polls, remained indifferent, if not hostile, to the document. Ratification seemed, indeed, to be in jeopardy.

During the second week in April, Assessor Chehardy of Jefferson Parish commenced a brief but aggressive and historically significant career as a television personality in the densely populated New Orleans area. To call attention to his frequent video appearances and to announce the subject of his discourses, Chehardy placed a succession of prominent advertisements in leading New Orleans newspapers. One that appeared on April 13 in the *Times-Picayune* was typical: "Chehardy Tells it like it is on Television. *Important Tax News.* The Supreme Court has ordered every assessor in Louisiana to re-appraise all property at 100% of actual cash value. We can only stop this *tax raising plan* by changing the law itself. *Learn the truth why we must vote for the new constitution.*"[37] Editorials in opposition newspapers were quick to condemn Chehardy's "scare talk" and to brand the assessor's tactics as "an insult to the intelligence of all Louisiana residents." Nonetheless, as PAR recalled afterward, "There was no counter television campaign. . . . Even those delegates who knew the assessor's claims to be misleading were conspicuous by their silence to offer correct information to the voters. Indeed, many delegates parroted the claims of the Jefferson Parish assessor."[38]

36. Shreveport *Times*, April 3, 1974, Sec. 1, p. 1, quoted *ibid.*, Baton Rouge *State Times*, April 18, 1974, Sec. A, p. 2.

37. New Orleans *Times-Picayune*, April 13, 1974, Sec. 1, p. 18, final italics mine.

38. Baton Rouge *State Times*, April 18, 1974, Sec. A, p. 2, quoted in Public Affairs Research Council, "Special Election on the Constitution," 3.

When the votes had been counted after referendum day, a number of sobering facts were apparent. Polls suggesting that many voters remained indifferent to constitutional revision in general and to CC-73 in particular were amply vindicated—63.7 percent of Louisiana's registered electorate had not taken part in the referendum. Evidence that other voters would oppose the new constitution was also proven by its rejection in thirty-six of the sixty-four parishes, most of them in North Louisiana. Also demonstrated was the power of television to sway a mass electorate, even when the message carried by television was misleading. For, despite its rejection in North Louisiana and its marginal support elsewhere, the proposed constitution was ratified on the basis of an immense majority of favorable votes cast in the four-parish New Orleans area, at which the misleading Chehardy television blitz had been aimed, and where the document was approved by a regional landslide of 76.9 percent of the votes cast. Indeed, the margin of victory in the New Orleans area alone, 103,371 votes, "exceeded the statewide margin of passage (98,304) by 5,067 votes." As PAR put it, "If voters in any region could be singled out as having been responsible for the ratification of the new constitution, it would be those in the New Orleans region."[39]

Two days after the referendum, Governor Edwards, whose prestige was linked to ratification, stated with apparent gratitude, "I've had people telling me what a political liability Lawrence Chehardy is to me. . . . Boy, what a political liability."[40]

Thus was elitism sustained in the Louisiana constitution of 1974. Not only was the document written by a convention of the elite, who incorporated within it such special interest provisions as judges' retirement, the five education boards, and numerous exemptions from property taxation, but in the process of ratification itself, members of the elite felt compelled to fall back on demagoguery and did so successfully. The present Louisiana constitution, to put it simply, was not endorsed entirely on the basis of its merits. We have it largely because anxious and misinformed homeowners in Louisiana's major popula-

39. Public Affairs Research Council, "Special Election on the Constitution," 6, 8–10, 11–12.
40. Shreveport *Times*, April 22, 1974, Sec. I, p. I.

tion center were misinformed about the effect the new constitution would have upon property taxation. As I observed in 1975:

> The issue . . . is *not* whether the proposed constitution should or should not have been ratified, but rather the performance of the voting public in Louisiana which made ratification possible. Voter behavior in the constitutional referendum provokes one to question how far democracy has come in Louisiana and how viable it actually is when, as recently as 1974, a large majority of the electorate still ignored vital public issues and declined to participate in resolving those issues, while many who did participate continued to let modern "intendants" and "patrones" make their decisions for them.[41]

The remaining two decades of this century are not going to be easy times in Louisiana. Since the days of Huey Long, state revenue and services have depended disproportionately upon severance taxes and royalties levied on extraction of oil and natural gas, which are rapidly disappearing. Who will pay the bill after these minerals have been exhausted? If services must be reduced, shifted from the state to the local level, or eliminated, which services will be affected? Most important of all, who will resolve these problems in the final analysis, and to whose benefit will the solutions ultimately accrue? While it is not pleasant to advance "gloom-and-doom" prophesies, the ongoing vitality of Louisiana's elitist tradition of constitutional revision offers limited scope for optimism.

41. Mark T. Carleton, Perry H. Howard, and Joseph B. Parker (eds.), *Readings in Louisiana Politics* (Baton Rouge: Claitor's, 1975), 447.

3.

The Legislature

PATRICK F. O'CONNOR

The Louisiana legislature has been the scene of some of the most colorful and tumultuous events in the state's political history. The sensational among these may come most quickly to mind—the impeachment and assassination of Huey Long, the "breakdown" of Earl Long—but many thousands of others, far less dramatic, have been significant in shaping government in Louisiana. The focus of this chapter, however, will not be particular events, but rather the character of the state's legislative institution. Features of structure and operation that affect the legislature's role in the policy-making process will be emphasized more than the "nuts and bolts" of legislative operation.

Legislative Selection

Apportionment of Legislative Seats

Few structural features of legislative bodies affect the character of representation and the distribution of political power more directly than the configuration of legislative districts and the method of electing representatives. Since the political stakes are high, legislative reapportionment is generally a contentious issue in American politics. Louisiana's experience has been no exception. After the adoption of the constitution in 1921 and the apportionment plan it contained, no major changes in the apportionment of the state legislature were made until 1963. The only responses to the pattern of growth and decline among the parishes were minor adjustments in 1954 and 1960 that distributed five additional house seats to Jefferson and East Baton Rouge Parishes. These adjustments increased the size of the house of representatives from 100 to 105 but made no changes in the apportionment of the original 100 seats. When the federal courts entered the apportionment arena in 1962 with an insistence upon equal-population legislative districts, the familiar American pattern of rural overrepresentation marked Louisiana's districting arrangements. Long-term population movement from the countryside into the cities and suburbs, coupled with the legislature's failure to obey the state constitutional requirement that it reapportion itself after the censuses of 1930, 1940, 1950, and 1960, meant that the legislative apportionment in the 1960s would fail to meet the United States Supreme Court's "one person, one vote" requirement.

Indeed, the 1921 apportionment in the year of its creation would have failed recently established judicial standards requiring "one person, one vote." There were districts that varied widely from the average district population, and these differences ran as high as 78 percent in the house and 63 percent in the senate. In addition, the 1921 constitution precluded equal population legislative districts in the house by a requirement that each parish of the state and each ward of Orleans Parish receive at least one representative. This meant that eighty of the one hundred house seats were distributed on the basis of political jurisdictions and without regard to population. By 1960, however, the state's most populous parish was not underrepresented, although there were large inequalities in the ratios of people to representatives from ward to ward. Orleans Parish contained 19.3 percent of the population in the 1960 census and was alloted 19.1 percent of the seats in the lower house and 20.5 percent in the upper chamber.[1] The remaining parishes with a 1960 population of over 100,000 did not fare so well, however. Together, the parishes of Caddo, East Baton Rouge, Jefferson, and Calcasieu contained 34 percent of the state's population but were allocated only 20 percent of the house seats. A similar pattern prevailed in the senate. Since the most urbanized areas of Louisiana were either underrepresented or given no more than a proportionate

1. Alex B. Lacey, Jr., "The Louisiana Legislature," Lacey (ed.), *Power in American State Legislatures*, Tulane Studies in Political Science, VI (New Orleans: Tulane University Press, 1967), 63–64.

number of legislators (in the case of Orleans), the more rural areas necessarily were overrepresented.

Following the United States Supreme Court's adoption of its strict apportionment standard, the Louisiana legislature was reapportioned on three occasions, twice by its own hand and most recently by the federal courts. In early 1963, prompted by a suit by four citizens of East Baton Rouge Parish, the legislature reallocated legislative seats in the house only. Since the 1921 state constitution mandated the distribution of eighty-five seats to political units, this reapportionment consisted only of a redistribution of the remaining twenty-five seats. The resulting ratios of legislators-to-population were more nearly equal from district to district than previously, but the constitution's allocation of one representative to every parish and to every ward in Orleans meant that significant discrepancies remained. The 1963 reapportionment plan survived judicial challenge, however, partly because, so soon after *Baker* v. *Carr* in 1962, the courts had not yet developed very clear tests of fair apportionment.

After the legislature failed to reapportion further in 1964 and 1965, several individuals from Jefferson Parish, one of the most underrepresented in the state, secured a federal court order directing the legislature to reapportion itself by the end of the year or face a judicial solution, probably statewide at-large elections.[2] The legislature responded with a new apportionment law for both house and senate that substantially restructured the method of electing legislators. The new districts were considerably closer to being equal in population, but in order to achieve the higher degree of equality upon which the federal courts were then insisting, the legislature had to ignore the state constitutional guarantee of at least one representative per parish or ward of Orleans. No parish or Orleans ward boundaries were crossed, but in some instances several were combined in creating house districts.

The 1966 apportionment was used in the 1968 elections only, for the federal census in 1970 provided new population figures. The state constitution required—and more importantly the federal courts now clearly expected—that these would form the basis for a reapportionment in time for the 1971 elections. The 1971 reapportionment round,

2. Lacey, "The Louisiana Legislature," 63.

which established the legislative districts to be used until after the 1980 census, resulted in radically different districting arrangements, and the transition was anything but smooth. The 1971 apportionment law was challenged on a variety of grounds in four federal suits. The bases for these suits included racial discrimination as well as population discrepancies. Districts deviated from the average population by as much as −14.82 to +12.31 percent in the house and −10.57 to +11.81 percent in the senate. Nor were the districts uniform in type: single-member and multimember districts were used, as well as several other variations. During the course of the federal suits, U.S. District Judge E. Gordon West appointed Edward J. Steimel, director of the Public Affairs Research Council of Louisiana (PAR), a special master to assist the court in preparing an alternative apportionment plan that the court could substitute for the one being challenged. Before the court could act, however, the U.S. Justice Department declared the 1971 act racially discriminatory under provisions of the federal Voting Rights Act. The federal court's ruling embraced the alternative apportionment plan developed by the special master and ordered its use in the 1971 legislative elections. This plan is still in effect and will be used until after the 1980 census.

In several respects the 1971 court-ordered reapportionment was a significant departure from previous practice in legislative districting. First, single-member legislative districts were used exclusively in both chambers. Under the apportionment law employed in the 1967 legislative elections, 80 percent of the representatives and 56 percent of the senators were chosen from multimember districts. In 1963, 42 percent of the house members and 21 percent of the senators were chosen from multimember districts—percentages that were virtually the same back to 1921. Second, parish boundaries were crossed frequently in drawing the single-member districts of 1971. Ward lines in New Orleans were also ignored. In creating 39 senate districts, eight of the sixty-four parishes found a portion of their territory combined with some or all of one or more other parishes in the new districts. For the 105 house districts over half (thirty-six, or 56.3 percent) of the parishes were fragmented in this way. The 1971 apportionment thus represented the first time that traditional political units were not coterminous with legislative districts. Finally, districts were approximately equal in population, and any vestige of remaining rural overrepresentation was eliminated. The average house district contained 34,697 inhabitants by the 1970 census, and the average senate district contained 93,415 persons. The maximum deviation from the house average ranged from −4.6 to +4.6 percent. In the senate the deviation ranged from −8.8 to +5.6 percent.

All of the consequences of these changes in Louisiana's legislative apportionment have not been fully studied, but several results are apparent. First, there has been an improvement in the fortunes of blacks and Republicans in house contests. The number of black legislators increased from one immediately prior to the 1971 reapportionment to ten in 1979 (nine in the house and one in the senate). Division of the larger urban parishes into single-member districts has created constituencies with the social and political characteristics most likely to elect members of this minority. For example, under the 1971 apportionment twelve house districts had black majorities in their population, and in another sixteen, blacks made up over 40 percent of the population. Nine of the twelve house districts with black majorities elected black legislators in 1975, and these came from those black-majority districts with the highest percentages of black population (all over 58 percent). All ten black legislators represented districts that lay within the parishes of Orleans, East Baton Rouge, or Caddo. While registration percentages for blacks are generally lower than their percentages in the population, single-member districts prevent black minorities from being entirely swamped by white majorities.

Similarly, Louisiana's Republican minority seems to have profited from the electoral changes. From 1921 to 1963 no Republicans were elected to the Louisiana legislature (See Table 3-1). Two were chosen for the 1964–1967 legislature, one for the 1968–1971 body, and four and five respectively were elected in 1972 and 1975. One Republican senator was elected in 1975. After the 1975 elections, four legislators who ran as Democrats switched to the GOP. The Republicans consolidated these gains in 1979 when all four were reelected as Republicans, and five other Republicans were elected as well. Though the incumbent Republican senator was defeated, the present GOP contingent in the house represents the largest number in this century. The somewhat improved Republican fortunes undoubtedly are due in part to a generally more favorable climate for Republicans in the South, but there is evidence that many of the house districts created within pre-

Table 3-1
Republicans in the Louisiana Legislature

Year	House		Senate	
	Elected	Switched	Elected	Switched
1921–1963	0	0	0	0
1964–1967	2	0	0	0
1968–1971	1*	0	0	1
1972–1975	4	0	0	1
1976–1979	4	4	1	0
1980–	9	1†	0	0†

*Elected in 1970.
† Figures as of February 1980.

viously unsubdivided urban parishes contain populations with the social characteristics typically associated with Republican party preferences. For example, seven of the nine Republicans in the 1979 House, including the four originally elected as Republicans, come from the sixteen districts with the highest percentages of the population employed in white-collar occupations. If future Republican success is tied to this same social base, expansion of the Republican contingent in the legislature may be limited. However, the single-member district reapportionment of 1971 seems to have distinctly improved Republican chances to elect at least a few legislators.

Although it is more difficult to document, it is generally thought that the move to single-member districts reduced the legislative influence of organized labor. Union strength apparently became more confined to particular urban districts. Under a system that employed multimember districts, this large interest group was formerly successful in contributing to the election of entire delegations from some of the larger parishes.

Certainly, future reapportionments will be politically important, and doubtlessly, they will be vigorously contested, but it is unlikely that they will produce the turmoil or confusion that accompanied the transition made in 1971. The Louisiana constitution adopted in 1974 requires the exclusive use of single-member districts, and therefore, a return to multimember districts is legally foreclosed. Also, it is less likely that federal courts will devise Louisiana's future legislative reapportionments since the state is now generally in compliance with what the courts expect and will need to make only marginal adjustments to account for population shifts. Moreover, the 1974 constitution provides for reapportionment by the state supreme court if the legislature fails in its duty.

Electing Legislators

In Louisiana the process of electing a legislature has traditionally been a competitive one, at least in comparison to other states of the one-party South. Malcolm E. Jewell's study of southern legislative elections provides comparative data on Democratic primary competition from 1948 through 1964, which, along with information on the 1971, 1975, and 1979 Louisiana elections, are shown in Table 3-2. *Competitiveness* is not easily definable in primaries with varying numbers of candidates from district to district and with the possibility of runoffs in some districts but not others. Following Jewell, five different calculations are presented, each of which may tap some dimension of competitiveness in legislative elections: (1) the percentage of races with more than one candidate, (2) the percentage of races in which the eventual winner received less than 60 percent of the vote in the first primary, (3) the percentage of races in which three or more candidates ran, (4) the percentage of races in which there was a runoff, and (5) the percentage of incumbents seeking reelection who were defeated in the primaries.[3] If one considers high percentages on each of these measures indicative of competitiveness, then Table 3-2 makes clear that Louisiana's legislative races have been more competitive than those of most other southern states. Louisiana has more frequently had contested legislative seats, close races, numerous candidates, and the necessity of runoffs. Until recently, there was also a high incidence of defeated incumbents. The differences are most striking in Jewell's data for 1948–1964, but no information on more recent elections for states other than Louisiana is available. The 1971 legislative primaries were comparable in competitiveness to the Louisiana averages for the 1948–1961 period, although there was a drop-off for all indicators of competitiveness in the 1975 and 1979 legislative races. Since the 1971, 1975, and 1979

3. Malcolm R. Jewell, *Legislative Representation in the Contemporary South* (Durham, N.C.: Duke University Press, 1967), 12–16.

contests were held under a newly created single-member-district legislative apportionment, there are problems of comparability with elections held earlier. In addition, the 1975 and 1979 races were not Democratic primaries, but rather the first set of legislative elections held under the state's open elections system. Thus, some Republicans are included among the candidates in these years.

The past competitiveness of Louisiana's legislative elections undoubtedly was associated with the unique bifactionalism that characterized the state's politics. The years in which clearly identifiable Long and Anti-Long candidates regularly faced one another in gubernatorial elections were times of extraordinary polarization for a one-party state, and the conflicts were as intense at the level of legislative elections as they were in gubernatorial races. In fact, the connection between gubernatorial and legislative campaigns was often direct and took the form of open, mutual endorsements of gubernatorial and legislative candidates. Although the extent of the practice varied from parish to parish and election to election, a system of slating was employed in which gubernatorial candidates created tickets, which they shared with local candidates of their faction. It is probably not the slating per se that caused heavily contested legislative elections, but rather the widely felt relevance of legislative and other local elections in Louisiana's highly competitive gubernatorial politics. Gubernatorial candidates also felt it necessary to connect themselves with local political organizations.

Slating seems to have declined in recent Louisiana elections, although the absence of firm comparative data and the apparent variability of the practice in the past make generalizations risky. The passing of Earl Long from the political scene in Louisiana may have been the watershed that marked the beginning of a lower level of direct association between gubernatorial and legislative politics. Jewell noted that slating declined sharply in the 1959–1960 elections.[4] In a 1972 survey of legislators, 24 percent of the senators said that they supported a gubernatorial candidate, and a large majority of legislators in both chambers (79 and 71 percent in the house and senate respectively) indicated that they frequently asked their own supporters to vote for their choice in the gubernatorial race.

4. *Ibid.*, 88.

Table 3-2

Competition in Legislative Primaries in Louisiana
and Other Southern States
(In Percentages)

	Contested Races	Won by Under 60 Percent	Three or More Candidates	Runoffs	Incumbents Beaten as Percentage of Incumbents Running
Lower House Southern States 1948–1964	71	47	28	19	19
Upper House Southern States 1948–1964	66	47	21	15	23
Louisiana House 1948–1964	94	76	65	42	43
Louisiana Senate 1948–1964	93	82	79	52	38
Louisiana House 1971–72	95	84	81	66	44*
Louisiana Senate 1971–72	87	71	67	51	27*
Louisiana House 1975	77	54	56	34	15
Louisiana Senate 1975	82	54	41	33	24
Louisiana House 1979	80	49	52	32	9
Louisiana Senate 1979	85	31	39	21	10

Source: Data from the 1948–1964 period are calculated from Malcolm E. Jewell, *Legislative Representation in the Contemporary South* (Durham, N.C.: Duke University Press, 1967), Table 2.1, p. 16.

*Because of reapportionment, a number of incumbent legislators were placed in the same districts as other incumbents. In the house 70 incumbents ran in 60 districts; a minimum of 10 had to lose, therefore. In the senate there was only one district in which two incumbents ran. If the percentages of defeated incumbents are calculated by subtracting the number of such forced losses from the actual losses and dividing the resultant figure by the number of districts in which incumbents were running, the percentages are 35 for the house and 24 for the senate.

The decline in the percentage of defeated incumbents in the 1975 and 1979 elections is noteworthy also. While the large percentages of defeated incumbents in 1972 were partly due to the dislocations of reapportionment and a mood of public dissatisfaction with state government, neither of these factors was present in the two subsequent elections. In addition, it is probable that the new single-member-district reapportionment of 1971, once it had produced an initial group of legislators, was a factor promoting more favorable conditions for incumbents. With single-member districts, individual constituencies are smaller and more socially homogeneous than under older districting arrangements, and nonincumbent candidates may have less ability to build successful coalitions in opposition to sitting legislators.

Stability and Turnover

A common concern among observers of legislatures is that a high turnover rate robs the legislature of the accumulated experience that comes with a stable membership. Table 3-3 shows that Louisiana's house and senate have consistently seen a significant turnover of membership with each legislative election. From 1948 to 1980 a nearly identical portion of the house and senate, around 47 percent, had served in the previous legislature. Thus, on the average, over half of the membership has been composed of legislators who had not served in the previous legislature. Data for other states for the same years are not readily available, but from 1963 to 1971, averages of 63.9 percent of the members of the lower chambers in all state legislatures and 69.6 percent of the senators had also served in the previous session. In the U.S. Congress the comparable figures were 85 percent for the house and 90 percent for the senate. In general, it has been found that legislative turnover rates are higher in the southern states and in states in which the terms are longer (four years instead of two).[5]

Voluntary departures, either into political retirement or to seek other office, account for a portion of legislative turnover. Slightly over one-

5. Alan Rosenthal, "And So They Leave: Legislative Turnover in the States," *State Government*, XLVII (Summer, 1974), 149–52; Kwang S. Shin and John S. Jackson III, "Membership Turnover in U.S. State Legislatures, 1931–1976," *Legislative Studies Quarterly*, IV (February, 1979), 95–104. It should be noted that the figures Rosenthal cites for Louisiana are incorrect.

Table 3-3
Membership Stability in the Louisiana Legislature

Beginning Year of Legislature	Percentage of Legislators Serving in Previous Session		Percentage of Legislators with Previous Service	
	House	*Senate*	*House*	*Senate*
1948	48.5	48.7	. . . .	. . . .
1952	25.7	28.2	. . . .	. . . .
1956	41.5	30.7	56.4	64.1
1960	45.5	41.0	57.4	59.0
1964	36.1	46.1	46.2	74.4
1968	52.4	56.4	56.2	71.8
1972	39.0	48.7	42.9	61.5
1976	67.6	56.4	70.5	69.2
1980	74.3	71.8	75.2	84.6
AVERAGE	47.8	47.6	57.8	69.2

Sources: Percentages of incumbents 1948–1964 from Alex B. Lacey, Jr., "The Louisiana Legislature," in Lacey (ed.), *Power in American State Legislatures*, Tulane Studies in Political Science, VI (New Orleans: Tulane University Press, 1967), Table 2, p. 56; percentage with previous service calculated from data in Public Affairs Research Council, *Citizens' Guides* to legislatures from 1956 to 1976 (Baton Rouge: Public Affairs Research Council, 1956–76).

fifth (21.51 percent) of the Louisiana legislators serving from 1952 to 1975 did not seek reelection to the legislature.[6] Defeat of incumbents is another contributing factor, and as Table 3-2 demonstrates, until recently incumbents have been less successful in being reelected in Louisiana than in other southern states. This picture has been somewhat changed and the rate of reelection has been higher in the 1970s than it was previously.

The percentage of returning incumbents in a session does not accurately depict the level of legislative experience, however. Table 3-3 shows that among those elected to sessions beginning in years from 1956 to 1976, 57.8 percent of Louisiana representatives and 69.2 per-

6. June Savoy, "Personnel Factors in the Louisiana State Legislature, 1952–1972" (M.A. thesis, University of Southwestern Louisiana, 1974), 81.

cent of senators had had previous service in at least one chamber of the legislature.

The Legislators

The social profile of Louisiana legislators is not notably different from that of senators and representatives in other states. Most legislators in Louisiana have been males. Only seven women have been originally elected to either chamber since 1952. The legislature has reflected the religious preferences of the state and generally has been composed of about half Catholics and half Protestants. The inability of blacks to win legislative seats and their recently improved opportunities have been mentioned. The ten black legislators elected in 1979 make up 6.9 percent of the legislature; the black portion of the Louisiana electorate in 1979 was 23.5 percent.

Louisiana legislators are fairly young as a group. In 1976 the average ages of representatives and senators were forty-four and forty-two respectively. These figures are very similar to those of the past. The older legislators, many of whom have had extensive political experience, are balanced by a number of young people who seek a legislative seat as their first political office. A survey of representatives in 1972, a year with a larger than average legislative turnover, showed that 56 percent of representatives and 50 percent of senators had not held another office prior to their election to the legislature.

The occupational affiliations of legislators traditionally have interested political scientists, largely because of the obvious stake that occupational groups have in the outcome of many public policy decisions. Moreover, certain occupations are perennially overrepresented in the legislature when compared to society at large, and almost all legislators continue to practice their regular occupations during their legislative term. As Table 3-4 shows, business occupations and the legal profession predominate in the legislature. The implications of having a legislative occupational structure at variance with that of the larger society that it represents are not fully known. One analysis, however, related that lawyers, who make up the largest occupational group in the Louisiana legislature, exhibit some interesting differences in behavior when compared to nonlawyers. Lawyers in the 1972–1975 Louisiana house were more likely to be politically liberal in their self-defined po-

Table 3-4
Occupations of Louisiana Legislators
(In Percentages)

	House		Senate	
	1972	*1976*	*1972*	*1976*
Agriculture	6.7	9.5	15.4	10.3
Attorneys	30.4	28.6	38.4	51.3
Education	5.7	7.6	2.6	7.7
Financial	4.8	4.8	2.6	0.0
Insurance	9.5	7.6	12.8	12.8
Real Estate	8.6	10.5	7.7	7.7
Retail Sales	15.2	11.4	5.1	5.1
Public Employees (except Education)	2.9	4.8	2.6	0.0
Other	15.2	16.2	12.8	5.1
Not reported	1.0	1.0	0.0	0.0
TOTAL	100.0	100.0	100.0	100.0

Source: Public Affairs Council of Louisiana, *Citizens' Guides* to the 1972 and 1976 legislatures.

litical philosophy; they were rated by close observers of the legislature as being more "effective" as legislators; they introduced more bills and amendments; they were more likely to be generalists than specialists in approaching their jobs; they were less inclined than nonlawyers to participate in the meetings of standing committees in the interim between legislative sessions. In addition, lawyers were found to be more politically "independent" than nonlawyers. This independence was evidenced in lawyer-legislators' tendency to give less support than their colleagues to Governor Edwards, in their expressed attitudes toward executive leadership in general, and in the greater tendency of lawyer-legislators to support legislative reforms designed to make the legislature more independent of the executive branch. Many of these patterns of behavior represent differences in legislative style, however, and analysis of roll call voting did not reveal that lawyer and nonlawyer legislators were distinguishable groups in general legislative voting.[7]

7. Patrick F. O'Connor, *et al.*, "The Political Behavior of Lawyers in the Louisiana House of Representatives," *Louisiana Law Review*, XXXIX (November, 1979), 43–79.

Legislative Structure and Organization

The Louisiana constitution creates a legislature limited to 105 representatives and 39 senators elected for simultaneous four-year terms. Legislators must be at least eighteen years of age, residents of the state for a minimum of two years, and residents of their districts for at least one year prior to qualifying for election. The Louisiana legislature is a part-time body, with regular annual sessions constitutionally restricted to a maximum of sixty "legislative days" (a day on which either chamber meets) during a period of eighty-five calendar days beginning on the third Monday of April. Before the 1974 constitution, the legislature met even less frequently, with sixty-day sessions in even numbered years alternating with thirty-day sessions restricted to fiscal matters in odd numbered years. The days spent in regular session do not convey the full extent of legislative activity, however. The governor occasionally calls special sessions, and it has become increasingly common for the standing committees of the legislature to be active during the interim between sessions. The constitution creates the legislature as a "continuous" body at the same time as it limits the duration of regular sessions. Staff activity is also continuous, and in recent years there has been significant expansion of the legislative staff's size and capabilities.

Legislative Authority

The legislature is the chief law-making agency of the state, although effectively binding public decisions are also made by other institutions. In general, the legislature is authorized to enact laws on any subject so long is it is not expressly prohibited from doing so by the federal or state constitutions. The limitations in the state constitution are significant in many areas, although a complete catalogue is inappropriate here. Under the constitution, the legislature cannot infringe upon the authority of the other branches or abridge the individual rights enumerated in the state bill of rights. Specific constitutional provisions place certain subjects beyond the legislature's reach (*e.g.*, the legislature may not authorize the state or a local government to conduct a lottery). The legislature is bound by the state constitution to perform certain actions according to prescribed procedures, but the 1974 Louisiana constitution places fewer restrictions upon the legislature than the 1921 constitution. Not only were some explicit limitations taken out but also much material of a statutory nature was removed from the constitution and made subject to legislative action. Also, many constitutional dedications of revenue were eliminated, giving the legislature greater authority to make meaningful fiscal decisions.

Leadership

While legislatures are basically collegial bodies in which decisions are made by all members casting equally weighted votes, they are not without their hierarchy, both formal and informal. The principal officials of the Louisiana legislature are the speaker of the house and the president of the senate. These presiding officers of each chamber possess a variety of procedural powers. They appoint the chairmen, vice-chairmen, and members of all standing committees, except the House Appropriations Committee. The speaker of the house names seven of its members (one from each Public Service Commission District and two at large), and the remaining eight members (one from each congressional district) are elected by the members of the house of representatives. Within some constraints, the presiding officers also appoint conference committees to work out compromises between the house and senate versions of bills that have passed the two chambers in different form. In addition to these and other minor appointing powers, the presiding officers derive some influence from their power to interpret and apply parliamentary rules.

Until recently, the speaker of the house has also been a prominent figure in gubernatorial factions. Louisiana governors have not been reluctant to seek the election of officers in the house and senate friendly to the administration, and loyal presiding officers have been one of the major means for securing executive influence in the legislature. The speakers' ties to gubernatorial factions are evident in the high rate of turnover in the position. Since R. Norman Bauer served as speaker from 1940 to 1948 under the administrations of Sam Jones and Jimmie Davis, both Anti-Long or "reform" governors, no speaker has held the post in two different administrations. In some cases, this may have been because certain speakers failed to return to subsequent legislatures, but on several occasions speakers have been displaced with a change of gubernatorial administration while remaining in the house.

During the Edwards administration, these traditional factional ties were altered significantly. E. L. "Bubba" Henry, elected speaker in 1972, was not Edwards' hand-picked candidate, although the governor did not oppose him. Even though the men were not factional opponents and their relationship involved a great deal of cooperation, Henry developed and maintained a degree of independence unprecedented in recent Louisiana political history. Henry's successful bid for the office can be attributed to a conjunction of forces in Louisiana politics that may not recur again: a higher than usual turnover rate in the 1972 legislature, a vigorous movement among mainly younger members to achieve a higher degree of professionalism and independence, and a governor not inclined to exert the maximum possible control over legislative operations.

Under the 1921 constitution the presiding officer of the senate was the lieutenant governor. There has been little time for testing the newly created position of president of the senate, but its first occupant, Senator Michael O'Keefe, was considered a prominent Edwards administration leader. He had been president pro tem of the senate before being elected president.

It has been the practice among Louisiana governors to designate several legislators in each chamber as administration floor leaders. There is no meaningful majority party organization in the legislature, and as a result governors must develop an *ad hoc* group of legislators whose role it is to promote and engineer passage of the governor's preferences on legislative issues. While there are signs that a movement for a more independent legislature made some headway in the 1970s, it has been traditional in Louisiana for the governor to dominate the legislature, initiating most of the major legislation. The celebrated attempt by Huey Long's factional opponents to impeach him should not suggest that the legislature has normally been a check on governors. Instead, aided partly by the factional loyalties of legislators, the governor of Louisiana has been the "undisputed master" of the legislature.[8] It is no doubt symptomatic of this relationship that, during the entire period from 1921 until the present, there has been no successful attempt to secure the two-thirds vote in each house necessary to override a gubernatorial veto.

8. Allan P. Sindler, "Bifactional Rivalry as an Alternative to Two-Party Competition in Louisiana," *American Political Science Review*, XLIX (September, 1955), 653.

Other sources of political leadership exist within the legislature, although none can match the executive faction in effectiveness and scope. Some legislators develop well-recognized expertise on particular subjects and can be exceptionally persuasive on these matters. Many legislators become the advocates of the causes of particular interest groups in the legislature, and these interest groups in cooperation with friendly legislators provide one type of leadership on many issues. In the house, a black caucus and a speaker's "study group" have been significant since 1972. The mayor of New Orleans has informally designated legislators from Orleans Parish to act as floor leaders for the city when issues affecting local interests are before the legislature, and some parish delegations have an active group life. These delegations hold meetings, and in some cases, formal organizations have been developed to the point of hiring staff to work for the entire delegation. One of the more interesting leadership forces in the House is the Independent Legislative Study Group (commonly called the conservative caucus) formed after the 1975 elections. The group of about sixteen legislators pooled their office expense allowances and some personal funds to employ aides to work for the entire group. The conservative factional organization functioned very much like the sort of gubernatorial opposition or minority party organization that might be found in a two-party legislature.

The Committee System

In the American legislative tradition, there are no more important internal legislative institutions than the standing committees. These bodies exist to provide close, expert scrutiny of legislation by legislators who specialize in a limited subject matter. If the committee system in Louisiana differs from that of other states, it is only in the details of its structure and operation, not in its underlying rationale. Under Louisiana's legislative rules, bills are assigned to the standing committee appropriate to the measure's subject matter. The committees usually hold hearings during which interested individuals and groups may testify. According to the constitution, such a hearing must be held if the bill is to be reported by the committee. The committee's staff may do research relevant to the legislation. A majority of the committee may report the bill to be voted on by the entire chamber. They are permitted to report it with any one of several recommendations: reported favorably, reported unfavorably, reported with amendments, reported without action, and reported by substitute. In addition, house committees reporting a measure without action may recommend referral of the measure to another committee. The committee may also choose not to report the legislation at all, effectively killing it under most circumstances.

In theory the standing committee system allows legislators to develop expertise in certain areas. This expertise should be beneficial in helping to screen legislation. However, the committees of the Louisiana legislature have been seriously deficient in practice, although significant strides in committee improvement have been achieved in recent years.

In 1979 there were fifteen standing committees in each house. The number has fluctuated from year to year following occasional efforts at substantial structural overhaul. (See Table 3-6.) In 1954, for example, there was a major reduction in the number of standing committees in both chambers. This was consistent with a nationwide trend and was intended to reduce the number of different committees on which a legislator served. While changes in size since 1954 have been minor, the identity of the committees has been altered somewhat, and there has been an effort made to equalize their workloads and to create subject-matter jurisdictions that more closely correspond from chamber to chamber. Table 3-5 indicates the number of bills assigned to each standing committee in 1978. The four committees with the largest number of assigned bills accounted for 44.5 percent of all bills in the senate and 42.1 percent in the house. In 1960, by comparison, the top four committees handled 73.8 percent of the bills in the senate and 76.1 percent of those in the house. In fact, in the senate in 1960, 61.3 percent of all bills were referred to the top two committees, Judiciary A and Judiciary B.

In addition to the inequitable workload that obviously existed in the committee system, these figures also point to the fact that subject-matter jurisdictions of the committees, implied in their names, were frequently ignored in assigning bills. Until 1973, the rules did not define the committees' jurisdictions (other than as might be reflected in committee names), and it was common practice for legislators to use floor motions to request assignment of their bills to the committees

Table 3-5

Legislative Committees and Bill Assignments, 1978

House Committee	Numbers of Bill Referrals	Percentage of Total Referrals
Administration of Criminal Justice	215	10.8
Agriculture	19	1.0
Appropriations	180	9.1
Civil Law and Procedure	225	11.3
Commerce	198	10.3
Education	93	4.7
Health and Welfare	100	5.0
House and Governmental Affairs	107	5.4
Judiciary	87	4.4
Labor and Industrial Relations	54	2.7
Municipal and Parochial Affairs	103	5.2
Natural Resources	124	6.3
Retirement	180	9.1
Transportation, Highways, and Public Works	100	5.0
Ways and Means	199	10.0
TOTAL	1984	100.0

Senate Committee	Numbers of Bill Referrals	Percentage of Total Referrals
Agriculture	19	1.2
Commerce	112	6.9
Education	54	3.3
Finance	139	8.5
Judiciary A	205	12.6
Judiciary B	158	9.7
Judiciary C	111	6.8
Health and Welfare	83	5.1
Revenue and Fiscal Affairs	108	6.6
Labor and Industrial Relations	33	2.0
Local and Municipal Affairs	147	9.0
Natural Resources	70	4.3
Retirement	87	5.3
Senate and Governmental Affairs	215	13.2
Transportation, Highways, and Public Works	89	5.5
TOTAL	1630	100.0

Table 3-6

Number and Sizes of Standing Committees, 1952–1976

Year	House			Senate		
	Number of Committees	Average No. of Committee Assignments Per Legislator	Average Size of Committee	Number of Committees	Average No. of Committee Assignments Per Legislator	Average Size of Committee
1952	35	4.4	12.4	28	6.6	9.3
1956	14	2.3	16.6	17	4.4	10.8
1960	14	2.4	16.8	17	4.5	10.2
1964	16	2.5	16.5	19	4.7	9.7
1968	21	3.4	16.9	20	5.1	10.0
1972	16	2.4	15.8	12	2.4	7.8
1976	15	2.3	15.8	15	2.8	7.3

Note: The figures apply only to substantive standing committees. The table excludes contingent expense and enrollment committees in the house of representatives.

that they desired. These choices were often not the appropriate ones at least in regard to the committees' titles. However, the practice has been virtually eliminated in the house by the specification of the committee jurisdictions in the house rules and by an "automatic" process of assignment of bills to committee by the speaker. While the senate has also defined committee jurisdictions, it is still common in that body for bills to be assigned to committee by floor action. Moreover, the senate retains the practice—now in disuse in the house—of having several judiciary committees, distinguished from each other only by a letter designation: Judiciary A, Judiciary B, and so forth. The house has a single judiciary committee but two others have been replaced by committees on administration of criminal justice and civil law and procedure. In both houses Judiciary B has traditionally but informally been the "governor's committee," stacked with his supporters and assigned much administration-backed legislation. A 1966 Legislative Council study showed that the house judiciary committees were assigned bills ranging in subject matter from agriculture to wildlife and fisheries.[9] This situation, inconsistent with the notion of standing committees as specialized bodies applying their knowledge to relevant legislation, has been greatly improved in recent years, especially in the house.

It is likely that the politics of naming members to committees is a major influence on their functioning. The selection of committee members, chairmen, and vice-chairmen is made under the rules by the senate president and the house speaker. In Louisiana, the tradition of strong gubernatorial influence in the legislature has meant that committee chairmen either have been designated by the governor or have been chosen by the presiding officers in consultation with the governor. Since 1972, with a more independent speaker and with governors willing to allow the legislature greater freedom, committee leadership selections in the house have been made with less external influence.

The combined effects of traditional gubernatorial influence in committee leadership selections, periodic change of administrations, and the tendency, discussed above, to alter the number and designation of committees with some regularity, have worked to make the leadership

9. "Analysis of the Committee System in the Louisiana Legislature," (undated document in the files of the Legislative Council, *ca.* 1969).

structure of the standing committees quite unstable over time. Table 3-7 depicts the extent and circumstances of turnovers in committee chairmanships from 1956 to 1976. Of all the chairmanships in existence during the first session of newly elected legislatures during the period, a considerable majority of them in both chambers were occupied by different legislators than held the posts four years earlier. In the house 64.3 percent and in the senate 73.1 percent of the chairmen were new to their positions in the first meetings of newly elected legislatures over the period. Much of the turnover was due to the failure of

Table 3-7
Turnover of Committee Chairmen, 1956–1976

	House	Senate
Total number of chairmanships, 1956–76	70	67
Number of new committee chairmen	45 of 70 (64.3%)	49 of 67 (73.1%)
Total number of chairmen returning to legislature	37 of 70 (52.9%)	35 of 67 (52.2%)
Number of returning chairmen who do *not* retain chairmanship	12 of 37 (32.4%)	15 of 35 (42.9%)
Of returning chairmen not retaining chairmanships:		
Number who became chairmen of another committee	0 of 12 (0.0%)	12 of 15 (80.0%)
Number who did not remain on the committee as a member	5 of 12 (41.7%)	6 of 15 (40.0%)
Of the replacements for the returning chairmen who did not retain their chairmanships:		
Number who were not members of the legislature four years earlier	2 of 12 (16.7%)	4 of 15 (26.7%)
Number who were in legislature but not on the committee four years earlier	4 of 12 (33.3%)	6 of 15 (40.0%)
Total number of replacement chairmen not previously on committee	6 of 12 (50.0%)	10 of 15 (66.7%)

Note: The calculations in this table are based upon comparison of the chairmanship assignments in the first and second years of each pair of successive legislatures during the period; that is, 1956–1960, 1960–1964, and so forth. Committees that existed in one year but not the next were eliminated from consideration. Thus, in reading the house figure, there were seventy instances in which a committee (and hence its chairmanship) existed in the first year of successive pairs of legislatures from 1956 to 1960.

chairmen to return to the legislature at all. But even among the returning chairmen, 32.4 percent from the house and 42.9 percent from the
senate did not retain the chairmanships that they held four years earlier. In no instance in the house did these displaced chairmen move
on to chair a different committee, but in the senate 80 percent did.
Around 40 percent of the displaced chairmen in both chambers did not
even remain on the committee they had chaired. The replacements for
the displaced chairmen often did not come from the ranks of those previously on the committee. This was true for half of the house replacements and two-thirds of the senate replacements. To a very large extent, then, the new chairman moved onto the committee as chairman.
In a few instances these new chairmen had not even been members of
the legislature at the beginning of the preceding term.

Although the legislature sometimes seems to have a continually
shifting committee leadership structure changing according to the
prevailing political winds from the executive branch, a legislator's seniority also affects his chances of becoming a committee chairman.
The Louisiana committee system, to be sure, does not automatically
promote to a chairmanship the person on the committee with the long-
est service there, but the evidence suggests that tenure influences the
committee leadership structure. In the 1972 house of representatives,
for example, legislators with no previous terms in the legislature held
no committee chairmanships; 21 percent of those who had served one
term, 30 percent of those who had served two terms, and 75 percent of
those who had served three or more terms held chairmanships.

Committee membership was just as unstable as its leadership. Table
3-8 displays two calculations: (1) the percentage of committee assignments from 1956 to 1976 retained by the same legislator from the
beginning of one legislative term to the beginning of the next, and
(2) the same percentage based only upon legislators serving in the two
consecutive terms being analyzed. The table reveals that in both
chambers over the entire period less than one-third of the committee
assignments extended from term to term. This was partly because of
turnover in the legislature itself. Those who returned to the legislature—and who presumably could have returned to the same committees—retained slightly over 60 percent of their previous committee assignments. This degree of continuity belies the ostensible purpose of
standing committees—to build expertise through service on the spe-

Table 3-8
Continuity of Committee Assignments

| | Returning Legislators Only | |
First Year of Legislature	House	Senate
1960	47.5	53.7
1964	61.4	62.5
1968	77.8	66.0
1972	45.5	40.5
1976	62.1	82.9
All years	60.2	61.5
All Legislators		
1960	24.6	24.9
1964	23.0	28.7
1968	39.8	34.8
1972	14.5	16.0
1976	37.7	39.1
All years	27.8	28.9

Note: All figures are percentages of committee assignments retained by the same legislators holding them in the first year of the previous legislature. The section on returning legislators pertains only to legislators serving in consecutive sessions.

cialized committees. In leadership and membership there has been considerable fluidity of personnel on the standing committees. It has been the practice for legislators to request committee assignments, and their preferences have weighed heavily in the appointments by presiding officers. It is unclear, therefore, whether the instability in membership results from political considerations that enter into the appointing process or from the legislators' own fickleness in requesting assignments. In either case, the result is the same.

Twenty-five years ago an assessment of the committee system in the Louisiana legislature concluded that it was the facet of legislative structure and procedure in greatest need of reform.[10] Descriptions of committee functioning prior to the early 1970s, gleaned from newspaper accounts or from close observers of the legislature, are not reas-

10. William C. Havard, *The Government of Louisiana* (Baton Rouge: Louisiana State University, Bureau of Public Administration, 1958), 88.

suring to those who prize standing committees for their presumed ability to apply their specialized knowledge to legislation. Attendance at committee meetings was often poor for many reasons. There was a large number of committees, and most legislators were assigned to several of them. Committee meetings were not scheduled with a view to minimizing schedule conflicts. In addition, there was frequently little or no advance publicity for committee meetings, a situation that created considerable frustration among groups and citizens desiring to testify. Meeting rooms were often unavailable, and when a place was found, it was often inappropriate for conducting orderly business. Meetings were reportedly held in the corners of rooms, in stairwells, and in the men's restroom. It was common for several committee meetings to be held simultaneously in different corners of a legislative chamber when the full houses were not in session. Sometimes a practice known as the "round robin," now expressly prohibited by the rules, was used to get committee approval of a bill without an actual committee meeting. A legislator wishing to get a bill out of committee could circulate a petition among committee members, and if a majority indicated by signing the petition that they favored the legislation, then the petition served as both committee meeting and committee report, and the legislation could be brought to the floor. It has been estimated that prior to its abolition, the round robin was employed for at least half of the legislation acted upon.[11]

The standing committees of the legislature were not generally authorized to meet during the interim between regular legislative sessions. Separate and distinct interim committees were often created by resolution to study specific problems, but they were not necessarily composed of legislators who served on the standing committees having jurisdiction over the subject matter. In addition, except for secretarial help, professional committee staff were unavailable. Consequently, a standing committee rarely could be said to have initiated legislation. The time necessary for the kind of research and study required to develop important legislation was only available in the lull between hectic sessions when, as mentioned, the standing commit-

11. Kenneth Dunaway, "The Louisiana Legislative Committee System" (paper delivered at the Annual Meeting of the Louisiana Political Science Association, Baton Rouge, March 11–12, 1977), 6.

tees were dormant. It was the *ad hoc* interim committees that were charged with conducting the investigations and research required for the legislature to take the initiative.

Cumulative change since 1972 has transformed the committee system significantly. The standing committees have been given authority to meet between legislative sessions, and resolutions of the legislature calling for interim study of some problem now generally designate a standing committee—often senate and house committees or their subcommittees, meeting jointly—to do this work. This new system not only requires legislators to devote more attention to their committees, but it serves to educate those legislators who handle measures on the same subjects during legislative sessions. Bills may be prefiled, and committee consideration of them can occur prior to the actual legislative session. Significantly, legislators can point to specific legislation enacted as a result of information and consensus developed by invigorated committees. Since the early 1970s the standing committees have added professional staff to the existing clerical personnel. These individuals are frequently attorneys, but specialists in other areas relevant to particular committees have also been employed. The creation of the Legislative Fiscal Office has added significantly to the legislature's resources, particularly in budgetary matters.

The physical facilities used for committee meetings have also been greatly enhanced. The senate has made the greatest strides in providing convenient and appropriately equipped rooms. The house situation has improved less, but additional facilities are scheduled for the lower chamber. Mere physical facilities may seem unimportant to some. However, apart from making orderly committee proceedings possible, there may be an important psychological effect on legislators and other participants in the legislative process that results from having well-designed meeting rooms. At the very least, committee facilities serve as visible reminders of the new legislative consensus that committee work ranks high on the list of the expected priorities of individual representatives and senators. In the minds of those who have witnessed committee meetings before and after facilities were improved, there seems to be little doubt of the facilities' importance.

The Legislative Budget Committee and the Appropriations Process

One politically significant committee of the legislature merits special comment. Before the recent reforms, it was difficult to place the Legislative Budget Committee structurally because it was not a purely legislative creature, but rather a panel of legislators appointed primarily by the governor. Not only did the Budget Committee violate the usual principles of separation of powers, but procedurally, it did not fit neatly with the standing committees of the legislature, particularly the House Appropriations and Senate Finance Committees. The Legislative Budget Committee was a statutorily created body of twenty-eight legislators, half coming from the house and half from the senate. Twelve senators and twelve representatives were appointed by the governor in such a way that each of the state's eight congressional districts were represented among the committee members from each chamber. In addition, the speaker of the house, the president of the senate and the chairman of the House Appropriations and Senate Finance Committees served *ex officio.*

The major function of the Budget Committee was to make recommendations concerning executive-agency budgets to the governor's budget office in the Division of Administration. Each spring the committee held hearings at which agency personnel testified concerning their budgetary needs for the upcoming fiscal year; the committee then made its recommendations. As these hearings took place, the governor's budget office was engaged in the final stages of preparation of the executive budget to be submitted to the legislature. The Budget Committee's recommendations were advisory to the executive budget agency, although apparently the executive budget office was often willing to accommodate the legislative viewpoint.

Upon completion of the executive budget, the document became the basis of the appropriations bill introduced in the house and referred to the Appropriations Committee. The Budget Committee's function in budget preparation formally ceased at this point. However, as an interim committee the budget panel had to approve requests of executive agencies to transfer appropriated funds from one expenditure category to another.

The Budget Committee was the object of considerable criticism in recent years and major changes in its composition and function were approved. The violation of separation of powers drew the objections of those desiring to create legislative institutions independent of the executive branch. Many felt that executive appointment co-opted many legislators in their later consideration of the appropriations bill and undercut the budgetary prerogatives of the House Appropriations and Senate Finance Committees. Until the recent committee reforms, Appropriations and Finance Committee consideration of legislation was often hurried and perfunctory. While these committees have in the past often added funds for various purposes, they have been unable to engage in any systematic evaluation of the spending priorities represented in the appropriations bill. The Budget Committee did not have—and still does not have—its own professional fiscal staff, although the newly created Legislative Fiscal Office provides this service to this and other committees.

In the reform mood of the early 1970s there were several attempts to abolish the Budget Committee. The initial efforts failed, but when legislation passed in 1976 went into effect in 1980, the Budget Committee became the Joint Legislative Committee on the Budget. Consisting of members of the House Appropriations and Senate Finance Committees, this joint committee will receive agency budget requests at the same time that they are submitted to the governor, but for informational purposes only. The joint committee is not expressly charged with aiding in the preparation of the executive budget. Its function is to prepare more adequately for effective legislative consideration of the executive spending proposals. The law creating the new Joint Committee on the Budget also requires the executive budget to be submitted to the legislature at least sixty days in advance of the legislative session.

Legislative Staff Agencies

The Louisiana legislature has several staff agencies, and in line with recent national trends, there has been a marked expansion in both the number of staff persons and the types of assistance available. The staff agencies most directly involved in the legislative process are the Legislative Fiscal Office and the two agencies formerly known as the Legislative Council. Created in 1952, the Legislative Council became the largest and most important of all the staff agencies. The formal Legislative Council was composed of the speaker of the house and the president of the senate, along with eight senators and eight representatives (one from each of the state's congressional districts) appointed by the presiding officers from the two chambers. This body employed an executive director and a staff. In informal usage the staff was often included when reference to the council was made, a practice continued here. The actual council served as a policy-making board for the agency. As general staff for the legislature, the council's principal functions included drafting bills, resolutions, and amendments for legislators and conducting research for legislators and committees that ranged from merely "looking something up" to research projects that were much broader in scope. In addition, the council prepared a postsession summary of bills, maintained a small library, and provided a variety of other services for legislators. Professional committee staff, newly provided in the 1970s, were organizationally part of the council.

Budget figures clearly reveal the expansion in the scope of the Legislative Council's work. The council had two major sources of revenue: appropriations from the state's general fund and dedicated revenues from taxes on horse racing. Because the state appropriated nothing from the general fund in the early 1960s, the council survived on approximately $100,000 in racetrack money and other minor revenues. By 1977 nearly $2 million in general fund revenues were provided in addition to the dedicated funds, which had increased to just over $300,000.

In early 1981 the Legislative Council was divided into two sections, the senate staff and the House of Representatives Legislative Services. It was hoped that the reorganization would balance the work load between staff assigned to committee projects and staff assigned to other projects, improve staff morale by allowing staff members to be involved in ongoing substantive projects, and increase staff members' expertise in their subject areas. The Research Services Section of the senate staff now handles research and the Administrative Services Section drafts bills for the senate. The House Legislative Services agency was divided into four sections, each of which serves a cluster of committees in the house. The Legal Section aids the committees on civil law, criminal justice, and the judiciary. The Fiscal Affairs Section serves committees on appropriations, ways and means, transportation and highways, and retirement. The Governmental Section is assigned to the committees on education, health and welfare, house services and governmental affairs, and municipal and parochial affairs. The Economics and Commerce Section serves the committees on commerce, natural resources, agriculture, and labor and industry.

The Legislative Fiscal Office is the other staff agency most persistently involved in processing legislation. Before the Fiscal Office's creation in 1974 the legislature lacked the independent staff capacity to evaluate the executive budget and revenue estimates of the governor's budget office or to engage in meaningful oversight and program evaluation. While the Fiscal Office does some program evaluation, budget analysis is its most important function. The Fiscal Office also prepares a "fiscal note" (a statement of the short- and long-term cost of legislation and the proposed source of revenue) to accompany each measure introduced in the legislature that affects the receipt or expenditure of funds.

The Fiscal Office is not an altogether neutral participant in the legislative process. Unlike the council staff, it formally recommends courses of action to the legislature, including spending levels for executive agencies. These suggestions provide an alternative to the executive budget. There was some resistance to the Fiscal Office's creation on grounds that it might "tell the legislators what to do," and it has remained a controversial agency.

A third legislative agency is also significant, although its involvement in the legislative process is intermittent. The Office of the Legislative Auditor, headed by an official elected by majority vote of the members of each chamber, is responsible for auditing the books of governmental agencies, including municipalities under some circumstances. The Legislative Auditor's activities promote compliance with the law in the expenditure of funds, and from time to time, the auditor's office may have an impact on the lawmaking process. However, the agency's narrow postauditing function does not routinely involve any broader notion of "performance auditing," and the agency does not regularly interact with legislators in developing or evaluating legislation.

Legislative Improvement

The 1970s have been a period of considerable activity directed toward the improvement of the legislature. The specifics mentioned here do not do full justice to all the procedural and structural changes made. The thrust of these efforts has been the desire to make the legislature more efficient, competent, and independent of outside interests—and consequently, better able to leave its own mark on public policy.

The legislature also seems to have broadened its own definition of its function. In addition to passing or rejecting new legislation, the legislature has expressed strong interest in oversight of the executive branch, a function that it had largely avoided in the past. Recent legislation, such as the "Sunset" law, the Administrative Procedure Act, and executive-branch reorganization, all commit the legislature to a new attentiveness to what occurs *after* bills become law. However, at this writing, only a few years after the formal commitment to these types of oversight activity, the legislature has done more to equip itself to perform the new functions than to actually perform them. It remains to be seen how effective the reforms will be.

Despite the energy laudably expended on improvement of the legislature, many structural legislative problems remain and many other problems are not amenable to solution by altering procedures, changing structure, or hiring staff. Many difficulties are political, and political conditions, to a substantial degree, will dictate the limits of real change. In a legislature with a tradition of strong executive influence and lacking the organized legislative opposition that a two-party system provides, the ability to create a maximally independent institution may be limited. It is noteworthy that, despite the fact that legislative improvement was promoted most vigorously by a group within the legislature, almost all the progress has occurred within the term of one governor. It will be most interesting to observe, in the course that the legislature takes under future executives, whether there is a reversion to the patterns of the past. It seems likely that legislators' attitudes and expectations have changed enough that complete backsliding will not occur. It is in the legislature's favor that the trend to more professional and competent legislative institutions is not confined to Louisiana, but exists throughout the nation. This trend may develop more momentum in the 1980s as a heavily Democratic legislature faces, for the first time in a hundred years, a Republican governor.

4.

The Governor

ED RENWICK

Such is the awesome power of the Louisiana governor's office that the state constitution for much of Louisiana's history has prohibited a governor from seeking a second consecutive four-year term. Some relatively recent governors were even nicknamed the Kingfish and the Earl, but Louisiana has always had a powerful governor's office. As former governor Edwin Edwards commented, "The Governor of Louisiana is the keystone of political life in our state. . . . The governor occupies and has always conveyed an unusually dominant position in state politics."[1]

The 1979 gubernatorial election stands as a testament to Governor Edwards' statement. More money was spent in that election by candidates seeking the executive office than has ever been spent in a nonpresidential election in American history. Pollsters were analyzing candidates' chances eighteen months before the first primary. A year before the election, public relations firms were hired; and paid campaign staffs were assembled, organized, and operating. Television commercials for candidates were filling the screen more than eight months before the voters went to the polls. Final campaign finance statements filed by the candidates showed that $20 million were spent in pursuit of the governor's office. The top six contenders spent in excess of $1 million each, and the largest expenditures listed—$5.8 million—were those of the winner, Dave Treen.[2]

1. Edwin W. Edwards, "The Role of the Governor in Louisiana Politics: A Historical Analysis," *Louisiana History*, XV (Spring, 1974), 101.
2. Public Affairs Research Council, "The Great Louisiana Campaign Spendathon," *Analysis* (March, 1980), 1, 2.

One might reasonably question why the state's highest elected office is so valuable. The powers and duties of that office—both formal and informal—are the subject of this chapter.

Although the governor is supplied with a rather poorly designed and badly built house, it is a large and very expensive one, a mansion. Many states do not provide any housing for their chief executives, but Louisiana has so far constructed three mansions for hers. In the early 1960s Governor Jimmie Davis had the state build the present mansion at a cost of over $1 million. The mansion is more than a residence. It has served since its construction as the political nerve center of the state. Both Governor McKeithen and Governor Edwards used the mansion as an office as well as a home. It has served both symbolically and politically as the command post of Louisiana politics and government. When a secretary anywhere in the state notifies her employer that "the Mansion is on the line," no one in Louisiana asks who's calling.

Besides the mansion and its staff, the governor receives many other perquisites. He is given numerous state police bodyguards to protect him. He is provided with liberal travel and expense accounts; and he is allowed to use several automobiles, as well as state airplanes, boats, and helicopters. Louisiana's voters seem not to want their governor to be "like one of us." The life-style of the state's chief executive is a grand, coveted one.

Not surprisingly, governors have historically been reluctant to give it up. In point of fact, gubernatorial succession has continually been a subject of controversy in Louisiana. The governor was prohibited from succeeding himself from 1812 until 1864. This constitutional provision was repealed in 1864, reinstated in 1868, repealed again in 1879, and reinstated in 1898. During the mid-1960s then-governor John McKeithen persuaded the voters to amend the constitution to allow governors to succeed themselves in office once. So far, the two-term amendment's effect has been to create an eight-year governorship. Indeed, after sitting out one term, former governors are currently eligible to seek a third and fourth term.

Governor McKeithen, after the reinstitution of gubernatorial succession, ran again and was reelected, receiving over 80 percent of the vote. His successor, Governor Edwards, was also overwhelmingly re-elected to a second term. Governor Treen's ability to maintain this tradition remains to be seen. Although incumbency gives the governor a tremendous advantage in seeking reelection, Treen's situation is somewhat different from that of his predecessors at least partly because he is a Republican. The Democrats, who are out of office for the first time in a hundred years, may find impetus to defeat even an incumbent Republican. Not only will Treen face a Democratic party anxious to regain power, he will also have to campaign against Edwin Edwards. And unlike most Louisiana governors, who have usually left office unloved, Edwards was still a very popular figure at the end of his second term. Whether the present governor will serve an eight-year term cannot, thus, be predicted. But gubernatorial succession very likely will remain an issue of considerable significance in Louisiana politics.

Although the constitution and the statutes invest the governor with many formal powers, these alone do not make the governor the heavyweight he is in Louisiana. Indeed, national studies place the legislature in a much stronger position than that body actually enjoys, and the office of governor is relegated to a standing far below its true status. One such study places Louisiana's governor's powers in the middle range.[3] Judging from the formal structure, this is a fair assumption, but in the Pelican State things are often not quite what they appear at first glance to be. For example, the legislature has formal control of the budget, but the budgetary process has historically been dominated by the governor. Through 1979, the budget was prepared by the Legislative Budget Committee, most members of which were appointed by the governor. In addition, much of the committee's information and staff work were supplied by the Division of Administration, which is part of the Office of the Governor. Thus, the budget was developed by the governor's Division of Administration and debated by a committee of gubernatorial appointees.

The legislature, in a move toward obtaining more independence in the budgeting arena, passed a law in 1979 abolishing the Legislative Budget Committee. They replaced it with the Joint Legislative Com-

3. Joseph H. Schlesinger, "The Politics of the Executive," in Herbert Jacob and Kenneth Vines (eds.), *Politics in the American States* (Boston: Little, Brown, 1971), 232.

mittee on the Budget, which is composed of Senate Finance Committee and House Appropriations Committee members.

The governor's traditional influence in selection of the presiding officers in the legislature has further enhanced his strong impact on the budget. Under most administrations, legislators have elected officers chosen by the governor. An exception occurred in 1972 when E. L. "Bubba" Henry campaigned for speaker of the house on an independent platform and won. In 1980, however, the house returned to tradition, choosing for speaker the candidate preferred by the newly elected governor. Meanwhile, the senate took a page from the 1972 house and elected Michael O'Keefe as its president.

Louisiana has not historically had two-party politics, ideological politics, or confrontation politics. Political success has usually gone to the man who could "bring home the bacon." For this reason, the governor's control of or influence upon the budget has been crucial.

In addition to the operating budget, which details proposed state spending and anticipated revenues for each fiscal year, the governor also proposes a five-year capital outlay budget each year. This piece of legislation has sometimes been referred to as the pork barrel, or the watermelon or cantaloupe bill, because supposedly everybody "gets a slice." The constitution mandates a five-year plan with recommendations for first-year funding and the order of priority for each proposed project. Although these requirements are intended to take politics out of the capital budget, 60 percent of the Priority I projects in the $1.2 billion capital outlay budget for fiscal year 1979–1980 had not been included in the previous year's budget. At least one legislator has suggested that "a lot of times there is no planning at all behind a project. It just pops up and gets approved." Or, as the Public Affairs Research Council has said, "There is no way of telling under present procedures which are valid needs and which are merely a part of the 'throw me something, mister' syndrome."[4]

Similarly, the final issuance of bonds for capital projects is in the governor's hands, since without his signature no bonds can be issued. He does not have to veto a project in the budget to kill it. Rather, he may sign the bill and later simply refuse to issue the bonds.

Although the constitution requires that all capital spending be in-

4. Public Affairs Research Council, "Capital Spending: Still a Mystery," *Legislative Bulletin*, XXVII (June 8, 1979), 1.

cluded in the capital budget and that specific projects be listed and specific funds appropriated, the general appropriations bill allows lump-sum budgeting, and the operating budget contains a lump-sum highway "emergency fund." Both give great latitude to the governor in deciding which requests to fund.

The Louisiana governor has still another form of budgetary influence—the item veto.[5] The chief executive can veto any line item in the budget. Although, theoretically, a two-thirds vote of both houses can override a veto, no veto has been overridden since 1921. The possibility of a veto is usually sufficient to produce a compromise between the governor and the legislature on any project funding. The promise of funding and the possibility of veto are two important tools that enable the governor to secure legislative support for his programs.

At first blush it might appear that the office of Louisiana's governor is not particularly strong, because so much executive power is divided into ten separate offices. Louisiana, a long-ballot state, elects nine other state officials besides the governor. However, all monetary requests flow through the gubernatorially dominated budgetary process. This budgetary power allows governors to exert considerable influence over elected officials throughout the state. These officials are loath to challenge the chief executive, for without his assistance they cannot adequately perform their own duties.

If he had no powers other than the budgetary ones described above, Louisiana's governor would be a powerful chief executive. There are, however, many other strengths attendant upon the office. Studies of state government often emphasize the importance of the governor's appointive power, a critical instrument of administrative control that can be used to develop support for the governor's legislative programs. Since Huey Long's rise to power, Louisiana governors have exhibited little reluctance to use their appointive power to reward political allies and solidify their influence upon the legislature.

Earl Long once said that he had $1 people and $50,000 people and jobs to match them up. In recent years there has been a reduction in the number of appointments made by the governor. In 1968 the governor made approximately 1,425 appointments to various positions in

5. Louisiana Constitution, Art. IV, Sec. 5F.

state government, most of them appointments to state boards and commissions. Since reorganization of the executive branch, it has been estimated that the governor makes only about 1,340 appointments. The governor still appoints eight top policy makers to his cabinet. He also names the members of some 135 boards and commissions.[6]

This appointive power can be an important source of political patronage for the governor. In Louisiana there is a licensing board for almost every profession from obstetrics to embalming. Politically active members of these professions are often eager to serve on these boards. Besides the licensing boards, there are policy-making ones. The most important of these is the Mineral Board, which oversees the state's awesome oil and natural gas resources. Another prestigious board is the LSU Board of Supervisors. Once appointed, board members are unlikely to want any conflict with the governor who appointed them. An extreme example of this reluctance to give offense came when a reporter questioned a particular commissioner about his expense account. The commissioner responded, according to the *Times-Picayune*, that "he was anxious to answer all questions but he had to talk to the governor first. He said he was appointed to the commission by the governor and was 'just taking orders.'"[7] The constitution allows the governor to remove any person he has appointed unless the appointment has a fixed term.[8] Traditionally, political prudence has dictated that members of boards and commissions submit their resignations upon request when a new governor assumes office.

Although most gubernatorial appointments require senate confirmation, this is rarely a serious obstacle. Members of the upper chamber usually confirm such appointments with a minimum of discussion and debate. As Senator B. B. "Sixty" Rayburn succinctly put it, "If he [the governor] can't get men he wants on these boards he's going to be in trouble. You just can't take politics out of politics and people who try are just as silly as they can be."[9]

6. Baton Rouge *Morning Advocate*, February 27, 1948, Sec. A, p. 1; Public Affairs Research Council, *Louisiana State Agencies Handbook* (Baton Rouge: Public Affairs Research Council, 1969), 5; Public Affairs Research Council, "State Government Reorganization: The End of the Beginning," *Analysis* (October, 1978), 7, 6.

7. New Orleans *Times-Picayune*, May 9, 1979, Sec. 1, p. 7.

8. Louisiana Constitution, Art. IV, Sec. 5A.

9. Baton Rouge *Morning Advocate*, July 8, 1964, Sec. A, p. 8.

With adoption of the state's new constitution in 1974, the governor's appointive power was reduced considerably. Under the old constitution the governor made appointments to fill vacancies in the judiciary. Under the new constitution such appointive power is vested in the state supreme court. Formerly, governors also filled hundreds of local governing positions with their appointees, but home-rule forces at the constitutional convention opposed this practice. Consequently, the present constitution provides that when a vacancy occurs on a school board, police jury, or any local governing body the remaining members appoint a person to fill that vacancy. Despite these curtailments, the appointive power of Louisiana's governor, like that of most state governors, remains significant. The patronage that follows political appointments is a source of considerable strength to the governor responsible for making the appointment.

Although most of Louisiana's sixty thousand civil service employees are not the governor's appointees, they too fall under his influence by way of their salary increases. Teachers and school bus drivers are paid to a large extent by state funds, and the amount and frequency of raises for these groups, too, is left up to the governor. Through him, the state provides supplemental pay for more than twelve thousand employees of local governments.[10] Local employees, city and parish leaders, and unions are vitally interested in the amount and extent of supplemental pay provided by the state. The more the state pays local employees, the less local officials have to raise taxes.

Consulting and purchase contracts provide another indirect source of power for the governor. Members of virtually any profession can be contracted to do studies in their areas of expertise, and professional services are seldom subject to bid. Monthly retainer fees can be paid to attorneys under this system. A $500-a-month retainer or a $10,000 study does not have much impact on a budget of over $5 billion.

Louisiana state government is a conglomerate. It operates schools, cafeterias, hospitals, prisons, laundries, and many other enterprises requiring varied and vast supplies. The state makes huge purchases of everything from paper to blood. No matter what the product, the state

10. Public Affairs Research Council, "State Salary Supplements for Local Employees in Louisiana," *Analysis* (October, 1977), 1.

of Louisiana buys a lot of it, and legions benefit from selling it through contracts totaling millions of dollars per year. Emergency purchases are even exempt from public bid laws requiring that "the lowest responsible bidder" get the contract.

It is not always safe to assume that the law has been rigorously obeyed in such purchases. A former buyer for a state hospital reported that she had "discovered a repeated pattern of seemingly planned irregularities, designed to obtain bids and sell commodities which don't meet the specification advertised, which this hospital has increasingly received, paying higher prices for inferior goods."[11] Given the immense amount of goods purchased by the state, favoritism in even a miniscule proportion of the purchases could amount to a lot of money paid into undeserving hands. Regardless of whether the letter of the law is followed in these exchanges, there still exists, as a by-product of this procedure, a large group of state suppliers who are a ready market for testimonial fund-raising tickets.

Retirement benefits offer another area in which the governor's influence may be felt. A supplicant can petition the governor's support for having prior employment at another job count toward the number of years required for state retirement eligibility. Public officials can gain greatly from special retirement eligibility laws.

Gubernatorial powers extend to parole and pardon, though the governor does not have absolute power of executive clemency. He may only pardon or commute a sentence upon the recommendation of the Board of Pardons, but it must be remembered that he appoints this five-member board.[12] The parole and pardon power, however, sometimes creates more trouble for the governor than it's worth. Former governor Edwards is one chief executive who has commented on the impropriety of this function for the governor: "You should have, in my opinion, a professional board working on a continuing basis with parole officers, probation officers, the knowledge of sociologists and psychiatrists, those involved in the system. If this board ultimately determines that these men should or should not be pardoned, that decision should be final."[13]

11. New Orleans *States-Item*, January 30, 1978, Sec. A, p. 1.

12. Louisiana Constitution, Art. IV, Sec. 5F.

13. Edwin Edwards, taped remarks before the Committee on the Executive Department of the Louisiana Constitutional Convention, May, 1973.

The governor is bound by the constitution to "see that the laws are faithfully executed."[14] However, local officials handle a good deal of law enforcement, and governors are wary of supplanting these local efforts. Candidates for governor routinely declare their support of home rule to the sheriff's convention, pledging to keep the state police out of the parishes and leave law enforcement to local officials. Gubernatorial candidates have frequently made this promise because they realize that opposition to home rule is not popular among sheriffs. Of course, once elected, a governor has the power to authorize the state police to conduct raids and make arrests, a power rarely utilized, but a power nonetheless.

Three facts of Louisiana life—oil, low taxes, and centralized government—the latter two, legacies of Longism, provide the foundation and columns of support for the Mansion and the formidable power it houses.

Louisiana is the second largest oil-producing state in the nation and first in the production of natural gas. "The state slithers around in it," wrote A. J. Liebling. He quoted a local source who said, "Oil is to Louisiana what money is to a roulette game. It's what makes the wheel go around. It's the reason there are so many big bank rolls available to stake any politician who has a Formosa Chinaman's chance to get into office." The source continued, "Oil gets into politics, and politicians, making money in office, get into oil." According to James R. Adams, "It's an expensive form of politics and the question of how a state with such low personal income could afford the legal—and illegal—boodling that goes on was answered 20 years ago by A. J. Liebling, the *New Yorker* writer, in one word: oil."[15]

State land leases have historically been used as rewards for political allies in Louisiana. Most of this story lies buried in parish recorders' files, but on occasion, a spectacular state land deal is exhumed. Although it no longer does so, in the past the state transferred 3,062,922 acres to her levee boards, which they in turn were free to sell or lease. In 1901 a levee board entered into a contract to sell for $120,000 to a

14. Louisiana Constitution, Art. IV, Sec. 5A.
15. A. J. Liebling, *The Earl of Louisiana* (New York: Simon and Schuster, 1961), 56; James R. Adams, "The Gusto of Louisiana Politics," *Wall Street Journal*, May 16, 1979, p. 22.

New Orleans law firm "all lands donated, ceded and transferred to the (law firm) their successors in title some 935,415 acres of land." In the 1930s lush state land leases were obtained by numerous allies of the Long organization. A state senate floor leader and the sheriff of a South Louisiana parish obtained state leases for over "500,000 acres of state owned oil land." Huey Long formed the Win or Lose Oil Company, and wags have suggested that the company never lost. In 1963 Mrs. Huey Long sold some of her oil properties. Attached to the conveyance was an eighteen-page exhibit describing her interests in eleven parishes.

The primary legacy of Longism in Louisiana, though, is low taxes. The state's mineral industry foots the bill, and consumers of oil and natural gas in other parts of the country pay the taxes. Then the governor gets the credit for spending programs. Louisianians are generally very antitax. Since World War II, governors who have proposed tax increases have suffered a decline in popularity, with the exception of Edwin Edwards. His tax package was directed at the oil companies, not the taxpayers. Edwards proposed, and the legislature accepted, altering the oil severance tax from a given amount per barrel (as enacted in the Huey Long years) to a percentage of its selling price. When deregulated oil prices soared, this new system created a nice surplus income for the state.

Edwards was able, thus, to lessen the direct tax liability of Louisiana's citizens while increasing tax revenues considerably. He also backed proposals that raised the amount of the homestead exemption and allowed federal income taxes to be subtracted from a taxpayer's income in determining his state tax liability. A state with low taxes and high revenues is a politician's dream. Because of the increasing cost of oil, Louisiana's revenues will continue to soar, increasing the governor's spending power without raising taxes and guaranteeing him pleasant dreams.

Low taxes and high spending contribute to Louisianians' tolerance of corruption. People do not feel their own money is being wasted. In the 1979 governor's race, one candidate proposed rebating part of the state's surplus to the taxpayers. This idea quickly died when it was pointed out that the state's very liberal income tax law exempts most people. The homestead exemption released most homeowners from property tax, and automobile licenses are set at three dollars a year by the constitution. The average citizen meets the tax collector only in the grocery store or at the gas station.

Taxation is integrally related to the other major legacy of Longism— centralized government. Since Huey Long, no matter the problem, the governor is consulted and often settles the controversy. The press, the politicians, and the man on the street look to the governor. If the teachers want a raise, they appeal to the governor, not to the local school board. If school bus drivers want better benefits, they do the same. Thousands of local government employees seek and receive supplemental pay from Baton Rouge. Parishes receive monies to help build and blacktop roads and construct bridges. Urban areas implore the governor for mass transit funds. Communities with colleges, vocational schools, or other state facilities seek funds and buildings for their institutions. Welfare, old age assistance, and foster care programs are all directed and funded in Baton Rouge. District attorneys, judges, and supreme court justices curry the governor's favor in pursuit of higher salaries and better pensions. Religiously affiliated schools seek the governor's blessing in behalf of state funds for private education. In every major area of governmental concern, the chief executive is asked to help. Everyone goes to the Mansion for relief. Huey Long's efforts to consolidate and centralize power in the governor's office endure.

And finally, the chief of state is the state's chief entertainer. This is not a constitutional responsibility or one written into the statutes, but it is historically demanded local lagniappe. The governors most remembered in the last half century were all at least amateur entertainers. The Longs, Huey and Earl, were showmen par exellence. Earl Long stories abound a generation after his death. Recollections of his stump speeches and witty ridicule of his opponents are classics. To this day, Jimmie Davis' principal profession is show business. "You Are My Sunshine" is more renowned than any act of his administration. John McKeithen stars as a raconteur, and his television talent brought him great popular support. His role of chief LSU football fan and recruiter enhanced his role as chief executive. To date, the most entertaining governor was Edwin Edwards. A master of the one-liner, never at a loss for a comeback or put-down, his deprecating humor has repeatedly allowed him to survive a hostile press. "At the beginning of 1975, a reelection year, Edwards made public a New Year's resolution to stop his gambling. When a reporter asked if he would keep his resolution, Edwards smiled back, 'The odds are eight to five.'"[16]

From the Evangelicals in the north to the cockfighters in the south the people of Louisiana are zesty and emotional. Most voters would claim that they could not define ideology, but all understand entertainment. "Laissez le bon temps rouler," is almost the state's motto.

Louisiana's political entertainment is not always of Oscar-winning caliber. And the line between entertainment and demagoguery has sometimes been very thin in Louisiana. Huey Long made raucous attacks on Standard Oil and the press. Huey even published his own newspaper, the *Louisiana Progress*, which he used to attack his enemies. Earl Long was a master of sarcasm. In the 1940 gubernatorial campaign he accused his major opponent, Sam Jones, of being "an educated fool" and nicknamed him "High Hat Sam, the High Society Kid who pumps perfume under his arms." In his 1956 campaign for governor, Uncle Earl attacked his opponent, New Orleans mayor deLesseps Morrison, dubbing him "Dellasoups." He referred to the Alexandria *Daily Town Talk* as the "Alexandria Bladder" and liked to tell a tale about the *Times-Picayune* reporter who fell into a ditch with a hog. "Somebody said," Earl screamed, "you can tell a man by the company he keeps, and the hog got up and left." This kind of entertainment has been common fare for Louisianians.

Because of the awesome power of Louisiana's governors there has historically been the possibility—and too often even the reality—of political corruption in the state, corruption either directly or indirectly traceable to the chief executive's office. Scandal connected to the Long governorships is infamous. Ironically, most of those scandals came after Huey died and before Earl became governor, yet Longism is invariably associated with scandal. Shady deals or the rumor of them has tainted many other administrations as well. The Sunshine Bridge

---

16. Public Affairs Research Council, *Louisiana Levee Districts* (Baton Rouge: Public Affairs Research Council, 1958), 21; P. J. Mills, "Louisiana Levee Districts as Agencies of State Government" (M.A. thesis, Louisiana State University, 1959), 26; T. Harry Williams, *Huey Long: A Biography* (New York: Knopf, 1969), 825.

and the Baker Bank scandals occurred during Jimmie Davis' tenure; *Life* magazine articles about Mafia involvement in his administration plagued John McKeithen. Usually public scandal adversely affects a governor's popularity. Early Long's career ended with the voters debating his sanity. Jimmie Davis was trounced in his comeback try in 1971. John McKeithen's political ship was scuttled when he tried for the U.S. Senate in 1972. The Edwards administration was also associated with a number of scandals. From "Koreagate" to "Brilab," the administration made headlines, but Edwards emerged politically and legally unscathed, his popularity intact. Thus far, Dave Treen's integrity is unimpugned. If his administration remains free of scandal, the popular image of a Louisiana governor may take on a different countenance.

As is likely true of many states, some degree of corruption has existed throughout Louisiana's history at both the state and local levels. Voters have been unusually tolerant of a certain level of corruption, perhaps because of Louisianians' exceptional candor about it. In their study of Louisiana, Bass and Devries wrote, "There is no question of a traditional public tolerance for political corruption and a record of exposure on a scale perhaps grander than anywhere in the United States." Louisianians seem to enjoy their politics like their food—hot and flavorful. Name calling, mud slinging, and admission of human frailty and sin are expected, even appreciated. Once, a state politician delivered a sizable contribution to the 1956 Earl Long campaign for governor from an association of theater owners who wanted the repeal of an admissions tax. Following the election, Governor Long declared he would not support the repeal and would, in fact, veto it if the legislature passed it. The politician who had collected and delivered the contribution asked Long what he should tell the theater owners. "Tell them I lied," said Earl. Governor Edwin Edwards claimed, according to an article in the New Orleans *Times-Picayune*, that he had rejected a campaign contribution from Tongsun Park in 1971 because he thought it was illegal. But he went on to say, "I thought it was only $400 or $500 so I said thanks anyway. If I'd known it was $10,000, I might have accepted anyhow."[17] This kind of playful attitude toward

17. Jack Bass and Walter DeVries, *The Transformation of Southern Politics* (New York: Basic Books, 1976), 160, 158; New Orleans *Times-Picayune*, October 28, 1976, Sec. 1, p. 1.

dishonesty has traditionally been part of Louisiana's political tone. But, to repeat, real and serious corruption has historically been political suicide for the governor so exposed.

T. Harry Williams once said, "I always suspected the carpetbaggers were learners down here. They didn't bring it with them; they were taking lessons."[18] Since the governor is the center of the state's political structure, his integrity is of great importance in setting the moral tone of state politics. The governor is the best known, most discussed, most controversial, and most powerful personage in the state. Given the vast legitimate powers of a Louisiana governor, a corrupt chief executive could do unimaginable damage to the state's political system.

18. T. Harry Williams, quoted in Bass and DeVries, *The Transformation of Southern Politics*, 160.

5.
The Judiciary

RONALD M. LABBÉ

The judiciary shares with the other branches of the government the primal function of resolving conflict in a peaceful way. The idea that the courts merely interpret the law and do not make it, which is only partly true, obscures the important political similarities between the judiciary and the other branches of the government. At the same time, the law remains an inescapably relevant aspect of the judicial process. Unlike the executive and legislative branches, the courts are obliged to decide their share of society's problems in terms of the particular provisions of the law pertinent to each case. The legal aspects of the political system are even more relevant when they are unique as they are in Louisiana. It is the only state in the union that adheres to a system of civil law that has its roots in the early legal systems of France and Spain. All other states base their private law on English common law. Louisiana's civil law system calls for explanation.[1]

Louisiana began, of course, as a French colony. In 1763 it was ceded by France to Spain in the Treaty of Paris. At that time the colony was governed by French law and it was not until 1769 that this system of law was abrogated by the Spanish governor. In 1800 Spain ceded the territory back to France, but France did not assume control until three years later, and then only for twenty days before the United States assumed sovereign control on December 20, 1803, as a result of the Louisiana Purchase. During this brief period France made no attempt to replace Spanish law. The first official act of W. C. C. Claiborne, the territorial governor appointed by President Jefferson, was to continue

1. This brief history of the civil law in Louisiana is drawn from A. N. Yiannopoulos, *Louisiana Civil Law System—Part I* (Baton Rouge: Claitor's, 1971), 53–69.

the applicability of Spanish law. Claiborne visualized this as a temporary measure, however. Since the territory was destined for statehood,
he assumed that eventually Louisiana would adopt the common law
espoused by all the other states. By this time most of the state's legal
community had established an affinity for the civil law based on cultural, if not objective grounds. Led by Edward Livingston, a distinguished New York lawyer and recent immigrant to the territory, they
resolved to retain the civil law system. In 1806 after Louisiana was divided into several subterritories, the legislature of the Orleans Territory, which roughly corresponded to present-day Louisiana, formally
declared that the territory should be governed by the Roman and
Spanish civil law then prevailing. Claiborne vetoed the act, and the
legislature adjourned in protest for what it assumed to be his anti–civil
law bias. The governor's opposition appears to have been motivated
mainly by practical considerations rather than a firm ideological commitment to the common law. Apart from his expectations concerning
Louisiana's future as a common-law jurisdiction, the prevailing civil
law that the legislature had tried to adopt by general reference was
unclear in some respects and outmoded in others. A short time later
when the legislature directed the preparation of an actual code based
on the prevailing civil law, Claiborne raised no objection. Two years
later the Louisiana Civil Code of 1808 was adopted.

The compilers of the code of 1808 had been instructed by the legislature to codify the civil law as it then existed in the territory. Because
of the similarity between many of the local legal rules of either French
or Spanish derivation and the civil law of France, they were able to
adopt many of the provisions of the Napoleonic Code in accomplishing
their task. But when the provisions of the French law conflicted with
the territory's Spanish rules, the compilers followed the Spanish rules
as they had been instructed. As a result a number of Spanish traditions
made their way into Louisiana law and the ground was laid for an endless debate over the cultural roots of Louisiana civil law.[2]

The code of 1808 led to confusion. It purported only to summarize
existing law, yet *code* implied a replacement for existing law. The confusion prompted a new code in 1825, which contained provisions spe-

2. Representative participants in the debate and their points of view are identified in
Albert Tate, Jr., "The Splendid Mystery of the Civil Code of Louisiana," *Louisiana Bar
Journal*, XXV (June, 1977), 29–39.

cifically repealing all prior law on subjects covered by the code. The Civil War and the adoption of a new state constitution eventually led to the adoption of a third civil code in 1870. Still in use today, the Louisiana Civil Code of 1870 consists of 3,556 articles governing the relations of private parties in the state in a variety of noncommercial matters.

From the beginning the civil code has been viewed as a unique system of law, more fundamental than ordinary statutory law and entitled to be protected from being replaced or even much influenced by common law. For all that it is no easy task to distinguish the Louisiana legal system from that of other states. Legal scholars tend to consider the state as a mixed system combining elements of both civil and common law.[3]

Ideally in a civil law system the whole body of private law on those subjects traditionally covered by the code, such as marriage and the family, inheritance, and certain property rights, is reduced to writing in the form of a code—an article-by-article statement of the law. These rules have their historical roots in Roman, or in Louisiana's case, French and Spanish law. Theoretically judges are expected to arrive at solutions to individual disputes deductively by applying the readily discernible rules of the code to particular facts. In contrast, in a common law system judges are expected to arrive at general solutions from the perceived necessities of individual cases. Thus in a civil law system the role of the judge is diminished in favor of the legislature or the legal scholar. Judges are expected to show much greater devotion to the code than to the decisions of other, even higher, courts; judicial precedent is not considered binding in civil law systems. Finally, because it is legislatively rather than judicially determined the system is thought to afford greater certainty as to just what the law is on any point.

The Louisiana code is simply not a summary of the whole body of law even in the areas it covers. Since it has not been revised since 1870, the code is deficient or even entirely silent on some subjects. As a result much of the state's law has had to be made as the need has arisen either by the courts or the legislature. The solutions they invented were frequently influenced by common-law practices; in fact, entire elements of common law have been adopted in this way. Be-

3. Yiannopoulos, *Louisiana Civil Law System*, 72. The comparison of the civil law and common law traditions which follows tracks Yiannopoulos' analysis.

cause problems cannot be solved simply by reference to the provisions of the code, the judge in Louisiana has a more creative role to play than might be expected. At the same time precedent tends to take on the same weight of authority as it occupies in common law, and uncertainty is no less or greater a problem than it is in common-law jurisdictions. This does not mean that there are not unique features in Louisiana law, but there are many more similarities with other states in both the substance and methods of the law. Most importantly, in the final analysis Louisiana's courts are no less relevant than the courts of other states as full-fledged participants with the other branches of the government in the process of making and enforcing policy.

The Lawyers

In every state lawyers are an important political elite. It is from their ranks, for instance, that judges are selected. Moreover, the technical nature of law and of the judicial process makes it virtually impossible for members of the public to avail themselves of the benefits of the legal system or the facilities of the courts without the services of lawyers. They have proven time and again that they make excellent candidates for public office because of their familiarity with government and the degree of control they are able to exercise over their personal schedules. With the sole exception of Jimmie Davis, all of Louisiana's governors since the 1940s have been lawyers. About a third of the seats in the legislature are customarily occupied by lawyers.[4] Lawyers constituted the largest single professional group among the delegates to the state constitutional convention of 1973. They can be found serving at all levels of local government, and in the advisory role they play on the local level as district attorneys or city attorneys, they are in a position to influence many important decisions. Through the state bar association, they can be a potent political force in areas of state policy that concern them.

Louisiana lawyers are organized in an integrated bar. This means that all persons admitted to practice automatically become members

4. June Savoy, "Louisiana Lawmakers: A 25-Year Profile," *Analysis* (January, 1975), 17.

of the Louisiana State Bar Association, and no one may practice law who is not a member in good standing. The organized bar possesses a unique combination of the elements of political influence. Not only is it well defined as an organization but it enjoys dual legal status as an independent corporation and, since 1941, as an official arm of the supreme court in the governance of the legal profession.[5] Its members are located in every parish of the state, and they are sensitive to their professional interests. Legally enforceable membership dues provide adequate financial resources. Its leaders are likely to be politically knowledgeable and personally persuasive, and the interests they represent ordinarily enjoy a large measure of acceptability in governmental and social circles.

For all that, the bar association is most effective in realizing goals that lie closest to its organizational purpose and that are likely to evoke almost unanimous agreement among lawyers, such as those that touch on their financial interest. The rules made by the bar association to maintain high professional standards for admission to practice and to regulate the professional conduct of practicing attorneys are routinely adopted and enforced by the supreme court. Similarly, proposed legislation that may have the effect of reducing the need for legal services, such as changes in the workmen's compensation laws or the adoption of no-fault automobile insurance are likely to meet with formidable opposition from the bar. On the other hand, elements of the bar association have advocated a merit system of selecting judges for years without any discernible success.[6] This is not a subject that is likely to provoke widespread consensus among the state's lawyers.

Although concern has been expressed in recent years that the supply of Louisiana lawyers has overtaken demand for their services, law remains popular as a career.[7] The total enrollment in the four law

5. For statutory materials relating to the Louisiana State Bar Association and the practice of law see *Louisiana Revised Statutes of 1950*, Title 37, Secs. 211–18.

6. The binding nature of the bar association's rules is discussed in *In re James*, 202 La. 789, 12 So.2d 435 (1953). Early alternatives to an elected judiciary are discussed in Ben Robertson Miller, *The Louisiana Judiciary* (Baton Rouge: Louisiana State University Press, 1932), 120–23. For more recent efforts at reform and their results see Ben Robertson Miller, *Memoirs of a Southern Lawyer* (Baton Rouge: privately printed by the author, 1973).

7. For further details concerning the characteristics of the legal profession in Louisiana see Louisiana Board of Regents, *The Supply and Demand of Lawyers in Louisiana:*

schools located within the state increased by 72 percent between 1969 and 1975. In the same period admissions to the bar increased by 46 percent. In 1975 the bar estimated that there were 7,500 lawyers in the state. A larger proportion of Louisiana lawyers are engaged in private practice than in the United States in general; relatively few are employed by government and in the field of business and education. In addition, continued growth in the population, increased industrialization, and the development of new forms of legal action may help to maintain growth in the demand for legal services at a steady though modest rate.

Recent years have seen a change in the extent to which white males predominate in the legal profession. The number of women enrolled in Louisiana law schools increased from 6 percent in 1970 to 21 percent in 1975. Minority enrollment did not fare as well, however. In 1971 minorities made up only 7 percent of the law students, and by 1975 this figure had risen by less than 1 percent.

The Judges

At present the judges of all Louisiana courts are elected, but this has not always been the case, and even today the appointive system has its supporters in the state. Originally, the judges of the Louisiana Supreme Court and of the inferior courts were appointed by the governor with the advice and consent of the senate. The coming of Jacksonian Democracy raised serious questions concerning the appointive system, and it became very difficult to argue successfully that the electorate was somehow unqualified to participate in the selection of judges. The system was first challenged seriously in the constitutional convention of 1845. Although that effort was unsuccessful, under the constitution of 1852 all judgeships were made elective, only to be made appointive again by the constitution of 1864. Since 1868, however, judges of the courts of original jurisdiction have been popularly elected. Judges of the supreme court have been popularly elected since 1904. Judges of

---

Past, Present, and Future Trends (Baton Rouge: Louisiana Board of Regents, 1976); A. Kenneth Pye, *Meeting the Needs for Legal Education in the South* (Atlanta: Southern Regional Educational Board, 1955).

the intermediate courts of appeal have been popularly elected since 1900, but when these courts were first organized in 1879, their judges were elected by a joint session of the legislature.[8]

Although the logic of a system of elected judges suggests that judges should be given short terms of office so that the electorate can repeatedly evaluate a judge's performance on the bench, Louisiana has always made a concession toward the features of an appointive system by providing terms of judicial office that are longer than those accorded to other office holders. The judges of the district, parish, and city courts are elected for six-year terms. Under the constitution of 1974, the justices of the courts of appeal and the supreme court serve terms of ten years—down from twelve and fourteen respectively under the previous constitution.

Not only do judges tend to serve longer initial terms than other office holders, they are much less likely to face serious opposition in their bids for reelection, and as a result, they enjoy a unique degree of stability in office. In a study of Louisiana judges who held office between 1945 and 1960, Kenneth Vines found that judges faced opposition in only 41 percent of a total of 304 elections.[9] Vines also showed that it is only in their first election that most judges are opposed. It is not surprising that a judge is more likely to leave office as a result of death or retirement than electoral defeat. Vines found that fewer than 10 percent of the district judges were turned out of office at the polls. This happens only occasionally to judges of the courts of appeal and virtually never to members of the supreme court. The explanation for the security of judicial office in the midst of an elective system of selecting judges probably lies in a paradoxical reluctance of the public to mix politics with the courts.

There is no lack of financial incentive for most attorneys to join the ranks of the judiciary. Although Louisiana ranks forty-third in the nation in terms of per capita personal income, its judges are the fourth

8. Early methods of judicial selection are traced in John T. Hood, "The Louisiana Judiciary," *Louisiana Law Review*, XV (June, 1954), 817; Miller, *The Louisiana Judiciary*, 34, 44; John T. Hood, "History of the Courts of Appeal in Louisiana," *Louisiana Law Review*, XXI (April, 1961), 544–45.

9. Kenneth N. Vines, "The Selection of Judges in Louisiana," in Kenneth N. Vines and Herbert Jacob (eds.), *Studies in Judicial Politics*, Tulane Studies in Political Science, III (New Orleans: Tulane University Press, 1963), 115.

highest paid in the nation. Members of the supreme court earn $56,200 annually, judges of the courts of appeal earn $53,500, and district court judges earn from $48,100 to $50,800, depending on their location. There is even a permanent, statutory Commission on Judicial Compensation charged with the responsibility of making recommendations periodically to the governor and legislature regarding the adequacy of judicial compensation.[10] In addition, a generous retirement system makes it possible for a judge to retire with full salary under certain circumstances and with as few as twelve years of service if he is fifty-five years old.

Indeed, in the past the attractiveness of judicial office may very well have led to a practice that tended to subvert the elective system. Vines showed that 20 percent of the district judges who served between 1945 and 1960 had *first* achieved their office by appointment. Eighteen percent of the judges of the courts of appeal and 16 percent of the supreme court justices had originally been appointed. Although appointive members of the appellate courts were ineligible to succeed themselves, this was not the case with appointees to the district courts. It was not unusual for an aspirant to a district court seat to use appointment by the governor, sometimes with the cooperation of the retiring judge, to beat potential opponents to the bench. At the expiration of his appointive term, the candidate could run for office with the inherent political advantage of an incumbent. Under the 1974 constitution, however, the supreme court fills vacancies in judicial office or newly created judgeships by appointment, and no interim appointee may run in the election to fill the vacancy permanently.[11]

Any effort to change Louisiana's system of selecting judges would almost certainly face stiff opposition. Such a suggestion, for example, was soundly defeated in the constitutional convention of 1973. A major problem in successfully arguing for change is that the state's judiciary is not visibly afflicted with the ills associated with an elective sys-

10. National Center for State Courts, "Rank Order of Judicial Salaries, Income, and Population," *State Court Journal* (Fall, 1978), 34; "Survey of Judicial Salaries: Update," *State Court Journal*, IV (Winter, 1980), 35, 39; Council of State Governments, *The Book of the States, 1978–79* (Lexington, Ky.: Council of State Governments, 1978), 92. The structure and functions of the Commission on Judicial Compensation are described in *Louisiana Revised Statutes of 1950*, Title 13, Sec. 42–46.

11. Vines, "The Selection of Judges in Louisiana," 114; Louisiana Constitution, Art. 5, Sec. 22.

tem. It is hard to argue that elections have an unseemly influence on the quality of justice when incumbent judges are seldom seriously challenged. Some members of the Louisiana bar occasionally profess to see a marked difference between the qualifications and energy of federal judges serving in the state, who are appointed, and their elected state counterparts. Still, it is difficult to maintain that the members of the state's judiciary are not generally well qualified.

Yet a merit system of judicial selection, perhaps limited to certain courts or to certain areas of the state, is very likely to continue to be an active item on the agenda of state judicial reform. A 1973 bar association survey among lawyers revealed that 50 percent of the responding attorneys favored a merit plan for selection of trial court judges and 56 percent favored it for the appellate courts. Support for merit selection was highest in urban areas, and lowest in rural areas.[12] Members of the urban legal community may be given generally to more reformist attitudes than their rural brethren. More importantly, they are keenly aware of the present-day expense of election campaigns and of the tendency of a campaign even for judicial office to degenerate into a struggle to outbid an opponent for the support of organized subconstituencies or into an expensive "media blitz" aimed at drowning out an opponent's superior qualifications. Judges themselves sometimes complain that election costs jeopardize their independence by making them overly susceptible to threats of opposition to their reelection.

The formal qualifications for judicial office were greatly simplified by the constitution of 1974. The age requirement for service on the supreme court was abolished as was an undefined, nebulous requirement that all judges be "learned in the law."[13] The length of residence in the election district was standardized. Today every judge above the level of justice of the peace must have been admitted to the practice of law in Louisiana for at least five years before being elected, and he must have maintained his residence in the jurisdiction of the court to which he is aspiring for two years. Judges of parish and district courts and all appellate courts are prohibited from practicing law.

The state is divided into six districts for the purpose of electing the seven justices of the supreme court. One justice is elected in each of

12. "Report of the Survey on Judicial Selection," *Louisiana Bar Journal*, XXI (September, 1973), 116–17.
13. Louisiana Constitution of 1921, Art. 7, Section 33.

five districts and two are elected from the four-parish district that includes New Orleans. In 1979 there were nine court-of-appeal judges
in each of the four circuits except in the second circuit where there
were five. Legislation enacted in 1980 carved a fifth circuit court of
appeals out of the old fourth circuit and increased the total number of
judges on the courts of appeal from thirty-two to forty-one.[14] By mid-
1982 when the legislation is in full effect, there will be ten judges on
the first and fourth circuits, six each on the second and fifth, and nine
on the third. The new legislation made no changes in the practice of
dividing each of the circuits into three districts for the purpose of electing judges. In each circuit most of the judges are elected from individual districts and a few are elected from the circuit at large.

Obviously not everyone who possesses the minimal legal qualifications for judicial office has an equal chance of being elected. To win
office, it is especially important that a candidate be able to meet the
public's expectations in personal or social terms because as a judicial
candidate he or she cannot espouse a platform of action. Every judicial
candidate is faced with the problem of finding reasons why the electorate should favor his or her candidacy over the opponent's. A candidate
with personal roots deeply planted in the district or who has established a reputation as a public servant or who is able to point to years of
professional experience will have a better opportunity to be elected
than someone who does not possess these qualities in the same degree
or in the same combination.

To the formal legal qualifications must be added those informal
traits that can be gleaned from a comparative picture of the sitting
judges themselves.[15] As more blacks and women enter the legal profession it is likely that they will achieve a greater proportion of judicial
offices. Already a few blacks have become judges either through appointment or election in areas where blacks vote in large numbers.
There are signs, too, that the equal rights movement is turning the female population in every district into a potential constituency for a
woman candidate. For all that, the typical Louisiana judge is a white
male. If he is a judge of a district court the chances are only one out of

14. Act 661 of 1980.
15. The composite picture of the Louisiana judiciary sketched here is based on John
Harris, "Recent Trends in the Selection of Louisiana's Judiciary" (M.A. thesis, University of Southwestern Louisiana, 1976).

five that he first achieved his office before age forty; only one out of ten if he is a judge either of the court of appeals or the supreme court. He is a native of the state and probably spent his childhood in the district from which he was elected. He is a member of the predominant religion in his district. He attended law school in the state, and if he is serving any place except Orleans Parish, his choice was very probably the law school at Louisiana State University. There is a 90 percent chance that judges serving in Orleans Parish attended either Loyola or Tulane. About half of all judges were elected directly from the ranks of the lawyers and had no prior judicial experience, but it is very likely that a judge of the district court served previously in a local political office. At least a third of the judges of the supreme court and at least a quarter of the judges of the courts of appeal served in the state legislature, and there is at least a 50 percent chance that an appellate court judge had previous judicial experience. Louisiana is no exception to the rule prevailing elsewhere in the country that the road to judicial position is political.

Judges in Louisiana may be removed in two ways. The constitution provides that a judge may be impeached for commission of a felony or for malfeasance or gross misconduct in office. It also provides a second mechanism for disciplining or removing judges. Article V of the constitution created a Judiciary Commission, made up of three judges, three lawyers, and three private citizens who are not lawyers. On recommendation of the commission the supreme court may censor, suspend, or remove a judge from office for a variety of misconduct ranging from failure to perform the duties of his office to criminal offenses. The commission may also involuntarily retire disabled judges.

Structure and Functions

Louisiana's first constitution, written in 1812, created only a supreme court, but it recognized the need for additional courts by authorizing the legislature to create inferior courts. The judicial system has experienced considerable change since 1812 as the result of legislative enactments and the work of subsequent constitutional conventions. In broad outline, the system is now patterned after a three-tier model consisting of trial courts of general jurisdiction, a set of intermediate courts of appeal, and a supreme court of last resort. The three-tier model has not been perfectly implemented, however. For instance, there is a good deal of fragmentation in the lower courts, and some of them have long since outlived their utility, if not their staying power. Moreover, a satisfactory allocation of appellate authority between the supreme court and the courts of appeal is just now in the process of being realized.

District Courts

In 1980 there were thirty-eight judicial districts in the state (excluding Orleans Parish), each comprising from one to three parishes.[16] Except for the Civil District Court for the Parish of Orleans, which is designated as such, these courts are referred to by number (*e.g.*, the First Judicial District Court). The number of judges in each of these courts ranges from one to thirteen. Courtroom facilities, judges' offices, and a clerk of court's office, which keeps the records of the court, are maintained in each parish. In multiparish districts, however, each judge usually maintains a permanent office in only one of the parishes. The district judges usually serve as the sole triers of both legal and factual issues in cases over which they preside. In practice jury trials are rarities except in more serious criminal cases.

It would be difficult to exaggerate the importance of the district courts. They are the state's principal trial courts of general jurisdiction, authorized to handle all civil and criminal matters. (In Orleans Parish separate courts are provided for civil and criminal cases.) The district courts have exclusive authority to hear all felony cases, cases involving title to real estate, civil rights, the right to public office, and estate matters, among a few others. Members of the public have frequent and significant contact with these courts as litigants, witnesses, or jurors. The vast bulk of the most important judicial business in the state is both initiated and terminated in these courts. More cases are decided with finality by the district courts than are heard by the courts

16. The structure of the Louisiana judicial system and the make-up of individual courts are determined partly by the various provisions of Article V of the state constitution and partly by the *Louisiana Revised Statutes of 1950*, Title 13. To avoid repeated citations to the same source, no attempt will be made to identify individual provisions in reviewing the judicial structure.

of appeal and the supreme court combined. A large measure of the public's support for the judicial system is determined by the district court's ability to function in a way that meets with the public's expectations.

As Figure 5-1 indicates, the district courts are authorized to review the decisions of all of the inferior courts except those of the juvenile and family courts and the criminal decisions of the city and parish courts. Some of these appeals are heard *de novo*—the case is simply retried in its entirety in the district court. Others are reviewed without taking evidence or by reference only to certain types of issues. These cases are only a small part of a district court's docket.

Courts of Limited Jurisdiction

Below the level of the courts of general jurisdiction exist a total of well over seven hundred courts of limited jurisdiction.[17] They are traditionally called *inferior* courts because most of them have very circumscribed authority. In some instances their decisions are subject to being reviewed and overturned on appeal by the district courts. Moreover, the judges of some of these courts are not lawyers, and procedural formalities are often at a minimum. It is possible to exaggerate the inferior status of these courts, however; they handle a vast number of cases and they mete out justice in thousands of minor cases that have very large significance for the parties.

Although the inferior courts exercise limited jurisdiction, there is very little specialization among them. The creation of specialized courts is uniformly discouraged by authorities in judicial administration because it is believed that continuous exposure to a variety of issues is the best guarantee of objectivity and breadth of outlook on the bench. For the most part, Louisiana has wisely declined to create specialized courts. Apart from the separate civil and criminal district courts and the traffic courts created in Orleans Parish to handle the docket of the state's most populous city, the judicial structure contains

17. The jurisdiction and structure of the courts below the district courts are fully discussed in American Judicature Society, *Modernizing Louisiana's Courts of Limited Jurisdiction* (Chicago: American Judicature Society, 1973). See also National Center for State Courts, *Louisiana State Court Organizational Profile* (Denver: National Center for State Courts, 1976).

Figure 5-1
Louisiana State Court System
ROUTES OF APPEAL

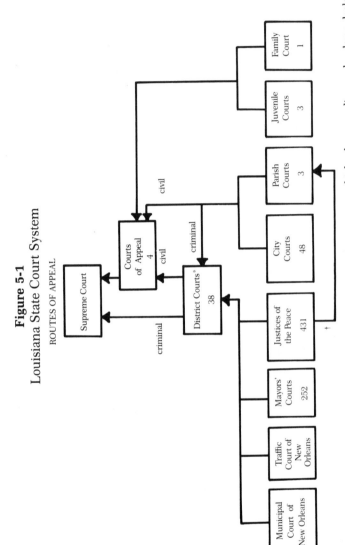

SOURCE: American Bar Association, Commission of Implementation of Standards of Judicial Administration, *Louisiana: State Court Organization* (Williamsburg, Va.: National Center for State Courts, 1979).

NOTE: The figure illustrates the routes of appeal without regard to the effects of the 1980 constitutional amendment. After July 1, 1982, there will be five courts of appeal, and they will review both civil and criminal cases. Direct appeal to the supreme court from the trial courts will be limited to cases in which a law or ordinance has been declared unconstitutional and to criminal cases in which a sentence of death has been imposed.

* Rather than a single district court in Orleans Parish (New Orleans), there are two separate courts: the Criminal District Court and the Civil District Court.

† Route of appeal in Jefferson Parish only.

a total of only four specialized courts. They are the juvenile courts of Caddo, Jefferson and Orleans Parishes and the family court of East Baton Rouge Parish.

The juvenile courts have exclusive authority to decide cases involving neglected, abandoned, or delinquent juveniles. They also may deal with adults charged with crimes against juveniles that do not amount to felonies. The family court in East Baton Rouge Parish has, in addition, exclusive authority to decide all domestic relations cases such as those for separation, divorce, alimony, or child support. Cases are appealed from the juvenile courts directly to the courts of appeal except for criminal prosecutions against adults which are appealable only to the supreme court.

City and Parish Courts

The legislature was first authorized to create city courts by the constitution of 1898 as a means of replacing the justice-of-the-peace courts with more elaborate bodies in the state's more populous wards. In 1979 there were forty-eight city courts, including two in New Orleans. The state's largest city actually has four different courts that together exercise the jurisdiction of a city court. The First and Second City Courts decide civil cases only. The New Orleans Traffic Court decides only traffic cases, and nontraffic criminal matters are handled by the Municipal Court.

The term *city court* is actually something of a misnomer since nine out of ten of them are assigned territories extending beyond the limits of a city to one or even two outlying wards. The authority of these courts was standardized in 1979 to include all civil cases involving less than $3,000.[18] Their criminal jurisdiction extends to all offenses not punishable by imprisonment at hard labor, including violations of city and parish ordinances. Both their civil and their criminal jurisdiction is concurrent with the district courts. Jury trials are prohibited in city courts.

Most city courts have only one judge. Like the judges of the district courts, they serve terms of six years. To qualify for the office, a can-

18. *Louisiana Code of Civil Procedure*, Art. 483, as amended by Act 46 of 1979.

didate must be a lawyer with at least five years of practice. Unlike district court judges, who are prevented both by law and their workloads from practicing law, city judges can and do maintain private law practices.

Their civil decisions are appealable to the courts of appeal. Criminal cases involving city and parish ordinances are appealable to the district courts, where review is restricted to issues of law. More serious criminal convictions are appealable to the supreme court.

Closely akin to the city courts are the state's three parish courts, the courts of East and West Jefferson and of Ascension Parish. A relative newcomer to the judicial structure, the parish court was conceived as a means of eventually making available throughout the state the kind of middle-range judicial facilities offered by the city courts. Presumably, in the future the creation of new city courts will be discouraged in favor of parish courts staffed by as many judges as are needed to serve the parish. Parish courts differ from city courts in only minor ways. Their territorial jurisdiction covers the entire parish and they handle civil cases worth up to $5,000. In addition parish court judges are prohibited from practicing law. Otherwise these courts are virtually the same in authority as the city courts.

The number of cases filed each year in all city and parish courts is now well in excess of half a million, more than the total number of cases filed in all other courts of the state. In 1977 traffic cases accounted for 67 percent of their docket; criminal cases accounted for 20 percent; civil cases for 11 percent; and various juvenile cases for 2 percent. While city judges devote more of their time to traffic cases than to other types of cases, their traffic dockets are not ordinarily onerous. Most traffic violators routinely admit their guilt and pay prefixed fines without ever appearing in court. Similarly, more than half of their criminal dockets are disposed of by guilty pleas. More and more creditors are availing themselves of the city and parish courts as a means of expeditiously and inexpensively collecting debts.[19] In both their capacity for handling large numbers of cases and their ready availability to litigants, the city and parish courts have become valuable supplements to the district courts.

19. Judicial Council of the Supreme Court of Louisiana, *Annual Report, 1977* (New Orleans: Judicial Council of Louisiana, 1977), 28; American Judicature Society, *Modernizing Louisiana's Courts*, 37.

Mayors' Courts

Since city courts are not established in municipalities with populations of fewer than five thousand, mayors' courts exist in about 252 of the state's smaller municipalities. Their jurisdiction is severely limited: along with the district courts they may deal with state traffic offenses—except cases of driving while intoxicated—and violations of city ordinances. They may also but seldom do serve as committing magistrates. Procedure is usually informal: the mayor himself ordinarily serves as prosecuting attorney as well as judge, and the defendant is seldom represented by a lawyer. Case loads are quite light; most mayors handle fewer than ten traffic cases per month and fewer than five nontraffic violations.

Justices of the Peace

The justice-of-the-peace courts are the most minor, the most numerous, and the most perplexing of the inferior courts. To be eligible to serve as a justice of the peace a person need only be a state citizen and a property owner, qualified to vote in his or her ward, and able to read and write English. No legal training is required. Subject to a long list of statutory exceptions, the justices of the peace have concurrent jurisdiction with the district courts in civil cases involving $750 or less, including suits over movable property and suits by landlords for eviction. Their criminal authority is limited to serving as committing magistrates only. They may admit persons to bail for noncapital offenses and those not necessarily punishable by hard labor. They may also place persons under peace bonds. Like any other judge, they may perform marriages. Justices of the peace hold court only irregularly. Their procedure is informal, and few, if any, records are kept. Their decisions are appealable to the district courts where the matters are retried in their entirety.

A study conducted in 1973 by the American Judicature Society of the state's lower courts confirmed the widely held suspicion that justices of the peace have very little to do. Seventy percent of the "JPs" responding to a questionnaire concerning their work indicated that they spent fewer than twenty hours per week on their judicial duties. An overwhelming majority of them admitted to handling fewer than twenty civil matters per month and fewer than ten criminal matters.[20]

It is not surprising then that the 1973 study recommended the abolition of both justices of the peace and mayors' courts. Efforts to implement this recommendation have encountered strenuous resistance from the justices of the peace, however. Mayors are not likely to be as covetous of their judicial duties as justices of the peace since they have other duties to attend to. They may welcome the establishment of a parish court as a decided improvement. Moreover their ability to enforce municipal ordinances was severely impaired in 1972 when the United States Supreme Court held that a trial on a traffic ordinance before a mayor whose municipality stood to benefit from the fine violated the defendant's right to be tried by an impartial judge.[21]

On the other hand, the 461 justices of the peace are not likely to agree with the argument that their offices have long since outlived their usefulness. They earn basic salaries ranging from $1,200 to $1,800 a year. Their success in resisting change so far can be explained in part by the advantage of their being represented in every parish of the state. Moreover they are able to link themselves to the widespread sentiment that judicial facilities ought to be maintained close at hand and easily available to potential litigants. They have proven to be a major force discouraging efforts aimed at unifying the lower courts.

Small-Claims Courts

No separate courts have ever been created for small monetary claims such as might arise between a vacating tenant and his landlord over a breakage deposit or between a customer seeking an adjustment on his account from a department store for defective merchandise. However, in order to encourage litigants to bring these petty disputes to court for settlement, the city courts were authorized long ago to forego some procedural formalities in cases involving less than $300. Nonetheless, the public's lack of familiarity with the judicial process and their fears of court costs, attorneys' fees, and the delays involved in bringing suit often cause such small claims to go unsettled.

20. American Judicature Society, *Modernizing Louisiana's Courts*, 10–11.
21. *Ward* v. *Village of Monroeville*, 409 U.S. 57 (1972).

In 1977, however, the legislature passed an act intended to extend the facilities of small-claims courts evenly throughout the state.[22] The act authorizes most city courts to create one or more small-claims divisions by simple rule of court. It greatly simplifies the procedures involved in these courts, standardizes costs at a minimum, encourages Saturday and nighttime sessions, and allows the city judge to appoint arbitrators to assist in disposing of small claims. The act is intended as a major incentive to motivate city judges to implement the small-claims concept. With the exception of a few localities the availability of a special forum for small claims is still not widely known. The success of the experiment will depend largely on public education and the willingness of judges and other court personnel to implement the idea.

Courts of Appeal

Louisiana is one of twenty-six states that maintain a set of intermediate courts of appeal between the courts of original jurisdiction and the supreme court. The courts of appeal were first established in 1879 as a means of relieving the supreme court's congested docket, but the experiment nearly ended in failure because of a reluctance to allocate sufficient appellate authority to the new courts.[23] In fact, throughout their history the courts of appeal have been plagued by doubts of whether they are sufficiently endowed with jurisdiction to justify their cost. Originally six courts of appeal consisting of two judges each were created. They were not given the authority to review any criminal cases, and more significantly for their survival, their civil jurisdiction was limited to cases involving less than a thousand dollars. Even after the jurisdictional amount was doubled in 1885, there were doubts that the courts of appeal had enough business. As a result, the constitution of 1898 phased out five of the courts of appeal, retaining only the appellate court for Orleans Parish with an enlarged territorial jurisdiction. This arrangement proved unworkable and in 1906 the constitution was amended to reestablish two additional courts of appeal. Since then, the existence of the courts of appeal, if not their full share of the appellate workload, has been assured.

---

22. Act 710 of 1977; *Louisiana Revised Statutes of 1950*, Title 13, Secs. 5,200–211.
23. Hood, "History of the Courts of Appeal," 544.

Map 5-1
Louisiana Court of Appeals Circuits

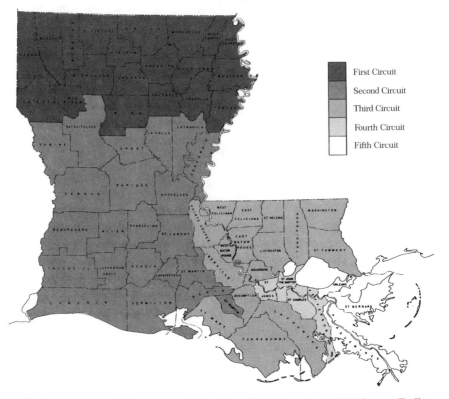

Outline map compiled and drawn by Louisiana State Department of Highways, Traffic and Planning Section

Only a few major changes have been made since 1906 affecting the courts of appeal, and they have been aimed at enabling these courts to realize their potential as intermediate courts of appeal. The constitution of 1921 enlarged the subject-matter jurisdiction of the courts of appeal to give them authority to review all suits for personal injuries including actions brought under the state's workmen's compensation law. In 1958 the supreme court's onerous workload prompted major adjustments in the allocation of appellate authority. Constitutional amendments adopted in that year, which went into effect in 1960, created a fourth appellate circuit, greatly reduced the mandatory appellate jurisdiction of the supreme court, and shifted a major portion of the appellate workload from the supreme court to the reorganized courts of appeal.[24] Even these far-reaching reforms did not result in criminal jurisdiction for the courts of appeal. The judges were anxious to avoid criminal jurisdiction if possible. Moreover, at that time relatively few criminal cases entered the stream of appeals, so that the supreme court's exclusive responsibility for criminal appeal did not constitute much of a problem.

By the 1970s, however, the number of criminal cases reaching the supreme court had grown enormously and was jeopardizing the high court's ability to fulfill its unique role in the judicial system. The supreme court scrutinized the problem for more than three years in consultation with representatives of the courts of appeal and a number of national authorities. A wide variety of alternatives were considered. Some of the judges of the courts of appeal advocated the establishment of a separate court of criminal appeals. However, this alternative was uniformly labeled by the authorities consulted as the worst of all alternatives because it would tend to relegate criminal appeals to a dark corner of the judicial system and to create "a slum area of the law." Finally, in 1980 constitutional amendments were adopted to transfer primary responsibility for all criminal appeals (except appeals against the death penalty) to the court of appeal, effective July 1, 1982. Though strenuously opposed by some members of the courts of appeal this is the solution that emerged as most consistent with basic principles of judicial administration. Related legislation enacted in 1980 created an additional circuit court of appeals and increased the number of appellate court judges.[25]

The courts of appeal play an important role in the judicial system, for without their assistance, the right of litigants under Louisiana law to have a final judgment reviewed by at least one appellate court would amount only to a hollow promise. This right is implemented by a constitutional provision that makes all final judgments rendered in civil cases, with the exception of those few that can be brought directly to the supreme court, appealable as a matter of right to the courts of appeal. In addition, when the 1980 amendment takes effect, the courts of

24. John H. Tucker, Donald J. Tate, and Henry G. McMahon, "Appellate Reorganization in Louisiana," *Louisiana Law Review*, XIV (February, 1959), 287.

25. Institute for Judicial Administration, *A Study of the Louisiana Court System* (New York: Institute for Judicial Administration, 1972), 222; Act 661 of 1980.

appeal will also be required to hear appeals in all criminal cases involving offenses triable by jury. These courts also have *discretionary* authority to entertain questions arising even before judgment is rendered by a lower court, but such matters make up only a small part of
their docket. In 1979, 2,269 mandatory appeals were filed in the four
circuit courts of appeal. Applications for discretionary writs amounted
to only 395, and 300 of them were refused. The overall workload of the
courts of appeal is suggested by the number of judgments rendered
each year, which in 1979 amounted to 1,802.[26]

Although the courts of appeal were initially created to reduce the
number of cases reaching the supreme court, they have become more
than mere filters in the stream of appeals. In their relationships with
the supreme court and with one another, they are key actors in the process by which the law is developed. Perhaps the most decisive argument for the significance of the courts of appeal stems from the fact
that most of their decisions are never reviewed by the state supreme
court. In many instances no effort is made to appeal a case beyond the
intermediate level. The chance of winning a reversal in the supreme
court may appear too slim to justify further expense in attorneys' fees
or costs of court. Or, if review by the supreme court is sought, the high
court may refuse to hear it. As a result, most civil cases decided on
appeal are decided with finality by the courts of appeal.

The Supreme Court

As the highest court in the state's judicial hierarchy, the supreme court
is vested by the state constitution with "general supervisory jurisdiction over all other courts." This very general grant of power implies a
uniquely dual role for the court. Its central role, of course, is its ad-
judicative function as the state's court of last resort. As such the court
has special responsibilities for assuring consistency and, to some
extent, direction in the development of the state's law by the other
state courts. In addition, the court has an administrative role of ever-
increasing importance to play. The constitution grants it authority "to

26. *Louisiana Code of Civil Procedure*, Art. 2082; John T. Hood, Jr., "The Right of
Appeal," *Louisiana Law Review*, XXIV (February, 1969), 287; Louisiana Constitution,
Art. V, Sec. 10A; Judicial Council of the Supreme Court of Louisiana, *Annual Report,
1979*, 33.

Map 5-2
Louisiana Supreme Court Districts

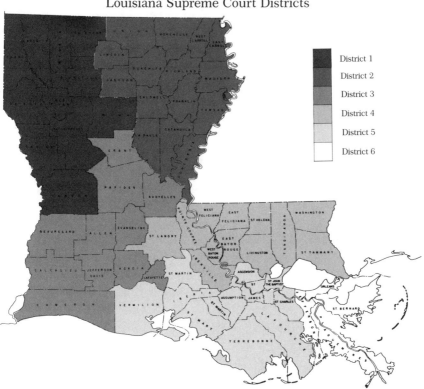

District 1
District 2
District 3
District 4
District 5
District 6

Outline map compiled and drawn by Louisiana State Department of Highways, Traffic and Planning Section.

establish procedural and administrative rules not inconsistent with law" for the entire judicial system.[27] It is ultimately the supreme court's responsibility to see to it that the judicial system functions well as an organization and to initiate and coordinate efforts by members of the bench and bar to evaluate the workings of the system and bring about necessary change. Its ability to perform both its adjudicatory and its administrative roles has been hampered in recent years, however, by its heavy case load.

The importance of the court's rule-making authority to its ability to carry out its functions has become increasingly obvious as the court

27. Louisiana Constitution, Art. V, Sec. 10A.

has sought in recent years to exert greater administrative control over the judicial system, but the full extent of the power remains an open question. It has yet to be fully explored by the court or fully accepted by the legislature. Thus, at this stage of its development, the power is subject to unpredictable political limitations. When, for instance, the court promulgated a new code of judicial conduct in 1976 containing a provision prohibiting any judge from serving as a member of the board of directors of any bank or other lending institution, a number of lower court judges who were directly affected filed suit to have the provision declared invalid. When their efforts failed, they obtained a legislative veto of the provision in the form of an act specifically permitting judges to serve on bank boards. In this instance the supreme court had the last word when it declared the act invalid as a violation of its constitutional authority to discipline state judges.[28] Questions concerning the court's rule-making authority persist, however, in both legislative and judicial circles.

As the state's court of last resort, the supreme court has authority to review on appeal the decisions of the state's lower courts in any type of case. Its original jurisdiction is limited to its exclusive authority over disciplinary actions against attorneys. The authority of the court to review cases on appeal can be divided into those cases that can be appealed directly from the trial courts, which the court is required to hear—its so-called appellate jurisdiction—and those which reach it only with its permission and in most instances only after the case has been reviewed by a court of appeals. Under the original provisions of the 1974 constitution the mandatory jurisdiction of the court extended to four types of cases: (1) lower court decisions declaring a law or ordinance unconstitutional; (2) felony convictions; (3) other criminal convictions in which a fine of more than five hundred dollars or sentence of more than six months in prison has actually been imposed; (4) district court decisions reviewing a ruling of the Public Service Commission.[29] All other types of cases reach the court only with its permission; that is, the appealing party must apply for and obtain a writ of review from the court before his case will be heard by the court on its merits. These types of cases are said to fall within the "writ jurisdiction" of the court.

28. *Babineaux* v. *Judiciary Commission*, 341 So.2d 396 (1976).
29. Louisiana Constitution, Art. V, Section 5.

Table 5-1
Cases Filed and Opinions Rendered
in the Louisiana Supreme Court

Type of Case	1971	1975	1979
Appeals			
Appeals Filed	151	358	493
Appeals Dismissed or Denied*	1 (.6%)	11 (3%)	10 (2%)
Opinions Rendered on Appeals	99	354	534
Writs			
Writ Applications Filed	694	1,240	2,271
Writ Applications Dismissed or Denied*	560 (80%)	883 (71%)	1,473 (65%)
Opinions Rendered on Writs Granted	79	146	178

Source: Judicial Council of the Supreme Court of Louisiana, *Annual Report, 1977* and *Annual Report, 1979.*

*The percentages are calculated by dividing the total number of appeals or writ applications denied or dismissed in the years shown, including any which may have been filed in the previous year, by the total number of appeals or writ applications filed in each of the years.

The number of cases appealed to the supreme court by each of the avenues of appeal as defined by the 1974 constitution is illustrated by Table 5-1. Each year most of the filings in the supreme court take the form of applications for discretionary writs. The court turns down the vast majority of these applications. By comparison, fewer mandatory appeals are filed but the court has no way of avoiding review of these cases. The result, suggested by Table 5-1, is that most of the opinions rendered by the courts are rendered in mandatory appeals rather than in cases in which writs of review have been granted.

By the 1970s the supreme court's docket came to consist predominantly of criminal cases. Fortunately almost two-thirds of criminal filings take the form of writ applications, which the court can and does decline to review in the vast majority of cases. But under the original provisions of the 1974 constitution, there was a large number of appeals that the supreme court was required to hear. In all other states that have intermediate courts of appeal, appeals of right to the supreme court are permitted in only a few of the more serious felonies or not at all. The extraordinary degree of mandatory jurisdiction outlined in the 1974 constitution was necessary because the courts of appeal were given no criminal jurisdiction whatever. The effect on the supreme court's docket is illustrated by the fact that in 1976 criminal cases accounted for 59 percent of all filings, 76 percent of all mandatory appeals, and 77 percent of all full opinions.[30]

The exclusive jurisdiction of the supreme court in criminal appeals does more than merely overwork the court. It also prevents it from fulfilling its unique role in the judicial system. In a two-tier system of appellate courts the courts of appeal and the supreme court have distinctive, though closely related roles to play. "The intermediate appellate court is assigned the function of correcting mistakes," whereas "the highest court is assigned as its primary function the obligation of law development, of resolving conflicts among lower courts, of teaching the other courts and lawyers and public about the law."[31] Louisiana has subscribed in principle to this model of the relationship of its appellate courts for years. But in practice, throughout the 1970s, if not longer, the court's heavy criminal case load was permitted to tax it to its limits and undermine the uniqueness of its role in the state's judiciary. For these reasons it is difficult to exaggerate the significance of the 1980 amendment to the judiciary article of the state constitution shifting primary responsibility for criminal appeals to the courts of appeal. After July 1, 1982, the supreme court will be required to hear only two types of cases: (1) those in which a lower court has declared a state law or ordinance unconstitutional, and (2) criminal cases in which the death penalty has been imposed. All other cases will be appealable as a matter of right only to the courts of appeal. They will normally reach the supreme court, if at all, only after having been reviewed by a court of appeals and then only by means of a discretionary writ.

The internal operating procedures of the court are designed to enable it to keep abreast of its work load. These procedures may be modified in the future to accommodate the decreased number of first-time criminal appeals reaching the court after the 1980 amendment takes

30. Eugene J. Murret, Judicial Administrator, "Supreme Court Docket: July 1, 1975, to June 30, 1976," Memorandum, September 27, 1976, in the administrator's files. The Judicial Administrator's office does not regularly report the proportion of civil and criminal filings in the Supreme Court. See also David S. Clark, "Statistical Survey," in "Work of the Louisiana Appellate Courts for the 1976–1977 Term," *Louisiana Law Review*, XXXVIII (Winter, 1978), 313, 316.

31. Charles Joiner, "The Function of the Appellate System," (Address delivered at the National Conference on the Judiciary, 1971) quoted in Institute for Judicial Administration, *The Louisiana Court System*, 219–20.

effect. At present, however, the court works in cycles of five weeks. The first working days of each cycle are devoted to hearing oral arguments. When the court is not sitting, conferences devoted almost exclusively to applications for discretionary writs are held once a week. Each writ application is reviewed preliminarily by two justices, but the decision to grant or deny the application is made by a majority of the justices in conference after all justices have considered the matter. Staff attorneys assist the court in identifying the criminal appeals in each cycle that do not merit lengthy consideration. These are placed on a summary docket for disposition on a special day after little or no oral argument by unsigned opinions known as *per curiam* decisions. Other cases are assigned to individual justices on a rotating basis for preparation of authored opinions fully discussing the factual and legal issues raised. In all criminal cases separate preargument memoranda are prepared by the law clerks working in the court's central staff. These memoranda are circulated to all of the justices along with the records and briefs before argument. Oral argument is limited to thirty minutes per side in civil and twenty minutes per side in criminal cases. It usually takes the form of a question-and-answer session between the court and the attorneys. A brief bench conference is held after argument for criminal cases. Afterwards each judge decides the cases assigned to him without further assistance from other members of the court. Finished opinions are circulated among the judges and at a final conference of the cycle the opinions are passed individually around the table for signature. If an opinion fails to get a majority of the votes, the dissenting justice who is next in seniority to the author writes a new opinion.

A thorough analysis of the supreme court's response to the cases appealed to it is beyond the scope of this study, but it is possible to get a

Table 5-2
Civil and Criminal Appeals
Affirmed and Reversed, 1976

Type of Appeal	Number	Reversed	%
Civil	73	54	74%
Criminal	362	90	25%

Source: Thomas R. Hopper assisted in gathering the data for this table.

glimpse of its substantive role and of the source of some of the conflicts in the judicial system by examining the fate of the lower court
decisions that it reviewed. Table 5-2 shows the rate at which the supreme court reversed the decisions of the lower courts in more than
four hundred cases decided on their merits on 1976.

The great majority of civil cases reach the court only with its approval. Inasmuch as it reversed 74 percent of the civil decisions it reviewed, it is obvious that it uses its wide discretionary authority over its
civil docket to review those cases in which it believes intervention is
needed. Since most of the civil cases reach the high court from the
courts of appeal, it is also evident that the supreme court's formal relationship with the courts of appeal is one of frequent conflict, a fact that
is not lost on individual judges of the courts of appeal who will occasionally engage in a kind of debate over particular points of law with
the supreme court in their written opinions.

The large role of the court in criminal appeals in 1976 is suggested
by the fact that the court decided four times as many criminal appeals
on their merits as civil cases. The court has no discretion to refuse to
hear most of these cases, however, so it is not surprising that the reversal rate is only 25 percent. Still, almost twice as many decisions were
reversed in criminal cases. The difference in the court's response
to civil and criminal cases should largely evaporate after the 1980
amendment takes effect and the court is able to exercise an equal degree of choice over both its civil and criminal docket.

The receptiveness of the present-day supreme court to claims of
state or federal constitutional rights by criminal defendants is a relatively new phenomenon. To some extent it can be explained by the
presence on the court of a new generation of judges. Between 1968 and
1980 nine incumbent justices were replaced. Some of the new recruits
have been very receptive to new constitutional rules developed by the
United States Supreme Court. However, an explanation of present de-
cisional trends solely in terms of the personal attitudes of individual
judges obscures the important influence of the federal courts on decision making in all state courts. The Louisiana supreme court is not
alone in its present-day willingness to enforce national constitutional
norms on the state level. The large amount of attention given nationally
to the field of criminal justice and especially to the work of the United

States Supreme Court regarding the constitutional rights of defendants has had a formative effect on all state courts. In the final analysis the willingness of the court to devote time and energy to a good-faith application of national rules in state criminal cases is in the best interest of federalism because their failure to do so will, in many instances, only provide the federal courts with an opportunity to intervene in the state's affairs.

Agenda for Reform

The types of problems that the Louisiana judiciary is likely to face in the future and its ability to deal with them will be determined in large measure by two relatively recent developments: (1) an unprecedented increase in the case load of all courts and (2) a relatively recent but growing commitment to the importance of the administrative function in the successful operation of the courts.

The Louisiana courts are currently laboring under an imposing case load. In 1979, for instance, a total of 417,770 cases were filed in the district courts representing an increase of 25 percent over the 1975 figure and of 163 percent over 1965 when only 166,675 cases were filed. In 1965 the dockets of the district courts were divided about evenly between civil and criminal cases—49 percent civil and 51 percent criminal. In 1979, however, criminal cases accounted for 63 percent of the dockets. While civil filings increased by 48 percent between 1965 and 1975, the increase in criminal cases amounted to 153 percent.[32]

Increased work loads in the lower courts are reflected in similar increases in the dockets of the appellate courts. In 1979 a total of 2,664 cases were filed in the four courts of appeal, representing a 33 percent increase over the 1975 docket and a 133 percent increase over the 1965 docket. The courts of appeal have been spared the worst effect of these figures, however, by the occasional creation of new judgeships which increased the number of judges from twenty in 1965 to thirty-two in 1979 and to no fewer than forty-one in 1982 when they assume

32. Judicial Council of the Supreme Court, *Annual Report, 1965*, Tables VI and VII (unpaged), *Annual Report, 1975*, 40, *Annual Report, 1979*, 36.

criminal jurisdiction. Until now they have also been sheltered by their lack of responsibility for criminal appeals. Thus, in 1979 these courts rendered an average of fifty-six judgments per judge, representing an increase of only 17 percent over 1965.[33]

As a single court with relatively fixed membership and a unique role to play in the judicial system, the supreme court has been particularly hard hit by the rising case load. Total filings in 1979 amounted to 3,051, an increase of 66 percent since 1975 and 466 percent since 1965. Fortunately, most of these filings were in the form of writ applications, which the supreme court can and does deny without reviewing the cases on their merits. But the large increase in criminal appeals entitled to review as a matter of right caused a rise in mandatory appeals between 1965 and 1979 from 45 to 493 cases or over 1,100 percent. As a result, the total number of opinions rendered per justice increased from 17 in 1965 to 98 in 1979, an increase of 476 percent.[34]

Firm recognition of the importance of the administrative task in the successful operation of the state's judicial system was first made in 1950 with the creation by supreme court rule of a judicial council. The council is charged with the responsibility of serving as an advisory body for the supreme court and especially for the chief justice, who is considered to be the chief administrative officer of the court system. Although planted as early as 1916, the idea of a judicial council did not germinate until the 1940s when increasingly crowded dockets, backlogs of undecided cases in all courts, delay, and lack of uniformity and coordination in the handling of cases made it impossible to ignore the pressing need for greater attention to the administration of the courts. In 1946 the bar association created a section on judicial administration, which in 1948 under the chairmanship of then associate justice John B. Fournet, recommended the creation of a judicial council. The idea was implemented in 1950, a short time after Fournet became chief justice. In 1954 after an Orleans Parish grand jury produced a secret report charging that the backlog of cases in the Orleans criminal courts was causing people to be held in jail for up to four years without a trial, the legislature was persuaded to appropriate funds for

33. Judicial Council of the Supreme Court, *Annual Report, 1965,* Table IV (unpaged), *Annual Report, 1975,* 30, *Annual Report, 1979,* 33.
34. Judicial Council of the Supreme Court, *Annual Report, 1965,* Table I (unpaged), *Annual Report, 1975,* 25, *Annual Report, 1979,* 31.

the operation of the council, making possible the appointment of a full-time judicial administrator to serve as an administrative assistant for the chief justice.[35] Today the judicial administrator's office is a constitutional office. The administrator is appointed by the supreme court and his office furnishes administrative leadership throughout the judicial system.

The council is composed of representatives from all of the courts, the bar, the public, the legislature, the clerks of court, and the district attorneys. Because of its size and the other interests of its members, it tends not to be self-motivated. But the council may be significant even beyond its particular accomplishments to the extent that it stands for a recognition of the importance of sound judicial administration to the work of the courts. Under its authority the judicial administrator's office furnishes administrative leadership throughout the judicial system. It is particularly valuable in gathering and circulating statistics and other information concerning the work of the courts. Various committees evaluate the procedures and practices of the courts at all levels and develop recommendations for improvement. These bodies can also serve as points of contact between the Louisiana courts and various external organizations advocating judicial reforms of different kinds. A 1972 study of the Louisiana courts conducted by the Institute for Judicial Administration under the council's auspices, provided an objective and thorough analysis of the strengths and weaknesses of the Louisiana courts.[36] One of its main recommendations concerned a statewide network of judicial administrators. Several of the busier lower courts now employ full-time administrators of their own. In short, the council furnishes the auspices for maintaining judicial reform as a permanent item on the agenda of the courts.

Current Issues

Like any other political institution, the ability of the judiciary to command respect for its decisions depends ultimately on its effectiveness in the performance of its assigned tasks. Among current issues of judicial reform, three stand out as particularly relevant for the future effec-

35. John B. Fournet, "The Reorganization of the Louisiana Judicial System," *Southwestern Law Journal*, XVII (March, 1963), 79.
36. Institute for Judicial Administration, *A Study of the Louisiana Court System*.

tiveness of the courts: (1) the perfection of the judicial system as an organization, (2) the reallocation of appellate authority, and (3) the development of ways and means of extending legal services to greater numbers of the public.

Although on paper the judicial system appears to be well organized, in fact it is not. Current attempts to coordinate the work of the courts at different levels or even at the same level outside of the channels of formal communication found within the actual decision-making process, are of relatively recent date. No corporation would permit its branch offices the degree of independence enjoyed by individual courts or attempt to carry on with the minimal organizational ties that exist between levels of courts. The organizational deficiencies of the system affect the quality both of justice and of court administration.

Three of the recommendations for change made by the Institute for Judicial Administration in its 1972 study of the Louisiana courts are aimed at curing the defects of the system as an organization. First, the institute recommended the unification of the various trial courts and intermediate courts of appeal into single courts at their respective levels. Under such an arrangement, the work load would be divided among geographic divisions of the trial courts or intermediate courts of appeal rather than among organizationally autonomous courts as occurs at present. Second, the institute advised the integration of all levels of courts and all judicial personnel into a single administrative system with clear lines of administrative authority, a well-defined fund of rule-making power, and a statewide system of financing. Third, the institute recommended the establishment of a statewide corps of administrative personnel.[37]

Although the seeds of organizational improvement have been planted, bringing the plant to maturity will not be an easy task. For instance, the case for a unified system is not self-evident to everyone whose cooperation is necessary to bring it about. Individual judges tend to be jealous of their present independence. Then, too, unification carries with it a threat to the existence of some courts, as in the case of justices of the peace, and it can engender stiff resistance. Even good-faith reform in one area can work against unification. Thus the creation of

37. *Ibid.*, 19–62.

parish courts as a means of extending the kind of midrange judicial facilities now furnished by the city courts evenly throughout the state will create another level of court below the district courts and further complicate the task of unification.

Organizational improvement depends also on the initiative and personal leadership of the chief justice, the judicial system's chief administrative officer. Louisiana is one of only six states that select the chief justice by seniority on the court. In the past this system has resulted in the selection of some notably strong and forward-looking personalities as chief justice. But it is not necessarily an effective means of selecting a chief justice who considers organizational improvement a matter of high priority. Finally, there is as yet no consensus among the judges or members of the legislature concerning the scope of the supreme court's authority to govern the judicial system by its rule-making authority.

Perhaps the most pressing problem now facing the Louisiana judicial system is the problem of successfully transferring primary responsibility for criminal appeals from the supreme court to the courts of appeal. The new constitutional provisions scheduled to take effect in 1982 represent the culmination of years of effort to solve this problem once and for all. The new arrangements may not automatically produce all of their intended beneficial effects, however. Much will depend on the willingness of the courts of appeal in each circuit to respond positively to this new challenge and to bring the same level of diligence to bear in criminal cases that they have characteristically shown in civil cases. Moreover, the supreme court will have to develop a firm determination to allow the courts of appeal to have the last word in all cases except those few that clearly merit a second review by the state's highest tribunal.

Finally, it is important to bear in mind that even the most elaborate, well-administered system of courts is of little avail to the public without the services of lawyers. Partly because of a lack of understanding concerning the services that lawyers have to offer and partly because of a fear of costs or an outright inability to pay, most of the state's legal services are rendered on behalf of only a minority of the population. Although the constitution of 1974 provides for the establishment of an indigent defender board at the state level, these services remain unevenly available and the problem of assuring that all criminal defendants, regardless of income, enjoy adequate representation continues to be a major challenge.

There is an increasing awareness of the uneven distribution of legal services in the civil field. Until recently low-income people had to rely on the willingness of individual attorneys to represent them for little or no payment in civil matters. In 1974 Congress established a national Legal Services Corporation to extend legal services for the poor throughout the country. By the end of 1980 the corporation had funded offices in all fifty states, including ten in Louisiana.[38] Each of the regional offices in the state makes available a staff of attorneys and paralegal personnel to assist the poor with non-fee-generating civil problems. They have not solved the problem of the availability of legal services for the poor. There are traces of friction between the private bar and legal services offices in some areas, and there is no guarantee of continued funding. On the other hand, in just a few years the state's legal services programs have amassed a large clientele and a mounting record of effective service that may make it difficult in the future to return to the former system of voluntary assistance.

38. The genesis and organization of Louisiana's legal services offices are described in Lila Tritico Hogan and David Duhon, "Legal Services for the Poor," *Louisiana Bar Journal*, XXVIII (December, 1980), 129–33.

6.

The Bureaucracy

CHARLES HOLBROOK AND MARK T. CARLETON

To the close observer of Louisiana's hectic political life, the control of the seemingly endless labyrinth of boards, commissions, departments, and divisions that make up the bureaucracy often appears to be the prize for which the politicians are competing. *Bureaucrat* is a negative term, bringing to mind a person behind a desk who is inflexible, inefficient, and generally insensitive to legitimate citizen needs. Someone, however, has to patrol the highways, enforce the state's environmental laws, and safeguard the state's wildlife. Whoever gets to determine or even influence the staffing of these agencies gets to influence the approval of contracts, the spending of state (and often federal) money, and the disposition of offenders against state law. The organization and operation of the state's governmental establishment, therefore, are eminently political.

Even the most self-interested politician must "deliver the goods" in the form of state services, however, and this is not possible unless decisions are made (at least to some extent) on a basis other than repayment of personal favors.[1] To be politically effective, bureaucracy has to be "impersonal." In addition, citizens dealing with their state government expect the state job holders to know what they are doing. Persons in state jobs, therefore, must have some specialized knowledge and competence. Although Louisiana's bureaucracy is highly politi-

1. For a discussion of the nature of bureaucracy see Max Weber, *The Theory of Social and Economic Organization*, ed. Talcott Parsons, trans. A. M. Henderson and Talcott Parsons (New York: Oxford University Press, 1947), 329–41; Victor A. Thompson, *Modern Organizations: A General Theory* (New York: Knopf, 1964), Chap. 8.

cized, the tendency has been to make it a politically effective and responsive bureaucracy. This has meant an ongoing attempt to clearly define the chain of command, to employ competent and specialized state workers, and to conduct services and operations so as to minimize the influence of "old boy" or "old girl" ties. Finally, there has been an attempt to make the state's bureaucracy sufficiently flexible to respond to the changing needs and circumstances of the state's citizens.

The Civil Service System

Around 1900 a Baton Rouge photographer assembled all local employees of the state for a group picture. Legislators were excluded, as were judges and top officials of the executive branch. No more than thirty clerks, stenographers, runners, pages, and janitors appear in the photograph—a tiny bureaucracy indeed. Eighty years later the State of Louisiana employs more than 80,000 people, 18,000 of them in Baton Rouge alone. Within this army of public wage earners are nurses, college professors, attorneys, engineers, librarians, psychiatrists, and computer specialists, not to mention the ubiquitous legions of departmental bureaucrats, clerical workers, law enforcement officers, and custodial personnel.

The multiplication of state agencies and the steady growth of state employment in Louisiana principally resulted from four causes: (1) constantly expanding state regulatory responsibility; (2) ongoing demand from a host of constituencies for additional and improved state services; (3) an increasing reliance everywhere upon government itself—federal, state, and local—as the "employer of last resort"; and (4) an unavoidable paper explosion triggered by governmental responsibility to generate increasingly more data and information. Hundreds of state employees now do nothing but produce, copy, distribute, and file tons of public documents.

As provider and regulatory agencies become more numerous, the state had to hire additional managers, monitors, and planners to supervise, discipline, and coordinate those who teach, heal, build, or inspect. Just as a modern army must maintain at least a dozen service and support troops for every combatant, so a modern civil government seems to need swarms of similar personnel to back up those employees who actually render the many services which the public has come to expect.

The phrase *state civil service* refers to all state employees. The civil service in Louisiana is regulated by the powerful Civil Service Commission, which is an autonomous regulatory body composed of six members appointed by the governor and one member elected from and by the classified employees. Virtually any issue that concerns any classified employee is ultimately subject to its approval. In 1971, for example, when the legislature appropriated funds to increase the pay of the State Police, the Civil Service Commission refused to allow the raises to go into effect. In the end, the money was used for new police cars. The commission has broad powers over both the classified or merit-system service and the unclassified service, into which state civil service is divided for administrative purposes.

Classified personnel are chosen through a competitive testing program designed to select the most competent employees possible. These employees are prohibited from engaging in any political activity, and they are subject to the rules of the Civil Service Commission, which has broad power to regulate employment, certification, compensation, promotion, demotion, suspension, reduction in pay, and qualifications. Examination scores, performance on personal interviews, education, and experience are all taken into account in assigning a grade to each applicant for a classified position. Veterans and their widows are given preferential treatment in the form of extra points, which are automatically added to their scores. Employers must fill vacant classified positions from a list of qualified candidates, and only applicants whose grades are among the top five scores may be hired.

Each new employee in the classified service is required to complete a six-month probationary period. During this time, his supervisor must evaluate the new worker's performance and make a recommendation either for continued employment or for termination. Figures showing the number of terminations after the six-month evaluation are unavailable, but once an employee passes this hurdle, he is unlikely to be dismissed. Supervisors rate employees as unsatisfactory less than 0.3 percent of the time on annual evaluations of all employees, even though this could not possibly reflect the true performance of the classified service.

The classified service was developed to prevent the Jacksonian spoils system of awarding jobs to political cronies of the person in power. The classified system lends a sense of stability and continuity to the everyday affairs of government. It also promotes the development of programmatic expertise through longevity and the employment of the most qualified through the competitive entrance system.

The disadvantages of the classified system all seem to be management related. Stability often impedes positive change and makes the bureaucracy unresponsive to the needs of the citizenry it serves. Motivating classified employees is also a major problem. Technically, no one's job in the classified service is guaranteed in perpetuity regardless of circumstance. Nevertheless, it is a common view among classified civil servants that it is impossible to be dismissed for nonperformance. Indeed, because of the time-consuming legal complexities involved in dismissing employees for nonperformance, dismissal for cause is rare. First-line supervisors seldom have the authority to impose other negative sanctions upon their subordinates. Their ability to demand quality work of their employees is, therefore, greatly jeopardized. Finally, the merit system does not guarantee expertise. Over time, any large bureaucratic organization tends to view its existence as its purpose. Individuals within the bureaucracy come to view their own jobs in a similar way, and they lose sight of the organization's goals. This myopic view of one's job discourages competency in a broader range of activities. It is possible that this narrow outlook is partly attributable to poor organizational structures, but comfort in one's job is also a significant influence.

As of June, 1978, approximately 1.5 percent of Louisiana's total population, about 59,000 people, worked in the state's classified service.[2] Males made up 45 percent of the total. Blacks were slightly overrepresented in state employment, for 31 percent of the workers, as compared to 29 percent of the general population, were black.

The mean age for classified employees was approximately thirty-six in 1978. In comparison to the general population, the classified employee is considerably overrepresented in the younger categories. There are a number of factors that could help to explain this phenomenon.

2. Data from Louisiana Department of Civil Service, annual unpublished data.

Table 6-1

Race and Sex of Classified Employees and General Population
(In Percentages)

Race and Sex	Percentage of State Classified Employees	Percentage of State Population*
White Male	32.90	34.42
White Female	35.76	36.26
Black Male	11.41	13.85
Black Female	19.17	15.42
Other	0.74	

*Calculated from Harris S. Segal, *et al., Projections to the Year 2000 of Louisiana Population and Households* (New Orleans: Division of Business and Economic Research, College of Business Administration, University of New Orleans, 1976).

Table 6-2

Age of Classified Employees and General Population
(In Percentages)

Age of General Population	Percentage of Population Between Age 15 and 75	Percentage of Classified Employees Between 16 and 75	Age of Employees
15–19	13.90	2.94	16–20
20–24	13.32	13.90	21–25
25–29	11.74	16.52	26–30
30–34	9.49	12.61	31–35
35–39	7.71	10.02	36–40
40–44	6.73	10.04	41–45
45–49	6.53	10.06	46–50
50–54	6.63	9.92	51–55
55–59	6.06	8.67	56–60
60–64	5.24	4.52	61–65
65–69	4.49	.57	66–70
70–74	3.50	.12	71–75
75+	4.60	.03	75+

Sources: Segal, *et al., Projections to the Year 2000*; Louisiana Department of Civil Service.

Between 1956 and 1978 the number of permanent employees of the state of Louisiana increased from 28,132 to 57,568. At this rate one could anticipate 1,347 new employees annually. This increase can largely be attributed to the growth of the federal government and its state-administered programs. Ultimately, the increase is, of course, attributable to the burgeoning demand for public goods and services. The rapid growth has created many entry-level positions, partially explaining the youthfulness of the Louisiana bureaucracy today.

In averaging the pay of classified employees in 1978, the mean was $846 per month, the median was $771, and the mode was only $525 per month. During the same period, the average nonsupervisory wage in the private sector was $895 per month nationally.[3] It is reasonable to assume that persons with a great deal of experience—that is, older workers—would not be attracted by Louisiana's rate of pay. In addition, job requirements in the classified system often emphasize considerable formal education. The young, who generally are far better educated than their parents but who have little job experience, are attracted to state employment, but they do not stay.

Since 1969, the average annual turnover rate for state employees has been 20.49 percent. This high turnover rate is partly attributable to such factors as low pay, which we have already discussed. Perhaps the most important factor, however, is the increasingly interchangeable nature of the skills demanded by government and those demanded by private industry. Many young people with good education but little experience and marginal skills are trained by the state to a degree that makes them eligible for private-sector employment. This training ranges from teaching clerical workers to type to making computer programmers out of young people who were educated in the humanities. Once these people have acquired sufficient experience, they move on to jobs in the private sector where pay and benefits are so much better. They leave open a large number of entry-level positions that will be filled, once again, by young people.

A large number of state employees are not members of the classified service. Unclassified personnel include all of the state's elected officials; the heads of the principal executive departments; the registrars of voters; the members of boards, authorities, and commissions; two

3. U.S. Department of Labor, Bureau of Labor Statistics, *Employment and Earnings,* XXV (October, 1978), 134.

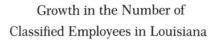

Figure 6-1

Growth in the Number of
Classified Employees in Louisiana

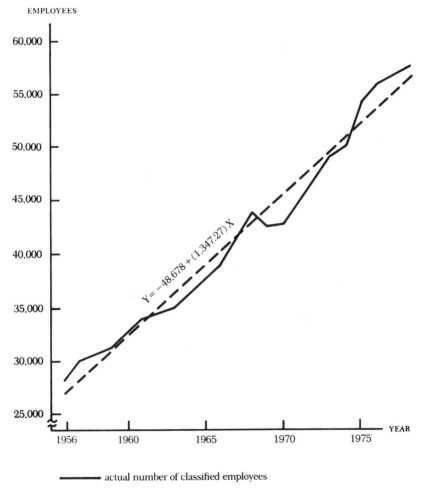

$$Y = -48,678 + (1,347.27) X$$

——— actual number of classified employees

- - - - - linear regression, r=.9885

SOURCE: Louisiana Department of Civil Service.

Table 6-3
State Employment Turnover

Year	Percentage Turnover
1969	20.54
1970	20.62
1971	16.94
1972	18.11
1973	20.23
1974	21.11
1975	20.54
1976	20.84
1977	24.28
1978	21.73

Source: Louisiana Department of Civil Service.

assistants to any of these; one secretary to the president of each college or university; the teaching and professional staffs of the state's schools, colleges, and universities; the employees of the offices of the governor, lieutenant governor, and attorney general. It is a long list, but at one time it was considerably longer. Article X of the 1974 constitution strictly limited the number of unclassified state jobs. It also gave the Civil Service Commission the authority to create additional positions if they are needed or to abolish them if they are no longer necessary.

At least one state agency has made an attempt to increase the number of unclassified employees allotted to it. In early 1977 the Division of Administration, which is organizationally a part of the Office of the Governor, asked the Civil Service Commission to allow certain of the division's employees unclassified status. The commission refused, and the division went to court. The division claimed that it was entitled to a larger portion of unclassified employees because it was part of the Office of the Governor, and the court found in its favor. The Civil Service Commission then refused to allow any of the division's employees to remain in the classified service. Meanwhile, the commission appealed the court decision and won a reversal. All of the employees of the Division of Administration returned to the classified service, except the very few allowed to remain unclassified by law.

It is difficult to generalize about the unclassified service because it embraces so many variations in method of selection, degree of job security, and pay scale. Some unclassified employees are elected, serve at the pleasure of the voters, and are paid a salary established by the legislature. Some of them are political appointees. They hold their jobs at the whim of the person who appointed them. In some cases, their salaries and duties are prescribed by law (board and commission members, for example); in other cases, their pay and duties are at the discretion of the official who appointed them.

The elected officials and their appointees are, perhaps, what most citizens think of when unclassified employees are mentioned. These people are policy makers, who often initiate new programs themselves and who have wide latitude in how they will interpret and implement the policies of the governor and the legislature. These employees must play politics not only to keep their jobs but also to influence the direction of the programs they administer. Undoubtedly, politics sometimes gets in the way of efficient performance, but it is also true that many of these unclassified employees are extremely competent administrators. They can and, indeed, they must respond to the needs and wishes of the voters.

Many other unclassified employees have no contact with politics at all. Teachers, for example, are employed on the basis of their qualifications, paid what the legislature decrees, and protected by a system of tenure that gives them job security that is at least equal to that of classified employees. As a group, they have considerable influence, but as individuals, they are no more or less politically oriented than any other citizens of the state. There are other unclassified personnel who are hired to work in the state's educational institutions on the basis of professional qualifications. These employees are experts in certain areas. Although there are no legal guarantees of job tenure as there are for teachers and for classified workers, these employees usually keep their jobs for as long as they wish. They are neither hired nor fired on the basis of political whim.

The strategic use of unclassified personnel is probably necessary and can be beneficial. The flexibility of these employees helps to make government responsive to the public's needs and encourages creativity and dynamism in administration. The unclassified service is a way to overcome the sluggishness, intractability, and organizational inertia of the bureaucracy. Those who employ unclassified workers have more freedom to select the person best qualified for a specific job, rather than a broadly generalized category of duties meant to cover many contingencies. As the needs of an office change, supervisors and administrators are able to respond quickly, filling new jobs, adjusting pay, changing an employee's duties. The unclassified service augments the work of the classified service; both are necessary to the smooth running of the bureaucracy.

Unions in the Public Sector in Louisiana

Unionization of state workers has become an important issue in Louisiana. Public employees have become prime targets of many industrial unions because declining membership has depleted union coffers, while organizational overhead has remained constant or increased over time. Public employees are relatively easy to organize perhaps because of the low pay scales and perhaps because of their lack of previous experience with unions. The American Federation of State, County, and Municipal Employees (AFSCME), the largest international union in the AFL-CIO, has approximately eleven thousand members and sixty contracts representing about thirty thousand employees in Louisiana. AFSCME claimed 10,500 dues-paying members in Louisiana in 1981, of whom 9,000 were state employees. (The remainder were parish and municipal employees.) According to the union, its contracts covered 40,000 state employees and 20,000 parish and municipal workers. Thus, AFSCME claimed to represent approximately two-thirds of all classified employees, but the union had only one-sixth of all classified employees as dues-paying members.[4]

It is apparent that public-sector unionization in Louisiana is growing. AFSCME's long-range goal of unionizing 75 percent of all Louisiana public employees will be difficult to accomplish, however, because the state's legal environment discourages union growth. For instance, Louisiana's right-to-work law means that union membership is not mandatory even if a union is designated as the bargaining agent for a unit's employees. It is also apparent that the state is willing to use

4. Data conclusions are based on an interview with Roger Fraser, Administrator, American Federation of State, County, and Municipal Employees, December, 1978.

its power to reduce the effectiveness of public-employee unions. The New Orleans police strike during Mardi Gras in 1979 was a good example of efficacy of state assistance in strike breaking. State Police were used in place of the striking city force. If they had not entered the fray, the ultimate settlement might have been significantly different.

The Productivity of Louisiana's Civil Servants

When asked about the number of persons working in the Vatican, Pope John XXIII replied, "About one-half of them." The popular stereotype of the government worker pictures him or her as lazy and inept perhaps because it is natural for people to denigrate the jobs of others or because government does not produce anything tangible that workers can point to as evidence of their diligence. Government is, after all, primarily a service enterprise, and it has no competition. Therefore, comparisons of public and private employee productivity are hazardous. We have found most state employees to be reasonably diligent in performing their jobs, but government itself is often inefficient or ponderously slow. Measures designed to reduce corruption often reduce agency efficiency as well. Purchasing a single piece of equipment, for example, may take months. Money must be appropriated; specifications must be drawn up; bids must be taken. After the equipment is actually in hand, more months usually pass while the bill is processed through many checkpoints before the supplier is paid. Procedures such as these do not promote efficiency, yet government proceeds in just such ways in order to protect the taxpayers from fraud and mismanagement. In some instances, government can be speedy indeed. Many Louisianians see evidence of this every year when they receive a refund of state income taxes withheld during the previous year. Since the Department of Revenue and Taxation gives refunds its highest priority, most taxpayers receive their refund checks a week after they file their returns. It is a record many private enterprises might envy.

Measures like Proposition 13, along with a relentless inflation rate, have alerted public policy makers to the importance of productivity in governmental service. In February, 1979, the Council for a Better Louisiana and the Office of the Governor sponsored a conference on improving productivity in state government. The consensus of the speakers from both the public and private sectors was that internal efficiency must be improved and pay scales must be made competitive with those in the world of business and industry. The seminar, more than lip service to the ideal of productivity, inaugurated a self-evaluation program, which had been mandated by executive order of Governor Edwards in all of the major departments of state government. Through evaluation of their own programs for efficiency and impact, it is hoped that agencies will be able to provide more and better services for fewer tax dollars.

Organization of the Bureaucracy

Louisiana's state bureaucracy grew steadily if unspectacularly between 1900 and the Huey P. Long era (1928–1940), by the end of which there were 122 departments, boards, and commissions of the executive branch. Directing and coordinating all these separate agencies became an aggravation to Governor Sam H. Jones (1940–1944), who initiated the first attempts to reorganize and trim Louisiana's burgeoning work force. His efforts were ineffective. As mineral-rich Louisiana entered the boom years following World War II, state revenues increased dramatically, and successive administrations and legislatures eagerly created more and more agencies to spend available revenues in ways to suit virtually every special interest and constituency. By 1951 the number of state agencies had reached 151, by 1969 there were 256, and by 1973 Louisiana's executive branch was a bloated and chaotic hodgepodge of almost 300 separate departments, boards and commissions.[5]

If it had been difficult for Governor Jones in 1940 to properly supervise 122 agencies (most of them headed by his own appointees), one can easily imagine the impossibility of a governor supervising 300 agencies thirty years later. Some departments performed identical or

5. Sources for this section are three publications by the Public Affairs Research Council: *1979 Louisiana State Agencies Handbook* (Baton Rouge: Public Affairs Research Council, 1979), "State Government Reorganization: The End of the Beginning," *Analysis* (October 1978), and "The Rise and Fall of Reorganization," *Analysis* (January 1981); and *Resume of Act No. 83 of the 1977 Regular Session of the Louisiana Legislature: Reorganization of the Executive Branch of State Government* (Baton Rouge: Louisiana Legislative Council, 1977). Act 83, as amended through 1980, constitutes Title 36 of the Louisiana Revised Statutes.

similar services, while others had become moribund, no longer performing any useful service at all—except issuing paychecks to their
employees. Some agencies were understaffed; some overstaffed. A
common problem among the former was hasty or slipshod performance of the agency's function, producing public criticism and low
employee morale. Larger agencies often did not know what their workers were doing, or should be doing, and were rarely able to give a
reasonable cost-accounting of their operations on those even rarer occasions when such an accounting was demanded. Forty years of Topsy-
like growth had left the Louisiana bureaucracy disorganized, unaccountable, inadequately managed, and almost out of control.

The winning candidate for governor in 1972, Democrat Edwin W.
Edwards, had urged during his campaign that the state executive
branch be reorganized into a cabinet system resembling the federal
model. After his election, the Constitutional Convention of 1973, over
which Edwards wielded considerable influence, provided in Article IV,
Section 1 and Article XIV, Section 6 of the new state constitution that
the executive branch be consolidated into no more than twenty departments (exclusive of the offices of governor and lieutenant governor)
and that the legislature complete the reorganization-consolidation process by December 31, 1977.

In 1975 the legislature created the Joint Legislative Committee on
Reorganization of the Executive Branch, an implementation body consisting of fifteen appointees; five were appointed by the governor, five
by the president of the senate, and five by the speaker of the house.
Recommendations of the committee, based on its own hearings and
deliberations, were to be presented to the legislature for consideration
and enactment.

Two interim reorganization bills were enacted in 1975 and 1976. In
1977 the legislature passed Act 83, the final and most substantive
reorganization measure. Act 83 abolished over eighty agencies, among
them the Board of Highways, the Bureau of Outdoor Recreation, and
the Higher Education Assistance Commission. Surviving agencies
were rearranged, as the constitution required, into twenty departments—eight headed by statewide elected officials, eleven by gubernatorial appointees, and one, the Department of Civil Service, by a person selected by gubernatorial appointees. The overriding consideration
of both the committee and the legislature in placing agencies within

the new departments was relevancy of function or service. This procedure ensured, for example, that the Office of State Parks was placed within the Department of Culture, Recreation, and Tourism rather than within the Department of Corrections.

Departments presided over by statewide elected officials include Agriculture, Education, Elections and Registration, Insurance, Justice, Public Service, State, and Treasury. (See Figure 6-2 for a depiction of their functions.) The 1974 constitution provided that the commissioners of agriculture, elections and registration, and insurance, along with the superintendent of education, could be made appointed officials after 1976. To date, however, they remain elected. Although the governor has no direct control over these departments or their personnel, both he and the legislature can affect their operations through the budget process.

Departments headed by gubernatorial appointees include Commerce; Corrections; Culture, Recreation, and Tourism; Health and Human Resources; Labor; Natural Resources; Public Safety; Revenue and Taxation; Transportation and Development; Urban and Community Affairs; and Wildlife and Fisheries. (See Figure 6-3 for a depiction of their functions.) Not only is the governor empowered to appoint the head of each of these departments (usually called the secretary) but he also appoints the various assistant secretaries, who head the functional offices within each department. The governor also names the department undersecretary, who heads the departmental office of management and finance, the office in each department that performs the department's budgetary, personnel, and planning operations. The secretary, at his discretion, may appoint a deputy secretary to assist him in running his department and to serve in his place when the secretary is absent or incapacitated.

Although this procedure conforms to the federal system in which the president appoints all upper-level officials within the executive branch, critics have charged that in Louisiana the secretary can be isolated and rendered ineffective by hostile subordinates who, owing their appointments to the governor rather than to the secretary, need not always follow the secretary's directions in order to retain their positions. Just such a situation brought about the resignation of Culture, Recreation, and Tourism Secretary Sandra Thompson shortly after reorganization was implemented, in fact. The same critics suggest

Figure 6-2

Departments Under Statewide Elected Officials
and the
Department of Public Service

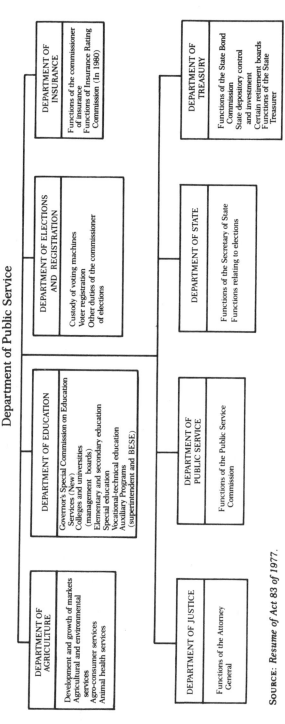

SOURCE: *Resume of Act 83 of 1977.*

Figure 6–3.

Departments under the Direct Control of the Governor and the Department of Civil Service

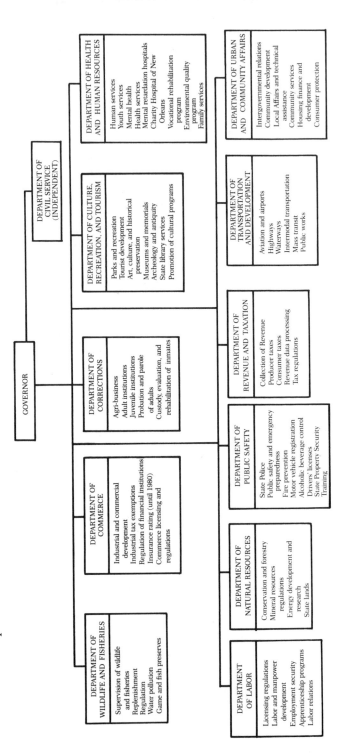

SOURCE: *Resume of Act 83 of 1977.*

that the secretary, rather than the governor, be authorized to appoint the undersecretary and assistant secretaries so as to create a more responsible and efficient chain of command. Louisiana politics being what it is, however, the present method of appointment, together with the controversy it provokes, is likely to remain unchanged for some time.

While Act 83 of 1977 abolished over eighty agencies, more than two hundred were retained, and others have been created since then. Many boards and commissions survived reorganization, but some lost their policy-making powers and were reduced to advisory status. These advisory boards were then attached to an appropriate department or to the Office of the Governor, which contains twenty-seven various entities in addition to the powerful Division of Administration.

Reorganization of the executive branch has, thus far, consolidated state agencies into a more identifiable and manageable complex. No longer must the governor or legislature deal with hundreds of separate agencies and their directors. Even the state's mammoth welfare and institutional programs have been much better centralized within the Department of Health and Human Resources, for example, which no longer seeks to administer dozens of far-flung services—as did its predecessors—but now coordinates them all under only eight offices: Family Security, Human Development, Mental Health and Substance Abuse, Health Services and Environmental Quality, Mental Retardation, Hospitals, Licensing and Regulation, and the Health Education Authority of Louisiana.

The reorganization has relieved the governor of direct supervision of the over two hundred agencies in state government and has delegated that supervision to the secretaries, but it is apparent that this buffer can have negative effects. It reduces the governor's contact with and control over the programs of the state and also reduces the likelihood of executive policy changes advocated from the program level. Moreover, it is not safe to assume that consolidation inevitably produces efficiency. It is clear that reorganization has produced at least some duplication of services. The offices of management and finance, for example, seem to have created another level of bureaucracy. The staff functions that these offices perform are duplicated from agency to agency, and this duplication has led to inefficiency and frustration for agency-level administrators. In addition, the changes in agency names have not necessarily reformed the agencies' practices. The internal operations of the agencies have tended to remain the same regardless of their names or departmental affiliations.

But reorganization was envisioned as an ongoing process, and much remains to be done. State employment continues to grow without much evidence of effective personnel planning or management, indicating that patronage, carelessness, and apathy still afflict the system. And while the governor may no longer have to deal directly with hundreds of department, board, or commission heads, he continues to appoint most of them—and their principal subordinates or colleagues. Duplication of functions and/or services has not been entirely eliminated, nor has conflict between departments on matters of common jurisdiction. For example, there are still conflicts between Health and Human Resources and Natural Resources over which agency oversees which aspects of environmental pollution. Members of one branch still violate the constitutional prohibition against holding offices or appointments in another branch, as for example, the legislators who sit on executive boards and commissions.

Reorganization notwithstanding, the bureaucracy of the State of Louisiana is in fact larger today than it ever was, and is still expanding. Those who would bring it under complete control or drastically limit its numbers, functions, or services are dreamers. Certainly, the projected paring down of federal services will not help, for that long hoped-for eventuality will only place greater burdens on all of the states.

Administrative Procedures

State agencies are part of the executive branch of state government, but their powers and responsibilities extend to the legislative and judicial, as well. The legislature is concerned with overall policy and a desired effect. It does not have the time, the staff, or the expertise to determine how the program will be administered. The legislature, for example, might decree that chiropractors must be tested and licensed in order to practice in the state. It would leave the questions of requirements for licensing, content of the tests, times and places of testing, and perhaps, the amount of the test fee to the Board of Chiropractic Examiners. Similarly, the board would have, as part of its executive function, the power to deny a license to a chiropractor or to revoke his license. In such cases, the board must also provide appeal procedures and must conduct a public hearing and adjudicate the case itself.

State agencies, thus, have a vast range of powers. They determine hunting seasons and bag limits, requirements for the disposal of hazardous waste, methods for administering the test for drunken driving, standards for receiving Aid for Dependent Children, and a host of other matters. Their authority for going about their daily business is provided by the Administrative Procedure Act (Chapter 13, Title 49, of the Louisiana Revised Statutes), which is a comprehensive code of administrative law and procedure. The act principally concerns how state agencies make rules and hand down decisions and orders. A *rule* is defined as "each agency statement, guide, or requirement for conduct or action . . . which has general applicability and the effect of implementing or interpreting substantive law or policy, or which prescribes the procedure or practice requirements of the agency." Administrative rules have the force and effect of law. A *decision* or *order* is "the whole or any part of the final disposition (whether affirmative, negative, injunctive, or declaratory in form) of any agency in any matter other than rulemaking."

Because agencies are exercising delegated legislative powers, the Administrative Procedure Act provides for legislative review of administrative rules. Through this review, state agencies remain accountable to the legislature. Agencies are also required to give notice in the *Louisiana Register* and, in some cases, to hold public hearings before making or changing rules. This requirement allows the public to influence the functioning of public bodies that are not elected and would not, therefore, be otherwise accountable to the state's citizenry. In addition, agency decisions and orders can be appealed to the courts for judicial review. Thus, contrary to what many believe, state agencies must conform to established legal procedures, guidelines, and limitations. No state agency operates in an unaccountable vacuum, nor can an agency arbitrarily or capriciously impose its will on defenseless citizens.

Summary

Louisiana's state bureaucracy provides a rational framework for the completion of complex tasks and, in this sense, conforms to the scientific notion of bureaucracy. This framework was shaped by the 1977 reorganization effort, which reduced the number of state departments and centralized responsibilities for state government in the hands of departmental secretaries. The reorganization also established a uniform organizational structure for all departments.

Productivity of public employees has long been an issue in Louisiana politics, and the state is making efforts to improve productivity through program evaluation. Unionization of state employees is still another issue which will probably figure prominently in the near future.

Because of its responsibility for interpretation and implementation of legislative and executive directives, bureaucracy plays a major role in shaping public policy. The pervasive influence of bureaucracy on governmental actions, coupled with its rapid growth, makes it essential that citizens understand its structure and operation. Otherwise, bureaucracy will no longer be the tool of government, but its master.

7.

Parish Government

JUNE SAVOY ROWELL

Parishes in Louisiana, like counties in most other parts of the nation, are political and geographical subdivisions of the state. They make up a middle level of government that was originally established to administer state policy and serve local needs. In this chapter, the offices and boards that compose parish government are described in terms of their relationships to policy making (or governance), financial administration, law enforcement, and education. Since the parish remains largely the child of the state, the parental relationship is meaningful in determining the extent to which parochial governments are developing their own identities as they move along the continuum from state control to semiautonomy through home rule.

Louisiana parishes, although middle levels of government, preceded the formation of state and municipal governments as we know them today. A form of civil rule in Louisiana can be traced to the Crozat charter given by the King of France in 1712. Local administration began to take form later in the 1700s when, after the territory had passed into Spanish ownership, Alexandro O'Reilly, captain general of the Spanish armies, reorganized the territory, dividing it into eleven rural districts and one somewhat urban district, Orleans. Twenty-one ecclesiastical parishes were also established although only nineteen were headed by a priest.

In 1804 after the purchase of Louisiana by the United States, the territorial legislature again set up twelve counties, which were similar to those formed by the Spanish under O'Reilly. The counties, however, were found to be too large for proper administration, and the population was growing rapidly at this time. By 1806, for the purpose of civil administration, the state had been redivided into nineteen parishes. Because these districts resembled the nineteen Spanish ecclesiastical districts that had been headed by priests, the name *parish* was retained.[1]

Early local administration was very much a part of state government. The first territorial legislature in 1804 did, however, give inhabitants of the County of Opelousas the authority to maintain a road (the Passage of Plaquemines) through the most convenient methods determined by their county judge, the justices of the peace, and a jury of twelve inhabitants. This jury was the predecessor of the current parish governing body known as the police jury. Although some autonomy existed in the management of local affairs, parish officials were appointed by the governor until 1811, when police jurors were first elected.[2]

An early decision by the Louisiana Supreme Court succinctly stated the relationships between the parishes and their parent body, the state: "Parishes, like counties in other states are involuntary political or civil divisions of the state, designated to aid in the administration of government, as state auxiliaries or functionaries, possessing no other powers than those designated, ranking low down on the scale of corporate existence."[3]

Thus, the parish was considered a quasi corporation. It differed from a municipal corporation in that the parish was created by the legislature to perform administrative tasks for the state. Moreover, as a quasi corporation, the parish has usually enjoyed broad sovereign immunity comparable in many ways to the immunity of the state.[4] As time passed, the distinction between municipal corporations and the quasi-corporate status of parishes became blurred. Increasingly, parishes secured grants of independent power from the legislature.

The institutions of parish government that had developed by the mid-1800s are generally those found in parish government today. Since development was piecemeal, it is not surprising that parish government failed to develop neat institutional relationships. Powers of

1. Roderick L. Carleton, *Local Government and Administration in Louisiana* (Baton Rouge: Louisiana State University Press, 1935), 1–31.
2. *Ibid.*, 33.
3. *Parish of West Carroll* v. *Gaddis*, 34 L. Ann. 928–31 (1882).
4. *Union Sulphur Company* v. *Parish*, 96 So. 787, 158 La. 857 (1923).

government are separated into different offices, but there is no "separation of powers" in the traditional sense. The executive and legislative institutions are not clearly defined nor are they separated by function. To further complicate the local pattern of government, the judiciary is largely separate since a judicial district may encompass more than one parish.

Governance

Figure 7-1 shows the usual structure of parish government in Louisiana. Each of the eight major parish offices has an elective head or is governed by an elective council. Two minor offices, justice of the peace and constable, are carry-overs from the era prior to urbanization and mass transit when law enforcement and judicial officers were needed throughout rural areas.

The police jury is the legal governing body for the parish. Authority, however, is divided among the police jury and several elected parish officials, such as the sheriff, assessor, clerk of court, school board members, and coroner. Governing authority also extends to the parish office of the district attorney and to those district judges whose jurisdictions lie within the boundaries of a single parish. Many functions, therefore, are vested in independently elected officials who depend not upon the police jury, but upon the state legislature for their existence and their financial support.

Louisiana's sixty-four parishes, like sixty-four families, exist in different physical and sociopolitical environments, as seen in Table 7-1. In some, offices and officials operate in harmony as would the closely knit family; in others, factional disputes and lack of cooperation are commonplace. Confronted with this pattern, the state acts as the benevolent parent, giving special benefits to favored children but refusing to mediate sibling rivalries.

Parish Governing Bodies

In 1807 the legislature officially designated a jury of twelve inhabitants of the parish as the police jury, which was required to meet at least once each year to make rules and regulations concerning roads

Figure 7-1
Organization of Louisiana Parish Government

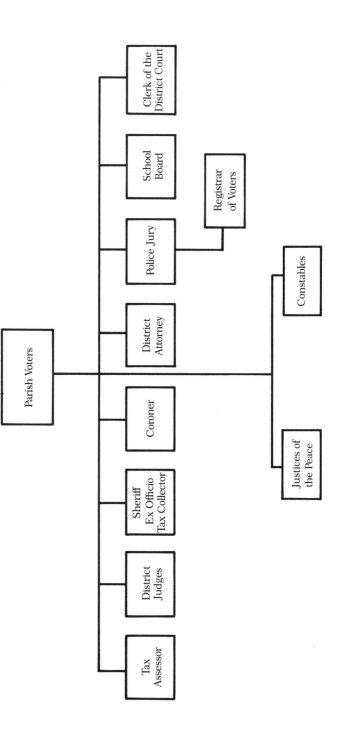

Table 7-1

Socioeconomic Statistics for Louisiana Parishes

(In Percentages)

	Total Population, 1970					
	8,500 to 20,000	20,000 to 40,000	40,000 to 60,000	60,000 to 80,000	80,000 to 100,000	over 100,000*
62	32.3	33.9	16.1	1.6	3.2	12.9
Parishes	(N20)	(N21)	(N10)	(N1)	(N2)	(N8)

	Population Increase (1960–1970)						
	−20% to −10%	−10% to 0	0 to +10%	+10% to +20%	+20% to +30%	+30% to +40%	over 40%†
63	6.3	25.4	30.2	20.6	6.3	6.3	4.8
Parishes	(N4)	(N16)	(N19)	(N13)	(N4)	(N4)	(N3)

	Urban Population, 1970			
	0 to 25%	25 to 50%	50 to 75%	75 to 100%‡
54	13.0	50.0	25.9	11.1
Parishes	(N7)	(N27)	(N14)	(N6)

	Nonwhite Population, 1970					
	5.5% to 10%	10% to 20%	20% to 30%	30% to 40%	40% to 50%	50% to 67.2%§
64	3.1	18.8	28.1	18.8	17.2	14.1
Parishes	(N2)	(N12)	(N18)	(N12)	(N11)	(N9)

	Average Weekly Wage, 1974				
	$230 to $200	$200 to $175	$175 to $150	$150 to $125	$125 to $104
64	6.3	15.6	20.3	32.8	25.0
Parishes	(N4)	(N10)	(N13)	(N21)	(N16)

* Lafayette, Ouachita, Rapides, Calcasieu, Caddo, East Baton Rouge, Jefferson, Orleans.

† St. Bernard (59%), Jefferson (62%), St. Tammany (64%). Vernon Parish is omitted because of Fort Polk, a large military base in an otherwise rural parish.

‡ Ouachita (78%), Calcasieu (85%), East Baton Rouge (86%), St. Bernard (91%), Jefferson (96%), Orleans (100%).

§ Claiborne (50%), Pointe Coupee (50%), DeSoto (53%), East Feliciana (54%), East Carroll (59%), Tensas (59%), Madison (61%), West Feliciana (67%).

Table 7-1 (*Continued*)

	7.5 to 8	8 to 9	9 to 10	10 to 11	11 to 12	12 to 12.3‖
	Median School Years, 1970					
64	7.8	18.8	39.1	14.1	12.5	7.8
Parishes	(N5)	(N12)	(N25)	(N9)	(N8)	(N5)

Sources: Milburn Calhoun, *Louisiana Almanac, 1975–1976* (Gretna, La.: Pelican, 1975); U.S. Department of the Census, *General Social and Economic Characteristics, Louisiana, 1970* (Washington, D.C.: U.S. Government Printing Office, 1973); James R. Bobo and Harris S. Segal (eds.), *Statistical Abstract of Louisiana* (6th ed.; New Orleans: Division of Business and Economic Research, College of Business Administration, University of New Orleans, 1977), 237.

‖Caddo (12), Lincoln (12), Jefferson (12.1), Bossier (12.1), East Baton Rouge (12.3).

and levees.[5] Today, parish governing bodies operate under the police jury plan, the commission plan, or as a parish council. Figure 7-2 makes note of the usual system, the police jury, which is used in all of the parishes except Orleans, East Baton Rouge, Jefferson, Plaquemines, Lafourche, and St. Charles.

Under the police jury system, the parish is divided into wards from which one or more jurors are elected. Where there is a multimember ward, each juror runs for election from a district within that ward. In 1974 the legislature stipulated that police juries could have a maximum of fifteen members or the number of members authorized for that parish's jury on May 13, 1974, whichever was greater. The same statute provided for a minimum of five jurors for each parish, except those with less than ten thousand people, which were permitted as few as three jurors.[6]

Jurors are elected to a four-year term in the state's general election. Some parishes show little change in jury membership from one election to another, while others experience extensive turnover. Of the 663 jurors who took office for the 1976–1980 term, 261, or 41 percent, were new; in one parish all of the members were newly elected. On

5. Louisiana Legislative Council, Memorandum, February, 1966, in the files of the Legislative Council.
6. Act 500 of 1974.

Figure 7-2
Police Jury Organizational Plan

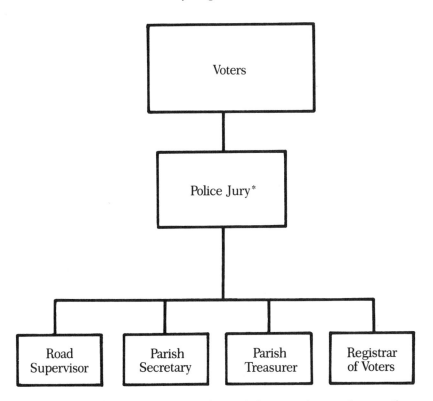

* Each jury has from three to fifteen members and elects one of its members president.

several of these juries, black and female members took seats for the first time. In 1976 there were fourteen women, seventy-two blacks and seven Republicans, all of whom can be considered minorities on the predominately white male Democratic juries of Louisiana.[7]

The members of the police jury select a president to preside over their meetings, which take place once or twice a month. Since police

7. June Savoy, "New Police Juries Show Significant Changes," *Louisiana Parish Government*, XII (August, 1976), 12–13.

jury membership is essentially a part-time job, jurors may be paid for only the days that they attend meetings or by the month, whichever the jury chooses.

Police jurors, like parish councils and commissions, serve as one body and exercise legislative, regulatory, and administrative powers. The jury may levy taxes in accordance with constitutional stipulations, call elections for the passage of bond issues in order to raise revenue for special purposes, appropriate its funds for public purposes, and incur indebtedness. Their regulatory powers include approval of zoning ordinances and local health ordinances, licensing businesses and amusements, and adoption of other regulations related to the parish welfare.

As an administrative body, the police jury is responsible for overseeing the use of public property including the courthouse and jail, the parish road system, parish health units, and in many instances, parish airports, libraries, and other facilities. The early road and bridge building and maintenance duties of police juries have remained of major importance. Historically, jurors have promoted their reelection by attempting to provide the best possible parish roads for their constituents. Urbanization and legislative requirements that road maintenance be carried out by the jury as a unit have changed the role of jurors.[8]

Today's police juror serves less as a road crew foreman and more as a decision maker. Although he is still responsible for parish property, the juror's time is increasingly devoted to providing social services on a parishwide basis. Citizens who live outside city limits demand water systems, garbage disposal, fire protection, and other urban services. Since the 1960s, the implementation of federal legislation has deeply involved juries in the administration of federal programs, such as food stamps, work-training programs, and community action projects. The more active juries have also undertaken social programs for juveniles, the elderly, and other special groups.

In order to discharge these duties, most police juries employ a considerable number of people. At the top of the administrative hierarchy, the jury may employ a professional parish manager or choose one of its

8. Act 336 of 1974.

own members as manager. An assistant manager may also be selected. Every parish has either a secretary-treasurer or a secretary and a treasurer, and most police juries entrust parish administration to this officer or officers. Every parish also employs a registrar of voters and road supervisors. The number and kind of other employees depend upon the variety of activities in which the parish engages.

The six parishes that do not have police juries have chosen commission or council forms of organization. Orleans Parish and the City of New Orleans moved toward a consolidated council as early as 1822. Police jurors and part of the city's councilmen then sat together to consider policies that involved their combined jurisdictions. Legislative act completed the consolidation in 1870 by making the boundaries of the city and parish coterminous and allowing the mayor and city council to assume the duties of the police jury. The remaining parish offices also differed in structure from those found in other parishes.[9]

With the passage of time, other changes in parish organizational structure occurred. New Orleans had a mayor-commission system as early as 1912. In 1914 other parishes were permitted to organize a commission form of government to replace the traditional police jury. This form called for the election of three commissioners: a commissioner of public affairs, a commissioner of finance, and a commissioner of public improvements. Each would be elected to serve full time, and would be paid on an annual rather than a per diem basis. Parishes were allowed to change from the police jury system to the commission form of government with the approval of the majority of the voters in a special election. No parish, however, chose to institute the commission plan as provided by this law. Instead, beginning in 1946 with East Baton Rouge, some parishes requested permission to draw up their own organizational structure. Since the constitution of 1921 provided the commission plan as the only alternative to the police jury system, East Baton Rouge Parish in 1946 secured a constitutional amendment permitting it to institute its individual plan of government. The amendment created city-parish consolidation and was Louisiana's first constitutional authorization for local *home rule*, which W. Brooke Graves early defined as "the power of local self-government. Communities

9. Carleton, *Local Government*, 52–55.

[parishes and municipalities] have the right to select their own form of governmental organization and either draft their own charter or select one to their liking under an optional charter plan." [10]

Baton Rouge's city-parish system is complex. Council members are elected from the city (Ward 1) and outlying areas. When the council considers parishwide business, the city's council members meet with their counterparts from other wards throughout the parish. Figure 7-3 provides an illustration of the parish element of this city-parish arrangement.

Through constitutional amendment in 1950, New Orleans gained home rule. The mayor, elected at large, is the chief administrative officer; presently, one councilman is also elected at large and five others are elected from single-member districts—all for terms of four years.

Jefferson Parish, like Orleans, is totally urban. In contrast, however, Jefferson has no major municipalities, and its area is largely governed by the parish. In 1956 Jefferson secured a constitutional amendment permitting the parish to adopt a home rule charter. The usual parish offices were retained, but the governing body achieved some separation of powers through the parishwide election of a council president who serves as the executive and the election of seven council members who act as the legislative body.

The state legislature, apparently tired of individual home rule amendments, passed a general amendment in 1960 that extended the prerogative of adopting home rule charters to all parishes except East Baton Rouge, Jefferson, and Orleans. In 1961 Plaquemines Parish took advantage of this amendment to set up a five-member commission, composed of commissioners of public affairs, finance, public improvements, public safety, and public utilities, to replace its police jury.

The concept of local autonomy became more popular among municipalities in Louisiana during the sixties, and several cities adopted home rule charters. However, no more parishes adopted such charters. In fact, between 1966 and 1971, proposed home rule charters were defeated in St. Charles, St. Bernard, Calcasieu, and Caddo parishes. In 1974 the state ratified a new constitution with provisions that expanded

10. W. Brooke Graves, *American Intergovernmental Relations: Their Origins, Historical Development, and Current Status* (New York: Charles Scribner's Sons, 1964), 700.

Figure 7-3
Baton Rouge City-Parish Government

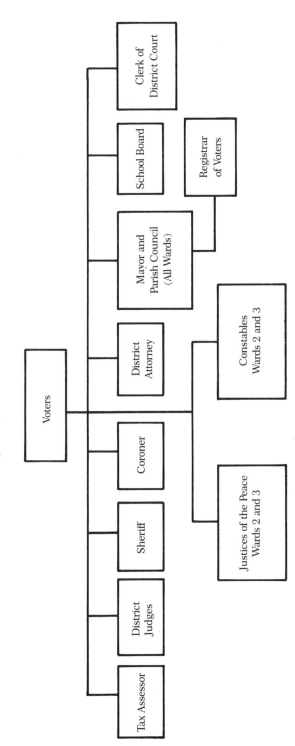

Figure 7-4
New Orleans City-Parish Government

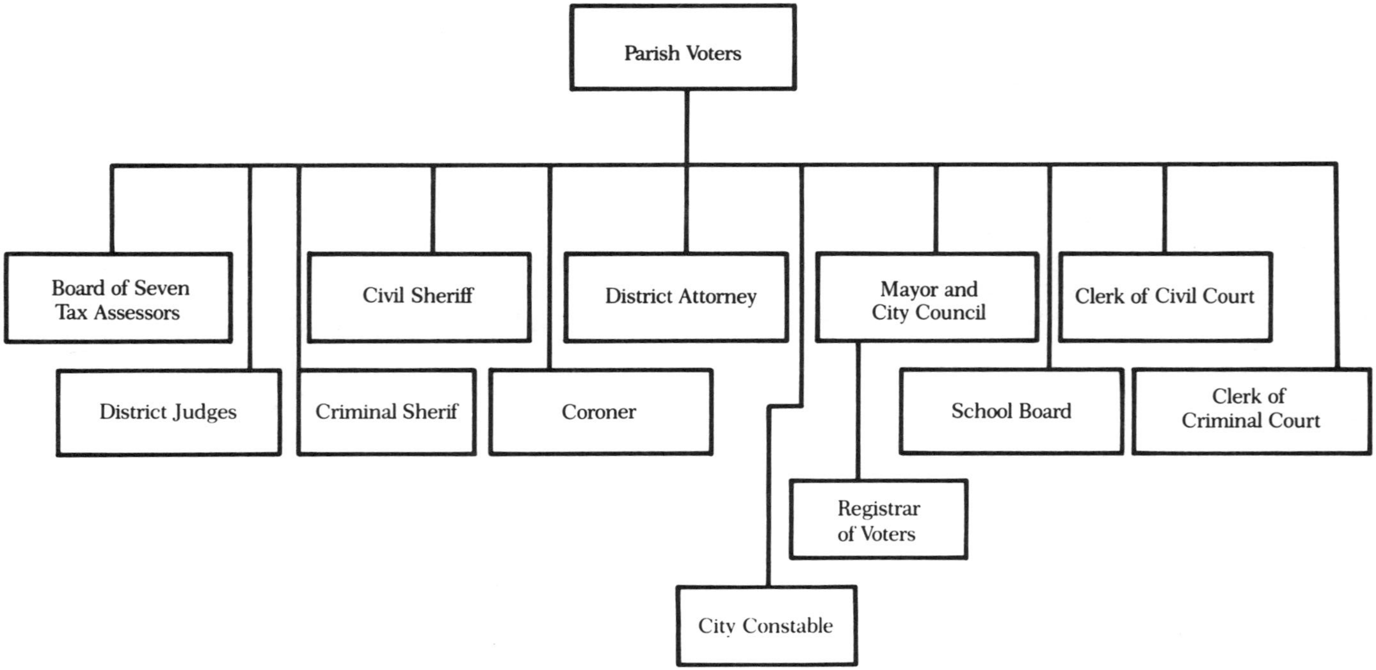

early definitions of home rule and were in line with model charters formulated by national organizations of city and county officials.

The constitution of 1974 allows a parish (or municipality) to develop a home rule charter that provides for any structure, organization, powers, and functions "necessary, requisite or proper for the management of its affairs, not denied by general law or inconsistent with this Constitution."[11] Although defined broadly, home rule is not absolute. The constitution stipulates that a charter may not contain any provision affecting school boards or the offices of district attorney, sheriff, assessor, clerk of district court, or coroner. As always, local decisions remain subject to the state's general laws and constitutional provisions.

Lafourche Parish in 1976 took advantage of the new constitution's provisions to set up a sixteen-member council. It includes fifteen councilmen elected parishwide. Judge Walter Lanier, Jr., chairman of the commission that drafted the home rule charter for Lafourche, has stated that the most significant change is the election of a president— a step that, in effect, establishes an executive branch. "Generally speaking," he said, "all legislative power was vested in the parish governing authority and except as otherwise provided in the charter all executive power was lodged with the parish president."[12]

St. Charles became a home rule parish in December, 1977, when voters approved a charter setting up a nine-member elective council and an elective president. Since the parish is divided by the Mississippi River, the charter provides that one council member be elected at large from the west bank and one from the east bank. The remaining seven members are to be elected from single-member districts. The president (who is elected parishwide) is vested with the powers of an executive, including the power to appoint all jury personnel.

During 1978, Lafayette, St. Tammany, Ascension, and Tangipahoa parishes established home rule charter commissions. Each commission is presently formulating a charter for presentation to parish voters. The outcomes, therefore, remain to be seen. Even if these charters are accepted, only ten of sixty-four parishes will be governed under home rule. Apparently, there is little interest in home rule in Louisiana. R. L. Carleton cited two reasons for the lack of interest: "(1) The Po-

11. Louisiana Constitution, Art. VI, Sec. 5E.
12. Walter Lanier, Jr., "Lafourche Parish's Home Rule Charter," *Louisiana Parish Government*, XII (December, 1976), 3.

lice Jury is an historical institution, and there is a large degree of sentiment for its retention; and (2) a large number of rural people believe
that all sections of the parish should be represented on the board, so
that the more populous sections could not dominate its affairs."[13] L. E.
Chandler cites a third reason: home rule would deprive a large number
of people of their right to hold public office and would take away political influence and local patronage. Police jurors themselves also noted
that the formulation of a home rule charter by a charter commission is
a lengthy and involved process. Moreover, juries are reluctant to take
the results of the charter commission's deliberations to the voters since
it is felt that rejection would damage the chances of incumbent police
jurors during the next election. Conversely, should the charter pass,
the possibility exists that incumbent jury members would not be selected to serve on the new council. Finally, home rule may not seem
important to most parish governing bodies since they customarily receive almost anything that they request from the benevolent parent,
the Louisiana legislature.

Finances

A further child-parent analogy can be made with regard to the financial ties between the parish and the state. As the child is largely dependent upon its parent for financial support, so police juries and other
parish offices derive extensive revenues from the parent-state. Table
7-2 provides an example of the sources and governmental units to
which revenues are allocated. Public school expenditures receive the
greatest amounts of state aid. The Louisiana School Board Association
asserts that financing public education "is recognized as a state responsibility although a local function" in Louisiana. "The state has an
obligation to provide a minimum education program, gathering wealth
wherever it occurs and distributing it wherever children are."[14] In a
similar vein, the Police Jury Association contends that local governments are not getting their share of state help, especially with respect
to the upkeep of parish roads.

13. R. L. Carleton, quoted in L. E. Chandler, "A Study of Parish Government in Louisiana," *College Bulletin* (Southeastern Louisiana College), XVII (January, 1960), 21.
14. Baton Rouge *Morning Advocate*, March 31, 1977, Sec. B, p. 1.

Table 7-2

State Tax Allocated to Local Governmental Units, 1972–1973

Gasoline Tax:	
Parishes	$ 16,881,852
Ports	1,635,974
Public Schools:	
Teachers', Bus Drivers', and Other Salaries	375,664,565
Teachers' Retirement—State Contribution	24,568,708
Vehicle Licenses	4,844,180
Chain Store Tax	805,007
State Revenue Sharing	86,716,188
General Severance Tax	7,705,577
Timber Severance Tax	1,654,807
Supplemental Pay:	
Deputy Sheriffs	4,244,543
Municipal Police	6,535,487
Firemen	5,038,104
Royalty	13,218,787
Parish Roads and Drainage	3,200,000
Tobacco Tax	26,229,643
Racing Fees	2,012,529
Fire Insurance Tax	1,165,116
Parish Roads:	
Act 128 of 1954	2,357,000
Act 113 of 1972	5,000,000
Various Other Allocations to Each Parish	1,534,197
SUBTOTAL	$591,012,264
Others That Have Not Been Allocated to Each Parish:	
Other School Employees' Retirement—State Contribution	6,207,561
TOTAL	$597,219,825

Source: E. J. Maciasz, Assistant State Treasurer, personal compilation.

Some interest groups oppose state aid to parishes, however. The Louisiana Association of Business and Industry (LABI) presents an adversary view. With the decline in state revenues from oil and natural gas severance taxes, LABI contends that local government should drastically expand its ability to raise its own revenues through the little used property tax and the authority in many parishes to levy sales taxes. LABI also favors legislative authorization to increase the sales tax percentages that local governments may assess.[15]

Federal monies also come to the parishes. The two major sources are categorical grants and federal revenue sharing. The various agencies of the national government sponsor grants to finance activities that are related to their particular categories of interest. For example, the U.S. Department of Labor, with cooperation from the U.S. Department of Health, Education, and Welfare (HEW), funded programs under the Comprehensive Employment and Training Act (CETA) that brought about $4 million to the city-parish government of East Baton Rouge in both 1976 and 1977. Because the Department of Labor is interested in reducing unemployment, the CETA funds permitted the city-parish to employ almost three hundred persons who had previously been without jobs.[16]

CETA is one of the larger categorical grants. There are also numerous grants for which parish agencies may apply that involve smaller amounts of money. When a parish agency applies for a grant in a given area, it must substantiate, among other things, its need for the project, its ability to carry out the project, and its willingness to abide by federal guidelines. In most instances, the agency is also required to match a percentage of the federal money with its own funds. This is a means of assuring the federal agency that the local agency will be seriously involved in carrying the funded project to a successful conclusion.

In the event that a federal agency accepts a parish's grant proposal, the money for the project comes directly from the federal government to the parish unit. Parish agencies such as the police jury, school board, and sheriff's office are more likely than others to apply for federal grants. Because of the national government's interest in education, school boards have long been the major grant recipients in parish government. Most grants are in the traditional areas of education, health, agriculture, welfare, and transportation, but more recently, national policy has emphasized housing, community and economic development, environmental protection, and natural resources.[17]

15. *Ibid.*
16. Baton Rouge *Morning Advocate*, October 3, 1976, Sec. A, p. 5.
17. Kenneth N. Vines, "The Federal Setting of State Politics," in Herbert Jacob and

Federal revenue-sharing funds are also available to parish government but only to police juries because they are the governing body of the parish and to sheriffs. Federal revenue sharing, which came into being in 1972, differs from categorical grants in that it does not have to be applied for but comes automatically from the federal government to police juries and sheriffs in an amount based on a nationwide formula. Another difference is that categorical grants carry extensive regulations governing their use, while revenue sharing was intended to have as few federal "strings" as possible.

Governmental bodies may spend federal revenue-sharing funds for any purpose consistent with state and local law. Staff members of the National Association of Counties indicate that parishes generally spend their revenue-sharing monies as they would spend their own funds. On the other hand, East Baton Rouge, which received $8.6 million in fiscal year 1976 and over $9 million in 1977, used its money primarily for major nonrecurring expenses such as buildings, equipment, and improvements to streets and drainage rather than wages or other recurring costs.[18]

Although parish government has both state and federal sources of support, local revenues remain basic. The most important of the local revenue sources is the tax that each parish levies on property.

The Assessor

The parish official given the authority to determine the amount of tax each property owner must pay is the assessor. Each parish, except Orleans, elects one assessor every four years at the time of the state's general election. In Orleans, one assessor is elected from each of seven districts every four years at the time of the city's election.

Assessors, unlike police jurors, are full-time administrative officials. They keep records of all property within the parish boundaries and place a value on each piece of property for the purposes of taxation. In the past, property—including land, homes, commercial buildings,

---

Kenneth N. Vines (eds.) *Politics in the American States* (Boston: Little, Brown, 1976), 22–29.

18. Baton Rouge *Morning Advocate*, October 3, 1976, Sec. A, p. 5; National Association of Counties to the author, January 25, 1978.

commercial furniture and fixtures, and public service equipment—
has been subject to varying rates of *ad valorem* property taxation in
the various parishes, and assessors had considerable leeway in determining the amount each property owner would pay. Because of the
discretion allowed them in setting assessments, tax assessors had considerable political power based upon patronage, and they tended to
hold office for long periods of time. The 1974 constitution and resultant legislation have somewhat reduced the discretionary power of the
tax assessor, however. Property owners now fill out forms indicating
the size and cost of their property. The assessor uses these forms to
determine value.

Taxes are not based on the full value of property, but rather on a percentage of assessed values. The constitution of 1974 required that
land and residences be taxed on 10 percent of their value and commercial properties, on 15 percent. Additionally, the residence in which a
homeowner lives was exempted from taxation on the first $3,000 of its
taxable value.[19] This exemption was later raised by the legislature to
$5,000 and by constitutional amendment to $7,500. The Louisiana
Association of Business and Industry can justly contend that the property tax is little used, for not only are rates of taxation exceptionally low
but a person who owns and resides in a $75,000 home assessed at
10 percent of its value ($7,500) pays no property tax because of the
$7,500 homestead exemption. Both factors considerably reduce the
revenue-raising capacities of the property tax for local government.

The workhorse of the tax structure is the local sales tax. Parishes
have the authority to call tax elections for sales taxes, not to exceed
three cents on each dollar. With legislative approval, sales tax elections
may ask the public to approve sales taxes at a higher rate. Unlike property taxes, sales taxes are considered regressive, that is, they fall pro-
portionately more heavily on the poor than on the rich. For this reason,
local governing bodies are reluctant to levy additional sales taxes, and
the legislature has been reluctant to approve taxes above 3 percent.[20]
One advantage of the *local* sales tax is that the people can see where

19. Louisiana Constitution, Art. VIII, Pt. 3E.
20. Fred Benton, Jr., "Local Sources," in Louis E. Newman (ed.), *Orientation for Police Jurors: Proceedings of the Conference* (Baton Rouge: Policy Jury Association and
Louisiana State University, 1976), 7.

the money is being used and can determine for themselves whether the tax should pass. In 1976 thirty-two of forty-four local sales tax proposals for public schools were approved by voters.[21] In contrast, a state sales tax needs only legislative approval, and although it affects citizens throughout the state, the effects are not nearly so visible. Hence, there is a reluctance on the part of legislators to approve this type of taxation.

Law Enforcement

The Sheriff

Police power—the power to protect the safety, health, morals, and general welfare of the citizenry—is inherently a power of state government.[22] Law enforcement, as part of the police power, is largely delegated by the states to local government. The sheriff is the chief law enforcement officer of the parish. He is responsible for enforcing both state and parish laws, and he also serves as an official of the district court. Each parish, except Orleans, elects one sheriff who is given authority for civil and criminal matters, but in Orleans both a civil sheriff and a criminal sheriff are elected. Many deputies assist the sheriff in his duties.

As part of his responsibility to enforce criminal laws, the sheriff serves as the jailer and is responsible for general peace keeping within the parish. As an officer of the court, he is charged with maintaining order in court; serving court papers, such as subpoenas and writs; conducting foreclosures; and confiscating abandoned property.

Another function of Louisiana sheriffs is tax collection. Prior to 1976, most of the funds allocated to each sheriff for the expenses of his office, aside from his own wages, came from a percentage of the *ad valorem* taxes collected in his parish. In 1976 the legislature designated each parish as a law enforcement taxing district, with the sheriff as executive officer of the district. Since 1978, a percentage of each dollar of property valuation (millage) has been assessed for support of

21. Baton Rouge *Morning Advocate*, March 3, 1977, Sec. B, p. 1.
22. Paul C. Bartholomew, *Ruling American Constitutional Law* (Totowa, N.J.: Littlefield, Adams, 1970), 241.

the sheriff's office. Initially, this millage was equal to the percentage that the sheriff received of the taxes collected in fiscal year 1976–1977. Any increases needed to run his office must come through a special election in the parish to increase the millage, rather than by legislative increase of his tax percentage as in the past.

In addition to the general operating funds just described, sheriffs in Louisiana (but in no other state) receive federal revenue-sharing monies. Ostensibly, this is necessary because in Louisiana local finances are not controlled by a central governmental body. Federal revenue-sharing funds allocated to the police jury are retained by the jury and do not benefit other local offices. In other states such offices often come under the supervision and financial control of the county (parish) governing body. Actually, however, it was the political power of Louisiana sheriffs in lobbying the state's congressional delegation, along with Senator Russell Long's influential position at that time as chairman of the Senate Finance Committee, that got the law changed in 1976 to give sheriffs 15 percent of Louisiana's revenue-sharing money. Of the 15 percent, half comes from funds previously allocated to state government and half from the share allocated to parishes and municipalities.[23]

Louisiana sheriffs have traditionally had large budgets and have been able to hire a considerable number of deputies. Since parish government generally has no civil service regulations, the selection of deputies is often a form of patronage. Because of the number of voters they can control, sheriffs are probably the most politically powerful of local officials.

The Coroner

An interesting minor office is that of coroner. It is an elective, part-time position closely associated with the sheriff's office. The coroner, who must be a medical doctor, is responsible for the investigation of all deaths where violence or unusual circumstances are involved. He is also *ex officio* parish physician and may be called in to examine prisoners or to carry out other parish health functions. In most parishes, there is also a health unit supervised by a full-time physician, which,

23. Baton Rouge *Morning Advocate*, August 26, 1976, Sec. F, p. 12; Carol Berenson, National Association of Counties, interview, January 22, 1977.

under the direction of the police jury, concerns itself with general health and sanitation problems.

District Attorney

Like the sheriff, the district attorney is an officer of the district court. Each of Louisiana's thirty-five judicial districts comprises one or more parishes but has only one district attorney. He is elected from the parishes within his district for a six-year term, and his salary is state funded and usually locally supplemented. Where there is a multiparish district, the district attorney usually appoints assistants who reside in the outlying parishes. Assistant district attorneys are paid by the state, and the number that a district attorney may appoint is controlled by the state legislature, but he may hire whatever additional staff his office can afford. The internal resources of a district attorney's office are dependent upon the degree of court activity within his district that results in fees collected for the criminal court fund.[24]

The district attorney or one of his assistants represents the state in both civil and criminal matters where the state is a party. Additionally, he acts as a prosecutor in cases involving a crime committed within his judicial district. The district attorney has considerable latitude in deciding whether to begin a prosecution. In some cases the evidence may be clearly insufficient to secure a conviction or no public interest would be served by pressing the charge. The district attorney has within his criminal jurisdiction, for instance, the responsibility to prosecute other public officials within the parish in cases of misconduct in connection with their duties. The possibility always exists that the close personal or political affiliation among officials in the parish, including the district attorney, could result in his failure to prosecute for such a crime. Conversely, the district attorney could be overly zealous in prosecuting officials who are not members of his political faction.

In addition to his work as an officer of the court, the district attorney and his assistants also act as advisors to other officials of parish government. Police juries or sheriffs, however, often choose to retain attorneys of their own in order to have legal advice more readily available.

24. Michael Simon, Louisiana District Attorneys' Association, interview, January 18, 1978.

The District Courts

The civil and criminal conflicts that come to the attention of the offices of the sheriff and district attorney are generally brought before the district courts. These courts along with special courts, such as the Jefferson Parish Courts, the Orleans Parish Civil and Criminal District Courts, the East Baton Rouge Family Court, and the Jefferson, Caddo and Orleans Parish Juvenile Courts, are the courts of original jurisdiction, that is, the courts where cases are initiated or first heard. Although the sixty-four parishes of Louisiana are arranged into thirty-five judicial districts, plus the criminal district court and civil district courts of Orleans, there may be one or several district judges serving within a judicial district. Table 7-3 provides examples of variations occurring in 1976.

Where there are multiparish districts, judges schedule court terms in each parish of the district. They work with the supporting staff and within the facilities that are available in an individual parish. Financing of the operations of the court is unequally shared throughout the district. Since each parish has its own criminal court fund, monies may not be shifted from a wealthy parish to a poorer parish in order to support activities of the court more adequately. The type of district, therefore, influences the way in which judges work, choose, and use their staff and facilities, and the funds they have available.

No clear criteria exist for establishing judicial districts; they are created as they are needed. Parishes that at one time were joined into one judicial district have remained, despite changes in population and case load. The usual method of coping with such changes has been to

Table 7-3
Parishes and Judges Within Louisiana Judicial Districts

Judicial District	Parishes	Number of Judges
Nineteenth	East Baton Rouge	12
Seventh	Catahoula and Concordia	1
Fifteenth	Acadia, Lafayette, and Vermilion	6

Source: Judicial Council of the Supreme Court of Louisiana, *Annual Report, 1976* (New Orleans: Judicial Council of the Supreme Court of Louisiana, 1976), 15–19.

add judges to the district. This may be accomplished through consent of two-thirds of the elected members of each house of the legislature. Altering the number of judicial districts, on the other hand, is much more difficult, for it requires not only a legislative act but also approval by referendum in each parish of each district affected.[25]

District judges are elected at the time of the congressional election for a period of six years. The constitution of 1974 provides that when a vacancy occurs, or a new judgeship is created, it be filled through a special election. The Supreme Court appoints a qualified person to fill the vacancy until this election takes place; however, the person appointed is ineligible to become a candidate in the election. Under the previous constitution (1921), the governor filled vacancies and the person appointed could run for reelection. This resulted in gubernatorially appointed judges enjoying the incumbent's usual advantage in being returned to office. Today, with the appointee ineligible, all candidates have an equal opportunity to be elected.

Clerk of Court

The duties of the clerk of court and his deputies are so numerous and varied that at best this official serves only as part-time clerk to the district court. Each parish elects a clerk of court every four years at the time of the general election. The clerk is, thus, not subject to overall control by the court but, instead, is responsible to the electorate. There may or may not be the cooperative relationship between these two offices that is needed for proper functioning of the court. Moreover, there are few clear lines of authority which tie the clerk's office to the court.[26] Although the clerk has the power to issue and sign certain documents that would ordinarily be signed by the judge, most of his duties in relation to the court involve transcribing court proceedings and keeping court records.

A major function of the clerk is to record conveyances, mortgages, and other documents. He also supervises elections within the parish, tabulates voting machines and absentee voting records, and forwards these to the secretary of state.

25. Louisiana Constitution, Art. VI, Sec. 22A, B.
26. Institute for Judicial Administration, *A Study of the Louisiana Court Systems* (New York: Institute for Judicial Administration, 1972), ch. 14.

The clerk of court is permitted to charge a fee for performing most of his services. These fees are deposited in the clerk's salary fund, from which the expenses of his office and the salaries of his deputies are paid. Although the clerk may set the rate of pay for his deputies, his own salary is determined by legislative act. The clerk must also pay the sheriff in order to have the various writs, summonses, and other papers issued by the clerk's office served upon the persons involved in a suit.

Education

School Boards

Under Louisiana's constitution of 1974, public education is the responsibility of the state: "The Legislature shall provide for the education of the people of the state and shall establish and maintain a public education system."[27] However, this responsibility has long been delegated to local school governing units, the vast majority of which are associated with the parish. Municipal school systems operate only in the cities of Monroe and Bogalusa. The constitution provides that these city systems, and no others, "shall be regarded and treated as parishes and shall have the authority granted parishes."[28]

In an effort, perhaps, to separate education from parish politics, the general authority for operating schools and selecting school personnel has been placed in the hands of an independent parish school board, which operates outside of regular parish government. The constitution further stipulates that "the Legislature shall create parish school boards and provide for the election of their members."[29] The parish school board may create intraparish school districts over which it remains the governing body, and it may consolidate or abolish such districts at will. All school districts have the authority to issue bonds, vote special taxes, and incur debts, but they are presided over by the parish school board.

Under current legislation, parish school board members are elected

27. Louisiana Constitution, Art. VIII, Sec. 1.
28. *Ibid.*, Secs. 9A, 13D.
29. *Ibid.*

from single-member districts. Their six-year terms of office are staggered with one-third of the membership coming up for election every two years. (In the Jefferson Parish and Bogalusa systems, school board members are elected to four-year terms.) All members serve on a part-time basis and their duties are legislative in nature. The executive officer is the superintendent whom the board appoints. School board members may be paid a per diem or on a monthly basis, except in Orleans and Jefferson parishes where school board members must be paid by the month.[30]

School board members are less likely than police jurors to assume specific responsibilities in the districts from which they are elected. Although they may show particular interest in schools within their constituencies, in general, they operate as a board for the entire district in setting school policies, authorizing financial transactions, and overseeing the professional instructional staff headed by the superintendent.

The administration of school systems, perhaps more than that of other parish governmental units, has become professionalized. The superintendent is a full-time professional administrator whose qualifications are set by the local school board and who serves at its pleasure. Most school systems have a vast hierarchy of school board personnel who are responsible for the various aspects of operating a large, complex educational organization.

The parish school system is by far the largest unit of parish government and the most expensive. Revenues for its support are derived from local property and sales taxes. Special taxes may also be passed by parish voters for school construction, maintenance, and other specific purposes. The state is heavily involved in financing teachers' wages and those of other school workers, along with their retirement funds. Under the constitution, state government is also required to appropriate sufficient funds to insure a minimum educational program; these funds must be allocated equitably on the basis of formulas adopted by the State Board of Elementary and Secondary Education (BESE) and approved by the legislature. In addition, the state is financially involved with the parish school system in supplying free textbooks and other materials of instruction, a practice which dates back to the administration of Huey Long.

30. Act 647 of 1975.

The federal government has, in many instances, been involved in public education longer than the state. The Northwest Ordinance of 1785 contained a provision whereby public lands were set aside for education—each sixteenth section was reserved for the maintenance of public schools. Early school lunch programs were the result of surplus commodities and depression-era nutritional needs. The most intensive federal involvement has come as a result of federal programs in the 1960s intended to assure black children and poor children educational opportunities equal to those available to other students. Like her sister states, Louisiana has benefitted tremendously from this influx of federal funds. The expenditure of these funds by schools is closely supervised by federal officials who work from offices either in Louisiana or at the regional level. The stipulations and reporting requirements attached to this supervision have also enhanced the professionalism of school board personnel.

Special Districts

The government of the parish is fractionalized not only because of the independent election, financial support, and autonomous authority of the various offices previously discussed but also because of the longstanding practice in Louisiana of establishing special districts with the power to tax, incur debt, and issue bonds for specific purposes. These districts are usually not confined to single parishes. Instead, they encompass certain geographic areas in which there exists a need for special services and in which local residents are willing to pay a tax in order to meet this need. Some of the more common special districts are rural road districts, fire districts, drainage districts, recreation districts, hospital districts, and water districts. In some instances, school districts are parishwide, and in other cases, the parish is separated into several school districts. Another example is the parishwide law enforcement district, over which the sheriff presides.

To complicate matters further, there are multiparish districts that include all or parts of several districts. Most prominent among these are levee districts and districts that supervise rivers and harbors. Port, harbor, and terminal districts are involved in much of the state's industrial development and, thus, have extensive powers.

The legislature may create or authorize the creation of any type of special district. Districts (other than school, law enforcement, levee, and river) are generally associated with parish government and are created by the police jury acting on its own authority or, in some instances, in response to a petition by landowners in the area. Parish taxing districts are governed by boards whose members are usually appointed by the police jury. However, the jury itself may also function in this capacity where the district is parishwide. While numerous districts and boards further fragment parish government, they also allow more participation in the governing process at the grass-roots level.

The variations in the types of special districts and the regulations governing the creation and operation of each make it impossible to speak in any but the most general terms regarding these miniature units of government. Their common element is that they provide the mechanism for passing bond issues from which money is raised to meet the special needs of a geographic area. The bonded indebtedness is then retired through the assessment of special taxes—hence the name *special taxing district*. This allows the burden of payment for special services to fall on those citizens who are the recipients of the service, rather than upon the taxpayers of the parish as a whole. Table 7-4 provides an indication of the types of districts and the powers of parishes in relation to each.

Parish-State Relations

The parental role of the state in the affairs of parish governments continues through supervision. In this instance, Louisiana is a permissive parent. As we have noted, the state legislature originally held the responsibility for overseeing local government operations. With the expansion and added complexities of government on all levels, the capacity of the legislature for such oversight became limited; supervision was largely turned over to the executive departments. Although there exist cooperative relationships between some executive departments and local government entities, supervision of parish government by the state tends to break down.

Legally, the state has the power to control parochial governments, and in the past, especially during the Huey Long and O. K. Allen ad-

Table 7-4
Selected Powers of Parish Governing Bodies over Special Districts

Selected Parishes	Soil Conservation	Drainage	Flood Control	Air Pollution	Solid Waste	Fire Protection	Water Supply	Housing and Urban Renewal	Cemeteries	Sewage	Education	Highways	Parks and Recreation	Hospitals	Libraries
Allen	—	ac	—	—	—	—	ac	—	—	—	—	—	—	ac	ac
Ascension	—	a	—	—	—	a	a	—	—	—	—	a	—	a	a
Assumption	—	ad	—	—	ad	ad	ad	—	—	ad	—	ad	ad	ade	ad
Beauregard	—	—	—	—	—	—	—	—	—	—	—	—	—	—	—
Bienville	—	—	—	—	—	—	—	—	—	—	—	—	abce	—	—
Jefferson	all	all	all	all	all	all	all	all	all	all	—	all	all	all	all
Morehouse	—	—	—	—	—	—	—	—	—	—	—	—	—	—	—
Pointe Coupee	abc	abc	abc	abc	abc	abc	abc	abc	—	abc	abc	abc	abc	abc	ab
Ouachita	ac	ac	ac	ac	ac	ac	ac	ac	ac	ac	ac	ac	ac	ac	ac
Rapides	—	—	—	—	—	—	—	—	—	—	—	—	—	—	—
Red River	—	—	—	—	—	—	—	—	—	—	—	—	—	—	—
St. Charles	—	all	—	—	—	all	all	all	all	all	all	all	all	all	all
St. John the Baptist	—	all	—	—	all	all	all	all	all	all	all	all	all	all	all
St. Martin	—	all	—	—	all	all	all	—	—	—	—	—	all	all	all
St. Tammany	—	—	—	—	—	—	—	—	—	—	—	—	—	—	—

Source: Advisory Commission on Intergovernmental Relations, *Profile of County Governments* (Washington, D.C.: U.S. Government Printing Office, 1971), 106.

Powers Over Special Districts
a Power to approve formation or establishment of special districts
b Power to consolidate special districts
c Power to abolish special districts
d Power to approve the budget of special districts
e Power to approve the tax rate used by special districts

ministrations, it attempted to intervene in parish affairs. In 1934 under Governor Allen and at the height of Huey Long's control of the Louisiana legislature, state approval was required for the appointment of deputy sheriffs in East Baton Rouge and Orleans parishes. Moreover, the legislature declared the offices of the mayor and two commissioners vacant in Alexandria and authorized the governor to appoint successors. Both moves were the result of local opposition to Long in these areas of the state.[31]

Today local and state candidates do not run on the same ticket, although there may be mutual support. Therefore, the connection between parish officials and successful gubernatorial candidates is seldom as clear-cut as in the Long era when the ticket system linking parish and state candidates was widely used. The current independence of parish officials and legislators and the strength of grass-roots goals and values make it politically impractical, if not impossible, for state government to exercise this type of control in the parishes. The result is that Louisiana's constitution and laws tend to protect parish government from state control rather than bring it more directly and effectively under the state's supervision. The lenient home rule provisions in the 1974 constitution exemplify this trend.

The independence of local government precipitates political problems when state elected officials attempt to regulate elected officials on the parish level. The supervisory structure for education in Louisiana presents a salient example. The constitution of 1974 provides for an *elective* State Board of Elementary and Secondary Education whose policies are to be implemented by the State Department of Education, headed by an *elected* state superintendent of education. In turn, the policies of the board and the state superintendent are to be implemented by the *elected* members of the parish school boards, their appointed parish superintendents, and staff. Here we have an example of a state board whose members are elected from districts (and responsible to the constituents in those districts) supervising a state superintendent elected by voters statewide (and responsible to them). Both are involved in policy formulation that affects school boards whose members are elected from districts within the parish (and responsible to their own electorate).

31. T. Harry Williams, *Huey Long: A Biography* (New York: Knopf, 1969), 741–45.

The constitution has done nothing to eliminate the conflict between the two elective entities at the state level. It has, however, protected the local school boards by prohibiting BESE from controlling the business affairs and selection or removal of officers and employees of parish or city school boards.[32] The State Department of Education gives only limited direction to parish school boards, except in areas such as basic funding, teacher certification, and curriculum requirements. In the main, its role is one of cooperation rather than supervision. Parish school boards, not the Department of Education, make rules for the day-to-day operation of local school systems and see to their implementation.

A similar conflict is present in the area of justice. There is a State Department of Justice headed by the attorney general. He is the chief legal officer for the state and is elected by voters statewide. His authority over locally elected district attorneys, however, is limited. In order to protect or assert any right or interest of the state, when authorized by the court of original jurisdiction, the attorney general may institute or intervene in any criminal action or supersede a district attorney in any civil or criminal case. These constitutional provisions protect against the failure of a district attorney to correctly perform his duties, but they are seldom invoked. By specifying the circumstances in which the attorney general is allowed to supervise the actions of a district attorney, they actually increase the autonomy of this local office.[33]

The parish sheriff has no direct counterpart in state government. He cooperates with the state police when called upon to do so and participates in district law-enforcement councils and other cooperative activities through the Department of Public Safety. As custodian of the jail and its prisoners, the sheriff also works closely with the Department of Corrections, often housing state prisoners in the parish jail. Moreover, through enforcement of state licensing and other regulations, as well as general state law, the sheriff comes in contact with most state agencies. Still, he is largely autonomous in the operation of his own office.

Like the sheriff's, the clerk of court's office is related to various de-

32. Louisiana Constitution, Art. VIII, Sec. 3.
33. Louisiana Constitution, Art. IV, Sec. 8; Representatives of the Louisiana District Attorneys' Association, interviews.

partments of state government. Since the secretary of the Department of State is the chief election officer, election activities with the parish that come under the jurisdiction of the clerk are governed by regulations of the Department of State. The clerk also serves in place of the secretary of state in administering oaths of office and maintaining public documents and records. The clerk's association with the judicial branch is also close since his staff transcribes local court proceedings and certifies certain court documents. Nevertheless, direct supervision by the courts is slight.

Parish tax assessors, long noted for their independent authority, are legally supervised by the Louisiana Tax Commission. A branch of the governor's office, the commission is empowered to assure equalization of property taxes among parishes and set assessment guidelines. It may refuse to accept as accurate a parish tax roll (list of taxpayers and amounts) on which property is not taxed at the same rate or in the same manner as prescribed by law. To do so would be a momentous step since it would mean that none of the parish governmental bodies, which are dependent upon property tax revenues, would receive payment until discrepancies were eliminated. The Tax Commission is more active in its role as board of appeals for local citizens who feel that the assessment of their property taxes has been unfair. In this role, the commission hears controversies and renders decisions favoring either the taxpayer or the assessor. More often, such disputes are settled between the local assessor and his tax-paying constituent or with the assistance of the police jury, which acts in such cases as a first board of review.[34]

Many state agencies impose upon the activities of the police jury. The jury-appointed registrar of voters, for example, is constrained by regulations of the Department of Elections and Registration. The parish health unit must comply with standards set by the Department of Health and Human Resources. The parish library is loosely associated with the state library under the Department of Culture, Recreation, and Tourism. Food stamps and general welfare services are closely supervised by the Department of Health and Human Resources.

The Louisiana legislature, more than any other body, supervises the

34. Act 705 of 1976; Gordon Johnson, Chairman, Louisiana Tax Commission, interviews.

police jury as a whole. This is accomplished through the passage of statutes or, conversely, the failure to pass a bill requested by the jury. Nevertheless, the police jury receives constitutional protection that prevents the legislature from passing local or special laws that would apply only to one parish. The legislature cannot increase the amount that local units must spend for wages, working conditions, or other benefits unless it appropriates funds for these increases.[35] In this way, laws discriminating against one parish are generally prohibited. Laws for categories of parishes, such as those with a population above a certain minimum, however, are permitted.

Probably the most effective way in which the legislature supervises police juries and other local government entities is through financial audits. Unlike municipal governing bodies, whose finances are reviewed by private auditors engaged by each city, parish offices are subject to periodic audit by the Office of the Legislative Auditor. The auditor has no power to force the correction of irregularities revealed by the audit but does send a copy of the audit report to the legislature. Misuse of funds by a parish office may be called to the attention of the local district attorney who will determine whether to prosecute. A still more effective weapon lies in the fact that the Legislative Auditor's records are open to the press. A local official's irregularities may become highly publicized, embarrassing him and perhaps lessening his chance of reelection.[36]

Supervision of the district courts by the state provides something of an exception to the general rule. The Louisiana Supreme Court "has general supervisory jurisdiction over all other courts. It may establish procedural and administrative rules not in conflict with law and may assign a sitting or retired judge to any court."[37] We have noted in this chapter that district judges have wide discretion, and the operation of their courts varies considerably. However, if there exists a hierarchy of supervision between the state and its lower governmental units, it is within the judiciary.

In local-state relations not only does influence flow from upper to lower levels of government but officials at lower levels may influence

35. Louisiana Constitution, Art. IV, Sec. 12A.
36. Personnel of the office of the Louisiana Legislative Auditor, interview.
37. Louisiana Constitution, Art. V, Sec. 5A.

policy on the higher levels as well. Charles A. Adrian mentions four ways in which this is often accomplished: (1) lobbying, (2) common interests, (3) upward mobility of office holders, and (4) imitation.[38]

In Louisiana, lobbying of the Louisiana legislature by organizations of local government officials is of considerable importance. Officials of each parish office have joined together to form statewide associations. The Policy Jury Association, the School Board Association, the Clerk of Courts Association, the Assessor's Association, and other organizations form powerful lobbying groups. Several of these maintain full-time staffs in Baton Rouge and carefully watch each bill that comes before the legislature to determine the bill's effect on the organization's interests. Surprisingly, dues paid by local officials to their organizations are considered an office expense and are paid from the funds that the official is provided to run his office. A parish official may thus use office funds to pay association dues in order that the association may lobby for an increase in his own personal wages or his operating expenses or to otherwise strengthen his position. In recent years, these organizations have become much more than lobbying groups. Those with permanent staff are making realistic efforts to upgrade the quality of operation of the local offices they represent. They are problem solvers, sources of reference, and providers of training for officials and their employees.

Also significant in Louisiana is the continuous interaction and commonality of interests among parish officers and legislators. As Adrian observes, "frequently they share a set of interests that provide the basis for understanding relationships."[39] Not only do parish officials and the legislative delegation from the parish have a close working relationship, in large measure they share the same constituencies and assist each other at the time of reelection. Needless to say, such reciprocity is based not only on personal friendship but also on favors granted.

In Louisiana, another vehicle for state-local interaction is provided by the Department of Urban and Community Affairs (DUCA) and the eight Economic Development Districts that the department supervises. This state agency, assisted by federal funds, coordinates ac-

38. Charles A. Adrian, *State and Local Governments* (New York: McGraw-Hill, 1976), 51–52.
39. *Ibid.*, 52.

tivities among local governments and with the state. DUCA is also helpful in such specialized areas as securing grant funds, planning, and providing technical advice related to parish development.

Adrian further points out that upper-level government officials have often had prior experience in the lower levels of government. A survey of Louisiana legislators serving in the period 1952–1974 showed that 48 percent had had previous experience in public service. Of those who held prior office, more had served at the parish level than at any other. This is especially noteworthy since there would seem to be more city offices available. The largest group of legislators who had been local officials were former police jurors.[40] In this respect, the Louisiana parish governing bodies may have "built-in lobbies" within the state legislature who share the experiences of and empathize with sheriffs, police jurors, assessors, clerks, district attorneys, judges, and school board members.[41]

Imitation is cited by Adrian as a fourth way that one level of government influences policy at a higher level. Parish government in Louisiana, however, has not been known for policy innovation whether through imitation or otherwise. This is evident in its reluctance to take advantage of home rule, its lack of professionalism, and its lack of merit-system employment. Generally, it has been the municipality, rather than the parish, that has exhibited innovation since the city is more a creature of change.

Future Trends

Parish government has not progressed as rapidly as municipal or state government. Yet, on a nationwide basis, the future of parish (county) government is not as bleak as it might seem. Rather, the possibility exists for the parish to emerge as the pivotal unit of intergovernmental cooperation linking local-municipal, state, and federal governments through its contacts with all of these units. Moreover, modernized parish government could assume the role of prime surveyor of those pub-

40. June Savoy, "Louisiana Lawmakers: A 25-Year Profile," *Analysis* (January, 1975), 17–18.
41. June Savoy, "Councils of Government," *Louisiana Parish Government*, XII (October, 1976), 11.

lic services that are best performed for areas larger than a municipality, including elections, solid waste collection and disposal, public health, and law enforcement.[42] For Louisiana we would add education, welfare, and tax assessment, which are already parishwide services.

The ability to provide improved services and to act as a pivot for all units of government, however, depends upon modernization of parish government. Fractionalization of parish (county) government is not unique to Louisiana—it is found nationwide. Until the parish can reorganize itself into a more functional administrative unit, its ability to modernize and administer additional services remains questionable.

Reorganization of parish government into a form similar to that illustrated in Figure 7-5 could be accomplished through constitutional amendment. In political terms, legislative initiative to reorganize the parishes and popular acceptance of a constitutional amendment designed to achieve it are unrealistic expectations. Legislators who attempted such actions would lose the support of current parish governmental officials and would invite the wrath of their strong lobbying organizations. Furthermore, local officials retain enough prestige in the parishes to insure the probable rejection of proposed amendments depriving them of the protection now afforded their offices by the constitution.

More realistically, as urbanization continues, city-parish consolidation (as in Baton Rouge and New Orleans) or the urban parish (as in Jefferson) may change parish government. In Lafayette the parish police jury, the city council, chamber of commerce, and the local council of governments are investigating consolidation.[43] A Caddo Parish police juror called for the merger of the Shreveport City Council, which operates under home rule, and the Caddo Police Jury. "The city and the parish have duplication of services and capabilities," he said, and "the time has come."[44] Yet, the resistance of parishes to change remains so strong that no reorganizations of this type have occurred in the last decade, although urbanization has increased steadily.

What then are the prospects for parish government in Louisiana?

42. "Improving County Government," *Public Management* (April, 1971), 3–20; *The County Yearbook, 1977* (Washington, D.C.: National Association of Counties, 1977), 69.
43. Savoy, "Councils of Government," 11; Baton Rouge *Morning Advocate*, January 6, 1978, Sec. D, p. 15, February 3, 1978, Sec. A, p. 10.
44. Baton Rouge *Morning Advocate*, February 3, 1978, Sec. A, p. 10.

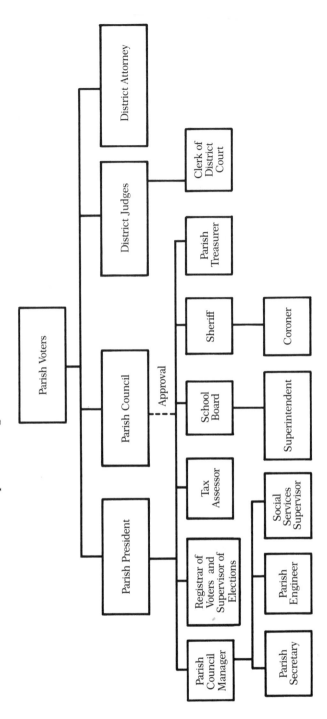

Figure 7-5
Proposed Reorganization of Parish Government

Probably more of the same structurally but with a tendency toward increased governmental activity and professionalism especially as the result of expanded federal-local relationships and the demands for services from culturally urban constituencies. Both should enlarge the area of authority encompassed by police juries and require more and more that they move toward leadership in parish administration. This specifically involves the addition of executive officers to juries, a change that has been slowly occurring through charter provisions in home rule parishes and the appointment of professional or jury-member managers in several others.

The current laws and attitudes of Louisiana state government permit parish government to move away from parental confines and toward a position of near autonomy. To achieve this degree of independence, parishes will have to participate to a greater degree in the financing and supervision of local activities, while still maintaining cooperative relations with state and municipal governments.

The progress that parishes make toward effective self-government now depends upon the desire of their citizens to see this accomplished. As Stephen Bailey points out, "effective local government depends not so much upon the machinery we employ as the spirit we are of."[45] Structural changes such as those advocated in Figure 7-5 are important, yet they cannot be imposed from outside. In advocating reorganization and the assumption of responsibility, we should not lose sight of the fact that governments do not change overnight. Rather, they adjust to meet the exigencies of the times and the desires of their constituents.

The exigencies that may occur to change parish government can be only dimly foreseen, but the citizens' bonds with the past are known to be strong. Just as government in rural districts preceded the formation of the state and its municipalities, this rural orientation may prevail in Louisiana long after the greater pressures and demands placed on cities and the state have caused their governments to adjust to the urban world.

45. Stephen K. Bailey, "Creative Leadership in Local Government," in Robert L. Moran (ed.), *Capitol, Courthouse, and City Hall* (Boston: Houghton Mifflin, 1977), 340.

8.

Municipal Government

RICHARD L. ENGSTROM

Louisiana's three hundred municipalities range in population from less than 100 residents in Bryceland (Bienville Parish) and Mound (Madison Parish) to almost 600,000 residents in New Orleans. They are classified into villages (those with populations of less than 1,000) towns (1,000–4,999), and cities (5,000 or more), of which there are 118, 131, and 52 respectively.[1] Municipalities are multipurpose units of local government created to supplement parish governments. Established initially as administrative subdivisions of state government, parishes were the local unit through which many state services were to be provided. Serving primarily rural areas, they originally performed only a few limited functions, such as road construction and maintenance, tax assessment and collection, law enforcement, judicial administration, and the registration of vital statistics. Although the authority of parish government grew extensively over the years, in time, more populous communities needed additional local services and public safety arrangements beyond those generally provided by parish governments. Municipalities have been created as additional units of government within parishes to provide these services.

Municipal government's prominent role in American political thought is a function of the strong normative preference in this country for government that is close to the people. Local government has traditionally been viewed as the most representative and responsive level of government, and the phrase "home rule," often invoked to defend mu-

1. These are the classifications as of May 13, 1978, reported in *Louisiana Roster of Officials, 1978* (Baton Rouge: Secretary of State, 1978), 180–240.

nicipal as opposed to state or federal activity or control, has consequently been a powerful rhetorical expression. As one author has stated, "It is a good hollering point because the phrase 'home rule' has achieved an unassailable position similar to that of motherhood."[2] Yet the expression is of far more rhetorical than descriptive value, for one of the most frequently cited problems of local government in this country has been its "legal and financial impotence."[3] The elevated status of municipal government in our normative thought has not been matched by its position in our legal doctrines.

The Constitutional Status of Municipal Government in Louisiana—Dillon's Rule

Municipalities are not autonomous governmental units with political authority derived directly from the people. Rather, they are the subordinate creatures of state governments and possess only that authority granted or allowed by the state. The United States Constitution delegates power to the central government, and under the terms of the Tenth Amendment, "The powers not delegated to the United States by the Constitution, nor prohibited by it to the States, are reserved to the States respectively, or to the people." No powers are allocated to local governments through that document. Municipal government within this constitutional system is viewed as a privilege granted to the people by the state, and the state maintains control over those municipalities created within it. The basic doctrine expressing this relationship is known as *Dillon's Rule*, which holds: "It is a general and undisputed proposition of the law that a municipal corporation possesses and can exercise the following powers and no others: First, those granted in express words; second, those necessarily or fairly implied in or incident to the powers expressly granted; third, those essential to the declared objects and purposes of the corporation—not simply convenient but indispensable. Any fair reasonable doubt concerning the existence

2. Lyle E. Schaller, "Home Rule—a Critical Appraisal," *Political Science Quarterly*, LXXVI (September, 1961), 404.

3. Anwar H. Syed, *The Political Theory of Local Government* (New York: Random House, 1966), 3.

of power is resolved by the courts against the corporation and the power is denied."[4]

Dillon's Rule has been recognized by the United States Supreme Court and has served as the basis for countless state court decisions denying municipalities the power to carry out public projects and to perform services, as well as upholding state intrusions into municipal matters. The effect of this restrictive legal principle is to require municipalities to have prior state authorization, through the state constitution or state statutes, before performing a particular function or assuming a responsibility. This requirement, many commentators argue, severely limits the flexibility of municipal governments to respond to changing conditions within their communities. In the words of one critic, the effect has been to "cut the heart out of local government's ability to grasp with imagination, enthusiasm, and perseverance its most pressing problems."[5]

Louisiana municipalities are, like those in other states, subject to Dillon's Rule. As the Louisiana Supreme Court noted recently, "It has long been settled in this state that municipal corporations are creatures or agencies of the state established by the legislature for the purpose of administering local affairs of government and, as such, possess only those powers delegated by the state." Louisiana municipalities, consequently, may perform only those functions and responsibilities that have been authorized by the state through either the constitution or statutes. As a recent mayor of Thibodaux once stated, "If a local problem arises in an area in which we have no authority, then *we are unable to take action until we secure legislation* to aid us in doing our jobs." In the opinion of a former executive director of the Louisiana Municipal Association, this legal situation "has all too often served to constrain local initiative and has prevented local officials from reacting positively and more responsively to the problems of their communities."[6]

4. John Forrest Dillon, *Commentaries on the Law of Municipal Corporations* (5th ed.; Boston: Little, Brown, 1911), 448–50.

5. Clyde D. McKee, Jr., "Local and State Government," in Murray S. Stedman, Jr. (ed.), *Modernizing American Government: The Demand for Social Change* (Englewood Cliffs, N.J.: Prentice-Hall, 1968), 155.

6. *Bradford* v. *City of Shreveport*, 305 So.2d 487 at 490 (1974); Warren J. Harang, Jr., testimony before the Local and Parochial Affairs Committee of the 1973–74 Louisi-

Efforts have been made to relax the impact of Dillon's Rule by altering the system of apportioning powers between state and local governments. State constitutions have been amended or statutes enacted to provide home rule for municipalities. As a legal concept, home rule is designed to eliminate the requirement that local governments have state authorization prior to acting upon local matters. Most states now have some form of municipal home rule, but the actual experience with home rule across the nation suggests that it exists more in name than in practice. While it has provided many municipalities with the opportunity to determine locally how the municipal government will be structured (*e.g.*, whether a mayor-council plan or a council-manager plan is used, whether an at-large electoral system or single-member districts for councilmen is chosen), it has not generally resulted in a serious expansion in municipal authority, especially revenue-raising authority. This has been true in Louisiana as well, although the home rule experience in Louisiana may now be changing significantly.

Louisiana's 1921 constitution, as amended, formally provided municipalities with the option of home rule. But these provisions "became meaningless" in the face of what was in fact "virtually unfettered legislative supremacy over local government and its affairs."[7] The constitution of 1974, however, contains new home rule provisions, discussed below, which may provide a meaningful change in Louisiana's municipal governance system. These provisions are complemented by others that enhance the taxing powers of municipalities and authorize both intergovernmental cooperation and interjurisdictional restructuring among local governmental units. One commentator has described the local government article in the 1974 constitution as "the most dramatic and advanced article in the new constitution. It is as near a political scientist's dream as one might reasonably wish."[8] Whether more vigorous and effective municipal government in Louisiana will result

---

ana Constitutional Convention, Baton Rouge, March 10, 1973 (my italics), Marvin Lyons, testimony before the same committee, March 10, 1973, both reproduced in *Louisiana Municipal Review*, XXXVIII (March, 1973), 4, 5.

7. R. Gordon Kean, Jr., "Local Government and Home Rule," *Loyola Law Review*, XXI (Number 1, 1975–76), 1–139.

8. Cecil Morgan, "A New Constitution for Louisiana," *National Civic Review*, LXIII (July, 1974), 348; see also Richard L. Engstrom, "Home Rule in Louisiana—Could This Be the Promised Land?" *Louisiana History*, XVII (Fall, 1976), 431–55.

from these provisions cannot be known, of course, until there has been more extensive experience with the new system. But a foundation for a more flexible and responsive system has been provided, and Louisiana's experience with that system will undoubtedly attract the interest of home-rule advocates throughout the country.

Basic Municipal Governance Arrangements— Structures and Powers

The Louisiana constitution (Art. VI, Sec. 2) requires the state legislature to establish procedures through which municipalities may be created (called incorporation) and to set forth the governmental arrangements through which municipalities will operate. Incorporation is accomplished only upon citizen initiative and approval. The procedure requires a petition signed by at least 25 percent of the registered voters in the area to be incorporated (who collectively must own at least 25 percent, in value, of the taxable property), followed by a special election in which a majority of those voting are in favor of establishing the municipality. During the recent decade of 1969–1978, seventeen municipalities were incorporated in Louisiana. (See Table 8-1.)

Upon incorporation, a municipality receives a charter from the state that establishes the form of government under which the municipality will operate. There are three basic types of charter in Louisiana: special legislative, general legislative, and home rule. Table 8-2 provides

Table 8-1
Municipalities Incorporated, 1969–1978

Ball	Jean Lafitte	Stonewall
Baskin	Lucky	Timber Trails
Chataignier	Martin	Urania
Downsville	Natchez	Vienna
Fisher	Richmond	Woodworth
Henderson	Richwood	

Sources: *Louisiana Roster of Officials, 1969* and *1978* (Baton Rouge: Secretary of State, 1969, 1978), 130–54, 180–240.

Table 8-2
Municipalities by Type of Charter
and Population as of May 13, 1978

Population	General Charter Lawrason Act	General Charter Commission Plan	Special Legislative Charter	Home Rule Charter	Total
<2,500	196		13	1	210
2,500– 9,999	42	1	13	5	61
10,000–24,999	7	2	4	6	19
25,000–49,999	1		1	3	5
50,000+			1	5	6
TOTAL	246	3	32	20	301

Source: *Louisiana Roster of Officials, 1978*, 180–240.

the number of municipalities with each type of charter, grouped according to population size.

Special Legislative Charters

A special legislative charter is one that has been granted to a particular community by the legislature through a local or special law. This type of charter has been constitutionally prohibited since 1952, although those previously in existence continue to be valid. Thirty-two municipalities (the largest being Monroe) were still operating under special charters in 1978. (See Table 8-3.) This type of charter may usually be amended only by additional special acts of the legislature. Over the years, frequent legislative amendments may make it difficult to ascertain a charter's contents. A mayor of Monroe recently commented, "The Act of the Legislature which created the present system almost six decades ago can hardly be called a charter, since it has been changed countless times by additional acts of the Legislature. No single compilation of this 'Charter' exists, so in order to study it, it is necessary to research every session of the Legislature, including all the special sessions, since its adoption."[9]

9. Ralph Troy, quoted in Monroe *Morning World*, January 11, 1976, Sec. A, p. 7.

Table 8-3
Municipalities with Special Legislative Charters, 1978

Abbeville	Franklinton	Mandeville	New Iberia
Bastrop	Grand Coteau	Mansfield	New Roads
Clinton	Greensburg	Many	Plain Dealing
Coushatta	Homer	Marksville	Plaquemine
Covington	Jackson	Minden	St. Martinville
Evergreen	Jeanerette	Monroe	Springfield
Farmerville	Keachi	Morgan City	Vienna
Franklin	Madisonville	Mount Lebanon	Zwolle

Source: *Louisiana Roster of Officials, 1978*, 180–240.

General Legislative Charters—Lawrason Act

General legislative charters are granted to municipalities under the provisions of general laws. There are three types of general law charters in Louisiana each providing a different form of government for municipalities, either a modified mayor-council plan, a commission plan, or a council-manager plan. Municipalities under 2,500 in population must operate under the mayor-council arrangement unless they have special or home rule charters, but those with populations of 2,500 or more may choose from among the three.

The modified mayor-council plan, known in Louisiana as the mayor–board of aldermen plan, is provided by the Lawrason Act, which was enacted in 1898 and has been amended frequently (L.R.S. 33: 321–481). Over 80 percent of Louisiana's municipalities are chartered under the Lawrason Act, although few of the larger municipalities operate under it. As shown in Table 8-2, all but 14 of the 210 municipalities with populations under 2,500 are chartered through this act, and over two-thirds of those between 2,500 and 10,000 are Lawrason Act municipalities. However, only a little over one-fourth of the cities larger than 10,000 (the largest being Houma) have Lawrason Act charters.

The mayor–board of aldermen plan provided through the Lawrason Act is somewhat different from the traditional mayor-council form found throughout the nation. Under the mayor-council plan, there is a fairly clear formal separation of legislative and executive powers between the council and the mayor. In Louisiana, the mayor is recognized as the chief executive of the municipality, and the board as the local legislative or ordinance-enacting body. Yet the mayor has significant legislative responsibilities, and the board has significant control over executive-branch appointments. Like other executives, the mayor may veto actions of the board, and his veto can be overridden only by a two-thirds vote of the entire board membership. But mayors also serve as the presiding officers at meetings of the boards and are permitted to cast tie-breaking votes at these meetings—responsibilities not generally granted to mayors under the traditional separation of powers. And although mayoral appointments to executive-branch positions frequently require councilmanic approval, under the Lawrason Act the appointment power is shared by the mayor and the board. The mayor is required to sign the commissions of appointees, but the selection of the appointees is shared with the board. The mayor's role is formally limited to casting a decisive vote when aldermanic votes on appointment matters are tied, or exercising the veto over the council's decisions in such matters.

Some mayors of Lawrason Act municipalities even have judicial responsibilities. They function as magistrates and preside over a forum called the mayor's court. This responsibility falls generally upon the mayors of villages and towns, for cities have city courts with elected judges instead of mayors' courts. Special statutory provisions have abolished mayors' courts for some municipalities (Breaux Bridge, Franklin, Leesville, Marksville, Newllano, Plaquemine, and Slidell) and have allowed other municipalities (Berwick, Harahan, Jean Lafitte, Kenner, Patterson, and Westwego) to have the local legislative body appoint a lawyer to serve, at the mayor's designation and pleasure, as the presiding officer in the mayor's court. These courts have jurisdiction over "all violations of municipal ordinances," and the mayor "may try all breaches of the ordinances and impose fines or imprisonment, or both, provided for the infraction thereof" (L.R.S. 33: 441). The largest fines and jail terms municipalities may impose for ordinance violations (except for driving while intoxicated, an offense that may not be tried in mayor's court) are $200 and/or thirty days. All decisions of a mayor's court may be appealed to a district court, which will completely retry any case in which a mayor's court has imposed a jail sentence or a forfeiture of rights and property.

A mayor does not have to be a lawyer in order to preside over mayor's court. In fact, there is no requirement that he or she have any legal training. This is not a situation unique to Louisiana; many states utilize nonlawyer judges to handle misdemeanors in small towns and rural areas. The practice has been frequently criticized, however, on the grounds that a lay judge lacks sufficient understanding of the complexities of criminal law and procedures to guarantee defendants due process of law. Due process is required by both the Fourteenth Amendment to the United States Constitution and Article 1, Section 2, of the Louisiana constitution, which states "No person shall be deprived of life, liberty, or property except by due process of law." A fine, even though relatively small, and a jail term, even though relatively brief, do constitute deprivations of property and liberty respectively.

The United States Supreme Court recently considered this issue in a 1976 case involving lay judges in Kentucky.[10] The Court ruled that the use of lay judges and magistrates under conditions such as those found in Louisiana does not violate the federal constitution. The Court characterized nonlawyer tribunals as courts of convenience, which use simple procedures to dispose of misdemeanors quickly and inexpensively, and held that when a defendant is given the right, after being found guilty by a lay judge, to a trial *de novo* (a new trial) in a higher court with a lawyer as judge, the use of lay judges is not unconstitutional. As noted above, any person in Louisiana who has had a jail sentence imposed or had rights or property forfeited by a mayor's court has the right to a trial *de novo* in district court, where the judge must be a lawyer. It would appear, therefore, that in approving Kentucky's use of lay judges the Supreme Court has in effect approved Louisiana's use of lay magistrates. In approving Kentucky's system, however, the Court stated that it assumed the lay judges "recognize their obligation to inform all convicted defendants . . . of their unconditional right to a trial *de novo*." All mayors presiding over mayor's courts in Louisiana are expected, therefore, to inform those they find guilty that they have the right to a new trial in district court.

A trial *de novo* is a completely new trial, not a review of alleged errors within the proceedings of the lower tribunal. This places mayors

10. *North* v. *Russell*, 427 U.S. 328 (1976).

serving as magistrates in mayor's court in an anomalous situation. On the one hand, Article I, Section 2, of the Louisiana constitution appears to demand that the proceedings in that tribunal comply with the various and sometimes complex requirements of due process. On the other hand, no higher judicial body formally reviews the procedures that a mayor follows, and in practice mayors may still be able to utilize simpler, more convenient personal procedures, a situation not at all uncommon in Louisiana's mayors' courts.

Boards of aldermen in Lawrason Act municipalities vary in size according to the classification of the municipality. Villages have three-member boards, towns five-member boards, and city boards may have from five to nine members. Aldermen may be elected from single-member districts within the municipality or at-large from throughout the municipality. Several other officials are also required by the Lawrason Act. A chief of police (marshal) must be elected unless municipal electors have voted in a referendum to make that position appointive. A municipal clerk, tax collector, and street commissioner must be appointed by the mayor and board of aldermen, and a municipal attorney may be appointed as well.

General Legislative Charters—Commission Plan

Municipalities of 2,500 or more population have the option of operating under a commission plan of government. This form of government centralizes both legislative and executive responsibilities within one small body. There is no formal separation of powers under this form. The commission usually consists of three to seven persons elected at large who individually serve as the head of one of the various departments of municipal government (e.g., commissioner of public safety or commissioner of streets) and who collectively serve as the legislative body or council for the municipality. Under this plan commissioners perform both legislative and executive duties.

The commission plan was the first complete structural alternative to the traditional mayor-council format and was widely perceived as a reform that would eliminate much of the corrupt boss rule that flourished within the mayor-council structures during the late nineteenth and early twentieth centuries. It was thought that centralization of authority would facilitate a more efficient, businesslike management of municipal government and the at-large elections were expected to eliminate ward-based politics and require a city-wide perspective in municipal decision-making. In addition, other reform ideas such as nonpartisan elections, civil service, and the initiative, referendum, and recall were often added to commission plan proposals, making them even more attractive to groups demanding changes in what were often perceived to be corrupt local governments.

The development of the commission plan dates back to 1900 when a hurricane inflicted massive damage at Galveston, Texas. Prior to the hurricane the city was in serious financial difficulty, and allegations of corruption were common. The Texas legislature changed the city's charter in 1901, placing the rebuilding responsibility in the hands of a five-member commission, three members of which were initially appointed by the governor and the other two elected. Most of the members were businessmen, and each of them assumed responsibility for one phase of the redevelopment effort. The effort was a tremendous success; not only was the physical rebuilding impressive but the city also was put back on a sound financial basis.

The Galveston experience quickly attracted considerable attention nationwide, and the concept of governing a municipality through a small elected commission with both policy-making and administrative authority became quite popular. It was known variously as the Galveston plan, the Texas idea (by 1922 seventy-five municipalities in Texas had adopted the plan), and the Des Moines plan (after Des Moines, Iowa, which adopted the plan in 1908 and attached its own name to it as part of its city-boosting effort). Adoptions of the plan began to spread rapidly throughout the country. By 1911 nearly 200 municipalities had adopted it, and by 1922, only about two decades after the Galveston hurricane, 522 municipalities in forty-one states were operating under the commission form of government.[11] Louisiana passed a law in 1910 allowing cities of 7,500 or more in population to adopt the plan and in 1912 amended the law to reduce the population requirement to 2,500. Between 1910 and 1919, twelve municipalities in Louisiana, including many of the largest cities in the state, adopted commission governments. (See Table 8-4.)

The author of a recent book on the commission government move-

11. Bradley Robert Rice, *Progressive Cities: The Commission Government Movement in America, 1901–1920* (Austin: University of Texas Press, 1977).

Table 8-4
Municipalities Adopting Commission Plan of Government,
1910–1919

Alexandria (1913)	Jennings (1913)	Natchitoches (1912)
Baton Rouge (1914)	Lafayette (1914)	New Iberia (1913)
Donaldsonville (1912)	Lake Charles (1913)	New Orleans (1912)
Hammond (1912)	Monroe (1919)	Shreveport (1910)

Source: Bradley Robert Rice, *Progressive Cities: The Commission Government Movement in America, 1901–1920* (Austin: University of Texas Press, 1977), 117.

ment states, "The idea spread rapidly because in city after city it initially provided positive results and seemed to meet its promise." Note
the qualifier *initially*, however, for during the 1920s the euphoria over
commission government faded rapidly. As expressed by another author, "By 1920 the Commission plan had become a weed in the garden
of reform thereafter to be fought rather than nurtured."[12] Municipalities began to abandon the plan, and the total number of commission-
plan municipalities has been said to have declined every year since
World War I. Since the 1930s new adoptions have been extremely
rare, an exception being Minden, Louisiana, which adopted commission government in the mid-1960s. Even Des Moines and Galveston
abandoned the plan in 1949 and 1960 respectively. New Orleans dis-
carded its commission government in 1952. Shreveport did not abandon the plan until 1978, however, and Monroe is today one of the
largest municipalities in the country governed under the commission
form.

The decline in the commission plan's popularity is commonly attributed to three general defects or problems. The first was that the
divided executive structure resulted in a lack of coordinated executive
leadership. Although the plan centralized power within a small group,
there was frequently an absence of coordinated policy leadership or administrative control emanating from the separately elected and officially equal commissioners. Although one commissioner is often assigned the title *mayor* as well as *commissioner*, this title carries with it
primarily symbolic responsibilities, such as cutting ribbons and pro-

12. *Ibid.*, 60; William O. Winter, *The Urban Polity* (New York: Dodd, Mead, 1969),
233.

viding keys to the city. It does not grant the designee significant executive authority over the other commissioners. A second problem was that few experienced administrators or businessmen were attracted to serve on the commission. The plan's premise was the idea that people with expertise and administrative experience and skill would become commissioners. But while the business community supported the commission idea, it generally did not serve as a source of candidates once the plan was adopted. In consequence, many administratively inexperienced people held important executive positions, and often professional politicians rather than experienced businessmen maintained political control over municipalities even after the adoption of the "reform" structure. The third problem was the lack of legislative oversight over executive-branch operations that often resulted from the absence of any separation of powers. This centralized arrangement lacked adequate checks and balances, and unwritten rules developed under which commissioners did not interfere in the operations of each other's departments, a situation tolerant of mismanagement and conducive to corruption.

Another factor contributing to the decline of the commission plan's popularity among reformers was competition from the council-manager plan of government. Many advocates of municipal reform abandoned the commission plan in favor of the manager plan. For example, the National Municipal League incorporated the manager approach into its Model City Charter and the Short Ballot Organization switched its support from the commission plan to the manager plan. By 1918 the manager plan was beginning to outpace the commission plan in number of adoptions, and by the 1920s there was no longer any contest—reform government was council-manager government. Indeed, one student of the commission government movement has concluded that "the major long-term importance of the commission movement was as a transition to the council-manager plan." [13]

Although there are few commission governments left in Louisiana today, the plan remained popular longer in this than in most states. As Table 8-5 shows, there were still fifteen commission cities in 1969. Only four were left, however, by 1979, two chartered under the general law (DeQuincy and Sulphur), one by special charter (Monroe),

13. Rice, *Progressive Cities*, xvii.

and one through a home rule charter (Donaldsonville, which switched from a general-law commission plan to a larger commission through a 1977 home rule charter). General-law commission charters are of two types. One is a five-member commission for cities of 100,000 or more in population, although cities 40,000 or over with five-member commissions as of 1958 are also permitted to retain that structure. The other is a three-member commission for cities smaller than 100,000. A five-member commission consists of commissioners of public affairs and public education (also designated as the mayor), accounts and finance, public health and safety, public utilities, and streets and parks or public works. A three-member commission consists of commissioners of public health and safety (designated as mayor), finance and public utilities, and streets and parks or public works. The specific responsibilities of the various departments are determined by the commission collectively.

Under the law, this plan of government is adopted pursuant to a majority vote in a referendum called through a petition signed by 25 percent of a municipality's registered voters. The plan includes referendum and initiative provisions. An ordinance passed by the commission is suspended and required to be reconsidered if, within ten days of passage, a petition protesting the ordinance is signed by a number of voters equal to 25 percent of the votes received by mayoral candidates in the most recent primary election. If the ordinance is not repealed upon reconsideration, it must be submitted to the voters. The initiative provision allows citizens to submit a proposed ordinance to the commission through a petition signed by a number of voters equal to 33 percent of the votes cast for mayoral candidates in the latest general election. If the commission does not pass the ordinance exactly as pro-

Table 8-5
Municipalities with Commission Form of Government in 1969

Alexandria	Hammond	Monroe
Bogalusa	Jennings	Natchitoches
Bossier City	Lafayette	Shreveport
DeQuincy	Leesville	Sulphur
Donaldsonville	Minden	Thibodaux

Source: *Louisiana Roster of Officials, 1969*, 130–54.

posed, it must then be submitted to a vote of the people. An ordinance adopted under the initiative procedure may subsequenly be amended or repealed only by another vote of the people.

As mentioned above, over half of the municipalities in Louisiana still utilizing the commission form of government in 1969 had abandoned it by 1978, among them Shreveport, Lafayette, and Alexandria. This was a rather serious increase in abandonments, for between 1961 and 1969 only two cities, DeRidder and Lake Charles, had changed from the commission arrangement. Many of these recent changes were undoubtedly prompted by a new type of objection to commission governments relating to the use of at-large elections—generally required within that plan because all commissioners have municipality-wide executive responsibilities. Black citizens have challenged at-large election arrangements as being unfair to minority voters who are unable to compete as effectively in municipality-wide elections as in district-based elections. The argument is that the significance of the black voting strength within a municipality is diluted when submerged under the white majority's vote. It has been well established empirically that black candidates for city councils are less likely to be successful when elections are held at large than when single-member districts are used. Of course, single-member districts by no means guarantee proportional representation and may themselves be gerrymandered so that the effect of the black voting strength is seriously diluted.[14]

The Supreme Court in recent years has reviewed complaints that at-large elections have a discriminatory impact on minority voters and has held, "To sustain such claims, it is not enough that the racial group allegedly discriminated against has not had legislative seats in proportion to its voting potential. The plaintiffs' burden is to produce evi-

14. See Richard L. Engstrom and Michael D. McDonald, "The Election of Blacks to City Councils: Clarifying the Impact of Electoral Arrangements on the Seats/Population Relationship," *American Political Science Review*, LXXV (June, 1981), Albert K. Karnig and Susan Welch, "Electoral Structure and Black Representation on City Councils: An Updated Examination" (paper presented at the 1978 Annual Meeting of the Midwest Political Science Association, Chicago, April 20–22, 1978), Richard L. Engstrom, "The Supreme Court and Equipopulous Gerrymandering: A Remaining Obstacle in the Quest for Fair and Effective Representation," *Arizona State Law Journal* (Number 2, 1976), 277–319, Richard L. Engstrom and John K. Wildgen, "Pruning Thorns from the Thicket: An Empirical Test of the Existence of Racial Gerrymandering," *Legislative Studies Quarterly*, II (November, 1977), 465–79.

dence to support findings that the political process leading to nomination and election were not equally open to participation by the group in question—that its members had less opportunity than did other residents in the district to participate in the political process and to elect legislators of their choice." The Court found that this burden had not been met by blacks challenging county-wide elections of state legislators in Marion County (Indianapolis), Indiana, but found that it was satisfied by blacks in Dallas County and Chicanos in Bexar County (San Antonio), Texas, who also were challenging county-wide state legislative elections.[15] In the Texas cases the Court focused on the long, unbroken history of pervasive discrimination that has resulted in lower rates of voter registration and turnout and less overall political sophistication among minority groups, thereby denying them equal participation in the electoral process.

In other states where the hangover effects of past discrimination are readily documented, at-large elections are similarly vulnerable to judicial rejection. Louisiana is such a state, of course, and black plaintiffs have been successful in securing the invalidation of such electoral arrangements throughout the state. When these arrangements are part of a commission plan of government, the entire governmental arrangement may have to be changed because it is incompatible with single-member districting. Ward-based elections would result in officials with municipality-wide executive responsibilities being electorally accountable to only a segment of a municipality's voters. In 1976 a federal district judge held that the at-large elections utilized in selecting the Shreveport commission were racially discriminatory and ruled that the city had to adopt a new form of government. Another federal district judge, who later that year invalidated the commission plan in Mobile, Alabama, went even further and ordered that city to change to a mayor-council government with nine councilmen elected from single-member districts. Fears of judicial invalidation have undoubtedly been a factor in some of the abandonments of the commission plan in Louisiana during the 1970s. Although the Shreveport case had been remanded by an appellate court to the district court for further consideration in March of 1978, Shreveport voters in May of that year

15. *White* v. *Regester*, 412 U.S. 755 at 765–66 (1973); *Whitcomb* v. *Chavis*, 403 U.S. 755 (1973).

decided to switch to the mayor-council plan, and the case became moot. The Mobile case, however, was appealed to the United States Supreme Court. In 1980 the Court ruled that the black plaintiffs had failed to prove that the disputed electoral plan was "motivated by a discriminatory purpose" or that it was "conceived or operated as [a] purposeful devic[e] to further racial . . . discrimination."[16] No doubt the decision will have an important impact on the future of the remaining commission-government municipalities in the South.

General Legislative Charters—Manager Plan

Municipalities with populations of 2,500 or more also have the option of operating under the council-manager form of government, which is modeled after the business corporation. Voters (stockholders) elect a council (board of directors), which establishes municipal policies and appoints a manager (corporation president) to execute those policies. While municipal power remains concentrated in the council, as it is under the commission plan, the actual administration of the municipality's affairs is performed by the manager. Under this arrangement, the council is generally elected at large in nonpartisan elections, and municipal policies are expected to reflect municipality-wide needs and priorities. The manager, at least in concept, is a professional administrator who will act in a politically neutral, economical, and efficient manner according to sound business management principles.

As noted above, by the 1920s this plan had surpassed the commission plan in the number of new adoptions, and today it is viewed as the reform structure of municipal government. Its origin is usually traced to Staunton, Virginia, which in 1908 adopted an ordinance adding to its municipal government a "general manager" appointed by the council. Sumter, South Carolina, in 1912 became the first municipality to adopt the plan through a new municipal charter. By 1921 over two hundred municipalities had adopted the plan, and by 1931 the number was over four hundred.[17] Louisiana made this plan available to munici-

16. *Blacks United for Lasting Leadership, Inc.* v. *City of Shreveport*, 71 F.R.D. 623 (1976), and see 571 F.2d 248 (1978). *Bolden* v. *City of Mobile*, 423 F. Supp. 384 (1976); *City of Mobile* v. *Bolden*, 446 U.S. 55, 62, 70 (quoting *Whitcomb* v. *Chavis*, 403 U.S. 124, at 149 [1971]) (1980).
17. Rice, *Progressive Cities*, 108.

palities of 5,000 or more through a law enacted in 1918, which was amended in 1950 to reduce the population requirement to 2,500.

In Louisiana the plan is referred to legally as the *commission-manager* plan. The council (or commission) consists of five members elected at large. The council appoints the manager, who, by statute, has the responsibility of enforcing municipal ordinances and the power to appoint, control, and remove the directors of most of the departments of municipal government. As with the commission plan, one councilman is designated as titular mayor. Initiative and referendum provisions similar to those for commission government are included with this plan as well, except that ordinances adopted by initiative may be subsequently amended or repealed by the council itself without further action by the voters.

The manager form may be adopted by a Louisiana municipality through a special election called upon a petition signed by the number of registered voters equal to 33 percent of the votes cast for mayoral candidates in the latest general election. Although the form is very popular nationally and especially so within the South, it has never been very popular in Louisiana. There is not a single municipality chartered under the general statute. DeRidder has a form of government adopted through a 1962 home rule charter that is frequently referred to as a manager plan, although it deviates significantly from the traditional council-manager arrangement. A mayor elected separately from the council presides over council meetings but, according to the charter, may vote on legislative matters only when councilmen are evenly divided. The council has authority to establish its own rules, however, and through this authority, it has granted general voting rights to the mayor by councilmanic resolution. This alteration is consistent with the traditional council-manager form, but it may be changed again simply by councilmanic resolution. The "manager" in DeRidder is appointed and may be removed *by the mayor*, not the council, an arrangement that resembles a mayor-council form under which the mayor has an assistant, frequently known as the chief administrative officer. The council establishes the manager's salary, and this power may provide the council with significant control over the manager's actions. Voters in Bogalusa were provided in 1977 with a choice between a council-manager plan or a mayor-council plan in their home rule charter election, and they opted for the latter arrangement. The council-manager plan remains available to Louisiana municipalities, however, either through the general law charter or the home rule charter. And although the plan traditionally utilizes at-large councilmanic elections, which may be vulnerable to judicial invalidation, there is nothing in the plan inherently inconsistent with single-member districts since councilmen in this arrangement do not have municipality-wide executive responsibilities as commissioners do under the commission plan.

Municipal Powers and Responsibilities

As noted at the beginning of this chapter, municipalities are granted authority to act through state constitutional and statutory provisions. The constitution of 1974 allocates few *specific* powers to municipalities and most of these authorizations are qualified by provisions conditioning the exercise of such powers on state law. For example, municipalities are authorized to adopt local regulations controlling land use, zoning, and historic preservation "subject of uniform procedures established by law," and are granted authority to acquire property "subject to restrictions provided by general law" (Art. VI, Secs. 17, 23). The constitution also contains some specific prohibitions on municipalities as well; for example, they are prohibited from defining and providing punishment for felonies and from enacting ordinances governing private or civil relationships (Art. VI, Sec. 9).

Statutory provisions relating to municipal authority are extensive. Some of these provisions are general in application, affecting all municipalities or all within a particular population range regardless of the type of charter under which they are governed. Certain police powers, *i.e.*, powers to protect the public safety, health, and welfare, are granted in this fashion. Other provisions are associated with a specific type of charter. The Lawrason Act, for example, contains an extensive set of provisions applicable only to those municipalities chartered under it. The breadth of statutory authorizations varies tremendously. The Lawrason Act provides such broad grants of authority as "to make all police regulations necessary for the preservation of good order and the peace of the municipality" and "to secure the general health of the municipality" [L.R.S. 33:401 A(6)(8)]. It also provides such narrow grants as authority "to provide for the lighting of streets, parks and public grounds and the erection of lamps and lamp posts" and "to regulate and order the cleaning of chimneys" [L.R.S. 33:401 A(10), 402 (5)].

Municipal Revenue Sources

Municipalities in Louisiana are prohibited by statute from appropriating funds for a given year beyond the estimated revenue that they expect to receive during that year. Municipal revenues come from several sources, including municipal taxes and bonds and state and federal fiscal redistribution programs. Taxes may be levied only as specifically authorized by state law. The state constitution explicitly places the authority to tax with the state legislature (excluding self-operative constitutional provisions) but permits the legislature in turn to delegate that authority to municipalities (Art. VII, Sec. 1, Art. VI, Sec. 30). Municipalities, therefore, have both constitutional and statutory authority to raise revenue.

Some municipal taxes are authorized to support programs and services generally, while other taxes are dedicated to support only specified activities. General purpose taxes include the property tax, sales tax, occupational license tax, alcoholic beverage tax, and chain store tax. The basic special purpose taxes are the special property tax and special assessments for public improvements. The constitution specifically prohibits municipalities from imposing a severance tax, an income tax, a tax on motor fuel, a license fee on motor vehicles, and from conducting a lottery [Art. VIII, Secs. 4(c), 5; Art. XII, Sec. 6].

Authorization to levy property taxes for general purposes is contained in the constitution (Art. VI, Sec. 27). This provision establishes a basic authorization of seven mills and permits increases if approved by local voters. A new property tax system became effective under the constitution on January 1, 1978, however, and this limitation is now relatively meaningless. The constitution contains a "roll back–roll forward" provision requiring municipalities to adjust their millage rates upward or downward in 1978 without voter approval and without regard to the previously mentioned limitation so as to collect in 1978 the same amount of *ad valorem* taxes as received in 1977 (Art. III, Sec. 23). The rate thereby established then remains in effect unless changed with voter approval. Increased revenues due to additional millage levies, additional property placed on the tax rolls, and increases in property value, however, were permitted in 1978.

The new property tax system is established in the constitution (Art. VII, Sec. 18). Land and residential improvements are to be assessed at 10 percent of fair market value, all other property at 15 percent, except agricultural, horticultural, marsh, and timber lands, which are to be assessed at 10 percent of use value. Assessments (except on public service properties, which are assessed by the Louisiana Tax Commission) are determined by locally elected assessors according to procedures and criteria provided by statute. All property is to be reassessed at least every four years. The type of property which is to be exempt from municipal taxation is specified in Article VII, Section 21, which also prohibits additional, statutorily created exemptions from this tax.

Authorization for municipal sales and occupational license taxes is also contained in the constitution (Art. VI, Secs. 29, 28). A sales tax may be implemented only upon the approval of municipal voters and may not exceed 3 percent. The legislature may increase the amount of sales tax available to a municipality, but any increase must also be approved by the local electorate. Although the legislature has exempted certain items and services from state sales tax, it permits municipalities to tax them. Occupational license taxes may not be greater than those imposed by the state unless approved by a vote of two-thirds of the entire membership of each house of the state legislature. The various rates for the state taxes are established by statute, as are the specific exemptions from these taxes.

In addition to the constitutionally authorized general purpose taxes, municipalities have been granted statutory authorizations for an alcoholic beverage tax and a chain store tax. The beer tax is a tax on beverages low in alcoholic content. The tax on chain stores is a license fee, based on the number of stores in a chain, that may be required by municipalities.

The constitution authorizes the use of property taxes for special purposes as well as general (Art. VI, Sec. 27B). This permits additional millage to be levied for special purposes provided municipal voters approve a proposition specifying the purpose and duration of the tax. Special assessments on real property to offset the costs of public improvements are also authorized (Art. VI, Sec. 36). Procedures for levying and collecting these assessments are established by statute.

The major state programs for redistributing revenue back to local governments are the state Revenue Sharing Fund and the tobacco tax. The Revenue Sharing Fund, provided for in the constitution (Art. VII, Sec. 26), requires an annual allocation of $90 million from the state general fund and permits a larger appropriation at the discretion of the legislature. The money is to be distributed to local governments through a formula reflecting both population and number of homesteads. Municipalities receive money, however, only after deductions are made for retirement systems and lawfully authorized commissions, and after revenue losses due to homestead exemptions are offset for other tax recipient bodies, such as parishes. If the fund is not increased beyond $90 million, little if any money is likely to be left for distribution among municipalities. The statutorily based tobacco tax is a state-collected tax on cigars, cigarettes, and smoking tobacco, the proceeds from which are redistributed to municipalities on the basis of population. Municipalities also receive revenue from the federal government through federal revenue sharing, and may apply for additional federal funds through approximately 450 federal grant programs.

Municipalities in Louisiana may also borrow money either on a short-term basis or through the sale of long-term municipal bonds. Debts so incurred vary by the type of revenue sources through which they are secured and by whether or not the "full faith and credit" of the municipality is pledged to the payment of the debt. The various legal authorizations for borrowing money frequently require the approval of both municipal voters and the State Bond Commission before debts may be incurred.

Home Rule

Home rule has long been a favorite item on the agenda of civic reformers. Municipal home rule was first authorized by the Iowa legislature in 1851; the first constitutional authorization was in 1875 in Missouri. Today most states have some form of home rule for their municipalities. As a legal concept, home rule is an attempt to reduce the impact of Dillon's Rule upon municipalities by eliminating the persistent need for state authorization prior to acting upon local matters. Although they have varied from state to state, home rule provisions may be subsumed generally under two basic forms—*autonomy* provisions and *initiative* provisions.[18]

The initial home rule grants were autonomy-type provisions designed to separate governmental functions and responsibilities according to their statewide or local character. State governments were to have exclusive jurisdiction over statewide matters, while local governments would have jurisdiction over local matters. The language of these provisions theoretically freed municipal governments to act without specific authorization on "local affairs, property, and government" or "local and municipal matters."

Experience with the autonomy-type provisions has not proven satisfactory to many home rule advocates, however. The problem has been the imprecision of the state-local dichotomy upon which these provisions are based. Whether or not a particular function or responsibility is statewide or local is frequently debatable, and consequently, that issue has often become a matter for litigation. The determination is made, therefore, by the judiciary, and restrictive judicial attitudes in the tradition of Dillon's Rule have most often resulted in rulings against the local units. Under autonomy-type provisions, the freedom from state control has been restricted largely to "internal housekeeping matters," *i.e.*, structural arrangements for local governance. Indeed, one commentator has asserted that the judiciary has emasculated home rule under these provisions. Local government officials as a consequence "do not believe they can rely with confidence on their home rule powers as a source of authority, particularly with respect to new or unusual situations."[19]

Disturbed by the continuing judicial supervision of municipal powers under the autonomy provisions, many home rule advocates now support initiative-type provisions. These provisions are sometimes called Fordham plans after Jefferson B. Fordham, Dean Emeritus of the University of Pennsylvania Law School, who is generally recognized as

18. See Barkley Clark, "State Control of Local Government in Kansas: Special Legislation and Home Rule," *Kansas Law Review*, XX (Summer, 1972), 660.

19. *Ibid.*, 661; Harvey Walker, "Toward a New Theory of Municipal Home Rule," *Northwestern University Law Review*, L (November-December, 1955), 580; James E. Westbrook, "Municipal Home Rule: An Evaluation of the Missouri Experience," *Missouri Law Review*, XXXIII (Winter, 1968), 72. See also Kenneth E. Vanlandingham, "Municipal Home Rule in the United States," *William and Mary Law Review*, X (Winter, 1968), 293.

the principal author of this approach. Initiative provisions are designed to minimize the role of the judiciary in determining the apportionment of power by abandoning the state-local dichotomy and simply
granting municipalities all powers *not denied* by or *inconsistent* with
a state's constitution and statutes. Under this formula the state legislature in effect functions as the judge of local government action, and
the allocation of powers becomes more a political than a legal question.
The wisdom in switching from judicial to legislative control has not
gone unquestioned, however. Effective home rule under initiative-type
provisions depends upon a legislative climate favorable to municipalities, and as one of the leading students of home rule in this country
has stated, "On the basis of past and present experience such faith [in
the legislature] may be misplaced." Research in the state of New York
has led one author to conclude that the fundamental premise of this
approach—that municipalities will receive more favorable treatment
from state legislators than judges—is "overstated, if it is not, indeed,
incorrect." The experience of Kansas municipalities also suggests cau-
tion. After passage of an initiative-type constitutional amendment designed to broaden the taxing authority of municipalities, the state legislature immediately began to withdraw that authority and home rule
was left in "a shambles."[20] Reservations aside, initiative-type provisions are now generally preferred by most home rule advocates, and
have been endorsed by the National League of Cities and the National
Municipal League.

Because the adoption of home rule—under either of the formulas
discussed above—has not necessarily resulted in more flexible and responsive municipal government, the utility of the legal exercise has
been questioned. Not only have the attitudes of judges and legislators
at times inhibited its successful application but local officials have not
always demonstrated a desire to take advantage of the home rule option. And while home rule may to some extent reduce the state's control over local governments and increase their flexibility, its advantages
are tempered by the fact that home rule provisions seldom provide for
any significant expansion in the revenue-raising abilities of govern-

20. Kenneth E. Vanlandingham, "Constitutional Municipal Home Rule Since the
AMA (NLC) Model," *William and Mary Law Review*, XVII (Fall, 1975), 20; Frank J.
Macciarola, "Local Government Home Rule and the Judiciary," *Journal of Urban Law*,
XLVIII (1971), 340; Clark, "State Control of Local Government in Kansas," 679.

mental units. Although not all local governmental action requires a financial expenditure, the grant of home rule authority without that expansion in revenue-generating capacity has been characterized as "illusory," "a pie without a filling," and "an empty and futile gesture."[21]

There were three separate amendments to the Louisiana Constitution of 1921 providing municipalities with "home rule." The cities of Shreveport and New Orleans were the subjects of specific provisions adopted in 1948 and 1950 respectively, and a general provision applicable to all municipalities was added in 1952. Ten municipalities (the largest being Lafayette and Lake Charles) adopted home rule charters under the general provision. (See Table 8-6.) These provisions were of the autonomy type, allowing municipalities authority over "local affairs, property and government," although the grant was prefaced by a statement of state supremacy that stated: "The provisions of this constitution and of any general laws passed by the legislature shall be *paramount* and no municipality shall exercise any power or authority which is *inconsistent or in conflict therewith. Subject to the foregoing restrictions* every municipality shall have, in addition to the powers expressly conferred upon it, the additional right and authority to adopt and enforce local police, sanitary and similar regulations, and to do and perform all other acts pertaining to its local affairs, property and government which are necessary and proper in the legitimate exercise of its corporate powers and municipal functions." The special provision for New Orleans contained essentially the same grant of power as did the general provision: "The City of New Orleans, in addition to the powers expressly conferred upon it . . . shall have the right and authority to adopt and enforce local police, sanitary and similar regulations and to do and perform all acts pertaining to its local affairs, property and government, which are necessary or proper in the legitimate exercise of its corporate powers and municipal functions. The City of New Orleans shall, however, *not exercise any power or authority which is inconsistent or in conflict with any general law.*"[22]

21. See Rubin G. Cohn, "Municipal Revenue Powers in the Context of Constitutional Home Rule," *Northwestern University Law Review*, LI (March-April, 1956), 29, 32; Clark, "State Control of Local Government in Kansas," 678; and Vanlandingham, "Municipal Home Rule in the United States," 273.

22. Louisiana Constitution of 1921, Art. XIV, Secs. 40D, 22 (my italics).. The special constitutional provision for Shreveport (Art. XIV, Sec. 37) did not contain a statement of home rule powers, and such questions were litigated under the general provision. See

Table 8-6
Municipalities with Home Rule Charters Under the General
Provision of the 1921 Constitution

Baker (1970)	Kenner (1972)	Oak Grove (1966)
Berwick (1966)	Lafayette (1971)	Slidell (1969)
DeRidder (1962)	Lake Charles (1960)	West Monroe (1971)
Jennings (1972)		

Source: Files of the Louisiana Department of State, Election Division, as of March 7, 1974.

Louisiana's experience with this "home rule" provision was quite consistent with the experience of other states employing autonomy-type frameworks. Significant flexibility was provided in the area of governmental structure, but not in the exercise of municipal powers and certainly not in the realm of municipal taxation. Judicial attention was focused on the state-supremacy qualification while the "local affairs, property and government" clause was never the subject of interpretation. One student of the home rule experience under the old constitution has stated that "Louisiana courts declined to recognize any distinction between the laws related to matters of state-wide concern and those which related to matters of local concern as a means of restricting legislative supremacy over internal and purely local governmental affairs."[23] As a consequence, Louisiana's municipal officials had not perceived themselves as having successfully escaped Dillon's Rule.

The home rule provisions in the 1974 constitution however were "clearly drafted with the designed purpose of altering the relationship between the legislature and local government."[24] Louisiana is apparently the second state to have substituted an initiative provision for an autonomy provision in the state's constitution. The first state to do so was Missouri.[25] Louisiana's new home rule grant is a self-executing

City of Shreveport v. Baylock, 107 So.2d 419 (1958) and City of Shreveport v. Belk, 258 So.2d 79 (1972).

23. Kean, "Local Government and Home Rule," 65. See also Engstrom, "Home Rule in Louisiana," 441–44.

24. Kean, "Local Government and Home Rule," 64.

25. See Vanlandingham, "Constitutional Municipal Home Rule," 4, 28.

provision. Absent a home rule charter, a simple majority vote in a referendum may grant a municipality the right to "exercise any power and perform any function necessary, requisite, or proper for the management of its affairs, not denied by its charter or by general law" (Art. VI, Sec. 7). Municipalities are also permitted to adopt, again through a majority vote in a referendum, a home rule charter that may provide likewise for the "exercise of any power and performance of any function necessary, requisite, or proper for the management of its affairs, not denied by general law or inconsistent with this constitution" [Art. VI, Sec. 5(E)]. There are no limitations on the legislative and executive arrangements that may be adopted through a home rule charter, and the state legislature is prohibited from changing or altering that "structure and organization" [Art. VI, Sec. 5(E)]. Municipal authorities may either appoint a commission to draft a proposed charter or provide for the commission's election, and must so provide if an election is requested upon petition of 10 percent of the registered voters or ten thousand of them, whichever is fewer [Art. VI, Sec. 5(A) (B)].

These new home rule provisions are among the most potentially significant changes in Louisiana's political system brought about by the new constitution. The language contained in that document provides a good start toward effective home rule, but a true test awaits the responses of local officials, legislators, and judges.

There has not yet been a tremendous rush to adopt home rule charters. Only nine municipalities had been added to the home rule charter category by the end of 1978. One of the major stimuli for the recent home rule adoptions appears to be the vulnerability of at-large elections to judicial invalidation, discussed above. Seven of the nine recent adoptions have been in municipalities that previously elected their legislative bodies entirely at large but that switched to a combination of single-member districts and at-large seats under the new charter. Alexandria, for example, changed to five single-member districts and two at large; Natchitoches to four single-member districts and one at large. Six of these seven municipalities were abandoning the commission form of government. The switch from at-large elections to single-member districts has also been present in the adoption of new home rule charters by municipalities already having such charters. For example, Shreveport changed to a seven-member council elected entirely from districts when it abandoned the commission form of gov-

Table 8-7
New Home Rule Municipalities 1974–1978

Alexandria	Leesville
Bogalusa	Natchitoches
Bossier City	Thibodaux
Covington	Zachary
Donaldsonville	

ernment; similarly, Slidell went from an all at-large council to one with seven members from single-member districts and only two at-large when it switched from one home rule charter to another in 1977. Under the 1965 Voting Rights Act, the new districting schemes adopted in these municipalities had to be approved as racially nondiscriminatory by either the U.S. attorney general or the U.S. District Court for the District of Columbia before elections could be held.[26]

Efforts to adopt home rule charters have been unsuccessful in some municipalities, e.g., Delhi, Houma, Monroe, and Sulphur. A proposed home rule charter for Monroe was opposed by approximately 75 percent of those voting in a 1976 referendum. One major issue in switching from the commission plan to a modified mayor-council arrangement (two elected commissioner positions would have been retained but would have been subject to supervision by the mayor and could have been made appointive in the future) was the power granted to the mayor under the new scheme. As campaign advertisements demonstrate, differences in opinion on this issue were considerable and the rhetoric at times exaggerated. Opposition to the proposed charter by the two incumbent commissioners also added a personal dimension to the charter revision issue. Eugene Tarver, a political scientist at Northeast Louisiana University and a staff assistant to the charter commission, stated after the election, "Personalities that became involved in the ratification campaign obviously influenced the thinking of many of the voters. . . . I'll never really believe that the issue was debated on the merits of the proposed charter." The 44 percent turnout in the Monroe referendum suggests that the campaign did stimulate the interest of

26. See Richard L. Engstrom, "Racial Discrimination in the Electoral Process: The Voting Rights Act and the Vote Dilution Issue," in Robert P. Steed et al. (eds.), *Party Politics in the South* (New York: Praeger, 1980), 197–213.

TRUE FACTS ABOUT THE POWER OF THE MAYOR!

It has been questioned as to whether the mayor's power is increased or decreased under the proposed City of Monroe Home Rule Charter. The answer is, quite simply, that the mayor's power will be DECREASED! The "power" would be vested in the council. The mayor would only have the authority to carry out on a day-to-day basis that which the council directs. The mayor will have a veto, but can be overridden by two-thirds vote of the council. The mayor will have no vote at the council meetings, and will not preside at the council meetings. Cities which have adopted new charters within the past five or six years, such as Alexandria, Lafayette, Lake Charles, Baton Rouge, Natchitoches, West Monroe and others, have all provided their mayors with more control than is given that office in our proposed charter.

WATCH KNOE-T.V. CH. 8 REPORT TONIGHT 6:30 P.M.

VOTE YES TO THE HOME RULE CHARTER

Paid for by Committee for the Passage of Home Rule Charter, George M. Rorex, CHAIRMAN

Your Study of this group of Questions
and answers should indicate . . .

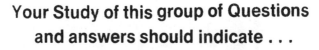

VOTE NO

on the proposed so called Home Rule Charter

drawn up by a hand - picked, political group, not elected by the voters.

Q. WHY DO WE NEED A NEW CHARTER?
A. PERHAPS MONROE NEEDS BROADER REPRESENTATION BUT WE DO NOT NEED THE FORM OF GOVERNMENT AS OUTLINED BY THE PROPOSED CHARTER. THIS IS NOT A TRULY DEMOCRATIC FORM OF GOVERNMENT BY THE PEOPLE . . . FOR THE PEOPLE. A FORM OF GOVERNMENT THAT GIVES THE MAYOR AN INORDINATE AMOUNT OF POWER . . . VIRTUALLY A DICTATOR.
Q. WHAT IS THE FUNCTION OF THE 9 MAN COUNCIL?
A. THIS 9 MAN COUNCIL WILL WORK APPROXIMATELY 2 HOURS PER MONTH AT A PAY OF $300 PER MONTH. WITHOUT DOUBT, THEY WILL BE BRIEFED ON ALL FUNCTIONS BY THE MAYOR AND WILL ACT ON HIS RECOMMENDATIONS. THE COUNCIL WILL ACT ON MATTERS SUBMITTED BY THE MAYOR.
Q. WHAT WILL THESE LEGISLATIVE COUNCILMEN COST THE TAX PAYERS OF THE CITY OF MONROE?
A. UNDER THE PRESENT FORM OF GOVERNMENT, BOTH THE LEGISLATIVE AND EXECUTIVE, THE SALARY COST IS $52,000 PER YEAR. UNDER THE PROPOSED FORM OF GOVERNMENT THE LEGISLATIVE AND EXECUTIVE SALARY COST WILL BE $104,900 AS A MINIMUM.
Q. WHAT IS THE FUNCTION OF THE MAYOR?
A. THE MAYOR WILL BE VIRTUALLY A DICTATOR SINCE HE SUPERVISES ALL DEPARTMENTS, OFFICES, AGENCIES . . . CAN FIRE ANYONE HE CHOOSES, CAN APPOINT AS MANY ADMINISTRATIVE AIDES AS HE WISHES AND CONTROLS EVERY FACET OF OUR CITY GOVERNMENT WHICH WOULD CREATE A POLITICAL EMPIRE. THIS PROPOSED CHARTER WOULD VIRTUALLY LEGISLATE A DICTATOR IN THE OFFICE OF THE MAYOR.

Q. WHAT HAPPENS IF THE PROPOSED CHARTER FAILS ON JAN. 24?
A. THE MAYOR AND 2 COMMISSIONERS HAVE ALREADY AGREED TO RE-CONVENE THE CHARTER REVISION COMMISSION. ACCORDING TO THE CITY ATTORNEY THEY COULD BE RE-CONVENED WITHIN 6 MONTHS AND MEET THE REQUIREMENTS OF THE STATE LAW UNDER WHICH THEY WERE APPOINTED. A NEW CHARTER COULD BE MADE A GOOD AND GREAT CHARTER . . . ONE THE PEOPLE COULD BE PROUD TO LIVE WITH FOR MANY YEARS TO COME.
JUDGE BEN DAWKINS, U.S. DISTRICT JUDGE, HAS ISSUED A STATEMENT TO THE EFFECT IT WOULD BE 2 TO 3 YEARS BEFORE ANY ACTION IS TAKEN RELATIVE TO THE CHANGE OF GOVERNMENT FOR THE CITY OF MONROE.
Q. WHY ARE THESE TWO COMMISSIONERS OPPOSING A CHARTER THAT WOULD GIVE THEM A HANDSOME INCREASE IN SALARY?
A. THE COMMISSIONERS ARE NOT OPPOSED TO A CHANGE IN THE FORM OF GOVERNMENT BUT ARE STRONGLY OPPOSED TO THE GOVERNMENT PROVIDED BY THE CHARTER WHICH GIVES AN INORDINATE AMOUNT OF POWER TO THE MAYOR AND UNDER THE PROVISIONS OF SECTION 4.09-4.10 THE MAYOR AND 9 COUNCILMEN CAN CHANGE THE ENTIRE CONCEPT OF GOVERNMENT WITHOUT THE VOTE OF THE PEOPLE.

VOTE NO TOMORROW

On the proposed so called Home Rule Charter

which has become too confusing and too politically controversial to be approved at this time.

Paid for by Citizens For Better Government, W. C. Sullivan. Chmn.

Monroe *Morning World*, January 21, 1976, Sec. A, p. 5.

THINK POSITIVE!
Before <u>You</u> Vote
Consider What Others
Have Decided

THOSE WHO ARE FOR THE HOME RULE CHARTER

Organizations & Businesses

- Monroe Chamber of Commerce
- Downtown Merchants Association
- Twin City Ministerial Alliance
- KMLB Radio
- Central Trades Council
- Monroe Morning World
- Monroe New Star
- Louisiana Republican Party
- Public Affairs Research Council (PAR staff)

Individuals

- Justice Jim Dennis
- Senator W.D. (Billy) Brown
- Dr. Eugene Tarver
- Robert Kirkham
- M. J. Cook
- Rev. H. M. Mitchell
- Wayne Parker
- Bobby Shafto

- Dr. Pat Garrett
- Pat Godfrey
- Louise Altick
- Willie Haynes
- Mrs. A. D. Tisdale
- George Rorex
- Dr. Doyle Hamilton
- Orville A. Renfrow
- Larry Holzer

REASON: None other than Good Government for the City of Monroe

THOSE WHO ARE AGAINST AND WHY:

- **Commissioner Harper** (loses authority & patronage)
- **Commissioner Prestridge** (loses authority & patronage)
- **James A. Noe** (defendant in suit by City to bring KNOE-TV within City)

JOIN THOSE ORGANIZATIONS AND INDIVIDUALS WHO ARE CONCERNED ONLY WITH BETTER GOVERNMENT FOR MONROE.

VOTE YES FOR OUR HOME RULE CHARTER

Paid for by Committee for the passage of Home Rule Charter. George M. Rorex, Chairman.

Monroe *Morning World*, January 3, 1976, Sec. A, p. 6.

local voters. Turnouts for home rule referenda in other municipalities unfortunately suggest that voters are often quite uninterested in charter revision. For example, the turnouts in the Delhi and Slidell referenda were only approximately 20 percent of the registered voters, while only 15 percent voted in Houma and approximately 10 percent in the Leesville and Bogalusa elections. A Bogalusa newspaper editorialized that people there "just didn't give a hoot."[27]

Whether the new home rule system will significantly expand the flexibility of municipal authorities to respond to community needs also depends heavily on state legislators and judges. State legislators are the primary guardians of municipal authority under initiative-type provisions, and they may withdraw much of that newly granted flexibility by enacting prohibitive legislation (called "no no" laws) denying municipalities authority to act on certain matters. And the judiciary will not be entirely avoided under the initiative arrangement. State judges may have to decide whether a particular exercise of power is in fact "necessary, requisite, or proper for the management of [municipal] affairs" and will certainly be required to resolve disputes over whether certain municipal activities are denied by or inconsistent with state law. It has been stated that "considerable jurisprudential interpretation" of the new provisions is to be expected and will be a major determinant of their success. In its first decision involving home rule powers, the Louisiana Supreme Court did recognize that the new constitution represented "a broad change" in state-local relations, but nonetheless invalidated a Shreveport ordinance punishing gambling because the definition of *gambling* in the ordinance was broader than the definition contained in state law.[28]

Metropolitan Governance Arrangements

Urban areas in the United States have not only been increasing in population; they have grown geographically as well. This population ex-

27. Eugene Tarver quoted in Marsanne Goldsby, "Voters Defeat Proposed Charter," Northeast Louisiana University *Pow-Wow*, January 30, 1976, p. 1; Editorial, Bogalusa *Daily News*, October 25, 1977, p. 4.
28. Kean, "Local Government and Home Rule," 64; *City of Shreveport* v. *Kaufman*, 353 So.2d 995 at 996 (1977).

pansion has been accompanied by a condition known as "governmental fragmentation," *i.e.*, a large number of local governmental units within a single metropolitan area. The United States Census Bureau has classified over 270 urban communities as Standard Metropolitan Statistical Areas (SMSAs). These generally consist of a central city with at least 50,000 residents and the surrounding counties (or parishes) that are socially and economically integrated with that central city. There are seven SMSAs in Louisiana. Lafayette, Lake Charles, and Monroe are single-parish SMSAs. The New Orleans SMSA includes Jefferson, St. Bernard, and St. Tammany parishes, as well as Orleans; the Baton Rouge SMSA includes adjoining West Baton Rouge, Livingston, and Ascension parishes; the Shreveport SMSA comprises Bossier, Webster, and Caddo parishes; and Grant and Rapides parishes make up the Alexandria SMSA.

Close to 70 percent of the nation's population lives within an SMSA and over half of these metropolitan residents now reside *outside* the central city. More people now live in suburban areas than live within central cities or in small towns and rural areas. This suburban growth is often closely associated with governmental fragmentation. The incorporation of municipalities along the urban fringe to meet the service demands of suburban residents (and often to prevent annexation by the central city), the absorption of small rural towns by the suburban dispersion, and the creation of special districts to perform specialized functions—all give the governmental map of a metropolitan area a patchwork character. The 1972 *Census of Governments* found 1,172 separate *local* governmental units within the Chicago SMSA, 852 in the Philadelphia SMSA, and 698 in the Pittsburgh SMSA. There were 27 other SMSAs with over 200 local governments within them. The average number of local governments within an SMSA was 84, consisting of two county governments, 30 special districts, 21 municipalities (*i.e.*, 20 municipalities, many of which would be quite small in terms of population, in addition to the central city), 18 independent school districts, and 13 townships (a unit of government not found in Louisiana).[29]

Metropolitan fragmentation has been criticized by many reform-

29. See United States Bureau of the Census, *Local Government in Metropolitan Areas*, Vol. V of *Census of Governments, 1972* (Washington, D.C.: U.S. Government Printing Office, 1974), Table 4.

Table 8-8

Numbers of Local Governments Within Louisiana SMSAs

Type of Government	Metropolitan Area						
	Alexandria	Baton Rouge	Lafayette	Lake Charles	Monroe	New Orleans	Shreveport
Parishes	1		1	1	1	3	2
Municipalities	9	3	6	6	3	14	15
Special Districts	12	2	7	28	6	21	11
School Districts	1	1	1	1	2	4	2
TOTAL	23	6	15	36	12	42	30

Source: United States Bureau of the Census, *Local Government in Metropolitan Areas*, Vol. V of *Census of Governments, 1972* (Washington, D.C.: U.S. Government Printing Office, 1974), Table 4, pp. 74–77.

minded individuals and groups as being uneconomical and inefficacious. Viewing a metropolitan area as an interdependent socioeconomic
unit, they point with alarm to the lack of coordination and cooperation
among units of local government. Specifically, they argue that it is an
inefficacious way to attack metropolis-wide problems such as crime,
pollution, or transportation. For example, when a municipal court
judge in New Orleans instructed vagrants to get out of town, city officials in neighboring Gretna complained that the vagrants simply
crossed the Mississippi River and relocated in their city. And disagree-
ments between officials of New Orleans and Jefferson Parish over
which should have priority, a metrowide transit authority or another
bridge across the Mississippi River, have hindered the development of
a more efficient transportation system for the New Orleans metropolitan area. Reformers further argue that the confusion generated by
jurisdictional fragmentation makes it difficult for the voters to hold
public officials accountable for conditions that afflict the entire metropolis. It is not easy to identify the set of political officials who should
be considered responsible for broad metropolitan problems or for failures arising from governmental action or inaction when jurisdictions
overlap and services are duplicated. Another argument of the reformers is that fragmentation is uneconomical, that multiple governmental
units providing the same or similar services do not take advantage of
economies of scale possible under a metrowide system. And some reformers also argue that the fragmented structure is inequitable. This
argument is usually advanced by those concerned with the decline of
the central city. It holds that central cities face the most demanding
social problems, yet suffer from a declining tax base as the white middle class moves to suburbia, followed by commercial and light industrial activities. Suburban wealth escapes central-city taxation, even
though suburbanites frequently utilize central-city facilities. Reformers find this situation inequitable and, again stressing the interdepen-
dency of a metropolitan population, often suggest to suburbanites that,
"if the city dies, the suburbs die with it."

These concerns with the fragmented situation have led to proposals
for massive restructuring of our metropolitan governance systems. A
metropolitan government, i.e., a multipurpose jurisdiction with metropolitan authority, would more effectively combat metropolitan problems, could take advantage of economies of scale, would have a legisla-

Byron Humphrey, New Orleans *States-Item*, December 18, 1976, Sec. A., p. 4.

tive body and chief executive easily held accountable, and would allow suburban tax dollars to be applied to central city needs.

While annexation may be utilized to expand a central city's jurisdiction in areas where fragmentation has not yet developed, reformers generally focus on consolidation or federation as means for achieving metro governments. Consolidation is the joining together of governmental units and usually takes the form of city-county consolidation. Efforts to consolidate have been concentrated largely in the South where metropolitan areas tend to be smaller and less fragmented. (Some have argued that this southern interest in consolidation is stimulated primarily by a desire to dilute the voting strength of central city minority populations.) Voter approval, however, has proven difficult to attain. Only about 10 percent of the consolidation proposals placed before voters during the 1970s received voter support. Areas where city-county proposals have been defeated recently include Augusta–Richmond County, Georgia; Charleston–Charleston County, South Carolina; and Durham–Durham County, North Carolina. Nashville–Davidson County, Tennessee, and Jacksonville–Duval County, Florida, are two of the largest areas to have consolidated.

Federation involves establishing a two-tier governance system. Some responsibilities are allocated to a metro-level governmental unit while others are retained by the existing municipalities and other local governmental units. Federated arrangements are usually suggested for areas in which existing fragmentation makes consolidation less feasible politically. Florida's Miami–Dade County two-tier system is the major example of a federated arrangement in the United States.

Louisiana's metropolitan areas, like those in the South generally, are significantly less fragmented than most SMSAs. Table 8-8 reports the number of local governments within each of Louisiana's seven SMSAs in 1972. As one would expect, the most fragmented was New Orleans with forty-two local governments, but this was a remarkably low figure in comparison with other SMSAs having populations of more than a million. The least fragmented was the Baton Rouge SMSA, which had only six governments. This was due largely to the fact that the City of Baton Rouge and East Baton Rouge Parish were consolidated in 1949, the first post–World War II city-county consolidation in the country. Technically, it was a partial rather than a complete consolidation, for the City of Baton Rouge is still recognized as a municipality for certain purposes, and the council members elected from within the city constitute a city council as well as serving on the larger parish council. Nevertheless, the Baton Rouge–East Baton Rouge Parish consolidation, authorized by a constitutional amendment in 1946 and narrowly approved by local voters in 1947, stimulated consolidation efforts in many other communities.[30] Another proposed constitutional amendment authorizing consolidation for Lafayette and Lafayette Parish was defeated in 1970 when it, along with fifty-two other proposed amend-

30. For a study of the adoption of this consolidation and a positive evaluation of its first few years of operation see William C. Havard and Floyd L. Corty, *Rural-Urban Consolidation: The Merger of Governments in the Baton Rouge Area* (Baton Rouge: Louisiana State University Press, 1964). The City of New Orleans and the Parish of Orleans were consolidated by the legislature in 1805, the first such governmental reorganization in the United States.

ments, failed to receive statewide ratification—even though it did receive the support of the voters in the Lafayette SMSA.

The 1974 Louisiana constitution, however, contains authorization for two or more governmental units within a parish to act jointly and adopt a home rule charter restructuring the existing units, provided a majority of voters in each affected unit approves [Art. VI, Sec. 5(D)]. This provision allows intergovernmental mergers such as city-parish consolidation to be adopted without prior statewide approval. As a consequence of this constitutional authorization, consolidation is back on the civic agenda in the Lafayette area. A charter commission was appointed in 1978 to study consolidation for that area, and if such a restructuring should occur it will undoubtedly stimulate other metropolitan areas in Louisiana to consider consolidation seriously. The new constitution also permits local governmental units to act together in performing any authorized functions or responsibilities (Art. VI, Sec. 20). This provision could increase the cooperation and coordination among various governmental units within Louisiana's metropolitan areas.

Municipal Governance Under the New Constitution— a Strengthened System?

Municipal government has generally occupied a prominent position within our normative political thought, but a subordinate position within our legal doctrines. Louisiana's municipalities, most of which are chartered under the Lawrason Act, have in the past operated within the context of legislative dominance. Even "home rule" municipalities could hardly be said to have escaped the restraints of Dillon's Rule in matters other than governmental structure under provisions of the old constitution. The new constitution, however, provides the potential for fulfilling the often shattered expectations of home rule advocates. The substitution of initiative for autonomy-type home rule powers, coupled with the authorization for interjurisdictional cooperation and restructuring and the expansion in constitutionally based revenue-generating authority, provides a foundation for a strengthened system of municipal governance in Louisiana. The alterations in the treatment of local government are clearly among the most significant changes in the state's new constitutional framework. Whether or not a strengthened system of municipal government is realized, however, depends on more than constitutional language. The attitudes and behavior of municipal officials, state legislators, and state judges will be crucial determinants of the shape of the future municipal governance system. The language of the new constitution provides the foundation for change. The response from those local officials, legislators, and judges will ultimately determine the nature of that change.

9.

Intergovernmental Relations

RILEY BAKER

Intergovernmental relations is a topic seldom discussed at the student union, on the golf course, or at the neighborhood bar. Yet this confusing web of relationships is both pervasive and significant. It is hoped that, by studying the legal relationship and some day-to-day examples of cooperation and failures to cooperate between one level of government and another, we will better understand and appreciate the effect of these relationships. The plan of this chapter is to describe various kinds of relationships between Louisiana and the central government, between the central government and local governments, between one state and another, between the state government and the local governments, and between city governments and parish governing bodies.

The mathematical possibilities for relationships between and among the units of government involved is staggering when one considers that we have 1 federal government with 13 departments, and scores of semiindependent regulatory commissions, corporations, and other agencies; 1 state government with 20 departments; 64 parishes; 287 cities; 6 school districts; and 419 other special districts.[1] Of course, not every city comes into contact with every parish in the state, nor does every school district interact with every parish or city. Nevertheless, the count of those relationships that are more likely to occur would exceed two thousand. We will attempt to discuss only a few representative examples.

1. Council of State Governments, *The Book of the States, 1974–75* (Lexington, Ky.: Council of State Governments, 1974), 299.

The Federal Principle—a Historical Perspective

One way to start untangling the maze of intergovernmental relationships is to review our political and constitutional history. In the beginning of our nation each state had a high degree of sovereignty—each had its own army, coined its own money, had authority to make treaties with foreign countries. In 1781 these states voluntarily allied themselves under the Articles of Confederation, but without relinquishing their powers. The central government was very weak—Congress could make no laws, there was no executive branch, and there were no permanent national courts. The states continued to perform the major service and regulatory functions, and the central government was merely a place where the state delegates could discuss their common problems, such as national defense and foreign trade. Many people distrusted strong central government, but it soon became clear that the Articles of Confederation provided an unsatisfactory solution. In 1787 a convention was called to consider revising the Articles of Confederation. What resulted from this convention, after considerable debate and compromise, was a draft constitution that contained, among other things, the federal principle.

The motivation behind the adoption of federalism has long been debated. Some have argued that the Founding Fathers considered all of the possible types of organizational arrangements, both actual and theoretical, and chose the best form as dictated by logic. Even though this explanation has some intuitive and emotional appeal, it lacks the support of historical evidence. Another well-known explanation is that of Charles A. Beard, who caused quite a stir when he suggested that the constitution was drafted by an economic elite who were primarily concerned with preserving their property. Beard's critics have accused him of exaggerating the unity of the economic elite. The explanation that I find most convincing is contained in a brilliant essay written almost twenty years ago by John P. Roche. He argued that, considering the unhappy experience with the central government under the Articles of Confederation, it was not surprising that there was a movement to strengthen the central government. The choice considered by the delegates to the convention was between a unitary and federal organizational structure. A majority of the delegates, including Hamilton and Madison, actually favored the strongest form of central government (unitary). Because they were practical politicians, however, they realized that the public would reject a unitary system; therefore they opted for the form that would meet less opposition—federalism. In this light, federalism seems to have resulted from pragmatic compromise, not from the selection of what a group of near-saints (or near-devils) thought was an ideal type. Historic or ethnic factors have led to adoption of the federal principle in many large, heterogeneous nations that "sought effective unity on common problems but individuality in local affairs."[2]

The fundamental law drafted at the constitutional convention provided for a very complicated system of relationships between the central government and the states and for a somewhat ambiguous distribution of functions. Its organizational structure was a compromise between an all-powerful central government and a confederation of all-powerful states. The Constitution vested sovereignty not in the states nor in the national government, but in the people. It established two separate but united levels of government, each with its own law-making body, courts, and executive branch. Each level of government had the power to act directly upon private individuals, but constitutional safeguards limited the powers of each.[3] In spite of its ambiguity and potential for misunderstanding and dispute, the Constitution was ratified by conventions held in each of the states and has endured an exceptionally long time with relatively few formal amendments.

Federal-State Relations

Constitutional Provisions

One of the basic concepts of the United States Constitution is popular sovereignty, the ideal that government as no inherent powers but

2. Charles A. Beard, *An Economic Interpretation of the Constitution of the United States* (New York: Macmillan, 1913); Forrest McDonald, *We the People: The Economic Origins of the Constitution* (Chicago: University of Chicago Press, 1958); Robert E. Brown, *Charles Beard and the Constitution* (Princeton: Princeton University Press, 1956); John P. Roche, "The Founding Fathers: A Reform Caucus in Action," *American Political Science Review*, LV (December, 1961), 799; John H. Ferguson and Dean E. McHenry, *The American Federal Government* (New York: McGraw-Hill, 1977), 102.

3. For general explanations of federalism, see Daniel J. Elazar, *American Federalism: A View From the States* (New York: Thomas Y. Crowell, 1972); W. Brooke Graves, *Ameri-*

is created by the consent of the governed and has only those powers granted by the people. In theory several arrangements were possible by which these powers could have been implemented. All power could have been vested in the central government, for example. The Constitution of 1789 created a type of union in which power was divided or shared between two levels of government.

The formula for the division (or sharing) of powers is contained in the Tenth Amendment: "The powers not delegated to the United States by the Constitution, nor prohibited by it to the States, are reserved to the States respectively, or to the people." Article I, Section 8 lists the powers delegated to the central government, and in addition to the powers specifically listed, Congress also has power "to make all laws which shall be necessary and proper for carrying into execution" those powers. The Supreme Court upheld the use of implied powers in the *McCulloch* v. *Maryland* case in 1819. [4] The federal and state governments share certain so-called concurrent powers, such as the power to levy taxes, borrow money, establish courts, and build roads. Other powers belong exclusively to the federal government and are specifically denied the states. The Constitution prohibits states from making treaties with foreign countries, entering into compacts with other states without prior consent of Congress, coining money, raising armies, impairing the obligation of contracts, and taxing imports. In addition to these restrictions contained in the main body of the Constitution, several of the amendments place restrictions on the states. For example, the Fourteenth Amendment prohibits a state from using race as a condition to deny citizenship to persons born in the state. The amendment goes on to further restrict the power of the states when it declares: "No State shall make or enforce any law which shall abridge the privileges or immunities of citizens of the United States; nor shall any State deprive any person of life, liberty or property, without due process of law; nor deny to any person within its jurisdiction the equal protection of the laws." The Fifteenth, Sixteenth, and Nineteenth amendments place other restrictions upon state suffrage requirements.

---

can *Intergovernmental Relations: Their Origins, Historical Development and Current Status* (New York: Charles Scribner's Sons, 1964); Morton Grodzins, *The American System: A New View of Government in the United States* (Chicago: Rand McNally, 1966); Aaron Wildavsky (ed.), *American Federalism in Perspective* (Boston: Little, Brown, 1967).

4. *McCulloch* v. *Maryland*, 4 Wheat. 315 (1819).

The U.S. Constitution guarantees the states territorial integrity, equal representation in the Senate, a republican form of government, no taxation on exports, equal taxation on imports at all ports, and defense from foreign invasion or domestic violence. Some of these constitutional promises are self explanatory, but perhaps a few words of explanation are appropriate for some of the items in this list. *Territorial integrity* means that the central government will not subdivide a state without its permission. A *republican form of government* is not defined in the Constitution, but probably includes, at a minimum, the selection of government officials by the voters and a peaceful and orderly method of succession without hereditary rulers. On two separate occasions the Supreme Court has been called upon for an official interpretation of this phrase, but only partial clarification was forthcoming. [5] Its precise and full meaning remains unsettled.

Since the states are prohibited from raising their own armies, it is reassuring to know that the central government is to come to the defense of states invaded by a foreign power, but the other part of the promise—protection from domestic violence—may be a mixed blessing. It was once thought that the central government would send aid to a state in case of domestic violence such as a riot only if the state and local law enforcement officials were unable to cope with the problem *and* upon the request of the governor of the state. But as early as 1895, President Grover Cleveland sent federal troops to bring order in the Pullman strike even though the governor of Illinois had not requested and did not want assistance. In Little Rock in 1957, Governor Faubus called out the Arkansas National Guard to enforce racial segregation of the public schools, only to have President Eisenhower nationalize the Arkansas National Guard and use the same troops to achieve a purpose diametrically opposed to the wishes of the governor. [6]

Changing Relationships

CHANGE THROUGH CONSTITUTIONAL AMENDMENTS   Since 1789 there have been twenty-six amendments to the Constitution. The first ten amendments, collectively known as the Bill of Rights, were added in

5. *Luther* v. *Borden*, 7 How. 1 (1849); *Pacific States Telephone and Telegraph Co.* v. *Oregon*, 223 U.S. 118 (1912).
6. *In re Debs*, 158 U.S. 564 (1895); *Cooper* v. *Aaron*, 358 U.S. 1 (1958).

1791 to guarantee the rights of citizens against arbitrary and unreasonable actions of agents of the federal government. These amendments were intended as clarifications, not as modifications of the intent of the main body of the Constitution. Of the remaining sixteen amendments, eleven modify the federal-state relationship to some extent.

The original Constitution did not mention which court was to have jurisdiction when a private individual sued a state. In 1793 the United States Supreme Court accepted a suit by Mr. Chisholm suing the state of Georgia. The justices explained that they were obligated to accept this suit because of Article III, Section 2, of the Constitution, which states that any case to which a state is a party shall originate in the Supreme Court.[7] There was such an outcry from Georgia and other states that did not want to be haled into a "foreign" court, that the Constitution was amended in 1798 to deprive the federal courts of jurisdiction in cases where a state was being sued by "Citizens of another State, or by Citizens or Subjects of any Foreign State." Since passage of the Eleventh Amendment an individual must bring his suit in the courts of the state being sued (if the state will grant its permission).

The so-called Civil War amendments—Thirteenth (citizenship), Fourteenth (due process of law and equal protection), and Fifteenth (suffrage)—limit the power of the states in a number of important ways. The most significant of the restrictions, contained in the Fourteenth Amendment, prohibit the states from denying persons due process and equal protection of the law. The Seventeenth Amendment, which changed the method of selecting United States senators, reflected the overall shifting in the relationship between the central government and the states. For a time the authority to control the manufacture, sale, and transportation of intoxicating beverages was transferred to the central government (by Amendment XVIII), but this transfer of authority was subsequently revoked (by Amendment XXI). Still later amendments prevented other discriminatory state requirements for voting. The Nineteenth Amendment granted suffrage to women, the Twenty-fourth Amendment prohibited poll taxes in federal elections, and the Twenty-sixth Amendment set the voting age at eighteen.

Amendment XVI has, perhaps, done more to change the federal-

7. *Chisholm* v. *Georgia*, 2 Dall. 419 (1793).

state relationship than any other amendment. Since it was ratified in 1913, the central government has had the authority to levy taxes on incomes, making the income tax the largest single source of revenue, and causing the revenue-raising potential of the central government to increase at a faster rate than that of the states. With this added revenue the central government has been able to "encourage" states to undertake programs that they do not have enough money to finance by themselves or, to put it another way, to buy compliance with national policy. Specifics of this enormous intergovernmental transfer of funds will be discussed later.

CHANGE THROUGH CONGRESSIONAL INTERPRETATION Although Congress can legislate only on those subjects mentioned or reasonably implied in Article I, Section 8, it has considerable discretion. Ultimately the Supreme Court defines the scope of that discretion. There have been numerous examples of federal agencies being created to perform regulatory functions that were previously performed either exclusively by state agencies or not at all. More often than not, Congress has cited as its authority to create these agencies not a grant of power in a new amendment, but a new interpretation of an old clause of the Constitution.

If a comprehensive list of examples of the use of this method to change the federal-state relationship were made, probably the most frequently mentioned clause would be the commerce clause. Article I, Section 8, makes clear that only Congress has authority to regulate interstate and foreign commerce. But the Constitution leaves the task of defining *among the states* and *commerce* to Congress, the courts, and executive agencies.

Originally, *commerce* was thought to include only buying and selling, and the central government could regulate it only if this activity occurred across state lines. In time, the meaning of the term was expanded, on a case-by-case basis, to include first navigation, then other forms of transportation, and eventually communication.[8] Federal regulation of firms that transport goods across state lines, such as railroads, trucks, buses, airlines, and pipelines, is based upon this interpretation of the commerce clause even though these industries are not

8. *Gibbons* v. *Ogden*, 9 Wheat. 1 (1824); *Pensacola Tel. & Tel. Co.* v. *Western Union*, 96 U.S. 1 (1878).

mentioned and did not exist when the word *commerce* was inserted in the Constitution. A similar justification can be given for federal authority to control telephone, telegraph, radio, and television. The power of the central government increased as the scope of these businesses grew.

There are many other examples of the growth of federal power by means of expanded interpretation of the commerce clause. In 1937 the Supreme Court upheld federal regulation of labor-management relations and, a few years after, federal regulation of agricultural production—both based upon their influence on the flow of interstate commerce. Beginning in 1964, various federal civil rights laws based upon the commerce clause have been upheld by the Supreme Court.[9]

More recently, proponents of states' rights sustained another telling blow when the Supreme Court upheld the Economic Stabilization Act of 1970, which was also based on the commerce clause. The Court ruled that states were not exempt from the limitations upon wage increases contained in the law. The most interesting remark in the *Fry* case appears in a footnote: "Petitioners have stated their argument, not in terms of the Commerce power, but in terms of the limitations on that power imposed by the Tenth Amendment. While the Tenth Amendment has been characterized as a 'truism,' stating namely that 'all is retained which has not been surrendered,' United States v. Darby, 312 U.S. 100, 124 (1941), it is not without significance. The Amendment expressly declares the constitutional policy that Congress may not exercise power in a fashion that impairs the States' integrity or their ability to function effectively in a federal system."[10] This remark was borne out just a few months later by the decision in *National League of Cities* v. *Usery*. In this landmark decision the Supreme Court rendered inoperable the 1974 amendments to the Fair Labor Standards Act of 1938, which expanded coverage of the law to include state and local government employees. The court agreed with the contentions of the National League of Cities that the authority conferred upon Congress by the commerce clause was broad but not limitless and that, in this instance, the federal statute would not only be disruptive of the em-

9. *N.L.R.B.* v. *Jones & Laughlin Steel Corp.*, 301 U.S. 1 (1937); *Wickard* v. *Filburn*, 317 U.S. 111 (1942); *Heart of Atlanta Motel* v. *United States*, 379 U.S. 241 (1964); *Katzenbach* v. *McClung*, 379 U.S. 294 (1964).
10. *Fry* v. *United States*, 421 U.S. 542 (1975), 547, n. 7.

ployment practices of the states but also constitute an unreasonable encroachment upon state sovereignty.[11]

CHANGE THROUGH JUDICIAL INTERPRETATION   In addition to determining whether statutes passed by Congress exceed constitutional authority, the Supreme Court has contributed to the alteration of the federal-state relationship in still other ways. For more than one hundred years the Supreme Court held that the rights guaranteed by the Bill of Rights did not apply to states. But in 1925 the Court declared for the first time that freedom of speech, as mentioned in the First Amendment, placed restrictions upon state government officials. In a series of cases since 1925, the Court has reconsidered the applicability of first one and then another of the amendments in the Bill of Rights, so that the cumulative effect has been to extend the applicability of almost all of them to state as well as federal officials.[12]

During the past twenty-five years, we have witnessed far-reaching changes based upon new applications of the equal-protection and due-process clauses of the Fourteenth Amendment. *Brown* v. *Board of Education* (1954) is a prime example of expanded utilization of the equal-protection clause. The redistricting cases beginning with *Baker* v. *Carr* in 1962 were also based upon a new interpretation of the equal-protection clause. The decisions in these cases had broad effects, including changing both the urban-rural balance and the racial composition of state legislative and U.S. congressional districts, as well as city council, police jury, and school board electoral districts. In the 1960s the Warren Court made significant changes in judicial procedure by insisting that the *states* honor the constitutional guarantees of due process, such as trial by jury and the right to counsel, and the bans on self-incrimination and unreasonable search and seizure.[13]

---

11. *National League of Cities* v. *Usery*, 426 U.S. 833 (1976).
12. *Barron* v. *Baltimore*, 7 Pet. 243 (1833); *Slaughter-House Cases*, 16 Wall. 36 (1873); *Gitlow* v. *New York*, 268 U.S. 652 (1925); *Near* v. *Minnesota*, 283 U.S. 697 (1931); *Palko* v. *Connecticut*, 302 U.S. 319 (1937); *Terminiello* v. *Chicago*, 337 U.S. 1 (1949); *Yates* v. *United States*, 354 U.S. 298 (1957); *Engel* v. *Vitale*, 370 U.S. 421 (1962).
13. *Brown* v. *Board of Education*, 347 U.S. 483 (1954); *Baker* v. *Carr*, 369 U.S. 186 (1962); *Reynolds* v. *Sims*, 377 U.S. 533 (1964); *Wesberry* v. *Sanders*, 376 U.S. 1 (1964); *Mapp* v. *Ohio*, 367 U.S. 643 (1961); *Gideon* v. *Wainwright*, 372 U.S. 235 (1963); *Escobedo* v. *Illinois*, 378 U.S. 478 (1964); *Miranda* v. *Arizona*, 384 U.S. 436 (1966).

FEDERAL-STATE FINANCIAL RELATIONSHIPS   The central government extends financial aid to the states, in several forms, including contractual arrangements, payment in lieu of taxes, tax offsets, categoric grants, and general revenue sharing.

The central government contracts with the state of Louisiana for certain services. For example, the United States Employment Service contracts with the Louisiana Office of Employment Security to conduct three programs for the federal government: Unemployment Compensation for Federal Employees, the Work Incentive Program, and the Comprehensive Employment and Training Act program. Another source of federal revenue for some states is known as payment in lieu of taxes. The decision in the *McCulloch* v. *Maryland* case prohibits a state from taxing any federal agency; however, Congress does make voluntary grants to reimburse states for the loss of property tax revenue on large federal holdings, such as military installations, national parks, and lakes administered by the federal government. Some payments in lieu of taxes have been made to parishes, but at present the central government makes no such payments to the State of Louisiana because the state government has not collected *ad valorem* taxes since 1972.

A *tax offset* illustrates how the federal taxing power has been used to alter the federal-state relationship. For example, when the Wagner-Peyser Act was enacted in 1933 it provided for a tax of 3 percent on the payroll of all employers of four or more persons. This tax was to be collected by the federal government, and there would be virtually no direct benefit to states that did not have unemployment compensation programs. However, if a state "voluntarily" created an unemployment compensation program, it could collect a tax of up to 2.7 percent of each subject employer's payroll, and the central government would collect only .3 percent. In other words the employer's payment to the state *offset* 90 percent of his federal unemployment tax liability. Naturally, all of the states "voluntarily" joined the program. In practice, Louisiana uses its portion of the taxes to make payments to eligible claimants, and the federal government uses its portion to operate the United States Employment Service and to reimburse the states for salaries and other administrative expenses.

Another example of a tax-offset relationship between the federal government and the state of Louisiana involves the collection of inheritance taxes. The federal Bureau of Internal Revenue gives partial credit for the inheritance tax paid to the state, thereby reducing the federal tax obligation of the individual taxpayer.

Federal grants to states have increased from $3 million in 1902 to more than $54 billion in 1979. In 1902 only 1.5 percent of the total revenue of all of the states was derived from federal grants-in-aid; by 1927 the comparable figure was still only 5 percent. The big jump came between 1932 and 1934, when such revenue soared from 9.2 percent to 29.0 percent. By the 1940s federal aid had increased to more than $5 billion but, even so, had declined to about 15 percent of total state revenue. During the 1950s state government reliance upon federal aid edged up slightly to about 17 percent. The following decade saw federal aid fluctuate between 20 and 25 percent of total state revenues, and the latest figure available, for the 1979 fiscal year, shows federal aid to states at 26.2 percent.[14]

At first glance the figures look alarming. Not only has the amount of federal aid to the state increased astronomically (by almost ninety times in just thirty-nine years) but the percentage of total state revenue derived from federal aid has more than doubled during the same period. However, more careful examination shows that Louisiana is not more dependent upon federal aid than the average state, and that federal aid as a percentage of total state revenue has not increased appreciably during the past twenty years. In 1979 Louisiana received $1.110 billion (27.3 percent of its general revenue) from federal aid, which was only slightly more than the national average of 26.2 percent. Louisiana's federal aid amounted to $276 per capita in 1979, as compared to the national average of $249.[15]

For what have these federal grants been used? In the 1940s public welfare, highways, and education were the big three; in fact, three-fourths of all federal aid to Louisiana was spent on these three programs. During the 1950s the amount of federal aid for the big three

14. U.S. Bureau of the Census, *Historical Statistics of the United States* (Washington, D.C.: U.S. Government Printing Office, 1975), 1,129; U.S. Bureau of the Census, *State Government Finances in 1979* (Washington, D.C.: U.S. Government Printing Office, 1980), 23.
15. Census Bureau, *State Government Finances in 1979*, 12–14.

Table 9-1

Percentages of Louisiana General Revenue Derived from Federal Aid, 1940–1979

Date	General Revenue (In Thousands)	Federal Aid (In Thousands)	Percentage
1940	$ 102,915	$ 12,397	12.0
1945	145,317	16,554	11.4
1950	363,766	78,764	21.7
1955	539,286	88,983	16.5
1960	768,125	200,425	26.1
1965	1,046,937	284,697	27.2
1970	1,542,279	410,793	26.6
1971	1,761,337	453,232	25.8
1972	1,978,428	521,623	26.4
1973	2,126,479	573,133	27.0
1974	2,376,006	612,744	25.8
1975	2,609,465	673,195	25.8
1976	3,092,100	815,654	26.4
1977	3,216,145	966,730	30.0
1978	3,670,852	1,050,687	28.6
1979	4,063,072	1,110,296	27.3

Source: 1940 to 1975 data from James R. Bobo and Harris S. Segal (eds.), *Statistical Abstract of Louisiana* (6th ed.; New Orleans: Division of Business and Economic Research, College of Business Administration, University of New Orleans, 1977), 313; 1976 to 1979 from U.S. Bureau of the Census, *State Government Finances in 1976*, p. 18, *in 1977*, p. 18, *in 1978*, p. 27, and *in 1979*, p. 27.

combined increased to about 80 percent of the total, with the largest amount of increase attributable to public welfare. During the 1960s, federal aid for the big three was close to 90 percent of the total. Welfare had doubled as an aggregate amount but declined as a percentage. By the second half of the 1970s the big three accounted for only 75 percent of federal aid to Louisiana. Public welfare and highways had each declined slightly as a percentage of the total, while education had increased substantially. The 1979 distribution of federal aid to the five largest functions was as follows: public welfare, 36 percent; education, 21 percent; highways, 17 percent; health and hospitals, 4 percent; and general revenue sharing, 4 percent. The remaining 18 percent was scattered among many other smaller programs (none of which amounted to more than 2 percent).[16]

The potential effect of this aid upon federal-state relations seems obvious. Those state programs that are heavily dependent upon aid are vulnerable to threats that federal funds will be cut off. For example, Title V of the Civil Rights Act of 1964 authorizes the Department of Health, Education, and Welfare (now the Department of Education) to withhold federal funds as a means of enforcing racial desegregation of public schools.

VOLUNTARY COOPERATION   In numerous instances state agencies and their national counterparts voluntarily work together to achieve common goals. The Bureau of Public Roads in the Department of Transportation has frequent, often daily contacts with the Office of Highways of Louisiana. Information is requested and given; plans are discussed. The Federal Bureau of Investigation has no control over the state police, but the two agencies assist each other in many ways. Louisiana officials responsible for administering health programs exchange information with the U.S. Public Health Service. State and federal interests are parallel in areas such as environmental quality, consumer protection, and wildlife conservation. As further evidence of interest in prompting more amicable relations, in 1975 Governor Edwin W. Edwards created the Office of Federal Affairs and charged it with improving federal-state relations.

In spite of a great deal of voluntary federal-state cooperation, there have been occasional disputes between state and federal agencies. Governor Edwards made front-page news in 1978 when he criticized the natural gas allocation policies of the Federal Power Commission. In late 1980 and early 1981 a state judge and a federal judge engaged in a highly publicized and bitter jurisdictional dispute over school busing. But there are many more examples of federal-state cooperation than there are examples of conflict.

16. The data for 1976–77 is taken from U.S. Bureau of the Census, *Governmental Finances, 1976–77* (Washington, D.C.: U.S. Government Printing Office, 1978).

Federal-Local Relations

Strictly speaking, the federal union consists exclusively of the states, and cities and parishes are creatures of the state. However, on a day-to-day basis, officials of local units of government operate with a great deal of autonomy, encountering little interference from either state or federal officials. City councils and police juries are accountable to local voters and, therefore, pay more attention to local public opinion than to state or national priorities. Nevertheless, during recent years local government officials have begun to turn to the central government for financial assistance. Federal aid to local governments was small prior to 1970, and even though it increased from $4 million in 1902 to $2.6 billion in 1970, federal aid still constituted only 2.9 percent of the total local government revenue in 1970.[17] During the ten years since 1970, however, there has been an extraordinary increase in the amount of federal aid to local governments.

Federal Grants-in-Aid to Parishes

The exact amount of federal aid to counties in 1970 was not reported by the Bureau of the Census, but apparently it was very small (less than $1 billion of the total county revenues of $17.7 billion). This conjecture is based on the fact that total federal aid to all units of local government, including counties, municipalities, school districts, and others amounted to only $2.6 billion in 1970.[18]

By 1979 there was a tremendous increase in federal aid to counties. The aid amounted to $4.9 billion, which was 9.8 percent of total county revenue. It is uncertain what caused this jump in federal aid to local governments in such a relatively short period of time. Some attribute the increase to the general revenue sharing associated with the "New Federalism," but of the $4.9 billion in federal aid received by counties nationwide in 1979, only $1.7 billion (or 3.5 percent of total county revenue) was in the form of general revenue sharing.[19] Much of the increase has actually been in the form of categoric grants.

17. Bureau of the Census, *Historical Statistics,* 1,133.
18. U.S. Bureau of the Census, *Governmental Finances, 1969–70* (Washington, D.C.: U.S. Government Printing Office, 1971), 20.
19. U.S. Bureau of the Census, *County Government Finances, 1978–79* (Washing-

Parishes in Louisiana are more dependent upon federal aid than are counties in most other states. Total federal aid to all parishes in Louisiana in 1979 amounted to $107.4 million (12.5 percent of total parish revenue as compared to 9.8 percent for the national average).[20] Although general revenue-sharing money is distributed on the basis of a formula that takes population into account, the percentage of the revenue each parish derives from federal aid varies widely because parishes apply for differing combinations of categoric grants.

Utilization of the federal funds also varies from parish to parish depending on the purpose of the grant application. In general the largest amounts have gone for parish roads, police protection, and health and hospitals. Louisiana differs from the national average in this respect, for two of the largest county expenditures in some states (education and welfare) are not financed directly by parishes in this state. General revenue-sharing money in Louisiana is used primarily for capital improvements and nonrecurring expenditures.

Federal Grants-in-Aid to Municipalities

Federal aid to cities increased from $557 million (2.7 percent of total revenue) in 1965 to $10.8 billion (15.4 percent of total revenue) in 1979. This increase was not solely attributable to revenue sharing. General revenue sharing in 1978 was $1.6 billion nationwide, or 4.0 percent of the total general revenue of the cities. Although the amount of general revenue sharing increased during the succeeding six years, the percentage of municipal revenue derived from general revenue sharing remained about the same.[21] We can conclude, therefore, that the significant increase in federal aid to municipal governments during the past fifteen years has been largely in the form of increased categoric grants, rather than unrestricted block grants.

It may come as a surprise to some that municipalities currently re-

ton, D.C.: U.S. Government Printing Office, 1980), 5; U.S. Bureau of the Census, *Governmental Finances in 1978–79* (Washington, D.C.: U.S. Government Printing Office, 1980), 64.

20. Census Bureau, *Governmental Finances in 1978–79*, 73.

21. *Ibid*; U.S. Bureau of the Census, *City Government Finances in 1975–76* (Washington, D.C.: U.S. Government Printing Office, 1977), 5; U.S. Bureau of the Census, *City Government Finances in 1978–79* (Washington, D.C.: U.S. Government Printing Office, 1980).

ceive considerably more state aid than federal aid. According to the Bureau of the Census, American cities received about $15.5 billion from state governments in 1979 (22.0 percent of their total revenue), as compared to $10.8 billion (15.4 percent of their total revenue) from the federal government. Federal aid to cities in the Pelican State amounted to $237.9 million (or 27.8 percent of municipal revenue) in 1979. Comparable data for years prior to 1975 are not readily available, but it appears that Louisiana cities are becoming increasingly dependent upon federal aid—in 1975 federal aid to Louisiana cities was 19.3 percent of municipal revenues; in 1979 it was 27.8 percent. We also know that Louisiana cities are more dependent upon federal aid than the national average, for they received 27.8 percent of their general revenue from federal aid in 1979, but the national average for such aid was only 15.4 percent.[22]

In the 1940s and 1950s federal grants to Louisiana cities were small, and the funds so derived were used chiefly for airport construction or improvement and for the construction of a limited number of public housing units. During the 1960s, the number of federally funded programs for cities increased, but few Louisiana cities applied for the funds. Even today, the degree of participation varies greatly from city to city within Louisiana.

Three types of financial assistance are available for cities from the federal government. First, there are more than a thousand different categoric grants for which a city may apply. Second, there are the limited purpose block grants—such as the Community Development Grants administered by the Department of Housing and Urban Development. These grants can be used for a wider range of projects, such as drainage and sewerage treatments, as long as they will benefit the low-income areas of a city. Finally, since general revenue sharing began in 1972, each city is entitled to its share of the more than $2 billion in unrestricted block grants. These funds are automatically distributed according to a formula combining population, tax effort, and income. Ruston, Louisiana, for example, a city of approximately 23,000 people, received $304,177 (9.7 percent of its total revenue) in 1979.[23]

22. Census Bureau, *City Government Finances in 1978–79*, 7; Census Bureau, *Governmental Finances in 1978–79*, 73.
23. Ruston *Daily Leader*, December 31, 1979, pp. 14–16.

Coordinating Agencies

Prior to 1966 each city and parish in Louisiana was on its own when trying to obtain federal funds. Since that time three types of agencies have been created to make local governments aware of available federal funds, to aid them in making application, and to provide coordinating and other technical services. The first of these were the Councils of Government (COG) that were created in the seven Standard Metropolitan Statistical Areas (SMSAs) of the state in response to the Demonstration Cities and Metropolitan Development Act passed by Congress in 1966. The councils serve as areawide planning agencies to review all applications for federal funds as required by Section 204 of the act.[24]

The second type of agency was created by the Public Works and Economic Development Act of 1965. This federal law made money available to pay the administrative costs of areawide coordination and development agencies within each state. By 1968 eight such agencies had been created in Louisiana to review aid applications and to provide other services for those portions of the state outside the area served by the COG organizations. The following list of activities of the Coordinating and Development Council of Northwest Louisiana in 1977 is typical:

1) the Northwest Regional Clearinghouse reviewed more than five hundred applications from local governments for categoric grants for more than $37 million in federal funds (in addition to $47.8 million in SA-COG)

2) the Council reviewed the applications of nine cities and three parishes in the region for a total of more than $1.5 million in Community Development bloc [sic] grants

3) the Manpower Division of the Council administered the Work Experience Program (with funds provided by the U.S. Labor Department) which provided training for 873 adults, and summer jobs for 1400 youths

4) the Economic Development Division of the Council worked with local government officials in the ten parish area to obtain

24. Shreveport Area Council of Government, *Profile* (Shreveport: Shreveport Area Council of Government, 1976); the clearance procedure was further developed by the Office of Management and Budget, "Circular No. A-95," July, 1969.

$7.1 million in Public Works and Economic Development grants
(to repair public buildings, such as courthouses, city halls, libraries, fire stations, hospitals; street and road improvements; construction of industrial parks)
5) seventeen seminars were held to train leaders in local communities how to induce industrial development
6) special research projects were conducted for the Louisiana
Tourist Development Commission, and for the Louisiana Department of Art, Historical and Cultural Preservation.[25]

In 1969 Governor John J. McKeithen established the Louisiana
Commission on Intergovernmental Relations to perform the clearance
function at the state level, and Governor Edwards renewed the mandate in 1974. The Commission has six major functions: "1) to operate
the state clearinghouse; 2) to coordinate the activities of local clearing-
houses; 3) to provide technical assistance to agencies, local governments, and other organizations; 4) to serve as the liaison between
federal, state, and local governments; 5) through the Director as chairman, to head up the work of the Five State Task Force; and 6) state
administration of HUD '701' Comprehensive Planning Assistance Program." In July, 1977, the Louisiana legislature authorized, as part of an
overall reorganization plan, the creation of the Department of Urban
and Community Affairs, and the commission became part of the new
department.[26]

State-State Relations

The jurisdiction of each state is limited, but problems often extend
beyond the borders of an individual state. There is obviously a need for
states to cooperate with one another to solve common problems.

Constitutional Requirements

Several federal constitutional provisions deal with the state-state relationships. The first of these is Article III, Section 2, which gives the

25. Coordinating and Development Council of Northwest Louisiana, *Annual Report*
(Shreveport: Coordinating and Development Council of Northwest Louisiana, 1977).
26. John J. McKeithen, Executive Order 73, September 26, 1969; Edwin Edwards,

Supreme Court original jurisdiction in cases "in which a state shall be party." In actual practice, however, states seldom avail themselves of this procedure for settling their disputes. Three parts of Article IV—the "full-faith-and-credit" clause, the "privileges-and-immunities" clause, and the clause that provides for the rendition of fugitives from justice—further define the relationship between states.

The "full-faith-and-credit" clause, Article IV, Section 1, reads as follows: "Full Faith and Credit shall be given in each State to the public Acts, Records, and judicial Proceedings of every other State." This provision does not mean that the laws of every state must be enforced in every other state. It does mean that each state must accept certain documents that are certified as legal by another state, such as birth certificates, marriage licenses, and wills. A state is not required to honor professional licenses issued by a sister state to medical doctors, lawyers, teachers, engineers, accountants, barbers, or plumbers, however. The full-faith-and-credit clause does not apply in such cases because the state has another, primary, responsibility to protect the health, safety, and welfare of its citizens.

The application of the full-faith-and-credit clause is somewhat different in the case of automobile driver's license and automobile license plates. All states recognize an out-of-state driver's license as valid for persons traveling through a state, but they also reserve the right to place a time limit upon the visit. In Louisiana the state police do not consider an out-of-state driver's license as valid after the person has lived in this state for as long as ninety days. Likewise, persons driving through this state in their personal passenger car are not required to purchase a Louisiana license plate unless they plan to be in the state over ninety days. Commercial carriers, such as trucks and buses, must purchase a Louisiana plate if they pick up passengers or cargo in the state, regardless of the duration or frequency of the visits.

Article IV, Section 2, provides, "The Citizens of each State shall be entitled to all Privileges and Immunities of Citizens of the several States." This provision has never been fully defined since the Supreme Court has attempted to clarify it on only a few occasions. In 1869 the Court said:

Executive Order 60, February 15, 1974; Intergovernmental Relations Commission, *Project Notification and Review System Procedural Guide* (Washington, D.C.: U.S. Government Printing Office, 1975); Act 83 of 1977.

It was undoubtedly the object of the clause in question to place the citizens of each State upon the same footing with citizens of other States, so far as the advantages resulting from citizenship in those States are concerned. It relieves them from the disabilities of alienage in other States; it inhibits discriminating legislation against them by other States; it gives them the right of free ingress into other States, and egress from them; it insures to them in other States the same freedom possessed by the citizens of those States in the acquisition and enjoyment of property and in the pursuit of happiness; and it secures to them in other States the equal protection of their laws.

Since that time the Court has rarely relied on the privileges-and-immunities clause. In 1894 the Court said, in effect, that the clause did not guarantee that the laws of one state would be the same as the laws of another; it merely forbade a state from dealing differently with citizens of other states who have newly arrived within that state than they would deal with their own citizens. Recently the issue of the reasonableness of residency requirements has been under attack. In 1969 Louisiana, along with all of the other states, was forced to discontinue its residence requirement for state welfare benefits. [27] Near the same time Louisiana reduced its residency requirement for voter eligibility to thirty days for all elections in order to comply with federal standards.

On the other hand, the courts have upheld the power of a state to collect a higher license fee for out-of-state hunters and fishermen. Tuition at state-supported colleges may also be higher for out-of-state students. This apparent violation of the clause is justified on the basis of the proprietary rights of the citizens who have lived in the state for a longer period and, therefore, have contributed more (in taxes) to the financial support of these educational institutions. Another exception to the general rule applies in the case of corporations. The Court has ruled that the privileges-and-immunities clause applies to natural flesh-and-blood persons only, not to artificial persons such as corporations. Hence it would not be a violation of Article IV, Section 2, to tax an out-of-state corporation doing business in Louisiana at a higher rate than a locally chartered corporation. [28]

27. *Paul* v. *Virginia*, 8 Wall. 168 (1869); *McKane* v. *Durston*, 153 U.S. 687 (1894); *Shapiro* v. *Thompson*, 394 U.S. 618 (1969).
28. *McCready* v. *Virginia*, 94 U.S. 391 (1877); *Geer* v. *Connecticut*, 161 U.S. 51

Article IV, Section 2, continues, "A Person charged in any State with Treason, Felony, or other Crime, who shall flee from Justice and be found in another State, shall on Demand of the executive Authority of the State from which he fled, be delivered up, to be removed to the State having Jurisdiction of the Crime." While the meaning of the language seems to leave little doubt as to the responsibility of one state toward another, in *Kentucky* v. *Dennison*, the Supreme Court ruled that this clause did not positively demand that a governor return a fugitive and that the provision was judicially unenforceable.[29] It should be noted, however, that, as a standard practice, governors do, with only rare exception, turn over fugitives to other states.

Interstate Compacts

One way states deal with areawide problems is to enter into interstate compacts. Many writers during the 1940s expressed the hope that use of interstate compacts would reduce the need for federal assistance and/or interference. Their hope, however, has not been realized.

As of 1977, Louisiana was a party to twenty-six interstate compacts.[30] In order to illustrate the variety of problems dealt with, the topics of these compacts are listed below:

Adoption of children
Children and minors' placement
Drivers' licenses
Education
Gas, uniform safety standards
Gulf States Marine Fisheries Compact
Juveniles, supervision and control
Library Compact
Mental Health
Minors
Out-of-state parolee supervision

(1896); *Bank of Augusta* v. *Earle*, 13 Pet. 519 (1839); *Paul* v. *Virginia*, 8 Wall. 168 (1869). Nonresident tuition was upheld in *Kirk* v. *Board of Regents of the University of California*, 78 Ca. Rptr. 260 (1969), and *Starns* v. *Malkerson*, No. 4-70 Civ. 26 (D. Minn. 1970); however, Arizona's nonresident tuition law was held unconstitutional in *Harper* v. *Arizona Board of Regents* (Superior Ct., Pima County, 1970).

29. *Kentucky* v. *Dennison*, 4 How. 66 (1861).

30. *Louisiana Revised Statutes*, index and pocket parts.

Placement of children
Police protection
Regional education
South Central Interstate Forest Fire Protection Compact
Southern Interstate Nuclear Compact
Vehicle Equipment Safety Compact
Disaster emergency
Environmental control
Mississippi-Louisiana Bridge Construction Compact
Police protection, Southern State Police Compact
Pollution, environmental control
Sabine River Compact
Southern Growth Policies Agreement
Southern State Police Compact
Traffic Violations Compact

The most recent agreement, the Traffic Violations Compact between Louisiana and five other states, affords more convenience to nonresident traffic violators. Before this compact went into effect on January 1, 1976, a nonresident who violated a traffic law in this state was subject to being transported immediately by the arresting officer to a Louisiana court to post bond. Needless to say, this procedure caused visitors considerable inconvenience and annoyance. Under the new system, the violator is given a citation by the policeman but allowed to make arrangements with the proper Louisiana court at his own convenience within a stated period. A violator who fails to contact the court in time has his driver's license suspended by his home state.

Associations to Encourage Cooperation

Several private or quasi-official associations seek to encourage specific forms of cooperation among the states. The first of these, the National Conference of Commissioners on Uniform State Laws, was organized in 1892 to draft model laws and suggest that state legislatures pass identical laws. It was thought that uniform state laws would reduce the inconvenience and confusion encountered by firms and individuals engaged in business in several different states. In the trucking industry alone, the weight limit on trucks, the legal length of trailers, and the number of clearance lights required varied from state to state. Those who formed this association also hoped to reduce the demand for federal legislation. In spite of its high hopes, this organization has experienced only modest success. More than one hundred uniform state laws have been written by the association and recommended to the states, but only three have been adopted by all of the states (dealing with negotiable instruments, warehouse receipts, and stock transfer). The Uniform Real Estate Trust Act of 1962 is the model law most recently adopted by the state of Louisiana.[31]

States also cooperate voluntarily through the various conferences established for particular state officials. The best known of these, the Governors' Conference, was organized in 1908 and meets annually to promote interstate accord, discuss common problems, and profit by the experiences of other states. Another such conference is the National Legislative Conference, which was organized in 1947 to bring together state legislators and legislative personnel to exchange ideas. Other conferences include those for secretaries of state, attorneys general, chief justices, budget officers, and insurance commissioners.

The Council of State Governments, founded in 1925, "conducts research on state programs and problems; maintains an information service available to state agencies, officials and legislators; issues a variety of publications; assists in state-federal liaison; promotes regional and state-local cooperation and provides staff for affiliated organizations."[32] The Council of State Governments publishes a quarterly journal entitled *State Government* and distributes an annual volume, *The Book of the States*, which contains comparative information about the states.

The Advisory Commission on Intergovernmental Relations was created by an act of Congress in 1959 to "give continuing study to the relationships among local, state, and national levels of government." This agency conducts studies, issues reports, reviews proposed legislation, holds conferences on crucial intergovernmental issues, and gives technical advice to federal, state, and local government officials.[33]

31. Paul J. Hardy to Riley E. Baker, September 16, 1977, in possession of Baker, Ruston, Louisiana.

32. Council of State Governments, *The Book of the States, 1976–1977* (Lexington, Ky.: The Council of State Governments, 1976), XXI, frontispiece, and see 559–60.

33. William Morrow, *Public Administration* (New York: Random House, 1975).

State-Local Relations

While cities and parishes have only those powers granted by the state constitution and statutes, as a practical matter, city and parish governments enjoy a great degree of autonomy. Although there have been suggestions of reducing the number of parishes in the name of efficiency and economy, tradition and local pride, as well as opposition from those with a vested interest in the status quo, have combined to prevent consolidation. Locally elected parish officials perform a number of necessary services, such as providing police protection, constructing and maintaining roads, keeping legal records, and operating hospitals. Locally elected city government officials are responsible for these services, as well as trash and garbage collection, health and sanitation, parks and recreation, and in some cities, airports, golf courses, industrial parks, and utilities. Although cities and parishes perform a large number of services and have large numbers of employees and large budgets, in recent years some units of local government have become increasingly dependent upon the state government for financial assistance.

State-Local Financial Aid

State aid to local governments has increased from $52 million (5.6 percent of total local government revenue) in 1902 to $26.9 billion (30.2 percent of total local government revenue) in 1970. State aid to local governments was more than ten times as much as federal aid to local governments in 1970. In fact, state aid exceeded federal aid to all units of local government (parishes, municipalities, school districts, and other special districts) by a wide margin from 1902 to 1970. There are no truly comparable figures for the period since 1970; the intergovernmental finance statistics for the period 1970–1976 pertain to state aid to cities and counties only. State aid to county governments in 1979 was $18.1 billion (36.1 percent of total county government revenue), and state aid to city government was $15.5 billion (22.0 percent of total city government revenues).[34] State aid to counties was almost

34. Bureau of the Census, *Historical Statistics*, 1,133; Bureau of the Census,

four times as much as federal aid to counties. State aid to cities nation-wide was large, getting larger, and already one and one-half times as large as federal aid to cities in 1979.

The 64 Louisiana parishes received only $163.7 million in state aid in 1979 (or 19.1 percent of total parish revenue), about one-half the national average. The 287 Louisiana municipalities received $76.5 million in financial assistance from the state government (8.9 percent of municipal general revenue), also less than one-half the national average. The 419 special districts in Louisiana received $2.8 million in state aid in 1979 (8.0 percent of general revenue). The state's 66 school districts received the largest share of state aid in 1979, $879.4 million (64.2 percent of school district general revenue).[35] The trend in state aid to local units of government in Louisiana during the period 1945–1979 can be seen in Table 9-2.

School districts have been the largest recipients of state aid through-out the entire period, ranging from a low of slightly more than half to a high of more than three-fourths of all state aid. Although state aid to cities has increased in dollar amounts, it has declined as a percentage of total state aid. State aid to cities has not made up as much as 10 percent of total state aid since 1957. State aid to parishes increased ap-preciably in dollar amount during the 1950–1973 period but was still only about 5 percent of total state aid to local governments. It was not until 1974 that aid to parishes amounted to as much as 10 percent of total state aid. More than half of state aid to parishes at the present time is derived from the State Revenue Sharing Fund (known as the Property Tax Relief Fund prior to 1972), which provides reimburse-ments for loss of parish revenue due to the state homestead exemption law.[36]

What are the various categories of state aid to a typical municipality in Louisiana in the 1980s? The city of Ruston received slightly more than $400,000, 18 percent of its total revenue in 1979, from nine state sources: tobacco tax refund (about one-half of the total), aid from the Louisiana Highway Department, the beer tax refund program, the fire

County Government Finances, 1978–79, 15; Bureau of the Census, *City Government Finances, 1978–79,* 7.

35. Bureau of the Census, *Governmental Finances, 1978–79,* 73.

36. See James Calhoun (ed.), *Louisiana Almanac, 1978–79* (Gretna, La.: Pelican, 1980), 390, for parish-by-parish distribution of this fund in 1976 and 1977.

Table 9-2

State Payments to Local Governments in Selected Years
by Type of Government
(In Millions of Dollars)

Year Ending June 30	Total	Parishes	Cities	School Districts	Other
1945	$ 37.5	$ 8.8	$ 1.2	$ 20.5	$ 7.1
1950	101.2	6.6	8.0	67.4	19.1
1955	143.1	9.3	19.8	95.0	19.1
1960	231.2	17.0	21.0	161.0	32.3
1965	305.9	24.0	23.8	217.6	40.6
1970	481.7	30.1	29.5	352.3	69.8
1971	586.8	28.5	37.4	438.8	82.1
1972	660.3	40.3	43.3	490.4	86.1
1973	675.3	37.0	46.1	478.7	113.6
1974	731.3	105.7	49.8	533.0	42.8
1975	824.8	96.1	62.7	606.9	54.1
1976	906.2	139.2	76.6	683.2	7.2
1977	956.2	167.1	78.9	702.5	7.7
1978	—	—	—	—	—
1979	1,122.9	163.7	76.5	879.4	2.8

Source: Data for 1945–1975 from *Statistical Abstract of Louisiana*, 343; data for subsequent years from Bureau of the Census, *Government Finances*, for the appropriate year.

insurance rebate program, the public service employee grant program, three small grants, and $42,000 in state revenue-sharing funds. Obviously, the state aid for highways, law enforcement, public service employees, and special purpose grants had to be spent for the purposes for which they were obtained. The money derived from the other categories of state aid was given without restrictions; these funds could be placed in the city's general fund and used for any purpose designated by the city council.[37]

How dependent is a typical parish of this state upon state aid? In Lincoln Parish, for example, only 13.3 percent of its general fund was derived from state revenue sharing in 1979. When the $575,605 from

37. Ruston *Daily Leader*, December 31, 1979, pp. 14, 15.

oil, gas, and timber severance taxes, which were collected by the state, were returned to the parish, total state aid amounted to more than two-thirds of the general fund of Lincoln Parish. In addition, more than half of the parish road maintenance fund ($1,259,953) was derived from state grants.[38]

The parishes are the beneficiaries of other intergovernmental financial arrangements: the state pays all of the salary of the district attorney and the district judge, and the state pays half the salary of the parish registrar of voters, the agricultural agent, the home demonstration agent, and the veterans' service officer. The Public Affairs Research Council recently called attention to the fact that the state pays supplemental pay to 4,250 deputy sheriffs and extra compensation to an additional 349 deputies. The report urged that the program be phased out. In another report PAR pointed out that local governments in Louisiana were less dependent upon state aid in 1974 than they were in 1964, but that Louisiana local governments derive a larger percentage of their total revenue from state aid than the national average. About the same time, the Louisiana Association of Business and Industry was urging that local governments be called upon to raise more of their revenue from local sources. A few days later the Police Jury Association replied that the parishes have less ability to raise revenue than the state and labeled the LABI proposal irresponsible.[39] Before making the changes proposed by PAR and LABI, the citizens of this state should try to anticipate all of the possible effects such a change would have on the political system. In particular, what would be the effects upon the efficiency and responsiveness of state government and upon parish government? Who would benefit from such a change, and who would pay more, and who would pay less, tax?

Shared Responsibilities

It is quite clear that local and state governments share the responsibility for many public services, such as education, welfare, highways,

38. Office of the Legislative Auditor, *Report: Lincoln Parish* (Baton Rouge: Office of the Legislative Auditor, 1979).

39. Public Affairs Research Council, "State Salary Supplements for Local Employees in Louisiana," *Analysis* (October, 1977); Public Affairs Research Council, "Resolving Louisiana's Financial Dilemma," *Analysis* (March, 1977); Ruston *Daily Leader*, March 30, 1977, Sec. 1, p. 1, April 5, 1977, Sec. 1, p. 1.

and health care. Local school boards provide the physical plant, set disciplinary and other policies, select the superintendent (and through the superintendent, the remainder of the administrators, faculty, and staff), and raise local funds through taxation and borrowing. The locally elected school board members are not subject to removal by any state official and are independent of other parish officials. The State Board of Elementary and Secondary Education has pervasive, although vague supervisory and budgetary powers under the 1974 state constitution. If it continues to operate as it has in the recent past, we can expect its functions to include prescribing qualifications for certification of teachers, preparing courses of study, administering the distribution of state-furnished textbooks, distributing state and federal funds to local school boards, and reviewing the accreditation of private schools. In theory, the state board sets policies, which are implemented by the State Department of Education under the supervision of the superintendent of education. About two-thirds of elementary and secondary education funds are furnished by the state, and the remaining one-third are derived from local sources.[40] In general, however, there is little state interference with the day-to-day operation of the public schools.

The case of welfare administration is quite different. There are welfare offices in each of the parishes, and in some towns the welfare office is located in the parish courthouse, but there the connection ends. The employees of the welfare office are hired and paid by the state. All decisions concerning the types of programs, eligibility requirements, and the size of the benefit payments to individual claimants are made at the state level. It seems fair to say that Louisiana's welfare program is totally state controlled; authority and responsibility are not shared with the units of local government.

In the case of highways a three-way split of responsibility is evident. The state is responsible for 16,000 miles of roads, including the interstate system, and primary and secondary roads; the parishes are responsible for 26,500 miles of roads in the parish road system; and cities are responsible for 6,800 miles of streets. Each city decides which streets need to be paved, lets the contract for paving, repairs and maintains the streets with its own employees and equipment, and allocates

40. These estimates are based on an interview with the secretary of the Police Jury of Lincoln Parish and an interview with the city treasurer of Ruston, January 28, 1981.

a certain percentage of local tax (and other) revenue for these purposes. Parishes maintain their roads in a similar manner, hiring their own personnel and raising their own funds. The Office of Highways in the Department of Transportation and Development does the planning for the state highway system. Contracts are let to private firms for the construction of roads and bridges. The state operates ten district offices where buildings, equipment, and personnel are available for routine maintenance, such as mowing rights-of-way, picking up litter, and making minor road repairs. In effect then, Louisiana's three distinct road systems serve as an integrated system because of the planning and cooperation of state and local authorities. It is estimated that Louisiana parishes received approximately one-half of their funds for road construction and maintenance from the state in 1977. Louisiana cities, similarly, received about one-third of their funds for streets from the state.[41]

Since expenditures on hospitals were merged with the overall expenditures for health, hospitals, and welfare in 1973, it is difficult to determine exactly how much money is spent by Louisiana on state-supported hospitals. It is safe to assume that expenditures on hospitals continues to be one of the larger state expenditures. As of 1973, the nine general charity hospitals, three mental hospitals, two tuberculosis hospitals, eight schools operated by the Division of Mental Retardation, fifteen mental health clinics, seven out-patient clinics for alcoholics, and one geriatric hospital cost the state over $156 million, or approximately 11 percent of the total state expenditures for the year. In 1974, $279 million of a total of $3.096 billion were spent on health and hospitals in Louisiana. At the local level there are three different arrangements for the administration of parish-owned hospitals. In six parishes (and three cities) the parish hospital is directly under the control of the police jury (or city council). In twenty other communities the hospital was built at parish expense, but leased to a group of businessmen who formed a corporation to operate the hospital without cost to the parish. Forty-nine additional hospitals are administered by special districts.[42] In all three types of parish hospitals the construction of the hospital building and, often, the purchase of much of the original

41. U.S. Bureau of the Census, *Governmental Finances, 1975–76* (Washington, D.C.: U.S. Government Printing Office, 1977), 35.
42. Louisiana Health and Social Rehabilitation Services Administration, *1973 Statis-*

equipment is customarily financed by a combination of local tax money, revenue derived from the sale of bonds, and federal aid (Hill-Burton funds). While the State Hospital Board does not control the hospitals owned by local units of government, there is an annual state audit of Medicare funds. Also there are periodic inspections of local hospitals by various state regulatory agencies, such as the State Fire Marshal and the Health Department.

From our discussion of education, welfare, highway, and hospital services in Louisiana it is readily apparent that the degree of local control varies rather widely. Some programs are entirely state controlled. Other programs are left almost completely to the parishes. And many other programs fall somewhere between these two extremes.

Parish-Municipal Cooperation

Every Saturday during the fall, campus police, city police, the parish sheriff's department, and the state police cooperate in directing traffic and controlling crowds at college football games. There are numerous other instances in which cities and parishes work together to achieve common goals. Lincoln Parish and Ruston jointly operate the parish ambulance service, for example. Since 1976 Lincoln Parish has operated a sanitary landfill that is jointly financed and used by all of the towns in the parish as well as by everyone who lives within the parish outside of city limits.

Unfortunately, there are also several examples of units of government failing to cooperate. In most parishes there is a tacit understanding among the various police agencies that the city police will have complete authority over law enforcement within the city limits, the sheriff's department will handle law enforcement outside the city limits within the parish, and the state police will enter a case only when requested by either the city police or the sheriff's department. How-

tical Summary (Baton Rouge: Louisiana Health and Social Rehabilitation Services Administration, 1974), xxxiv; Division of Business and Economic Research, University of New Orleans, Statistical Abstract of Louisiana (New Orleans: Division of Business and Economic Research, University of New Orleans, 1976), 268; American Hospital Association, Guide to the Health Care Field (Chicago: American Hospital Association, 1977), 93–97.

ever, in 1970 the Caddo Parish Sheriff's Department raided several locations inside Shreveport's city limits and seized pinball machines that were allegedly being operated illegally. Considerable outcry resulted, and the Shreveport commissioner of public safety expressed his annoyance with what he considered the unwarranted action by the sheriff's department. A spokesman for the Caddo Sheriff's Department made a statement explaining why the raids were conducted without prior consultation with the Shreveport police.[43] As often happens, the charges and countercharges were aired for a few days in the newspapers. Then the furor abated without a resolution of the issue. Responsibility for the misunderstanding was never clearly placed, nor were any steps taken to prevent another jurisdictional dispute.

Coordination Problems in Standard Metropolitan Statistical Areas

The need for cooperation and coordination among local units of government is always important, but it is crucial in the metropolitan areas of the state where 62 percent of the population resides and where local governments proliferate. For example, in the New Orleans SMSA— the central city and its contiguous suburbs—there are actually forty-two autonomous units of government, including fourteen municipalities, three parishes, twenty-one special districts, and four school districts. It seems reasonable to assume that in the New Orleans area, problems such as drainage, flood control, air and water pollution, waste disposal, sewage treatment, and fire and police protection could be dealt with more effectively if formal cooperation existed. Fragmentation problems also exist to a smaller extent in Louisiana's six other SMSAs (Alexandria, Baton Rouge, Lafayette, Lake Charles, Monroe, and Shreveport). Some attempts have been made to prevent duplication of services and to fill unmet needs. In East Baton Rouge Parish, the parish and municipal governments merged, for example. During the past ten years, the Councils of Government have performed valuable coordination functions in the seven SMSAs of Louisiana. However, the experience of metropolitan areas in other states suggests that

43. Shreveport *Times*, September 17, 1970, Sec. 1, p. 1.

there will be an increasing demand for improved intercity cooperation as the number of units of local government increases. A few of the arrangements that have been tried by cities in other states include annexation, city-county consolidation, metropolitan districts, comprehensive urban county plans, and federation.[44]

Trends, Conclusions, and Guesses About the Future

This chapter has not examined all of the possible intergovernmental relationships, but a truly comprehensive study would be excessively long—longer than Brooke Graves' 984-page textbook on this subject. Nevertheless, this brief survey of how governments interact in the nation, and particularly in Louisiana, has indicated a few trends.

Relationships among levels of government are temporary balances between conflicting pressures or forces. It is obvious that the balance between the federal and state governments has been shifting toward centralization throughout our nation's history. It is the most obvious long-range trend in government relations, and much of this chapter has dealt with how centralization has occurred. There has also been some implied explanation of why. Centralization has been gradual, and it has occurred for pragmatic rather than ideological reasons. Forces such as territorial expansion, population growth, urbanization, economic growth, and technological development contributed to the process. The urban way of life, with its increased emphasis upon specialization and interdependence (and with its concomitant insecurity) has weakened the American tradition of self-reliance and rugged individualism. It has led to more acceptance of government programs to redistribute financial resources.

The fairly widespread belief that centralization is the result of a plan or conspiracy by power-hungry bureaucrats in Washington does not conform to the facts. Bureaus do not create themselves. New federal

44. John C. Bollens and Henry J. Schmandt, *The Metropolis* (New York: Harper and Row, 1975), Chaps. 11–13; Alan Shank and Ralph W. Conant, *Urban Representatives* (Boston: Holbrook Press, 1975), 107–119; John J. Herrigan, *Political Change in the Metropolis* (Boston: Little, Brown, 1976), Chaps. 7 and 8. For an account of the minority view in opposition to consolidation, see Robert L. Bish and Vincent Ostrom, *Understanding Urban Government* (Washington, D.C.: American Enterprise Institute for Public Policy Research, 1974).

agencies are created by acts of Congress. Therefore, a majority of the members of Congress and, theoretically at least, a majority of the voters wanted the services supplied by the agencies. In other words, the overall increase in governmental activity has come about as a response to expressed needs. It is not certain why the central government has been more responsive than the states. Perhaps, groups seeking services have turned to the national government in those instances when the states have been unable, or unwilling, to provide the desired services.

The argument over the desirability of centralization will probably never be decided. The twentieth-century liberal argues that the twin pressures of technological revolution and large-scale corporate enterprise have pushed us in the direction of a national economy. We are no longer a nation of self-employed small farmers and small businessmen. New and bigger problems have arisen, and it is unreasonable to expect small units of local government to deal adequately with problems such as unemployment, inflation, regulation of oligopoly, and inequality of opportunity. New and bigger problems call for new and bigger governments. The liberal concludes that in order to achieve efficiency and equity, nationwide priorities must be considered in the formulation of policies—with the states and local units of government primarily responsible for the implementation of these policies.

Conservatives defend the values of self-reliance and individual initiative. They argue that the centralizing trend is doomed to failure because the task is so large and complex that no single unit or level of government can adequately deal with it, because the increased standardization and uniformity that accompanies centralization ignores the need for diversity, and because a centralized government is less responsive to changing conditions. Some conservatives argue that centralization is a first step to tyranny, a curtailment of personal freedom. Those who adhere to this line of argumentation tend to look with suspicion on all changes in the functions that government performs and to oppose any change in the relationship between various levels of government. Many conservatives are sincere in their belief that the Founding Fathers established our government upon absolute and immutable principles. Any deviation from these principles and any change of these long-standing arrangements is, in the conservatives' view, not only error but possibly treason.

Despite the arguments against it, however, the centralizing trend in federal-state relations is likely to continue. There probably will also be increased federal influence at the local level. It appears likely that both state and local units of government will survive with little change in their organizational structure or the formal distribution of functions but that the states will be called upon to adapt and to accept an altered role in the evolving federal system. The changes will not come without protest.

10.
Political Parties

PAUL GROSSER

In Louisiana, politics rivals football and bass fishing as a major topic of conversation, a primary source of entertainment, and a deadly serious way of life. The usual distinctions between the political and the non-political are unknown and the boundaries between private and public are weak and blurred. Interest in politics is intense and the impact of politics is pervasive. Virtually no aspect of life—social, economic, cultural, or personal—is unaffected. Areas assumed to be nonpolitical or normally shielded against politics, such as the civil service, technical processing decisions, and the state law school are, in Louisiana, immersed in state politics. In areas usually recognized as political—agricultural and industrial policy, environmental and energy issues, labor-management relations, transportation and highways, criminal justice, and education—the level and intensity of political activity is staggering. As a result, Louisiana has been characterized as the northernmost Latin American or westernmost Arab nation, and its political style labeled feudal, byzantine, or simply bizarre. Louisiana is not typically southern or typically anything else in this regard. Borrowing the self-descriptive term of the state's most famous politician, Louisiana is *sui generis.*[1]

Politics as intense and pervasive as Louisiana's are normally associated with elaborate, well-defined, disciplined, active, and highly visible

1. V. O. Key, Jr., *Southern Politics in State and Nation* (New York: Vintage Books, 1949), 156–82; A. J. Liebling, *The Earl of Louisiana* (New York: Simon and Schuster, 1961); Harnett T. Kane, *Louisiana Hayride* (New York: Morrow, 1941); Robert Sherrill, *Gothic Politics in the Deep South* (New York: Ballantine Books, 1969), 5–38; T. Harry Williams, *Huey Long* (New York: Knopf, 1969); Allan P. Sindler, *Huey Long's Louisiana: State Politics, 1920–1952* (Baltimore: Johns Hopkins University Press, 1956).

political parties or political organizations. (The Democratic "machines" of Cook County, Illinois; Tammany Hall in New York; and the Pennsylvania Democratic party are examples of the well developed and disciplined political organizations that exist in and give form to highly politicized environments.)[2] These organizations either constitute or dominate the political parties where they exist. A puzzling feature of the Louisiana political milieu is the apparent absence of similar organizations.

In democratic societies, political parties are organizations designed to gain political power by capturing control of the machinery of government through the process of contesting elections. As such, political parties carry out the processes of candidate selection and issue formulation; they manage the pacific power struggle of elections and carry out the political education and mobilization of the citizens in order to build the support coalitions needed to win elections. Parties serve as personnel agencies for staffing government when successful, act as critics and watchdogs when unsuccessful, and provide a link between citizens and government.[3]

As parties developed they typically came to represent interests of more or less well defined coalitions of classes and groups. For example, today the Republican party is generally identified with the interests of business and agricultural groups, white collar workers, the professions, and the more affluent members of the population. The Democratic party, in contrast, is identified with the interests of labor, minorities, and the less prosperous members of the population.[4] Political scientists generally agree that it is rational to vote for the candidate of the political party identified with one's interests. This rational basis for electoral behavior has not been generally available to voters in the South. As one scholar has noted, "In the conduct of campaigns for the control of legislatures, for the control of governorships, and for representatives in the national Congress, the South must depend for political leadership, not on political parties, but on lone-wolf operators, on fortuitous groupings of individuals usually of a transient nature, on

2. Frank J. Sorauf, *Party Politics in America* (Boston: Little, Brown, 1972), 65–85.
3. Sorauf, *Party Politics in America*, 7–27; Everett C. Ladd, Jr., *American Political Parties* (New York: Norton, 1970), 1–56; Giovanni Sartori, *Parties and Party Systems* (New York: Cambridge University Press, 1976), 3–67.
4. William H. Flanigan and Nancy H. Zingale, *Political Behavior of the American Electorate* (Boston: Allyn & Bacon, 1975), 69–70.

spectacular demagogues odd enough to command the attention of considerable numbers of voters, on men who have become persons of political consequence in their own little bailiwicks, and on other types of leaders whose methods to attract electoral attention serve as substitutes for leadership of a party organization."[5]

As part of the Deep South, Louisiana has been identified as a one-party Democratic state. Within specific boundaries a fairly strong case can be made to justify this label. Studies of interparty competition have consistently ranked Louisiana as one of the most solidly Democratic states in the South. On a scale on which o represents total Republican success and 1 represents total Democratic success, Louisiana was rated .9930 on interparty competition for state offices from 1962 to 1973. Another study found that from 1880 to 1980, Louisiana voters supported the Democratic presidential candidate in all but five elections. Over the same period, the Louisiana congressional delegation did not include a Republican until 1972, and only a handful of Republicans have served in the state legislature. As of 1981 only ten Republicans serve in the state house of representatives and none in the senate. Finally, after Reconstruction, no Republican was elected governor until 1979.[6]

To characterize Louisiana as a one-party state, however, is to ignore the bifactionalism of the Long era, during which the state had the functional equivalent of a two-party system, and to imply that the politics following the collapse of bifactionalism possessed order, coherence, and some semblance of party organization. At best, the identity of Louisiana as a one-party state refers to external political relations, that is, presidential and congressional elections, and is not a satisfactory description of the state's internal politics. Furthermore, if the state's political history is viewed from the narrower focus of the last twenty years, even this restricted sense of one-party Democratic is inaccurate. Since the 1960 presidential election, Louisiana has been in the Democratic column only once—in 1976.[7] Two of the state's eight

5. Key, *Southern Politics*, 15–18.
6. Austin Ranney, "Parties in State Politics," in Herbert Jacob and Kenneth N. Vines (eds.), *Politics in the American States* (Boston: Little, Brown, 1970), 51–91; Perry H. Howard, *Political Tendencies in Louisiana, 1912–1952* (Rev. ed.; Baton Rouge: Louisiana State University Press, 1971), 419–20; James Calhoun (ed.), *Louisiana Almanac, 1977–78* (Gretna, La.: Pelican, 1979), 342, 346–48.
7. Calhoun (ed.), *Louisiana Almanac*, 342.

members in the federal House of Representatives are now Republican. And in 1980, Republican Dave Treen was sworn in as governor. This is hardly the kind of behavior expected from a one-party Democratic state.

Obviously, Louisiana is undergoing some type of political transition. Although the one-party Democratic label is no longer accurate, Louisiana is decidedly not a two-party state, and there is little evidence of an emerging Republican majority. The state system is, depending on one's point of view, either undergoing major change or is simply stuck in a pattern of drift. This fluid and uncertain situation was reflected in the course of party politics over the past decade. For the most part, it was a period of very weak party organization and discipline. The one-party bifactionalism of the Long era was replaced by a system best described as no-party rule. The Democrats, though still the majority party and enrolling almost 90 percent of the registered partisans, have been unwilling or unable to perform the functions normally associated with political parties, such as recruiting candidates, contesting elections, and determining the political agenda.[8] The dominant party has been reduced to a label at election time. As a result, voters have been treated to such no-party manifestations as six or more nominal Democrats running for the same office, and Republicans running unopposed for major offices. When party functions have been performed, individuals, interest groups, or elected officials acting independently of the Democratic party have often been the prime movers.

In 1976 the Republican party enrolled less than 4 percent of the registered partisans in the state and was distinctly the minority party.[9] Until very recently the Republican pattern was to field a single statewide candidate for governor or U.S. senator on an episodic basis and to reserve its most serious effort for the presidential contests. Consequently, the party was not perceived as an alternative to the Democrats in most elections. However, since the mid-1970s the Republican party has shown considerable interest in organization and is making a serious effort to expand its base. As a result, it is the more dynamic, organized, and disciplined of the two parties.

8. Public Affairs Research Council, "Primary Election, October 27, 1979," *Analysis* (November, 1979), 2.
    9. *Ibid.*

The make-up of the Louisiana congressional delegation is a clear indicator of the condition of the political parties. In 1979 there were three Republican congressmen in the state's delegation. The 1978 election almost added a fourth Republican congressman, but Republican Jimmy Wilson lost to Democrat Claude Leach by margin of 266 votes in the Fourth Congressional District. (Following the election of Democrat Billy Tauzin to fill the congressional seat vacated when Dave Treen was elected governor, the number of Republicans in the delegation was reduced to two.)

These Republican victories occurred despite the fact that the party membership is only 5.1 percent of the state's registered voters. Some of the credit for the increased Republican strength must be attributed to "closet" Republicans, that is, those registered Democrats who will vote for attractive and serious Republican candidates. This pattern has been present on the presidential level since the Eisenhower candidacy of 1956 and indicates the potential strength of the Republican party in the state.[10]

Without minimizing the Republican successes, some credit for these victories must be given to the lack of discipline in the Democratic party and to the Democrats' unwillingness to take the Republican challenge seriously. The disarray of the Democrats was evidenced in the 1978 election when the party failed to oppose Congressman Treen and was able to offer only token opposition to the two incumbent Republican congressmen. In short, Louisiana's party system in 1978 consisted of a disorganized and directionless Democratic party, claiming the habitual loyalty of the bulk of the electorate in state and local elections, and a developing but still embryonic Republican party. The intense and pervasive politics of Louisiana are not reflected in elaborate, well-defined, and disciplined political organizations. The absence of organizations capable of articulating political energies and interests on a permanent basis contributes to a neofeudal political style. Political dynamics are expressed organizationally in various specialized, narrowly focused, single-issue or highly personalized groupings. Loose pragmatic coalitions sometimes emerge on general issues, but these combinations have no permanent basis. Different sets of issues are

10. Calhoun (ed.), *Louisiana Almanac*, 342.

likely to generate different combinations of interests. However, as noted earlier, there are indications that state party politics are undergoing a transformation. If this proves to be the case, the no-party experience may simply be a transitional phase and, though typical of southern politics, atypical for Louisiana. To appreciate this, a review of the state's political history will provide a broader perspective for examining what appears to be the fourth developmental phase of Louisiana's party system.

The recent formlessness of Louisiana's party politics is not representative of the state's political experience. Examination of Louisiana political history reveals three fairly clear-cut periods with distinctive party systems. The first party system, covering the antebellum period from the 1830s to the mid-1850s can be characterized as two-party competitive. The second distinctive party system developed after Reconstruction as a one-party Democratic type common to other southern states and lasted from the 1870s to the 1920s. The third party system, known as the Long era, which held sway from 1928 until the mid-1960s, was a one-party system with well-defined and sustained internal competition along bifactional lines. These party systems reflected the economic, cultural, social, and political cleavages within the state during each period. In marked contrast to the present party situation, the political parties of each period were able to articulate interests into fairly stable and permanent support coalitions.[11]

The dominant issues and conflicts of each period reflect a continuity that the changing partisan patterns may obscure. The issues, including the degree and extent of political participation, race relations, and class conflict, judging from historical experience, may be permanent features of the state politics. The political mood or style that has dominated the handling of these questions can best be characterized as conservatism. In conservative pre-Jacksonian days, politics was considered the proper preserve of gentlemen, or at least of men of property; this view is reflected in the history of the state's party struggle and has currency to this day. De Tocqueville's observation that party cleavages revolve around the expansion or restriction of popular par-

11. See Howard, *Political Tendencies*, 251–52, Key, *Southern Politics*, 3–18, 156–82, 644–47, and Perry H. Howard, "Louisiana: Resistance and Change," in William C. Havard (ed.), *The Changing Politics of the South* (Baton Rouge: Louisiana State University Press, 1972), 525, 587.

ticipation in politics is still accurate for Louisiana. The reluctant acceptance of democracy has informed state politics and the partisan struggle since Louisiana's admission to the union in 1812. This conservative impulse is so strong that it was able to survive the Long era and appears to be flourishing today. The nature of the state's first party system is a reflection of this abiding interest in restricting popular political participation. From the 1830s to the collapse of the Whigs in the 1850s, a genuinely competitive two-party system existed in Louisiana; Louisiana voters were almost evenly split in their support for Democrats and Whigs. The average statewide support for the Democratic candidates in presidential elections from 1832 to 1852 was 50.3 percent. The average statewide support for Democratic gubernatorial candidates was 48.1 percent. This highly competitive situation in Louisiana was in contrast to the national pattern of Democratic dominance and can be partially explained by the fact that universal manhood suffrage was not established until 1845. The Jacksonian revolution was slow in coming to Louisiana.[12]

Within this context of limited suffrage based on property qualifications and restrictive residence requirements, the Democrat/Whig cleavage was along economic and class lines. The hill country farmer (engaged in non-slave-based agriculture), and the immigrant urban working class (specifically the Irish in New Orleans) formed the basic coalition of the state's Democratic party. The Whig party, on the other hand, was based on a coalition of planters (engaged in slave-based agriculture), merchants, bankers, and professionals.[13]

The state Democratic party coalition during this period typified Democratic politics elsewhere. Within the context of the times, the party represented the less affluent. It championed the egalitarianism of the Jacksonian revolution and favored expansion of suffrage and elimination of property requirements for voting. The 1845 constitution was a minor victory for this liberal mood. The conservative forces lost some ground, and with universal manhood suffrage, Whig strength

12. Ladd, *American Political Parties*, 15–27, 57–102; Seymour M. Lipset, *The First New Nation* (Garden City, N.J.: Doubleday, 1967), 17–51; Alexis de Tocqueville, *Democracy in America*, ed. George Mayer (Garden City, N.J.: Doubleday, 1969), 174–79; Howard, *Political Tendencies*, 36–68; Roger W. Shugg, "Suffrage and Representation in Ante-Bellum Louisiana," in Mark T. Carleton, Perry H. Howard, and Joseph B. Parker (eds.), *Readings in Louisiana Politics* (Baton Rouge: Claitor's, 1975), 100–114.
13. Howard, *Political Tendencies*, 59–62.

declined. The last few years of the first party system saw the Democratic party become dominant in state politics.[14]

The first party system collapsed with the dissolution of the Whig party and the coming of the Civil War. During the following twenty years, Louisiana politics had to cope with the questions of slavery, secession, war, military occupation, and reconstruction. This maelstrom of emotion and conflict not only shaped the party system that emerged after Reconstruction but also drew the broad lines of conflict that inform state politics today. The second party system also reflected a continuity with the antebellum party system. The earlier conflict over participation and the extension of suffrage surfaced again, and during this second period of party politics, there was a resurgence of conservatism. Although the sources of the controversy were different, the result was a pulling back from democracy and the establishment of class rule based on limited suffrage. The second system of party politics was the ascendance of the Bourbons. The politics of this period reconstituted the Democratic party and brought the tone of state politics in line with that of one-party politics and the Solid South. The Democratic party became identified as the party of rebellion and underwent a transformation. In the first party system, the Democrats had represented the less prosperous segment of the population. They had been the more liberal force and had championed the extension of democracy. The Whigs had represented the more privileged segment of the population, the more conservative force, and had supported the tradition of class rule and limited suffrage. After Reconstruction, the old Whig/Democrat cleavage disappeared. A fusion of the two parties took place as one-party rule replaced the two-party system. Those interests represented by the Whigs—the planters, bankers, merchants and professionals—became the dominant force in the transformed Democratic party. The Bourbon economic elite dominated party politics.[15]

Within the one-party structure of the second party system, the less prosperous segment of the population had no effective voice in state politics. The democratic concept of broadly based political participation was abandoned as significant segments of the population were ei-

14. Ladd, *Political Parties*, 57–108; *ibid.*, 69–88.
15. Howard, *Political Tendencies*, 69–154; Carleton *et al.* (eds.), *Readings in Louisiana Politics*, 328–92.

ther disenfranchised or actively discouraged from participating in the political process.

The force behind this transformation was the racial conflict that grew out of the "misrule" of the carpetbaggers and Reconstruction. Racial fears were manipulated in such a way that the white population joined in common cause against the black population. The Democratic party became identified as the party of white supremacy. In the process it also became the party of privilege, class rule, and reaction. Blacks were effectively disenfranchised, the interests of the economic elite were protected, and racial demagoguery built on the myth of white supremacy distracted the less prosperous white population.[16]

The overriding intensity of the race issue permitted the dominant party to ignore the increasing economic discontent of the nonplanter agricultural sector. The unresponsiveness of the Democratic party to the grievances of the less privileged gave rise to sporadic but ultimately unsuccessful opposition party efforts. The intensity of the discontent is indicated by the radical nature of these challenges to Democratic misrule. The Populists and Socialists focused and expressed the discontent of the working class and the hill country farmers, but their challenges had little impact, and the social and economic inequities that served the interests of the Democratic elite continued. However, the abortive reform efforts of the Populists and Socialists politicized the discontent and the next challenge to the Bourbon elite—the Progressive movement—was successful. The Populists and Socialists drew their support from the hill farmers and the urban workers; the Progressives added support from the middle-class to this base. The corruption and insensitivity of the old order gave credibility to calls for reform in politics and efficiency in government.

One reason that the Progressives succeeded where the Populists and Socialists had failed was that the latter challenged the Bourbons from outside the one-party framework, rather than from within the Democratic party. A split in the Democrats occurred between the regulars and the reformers. Race-baiting no longer worked as a device to distract and refocus discontent in order to prevent challenges to the dominant party group. The long delay in addressing serious social and eco-

16. Carleton *et al.* (eds.), *Readings in Louisiana Politics*, 328–92.

nomic problems confronting the state and the unwillingness of the regular party leadership to deal with the genuine grievances of the bulk of the population led to the overthrow of one-party rule. The forty-year period of negativism and conservatism came to an end with the emergence of the state's third party system.

The split of the Democratic party, which created two fairly consistent and permanent factions in the party, constituted the state's third party system. This system is identified with the Long era, which lasted from 1928 until the mid-1960s. Although Louisiana was still a one-party state in name, the bifactionalism within the party provided the functional equivalent of two-party competitive politics. Slates of candidates representing the opposing coalitions competed for election, voters identified with one or the other faction, and forceful executive leadership maintained the discipline of the coalitions. The beginnings of this system can be traced to the reform movement led by John M. Parker, a Reform Democrat, who broke with the party on the tariff issue in 1912 and supported Theodore Roosevelt for president. Parker ran unsuccessfully for governor in 1916 as a Progressive Republican and was elected governor as a Democrat in 1920. His election was an indication of the widespread discontent and revolt against the corruption and negativism of the regular Democrats. Parker's electoral victory was significant in that it proved that the Democratic oligarchy could be successfully challenged. His administration also introduced the idea of positive government as an alternative to the negativism of the old order. In short, Parker's success broke the grip of the regular Democrats on the machinery of government, shattered the monopoly they had enjoyed in the electoral arena, and challenged the conservative ethos that had typified Louisiana politics.[17]

Parker's career set the stage for the most important political leader in the history of the state—Huey P. Long. Long created a permanent political coalition and radically changed the direction and tradition of state politics. He became the spokesman for the hill farmers, the urban working class, and other disadvantaged groups. He spoke for "the people" against the moneyed interests and the corporations. Before Huey Long, the disadvantaged counted for little in state politics. Alienation and submissive fatalism, combined with active efforts to dis-

17. Sindler, *Huey Long's Louisiana*, 248–86, 40–45; Williams, *Huey Long*, 136–58.

courage their involvement, resulted in a very low rate of political participation by these groups. Consequently, their interests could be ignored with impunity.

Long constructed a political base from those who had neglected the political process and had been neglected by it. His political strategy was built on the mobilization of this large segment of the electorate and resulted in a massive expansion of political participation by the eligible electorate. Long, his lieutenants, and his successors forged this political base into a formidable organization. The Long organization was the focal point and stabilizing principle of the bifactionalism that typified the era. The political strategy of mobilizing segments of the population previously ignored and basing the political organization on the principle of mass participation was one of two major attacks by Long on the traditional conservatism of the state. For all its flaws, rambunctiousness, and demagoguery, the Long era has to be seen as one of expanded participation and one that opened the political process to those who had been excluded from participating in their own governance. In short, Huey Long greatly extended the concept of citizen in Louisiana.[18]

Long also attacked the conservative mood with the broad spectrum of economic and social programs inaugurated and carried out during this period. The concept of positive government introduced during the Parker administration was expanded in scope and detail and given a new meaning during the Long era. Under Long's leadership, Louisiana developed into one of the most progressive states in the nation in providing social services. The state became an instrument by which services and assistance were given to the people of the state. Positive government now not only attempted to regulate and bring the corporations under public control, but also carried out road and bridge building and educational and health programs that directly benefitted the people. These highly visible programs in turn further solidified the Long political base and provided incentive and motivation for continued support. Campaign promises and political rhetoric were backed with real performance. This willingness to use the state machinery in a positive way assured, in large measure, that the political organization created by Long would survive his assassination. His political organi-

18. Howard, *Political Tendencies*, 235–37, 421–22.

zation survived for some thirty-five years, not as a protest movement but as a positive movement of considerable accomplishment.[19]

The bifactional one-party system that typified the 1928–1963 period—the Long/Anti-Long division of the Democratic party—reflected mobilized class politics; the haves were in opposition to the have-nots. The basic conflicts reflected clashing economic interests, and the political division ran roughly along class lines. The Long faction supported and expanded state programs in the service of the have-nots and placed the financial burden on the corporations and those engaged in exploitation of the state's natural resources. The Anti-Long faction could not attack popular and essential programs and expect to win elections. They, therefore, typically campaigned on general reform planks promising to fight corruption, perform with greater efficiency, and promote good government. The Anti-Long faction was successful when scandals and corruption became too blatant or when the Long forces were split by internal rivalries or power struggles. On balance, during the period of operational bifactionalism, Louisiana preferred positive government with corruption over good government with fiscal restraint.[20]

The bifactionalism of the Long era can be documented in the organized slates of candidates for statewide offices and in legislative elections in which candidates competed under the Long or Anti-Long labels. This pattern of electioneering disappeared in the mid-1960s, when the organized style of politics it reflected fell into disarray after the 1963 gubernatorial election. The dissolution of bifactionalism resulted in the virtually no-party system that exists in the state today. The Long versus Anti-Long division had polarized the many historic, cultural, economic, and political cleavages of the state, however, and without the bifactional organizations, these cleavages reemerged. The multiple cleavages, when released from the unifying and overriding class-based bifactional politics, produced a fluid and directionless party system.[21]

The collapse of the state's bifactional party system did not occur for the usual reasons associated with such changes in political systems.

19. *Ibid.*, 211–95; Key, *Southern Politics*, 156–82; Williams, *Huey Long*; Sindler, *Huey Long's Louisiana*; Liebling, *The Earl of Louisiana*.
20. Key, *Southern Politics*, 176–77.
21. Howard, *Political Tendencies*, 295–377.

The factions had not successfully achieved the goals of the political agenda of the period. Huey Long's deathbed complaint of having so much more to do was as true in the mid-1960s as when he purportedly uttered it; and it is true today. The dissolution was not a consequence of a new political movement challenging and displacing a tired, outmoded, or irrelevant approach to politics as had occurred, for example, when the rise of Longism had challenged the Bourbons. Furthermore, the breakup was not caused by the system's neglect of long-standing grievances.[22]

The transformation of state politics that coincided with the decline of bifactionalism resembles, in a number of ways, the pattern of the Bourbon ascendancy. Both were reactions to national policies and movements beyond the control of the state political system. Both reflected a resurgence of conservatism in the state's political mood, in the nature of the political conflicts, and in the attempted political solutions. The conservatism of the period immediately preceding and following the collapse of bifactionalism gained its dominant position because the political arrangements could not deal effectively with the race issue. The race issue began to resurface in state politics as early as the 1948 presidential election. However, the class-based politics of the Long era muted the issue, and it did not become a dominant force in state politics until the 1960s. By the mid-1960s, treatment of the issue had reached such an emotional pitch and had become so pervasive that it could no longer be subsumed under the overriding economic mantle; nor could it be contained within the bifactional framework. Race-baiting, white supremacy, and state rights became the standard themes of political rhetoric and dominated the political agenda.[23]

Although the Long faction had not been integrationist, it had not been racist, and it had resisted, after a fashion, efforts to intensify racial conflict in state politics. Some observers attribute Earl Long's physical and mental deterioration to the rigors of his efforts to beat back the racial hysteria that had captured the state legislature during his last term as governor. Despite efforts to defuse this issue, federal court decisions, national legislation, and executive actions, combined with the national media's focus on civil rights, contributed to an hys-

22. Ladd, *Political Parties*, 28–45; Everett C. Ladd, Jr., with Charles D. Hadley, *Transformation of the American Party System* (New York: Norton, 1975), 2–27.
23. Howard, *Political Tendencies*, 295–377.

terical and irrational reaction in defense of the "southern way of life." Racism in all its ugly manifestations dominated state politics. The class-based politics of the bifactional system broke down as race overshadowed other considerations. No public leader could afford to be perceived as soft on the race issue.

The White Citizens Councils and the resuscitated Ku Klux Klan exerted considerable influence on the politics of the period. As part of the racist reaction, the conservative strategy of limiting and restricting participation was tried once again. Legal barriers, inconvenient and complicated procedures, active discouragement, blatant harassment, intimidation, and violence were the methods used to fight the implementation of national policy within the state. This unsuccessful effort to resist the national movement toward greater racial justice generated bitterness, hostility, and antagonism that linger today, although on a much reduced and muted level. The attempt to restrict participation failed largely because of aggressive federal actions to prevent a repetition of the disenfranchisement of blacks and to assure that black registration would not be subverted by state actions.

An investigation of state politics over the past ten years indicates that a new party system has yet to take form to replace the bifactionalism of the Long era and to give shape and direction to the contemporary political environment. The intense racial politics that shattered the division and unity of the bifactional system gave way to a highly personalized pattern of political organization and fluid alliances. The apparent chaos partially reflects older cleavages that had been bridged in the bifactional arrangement and partially reflects new political interests that developed out of the changes within the state over the past thirty years. This is not to imply that during the Long era there were no personalized political organizations, but the Long/Anti-Long factions used a broader set of unifying loyalties—as a base to forge the personalized organizations into fairly permanent coalitions reflecting class interests.[24] Since the dissolution of the bifactionalism system, no political leader with the force of a Long or a George Wallace has appeared to construct a coalition that would submerge the local loyalties. Furthermore, with the passing of race as a political issue no issue or

24. *Ibid.*

set of issues has been strong enough to bring about coalitions transcending specialized or parochial interests.

The dimensions of political cleavage in Louisiana illustrate the state's uniqueness. No other southern state has as diverse a social ecology. It should be noted, however, that many of the cleavages overlap. For example, the cleavage between North and South Louisiana includes, but does not totally account for the Protestant/Catholic, the American/French, or much of the nativist/foreigner polarity. Likewise, the antagonisms between New Orleans or Shreveport and the rest of the state resemble typical urban/rural cleavages, but with interesting differences. In the case of New Orleans, the urban/rural conflict is aggravated by the dimension of cosmopolitanism and sophistication associated with the city that is reflected in a certain snobbism and sense of superiority toward the remainder of the state. (The attitude of New Orleanians is said to resemble that of those East Coast residents for whom civilization stops at the Hudson River.) The Shreveport cleavage with the rest of the state, on the other hand, originates in a sense of isolation from the remainder of the state and a feeling of greater proximity to Texas. Similarly, the black/white and labor/management polarities cut across other cleavages on certain issues and under certain conditions. The complexity of these conflicts and antagonisms makes political unity a sometime thing in the state.

The conflicts outlined in Table 10-1 are of long standing within the state; some have existed since the colonial period. The economic and social changes of the past thirty years have added to these cleavages and complicated them. The most visible change and the one that encompasses most of the other changes is the increased urbanization in the state. In 1950 the state's urban population accounted for 54.8 percent of the total population. By 1970 nearly two-thirds of the population resided in urban areas, and population projections for 1980 predict that seven out of ten Louisianians will live in urban areas. This changing residential pattern reflects two types of population movement. One is the immigration from other parts of the country, an experience Louisiana shares with the rest of the Sun Belt. The other is internal migration from the rural areas and small towns to the industrial centers. Much of the residential transformation is actually suburbanization rather than urbanization in the historical sense. The reverse

Table 10-1

Dimensions of Political Cleavages in Louisiana Politics

Regional
Plantation areas v. small farm areas
   North v. South
   New Orleans v. State
   Caddo/Shreveport v. State

Ethnic
American v. French
Nativist v. Foreigner (Irish, Italian, Cajun)
Protestant v. Catholic

Demographic
Urban v. Rural
New Orleans v. State
Industrial v. Agricultural

Economic
Planters, Merchants, Professionals v. Farmers, Laborers
   Property Owner v. Non–Property Owner
   Planter v. Farmer
   Management v. Labor
   Developers v. Environmentalists

Ideological
Elitist v. Egalitarian
White Supremacy v. Moderation
Liberal v. Conservative

Note: This table is a modification and elaboration of the delineation of Ecological and Power Structures in Perry Howard, *Political Tendencies in Louisiana*, 23–24.

side of this residential shift can be seen in the decline of the rural farm population over the same period. Roughly 21 percent of the state's population lived on farms in 1950. The percentage had dropped to 7.1 percent in 1960 and to 4.7 percent in 1970.[25] The changed residential pattern is only one indicator of the depth and breadth of the moderni-

25. Louisiana Office of State Planning, *The State of the State*, 1974 (Baton Rouge: Office of State Planning, 1975), 5–7, 60.

Table 10-2

Louisiana Social and Economic Development 1950–1970

	1950	Percent	1960	Percent	1970	Percent
Total Population	2,683,516		3,257,022		3,643,180	
Urban	1,471,696	54.8	2,060,606	63.3	2,406,150	66.1
Rural	1,211,820	45.2	1,196,416	36.7	1,235,156	33.9
Percent Adults						
With No Schooling		9.1		6.6		3.9
With Less Than 5 years		28.7		21.3		13.1
With Four Years High School		21.6		32.3		42.3
With Four Years of College		4.7		6.7		9.1
Employment By Major Industry						
Total	875,608		1,007,812		1,158,245	
Agriculture	160,595	18.3	78,810	7.8	47,999	4.2
Construction	64,939	7.4	81,033	8.0	96,609	8.3
Manufacturing	132,476	15.1	157,261	15.6	184,024	15.9
Educational Services	36,405	4.2	62,281	6.2	101,791	8.8
Medical & Health	23,696	2.7	26,119	2.6	60,801	5.3
Other Professional	11,927	1.4	21,294	2.1	30,365	2.6
Public Administration	33,446	3.8	43,607	4.3	53,520	4.6
Employment by Occupation						
Total	876,608		1,007,812		1,158,245	
Prof. Tech. & Kindred	69,879	7.9	103,530	10.2	161,025	13.9
Farmers & Farm Mgrs.	89,781	10.2	33,080	3.2	15,982	1.3
Mgrs., Officials & Pro-						
prietors Except Farm	74,110	8.4	91,993	9.1	104,128	8.9
Clerical & Kindred	85,530	9.7	120,112	11.9	180,406	15.5
Craftsmen, Foremen &						
Kindred	100,922	11.5	124,908	12.3	167,860	14.4
Operatives & Kindred	131,539	15.0	164,832	16.3	180,777	15.6
Service Workers Except						
Household	70,185	8.0	94,803	9.4	134,054	11.5
Farm Laborers &						
Foremen	57,518	6.5	28,567	2.8	21,152	1.8
Laborers Except Farm	84,291	9.6	75,965	7.5	70,286	6.0

Table 10-2 (*Continued*)

	1949	1959	1969
Median Family Income			
Louisiana	$2,122	$4,272	$7,530
United States	$3,073	$5,660	$9,590
Percent of Families With			
Income Under $3,000			
Louisiana	62.4%	35.6%	18.9%
United States	48.4%	21.4%	10.3%
Percent of Families With			
Income Over $10,000			
Louisiana	2.2%	9.9%	33.6%
United States	3.1%	15.1%	47.3%

Source: *Statistical Profile of Louisiana* (Baton Rouge: Public Affairs Research Council of Louisiana, 1973), 1, 6, 8, 13–14.

zation that has taken place in the state over the past thirty years. Other indications of these changes can be found in the patterns of employment, education, and income reflected in Tables 10-2 and 10-3. The tables indicate the social and economic development that has taken place in the state over the past thirty years. Most analysts expect those trends to continue. Political development, on the other hand, has not kept pace with social and economic progress. Indeed, the institutional arrangement that reflected political modernization—the bifactional party system—collapsed midway through this period. State politics over the past fifteen years have been highly personalized and fragmented. Political power has been associated with particular sheriffs, district attorneys, mayors, ethnic leaders, interest group leaders, and prominent individuals as opposed to formal political institutions or organizations. This political regression is caused by the absence of unifying forces in the political arena.

The disintegration of the bifactional system permitted the state's political cleavages to reemerge. Local notables and political leaders increased their power and assumed greater roles as power brokers.[26] In turn, candidates focused their attention on gaining the support of the

26. Howard, "Louisiana: Resistance and Change," 574–88.

Table 10-3

Changes in Selected Louisiana Social and Economic Dimensions, 1950–1970

Year	Urban Population	Percent Change	Employment in Agriculture	Percent Change	Employment in Manufacturing	Percent Change	Employment in Educational Services	Percent Change
1950	1,471,696		160,595		132,476		36,405	
1960	2,060,606	+40%	78,810	−50.9%	157,261	+18%	62,281	+71%
1970	2,406,150	+16.7%	47,999	−39%	184,624	+17%	101,791	+63%
1950 to 1970 Total Change		+63.4%		−70%		+38.9%		+179%

Year	Professional Technical and Kindred Workers	Percent Change	Farmers & Farm Managers	Percent Change	Clerical & Kindred Workers	Percent Change	Service Workers Except Household	Percent Change
1950	69,879		89,781		85,530		70,185	
1960	103,530	+48.1%	33,080	−63.1%	120,112	+40.4%	94,803	+35%
1970	161,025	+55.5%	15,982	−51.6%	180,406	+50%	134,054	+41%
1950 to 1970 Total Change		+130.4%		−82%		+110%		+91%

local political leaders who controlled or could deliver the necessary votes. This furthered the fragmentation of politics and created new barriers to effective political aggregation.

Although politics have recently been chaotic, two elements have emerged that have positive implications for the future of state politics. The element most directly political in its effect is the reluctant acceptance and adoption of modern campaign methods and practices. This includes the use of polls, campaign managers and consultants, advertising agencies, public relations techniques, and extensive use of the mass media. These methods and techniques were relatively late in coming to Louisiana. As in other southern states, the pattern of state politics had been the "friends and neighbors" approach, which entailed personal appearances at festivals, homecomings, crawfish boils, fish fries and barbecues, along with gathering the support of the courthouse power group. In this approach to elections, the campaign was entertainment, the serious work of electioneering involved getting the support of the sheriff or other local organizations that could deliver the vote. The modern campaign, in a sense the reverse of the "friends and neighbors" approach, stresses the media; the candidate's image and movements are deadly serious and not fun and games. The local organization is not central to this approach. Indeed, the candidate typically hires his or her own campaign staff, organizes local volunteers, and goes over the head of any barriers between image and the voter. The 1971 election, the first one in which modern campaign methods dominated, saw the defeat of most of the old line politicians and the election of many political newcomers, most of whom were considerably more physically attractive than those they defeated.

Since 1971, the modern campaign approach has become so important that the crustiest example of the southern political stereotype feels constrained to hire an advertising agency and spend most of the campaign funds on polls and television advertising. As a result, the role of the media has increased significantly in campaigns, and a new political class is emerging in the state. The bright young political technicians, the polling experts, the public relations consultants, the campaign managers, and the fund raisers who make up this group of specialists will, as their presence becomes more permanent, transform state politics. The local political boss may be displaced by the highly mobile political technocrat. If this occurs, the power-broker role of the political leader will be eroded, and one of the major barriers to effective political organization will disappear.

The second element that has positive implications is a consequence of the social and economic modernization of the last thirty years. Educational and demographic changes have produced a potential support base for a serious Republican party. The state now has a fairly broad new middle class—white-collar, professional, technical, affluent—that typically is more comfortable with the Republican than with the Democratic political style and credo. The Louisiana Republican party has yet to realize its potential with this segment of the population.

In the past, southern Republicanism was either a reflection of Civil War loyalties that survived through federal patronage or a genteel form of racism reflecting discontent with the national Democrats and the Civil Rights Movement. Indeed, as late as 1968, the southern Republican strategy was designed to capitalize on racial antagonisms. In the 1960s this strategy was based on political cynicism; today such a strategy is political stupidity. A minority party hoping to challenge the dominant party cannot afford the luxury of alienating one-third of the electorate.

Within the present context of Democratic party disorganization the opportunity for the creation of a viable Republican alternative has never been greater. Discontent with state and local government; such issues as waste disposal, pollution control, educational quality, criminal justice, energy, and government responsiveness; and the existence of a new and growing potential base of support all add up to Republican opportunities. If the Republican leadership continues its organizational efforts of the mid-seventies and fields candidates for major state and local offices in areas of Republican strength, the party will increase its credibility and Louisiana will begin to move toward a two-party system. In order to realize this potential, the Republican party has to broaden its base and get off its ideological hobbyhorse. At this time the party has the image of a lily-white band of malcontents who meet at the country club to curse the New Deal. This may be emotionally satisfying, but it does not win elections, and it will not create an effective political party. The pattern of effective challenges to dominant parties entails a broad coalition offering positive and creative solutions to real problems. The challenge facing the Louisiana Republican party is to convince voters that it is not necessary to be a closet racist, a social Neanderthal, or a member of the country club to be a Republican.

The organizational efforts of Republicans have succeeded in expanding the party's base of support. In 1976 only twelve parishes (Bossier, Caddo, Calcasieu, East Baton Rouge, Jefferson, Lafayette, Lincoln, Orleans, Ouachita, Rapides, St. Tammany, and Terrebonne) had a thousand or more registered Republicans. By 1979 the list had expanded to include Iberia, Lafourche, St. Landry, St. Mary, and Tangipahoa. The strength of the party is concentrated in those parishes within or bordering the state's major urban areas, and these seventeen parishes contain 83 percent of registered Republicans.[27]

It should be noted that, despite impressive growth, Republican strength in its most concentrated form is only 11.5 percent of the registered voters and amounts to one-seventh of the Democratic strength. In 1979, for example, St. Tammany Republican registrants numbered 5,925 to 40,670 Democrats. Nevertheless, Republicans now control two of the state's eight seats in the United States House of Representatives, ten seats in the state house of representatives, an increasing number of local offices, and the state's executive mansion. It is obvious that the registration figures underestimate Republican strength and potential.

In contrast to the Republican party, the Democratic party appears determined to live up to Will Rogers' estimation that it was not an organized political party. The party is still operating in the fragmented mode that followed the collapse of bifactionalism. However, there are signs that this pattern may be in the process of breaking down. Three forces are converging to propel the Democratic party into another mode of operation.

First, the open-primary strategy, which Democrats hoped would squelch the Republican party, is not working. The Democrats responded to the challenge posed by the revitalized Republicans by manipulating the electoral process. The democratically controlled legislature passed legislation, backed by Governor Edwards, that replaced the closed-primary system with an open-primary system, under which the candidate who receives a majority of the votes cast in a primary elec-

27. U.S. Bureau of the Census, *Congressional District Data Book* (Washington, D.C.: U.S. Government Printing Office, 1976); Public Affairs Research Council, "Primary Election, October 27, 1979," *Analysis* (November, 1979), 2.

Table 10-4
Republican Party Registration,
1975–1980

Year	Total Registered Voters	Registered Republicans	Percent of Total	Percent Increase
1975	1,798,032	53,100	2.9	
1976	1,866,117	68,078	3.6	28.2
1977	1,787,031	70,877	4.0	4.1
1978	1,821,026	79,900	4.4	12.7
1979	1,936,804	98,211	5.1	22.9
1980	2,015,402	149,903	7.4	52.6

Source: Public Affairs Research Council, *Primary Election of October 27, 1979*, 3, and Public Affairs Research Council, *Presidential Election, November, 1980*, 3.

tion is declared elected and is not required to stand for election in the general election.[28] Under the closed-primary system leading Democratic candidates were frequently required to contest three elections; the primary, a runoff, and the general election. The new system, it was argued, would simplify the electoral process, reduce the costs of elections, and ease the burden on both candidates and voters. Underlying these laudable objectives was the assumption that under such a system the overwhelmingly Democratic registration would effectively block Republican candidates from electoral victory. In this way, the Democratic power structure thought to fend off the Republican challenge without jeopardizing the various political fiefdoms that constitute the party hierarchy. The "single shot" primary permitted the Democratic party to abdicate any role in candidate selection and nomination for the gubernatorial election. While the Republicans carried out the party function in agreeing on one candidate and approaching the election in a disciplined fashion, the Democrats engaged in the no-party politics typical of its operations over the past fifteen years. Five major Democratic candidates brawled and bruised each other until the primary, after which the four runners-up endorsed the Republican candidate in the general election—a classic case of no-party politics run amok.

28. Act 1 of 1975.

Second, the increased use of modern campaign techniques and the mass media has reduced the control of many of the party chieftains over the vote in their jurisdictions. Within the tradition of high political participation that was instituted during the Long era, this novel campaign methodology has also increased the centrifugal forces operating in the party as previously controlled or controllable segments of the party have achieved power brokerage positions rivaling the traditional power brokers.

Third, the national Democratic party has required the state parties to modify and reform their operations to allow more direct rank-and-file participation in party affairs. The Democratic reforms are designed to facilitate greater political participation and to make the party leadership more attentive and responsive to the interests and issues affecting the politically engaged members of the party. This has had the effect of opening the party to a wider range of interest and diminishing the control over party affairs once enjoyed by the party hierarchy.[29] The structural and operational modifications required by these reforms have moved the Democratic party into a more defined and elaborate organizational mode. The centrifugal forces within the party have been called into question by the accommodations made to meet the reforms. As new faces and new voices emerge in party affairs the present fragmentation should give way to a more unified and clearly defined political organization. The State Democratic Convention in March, 1980, gave some credence to this assumption. The party adopted a platform, addressed the problem of party loyalty, censured the four Democratic gubernatorial candidates who had endorsed Republican Treen and appeared to be on its way to becoming an organized and effective political party.

The increasing organizational and electoral vitality of the Republican party and the recent developments within the Democratic party reflect the movement of Louisiana politics away from the southern regional style toward the national mainstream. Although the state's politics are still unique and are dominated by the one-party style that permits specialized pressure groups to dominate public policy formulation, the possibilities for the development of effective political competition and responsible government are now more real than in the

29. Roy W. Fletcher, Jr., "The Democratic Party Reforms, 1936–1974" (M.A. thesis, Louisiana State University, 1976).

past. It is premature to speak of the emergence of a competitive two-party system, but the highly politicized nature of the state requires a more defined framework than presently exists. The Republican successes in recent years reflect that requirement. The party arena is adjusting to the changes taking place in the state's social and political environment. Further adjustments are required and can be expected. Too many forces and interests have been activated to be contained within the fragmented party system that followed the collapse of bifactionalism.

A Note on Party Organization

Anyone with experience in large-scale organizations or party politics knows that neat schematic diagrams purporting to show organizational structure and operation are frequently misleading. More often than not the charts present someone's idea of how things should be, not how things are.[30] The following description of the structure of Louisiana's Democratic and Republican parties should be read with these caveats in mind.

The Louisiana Election Code (Title 18 of the *Louisiana Revised Statutes* as amended by Act 697 of 1976) provides a legal definition of political parties and prescribes specific structural arrangements and party activities. In order to be recognized, a political party must have at least 5 percent of the voters in the state "registered as being affiliated with the political party," or one of its candidates for presidential elector must have "received at least five percent of the votes cast in this state for presidential elections in the last presidential election."[31] The law further provides that a party receiving more than 5 percent but less than 10 percent of the vote in the last presidential election is not entitled to representation on the board of election supervisors at the parish level. The Democratic and Republican parties both qualify as recognized parties under the Election Code. In the 1980 presidential election no other party received the minimum 5 percent needed for recognition.

30. Samuel J. Eldersveld, *Political Parties: A Behavioral Analysis* (Chicago: Rand McNally, 1964).
31. Louisiana Election Code, Pt. III, Sec. 441.

Table 10-5
1980 Presidential Election in Louisiana

Party	Popular Vote	Percentage Popular Vote
Democratic	708,453	45
Republican	792,853	51
Anderson (Independent)	26,345	1
American Independent	10,333	less than 1
Libertarian	8,240	less than 1
People's	1,584	less than 1
Socialist Workers'	783	less than 1

Source: Election Proclamation, Office of the Secretary of State, "Electors for President and Vice-President of the United States," in Baton Rouge *State Times*, November 18, 1980, Sec. D, p. 12.

The Election Code prescribes that recognized parties "shall be controlled and directed by one state central committee and a parish executive committee for each parish." Members of each committee serve four-year terms and are elected at the time of the gubernatorial election. Party state central committees are required to meet at the state capital within fifteen days of the gubernatorial general election in order to elect the officers of the committee. A majority of the committee constitutes a quorum and voting must be in person. The same provisions are made for the parish executive committees except that parish committees are required to meet at the parish courthouse.[32]

The Election Code also prescribes the composition and apportionment of party state central committees. The committees of recognized parties shall have "at least one member from each parish and one additional member for each eighteen thousand two hundred fifty persons or a major fraction thereof in each parish." If the party has less than 10 percent of the registered voters of the state, the apportionment of central committee members is left to the party's state central committee. However, if the party enrolls more than 10 percent of the registered voters, it must follow the apportionment prescribed in the Election Code. The code describes 109 districts and the number of representatives from each district to serve on the state central committee. Dis-

32. *Ibid.*, Pt. III, Secs. 442, 443C, 444C.

trict representation ranges from one to three members.[33] In early 1981, the Democratic party, which has slightly more than 90 percent of the registered voters, is the only party affected by these requirements.

The Election Code provides that parish executive committees are to be composed of five members elected at large from the entire parish and as many members elected from each police jury ward or equivalent subdivisions as there are members of the parish governing authority elected from that subdivision.[34] For example, the East Baton Rouge Parish Executive Committees of the Democratic and Republican parties have seventeen members: twelve members matching city-parish council positions elected by ward and five members elected at large for the entire parish.

The Democratic State Central Committee with 203 members is obviously too large to administer the party's business. This task is carried out by a fifteen-member executive committee chosen by the central committee. The state central committee also selects the party's five-member delegation to the National Democratic Committee and appoints the membership of DemoPAC (Democratic Political Action Committee). DemoPAC, the action arm of the state central committee, is primarily active during gubernatorial elections. It is a ten-member body whose major role is fund raising. The Democratic State Central Committee convenes at least once a year. However, during gubernatorial and presidential election years meetings may be more frequent.[35]

Democratic Parish Executive Committees exhibit a pattern of activity similar to their state counterparts. The parish committees must meet regularly. They also become quite active in periods immediately preceding and during election campaigns. In non–election years these committees are considerably less active and meetings are held episodically. Typically, Democratic committees at the parish level do not engage in any year-round party activity.[36]

In addition to the regular party structures, the Democratic party also includes two auxiliary organizations—Democratic Women and the Young Democrats. The organizational vitality and activity patterns of these two organizations parallel those of the regular party. Member-

33. *Ibid.*, Pt. III, Secs. 443C, 444C.
34. *Ibid.*, Pt. III, Sec. 444G.
35. Larry S. Bankston, Chairman, East Baton Rouge Parish Democratic Executive Committee, interview, January 3, 1981.
36. Bankston, interview.

ship growth, high visibility, and political activity coincide with guber-natorial and presidential elections followed by two years of organiza-tional decline and inactivity. The auxiliary organizations do not carry out any sustained political activity, although both groups are well suited for party work.[37]

Since the Republican party enrolls less than 10 percent of the state's registered voters, the composition and apportionment of the Republi-can State Central Committee is not prescribed in detail by the Election Code. The Republicans have 148 members on their state central com-mittee. The basis of representation is the Louisiana house of repre-sentatives' election district. Representation on the central committee by district is based on the number of Republicans registered in the dis-trict and is determined by the state central committee. The executive committee of the Republican State Central Committee has six mem-bers including the state chairperson, vice-chairperson, secretary, trea-surer, and the national committeeman and national committeewoman. The Republican State Central Committee normally convenes once a year but more frequently when conditions such as gubernatorial and presidential elections require it. The Republican party has developed an additional organization unit that serves as the party's policy and strategy arm—the Political Action Council. The council has three lev-els of organization: parish, region (roughly equal to the state's con-gressional districts), and state. The state Political Action Council nor-mally meets three or four times a year but more frequently during election years. It has eighteen members, including the central com-mittee's executive committee and eight regional PAC chairpersons. It was the state PAC that made the strategic decision to field only one gubernatorial candidate in the 1979 election. The Political Action Councils are much more active on a year-round basis than the state central committee. The regional PAC members serve as political cir-cuit riders advising and aiding the parish executive committees and parish PACs on membership, candidate recruitment, funding, cam-paign organization and strategy, and other party matters.[38]

Republican parish executive committees represent varying degrees of maturity. Some parishes have no Republican organization, others

37. Bankston, interview.
38. Robert A. Hawthorne, Jr., Regional Political Action Council Chairperson, Repub-lican Party, Region 6, interview, January 3, 4, 9, 1981.

have an organization on paper but only two or three active members, and still others have an executive committee appointed by the state central committee. Some parishes have Republican executive committees that are elective but active only during election years. There are parishes such as East Baton Rouge with growing and dynamic Republican organizations. The East Baton Rouge Republican Political Action Council and the East Baton Rouge Republican Executive Committee hold meetings on a monthly basis and are involved in party activity year-round.[39]

The Republican auxiliary organizations—Republican Women and Young Republicans—are generally more active and better organized than their Democratic counterparts. Both provide members with social activities and satisfactions within the context of party politics. The membership and activism of the Republican auxiliary organizations are more sustaining and less tied to electoral considerations than their Democratic counterparts. This is particularly true of the Young Republicans, who seem to be preoccupied with ideological and policy matters.[40]

The differences in party organization reflect the condition of party politics in the state. Democratic organization typifies parties born to or long accustomed to a monopoly of political power. In such cases, party organization is convenient for elections and for containing power struggles within the ruling group. Any other activism by party organizations becomes a nuisance, and consequently, strong and sustained party activity is discouraged.

The Republican organization reflects the style of a cautious challenger: building from strength, marshaling resources, hoping not to alert or antagonize the "king of the hill" until it is too late for the Democrats to carry out effective countermeasures. So far, the Republican strategy has worked. Democratic responses have been ineffective and confused and, in some cases, have resulted in unnecessary self-inflicted wounds. The key to the future shape of party politics in the state rests with the Democrats. The Republicans know what they are doing.

---

39. Hawthorne, interview.
40. Sheila Feigley, Past President of Louisiana Republican Women's Clubs, Former Member of the Republican State Central Committee, interview, January 8, 9, 1981.

11.

Blacks in Louisiana Politics

JEWEL L. PRESTAGE AND CAROLYN SUE WILLIAMS

Whatever phase of the southern political process one seeks to understand, sooner or later the trail of inquiry leads to the Negro.
V. O. Key, Jr., *Southern Politics in State and Nation*

Somehow the Negro unwittingly has exercised a tyranny over the mind of the white South, which has found continuous expression in the politics of the region.
Samuel DuBois Cook,
"Political Movements and Organizations"

The political history of blacks in Louisiana has reflected the political life of blacks in the nation at large and in the South in particular. Any effort to describe the politics of black Louisianians must take into account not only such traditional political activities as registering and voting but also ways in which blacks have indirectly affected the politics of the state. The latter consideration has received only limited attention in the literature of black politics. Current definitions of *politics* range from restrictive notions that associate politics with government and the state to more flexible views that equate politics with power, authority, conflict, and decision making.[1] Politics encompasses the totality of the power relationships in society as those relationships impinge upon the ultimate use of coercive powers of the society. Most black politics literature has focused on traditional political behavior

1. For these definitions and discussions, see Harold Lasswell, *Politics: Who Gets What, When, How?* (New York: McGraw-Hill, 1936); David Easton, "An Approach to the Analysis of Political Systems," *World Politics*, IX (1957), 383–400; Karl Deutsch, "On the Concepts of Politics and Power," *Journal of International Affairs*, XXI (1967), 232.

with major emphasis on Reconstruction and the post–Civil Rights era of the 1960s and 1970s. However, from our viewpoint, everything that has affected the status of blacks in Louisiana is politically relevant.[2]

We will discuss political activities of black Louisianians through five historical periods: slavery (1717–1861), the Civil War (1861–1865), Reconstruction (1866–1890), post-Reconstruction and early twentieth century (1890–1943), and the Second Reconstruction (1944 to the present). These periods represent distinct segments during which the political forces acting on blacks and the blacks' reactions to these forces were markedly different.

The Period of Slavery (1717–1865)

The first slave ships arrived in Louisiana in 1719. Prior to that time, there were hardly more than a dozen black Africans in Louisiana, but by 1840, of 19,181 families residing in Louisiana, 9,688, or just over half, held slaves.[3] The highest percentage of slaveholding families lived in ten Mississippi River parishes in the northeast and southeast sections of the state. (See Table 11-1.) By 1860 there were approximately 331,726 slaves in Louisiana.

Studies of American slavery reveal that most slaves lived on plantations where political life was determined by the objective of economic gain, which pervaded the slave system. Generally, whatever was perceived as contributing to economic productivity took precedence over other considerations. Where economically feasible, beatings, sexual exploitation, and overwork were common. Family life among slaves existed at the sufferance of slave masters, and the black father-husband role had no status. The few laws protecting slaves were not usually enforced. Extant scholarship suggests that Louisiana was no exception to this pattern. Particularly trying conditions existed on the state's sugar-cane plantations where the eighteen- to twenty-hour workday was

2. Hanes Walton, Jr., *Black Politics: A Theoretical and Structural Analysis* (Philadelphia: J. B. Lippincott, 1972); Mack H. Jones, "A Frame of Reference for Black Politics," in Lenneal J. Henderson, Jr. (ed.), *Black Political Life in America* (San Francisco: Chandler, 1972), 7–20.

3. Sarah Searight, *New Orleans* (New York: Stein and Day, 1973), 106; D. L. A. Hackett, "The Social Structure of Jacksonian Louisiana," *Louisiana Studies*, XII (1973), 324–53.

Table 11-1

Slaveholding Among Louisiana Families, 1840

Parish	Percentage of Families Owning Slaves
St. Charles	78.2
St. James	75.9
St. John	73.1
Iberville	72.2
Pointe Coupee	71.0
Madison	70.0
West Feliciana	69.5
Concordia	68.9
West Baton Rouge	68.9
Carroll	67.7

Source: D. L. A. Hackett, "The Social Structure of Jacksonian Louisiana," 324.

not uncommon. It has been suggested by some scholars that the slave experience on small plantations or farms was more severe than on larger estates. If this was the case, then the Louisiana situation was comparatively more depressing since, in 1840, 41.4 percent of the slaveholding families owned from one to four slaves, 64 percent held from one to nine, and 80.4 percent held from one to nineteen slaves. Few families owned large numbers of slaves: 6.4 percent had twenty to twenty-nine slaves, and 7.3 percent held more than fifty slaves each. That is to say, 80.4 percent of the slaveholding families possessed only 31.0 percent of all the slaves in the state.[4]

Although members of the slave community could not engage in traditional political behavior, it seems clear that slaves did not constitute an inactive political element in Louisiana from 1719 to 1861. Of political significance were the slaves' reactions to their oppression. Among these were the resort to otherworldliness through religion, work slowdowns, feigning of illness, destruction of plantation property, self-mutilation, suicide, escape, revolt, violence against the master class, and the formation of secret slave alliances. Louisiana had its share of all of these forms of political expression. In 1811 a massive uprising of

4. John Hope Franklin, *From Slavery to Freedom* (New York: Knopf, 1974), 144; Hackett, "The Social Structure of Jacksonian Louisiana."

over four hundred slaves occurred in St. Charles and St. John the Baptist parishes, and in 1829 several plantation revolts took place. A revolt of over 2,500 slaves in New Orleans was aborted by a free-Negro informer in 1853. A dramatic suicide of two runaways occurred in 1858.[5] One of the most effective means of convincing the slave masters to provide better treatment, especially on the sugarcane plantations, was simply not to work efficiently and diligently at the task of harvesting the cane. While basically nonpolitical, such action took on a distinctly political character under the circumstances.

Slaves in Louisiana, as in other areas, were also not without considerable indirect influence on the formal political process. Louisiana slaves indirectly affected the political system in at least two ways. First, they were the subject of a substantial body of law designed to outline their status, upkeep, and behavior. The *Code Noir*, which Bienville drafted in 1724, was based on the codes of Santo Domingo. With some minor changes, it remained in effect until the Louisiana Purchase when it was replaced by codes that were even more strict. According to the *Code Noir*, slaves were forbidden to carry weapons or to assemble with slaves belonging to a different master. However, they were given Sundays and holidays off from work or were allowed to work for themselves on those days. The essential point is not what the codes contained, but rather that specific public policy existed relative to slaves and that this public policy necessitated structures and processes for formulation, implementation, and enforcement. The code was periodically revised by the political elite consistent with their view of what was needed to keep slaves in their place.

Another kind of influence exerted on Louisiana politics by black slavery has been identified by Roger W. Shugg, who found that slavery militated against the development of overt class hostility between the white propertied class and poor whites. The poor white was provided a social system in which he could always look down on "one lower than himself, the enslaved black," with contempt and hostility that might have otherwise been aimed at the privileged white elite.[6] In short, slav-

5. John Blassingame, *The Slave Community* (New York: Oxford University Press, 1972), 126; Franklin, *From Slavery to Freedom*, 161–62; William F. Cheek, *Black Resistance Before the Civil War* (Beverly Hills: Glencoe Press, 1970).

6. Roger W. Shugg, *Origins of Class Struggle in Louisiana: A Social History of White Farmers and Laborers During Slavery and After, 1840–1875* (Baton Rouge: Louisiana State University Press, 1939), 30.

ery was a political experience for both the enslaved and the enslavers.

In addition to the black slaves, Louisiana had a sizable free-black population. These free blacks have been the focus of several historical accounts. One observer noted in 1839 that the number of free blacks was increasing since children of free mothers were themselves free. By 1860 New Orleans had a population of 168,000, of whom 13,000 were black slaves and 11,000 were free blacks. One state law enjoined free blacks from remaining in the state and stipulated that freedom could not be given to any slave within the state except on the condition of "his quitting it forever." The fear undergirding the law was that, if free blacks remained in the state, they would transmit a love for freedom to the slaves and excite their desire to enjoy it for themselves. Free blacks, for a time, occupied a peculiar status involving "distinct grades of society." In New Orleans a caste system somewhat comparable to that of India came into being. Studies of this caste system have emphasized not only the relations between those blacks in the various levels of the system but also the relationship between the total system and white society.[7]

Many of Louisiana's free people of color were small businessmen or skilled artisans; they were well educated and well-to-do. Until two decades before the Civil War, they enjoyed considerable freedom despite the letter of the law. But as the slavery dispute heightened, the legislature put more and more legal restrictions on them and in 1857 forbade manumission. One author summarily equates their status just prior to the Civil War to that of slaves in stating that "all Negroes, bond and free, had good reason to welcome the bluecoats."[8] A body of law had grown up around free blacks that rivaled that relating to slaves.

Free blacks in Louisiana were not satisfied with their *de jure* status of quasi freedom nor even with their more relaxed *de facto* status that prevailed up to about the 1840s. They engaged in a variety of activities designed to ameliorate their plight and, to some extent, that of their

7. James Silk Buckingham, *The Slave States of America* (2 vols.; New York: Negro University Press, 1968), I, 376–77; Gerald M. Capers, *Occupied City* (Lexington: University of Kentucky Press, 1965), 5; Alice Dunbar Nelson, "People of Color in Louisiana: Part II," *Journal of Negro History*, II (1917), 51–78. Frederick L. Olmsted, *Journey to the Seaboard States* (New York: Negro University Press, 1968), 583. For information on free people of color outside of New Orleans, see Gary B. Mills, *The Forgotten People: Cane River's Creoles of Color* (Baton Rouge: Louisiana State University Press, 1977).

8. Capers, *Occupied City*, 10.

enslaved kin. Many of them fled to Haiti and Europe when the more restrictive regulations were enacted just prior to the Civil War, while others formed themselves into a distinct group to accentuate the fact that they were separate and apart from the slave population. Further, they agitated for the right to vote. For example, on November 5, 1863, New Orleans free blacks held a mass meeting and agreed to petition the military governor of the state for the right to vote. Disappointed at the state level, in 1864 they sent a petition to President Lincoln and the Congress, bearing the signatures of more than a thousand men, twenty-seven of whom had fought with Andrew Jackson at the Battle of New Orleans. The petition was carried to Washington, D.C., by Jean Baptiste Roudanez and Arnold Bertonneau and presented to President Lincoln on March 12. Senator Charles Sumner presented it to the U.S. Senate on March 15. The bearers of the petition went on to Boston where they had been invited to solicit support for their cause. In an unusual development, free blacks even voted in Rapides Parish from 1838 to 1860, in spite of the curtailment of this right by the state legislature in 1812.[9] Overall, free blacks in Louisiana were the target of a sizable number of legal rules and were active in efforts to influence the nature and character of their political environment.

The Civil War (1861–1865)

The secession of South Carolina shortly after the election of November, 1860, began the great schism, the principal event of which was the Civil War. During the later years of the war, Louisiana slaves found themselves with the first legal opportunity to act out against their oppression through enlistment in the Union army. During the early stages of the war the Union army had refused to accept blacks into its ranks, but by 1862, recruitment difficulties led to a formal call for blacks to join the Union army. Free blacks responded quickly to the opportunity, filling up three regiments by November 24, 1862. According to most accounts, these first black recruits were wealthy and well educated and were reported to be more kindly disposed toward military service than were their white northern counterparts. By 1863, all

9. James M. McPherson, *The Negro's Civil War* (New York: Random House, 1965), 185; Walton, *Black Politics*, 33.

blacks, regardless of prior status, were accepted by the Union army. As of February, 1865, there were 10,772 black Louisianians enrolled in the Union ranks.[10]

Few opportunities for combat were afforded the Louisiana Native Guards, as the black Union regiments were called. One account stated that they spent the bulk of their time marching and countermarching, guarding and repairing railroads and bridges, clearing sugarcane fields, scouting, foraging, guarding prisoners, unloading commissary stores, and doing garrison, picket, recruiting, and engineer duty. The first real battle in which Louisiana's black troops engaged occurred on May 27, 1863, at Port Hudson. Although they were unable to overcome the Rebels, the Guards, during this battle, revealed the ability to fight well against insurmountable odds. One white officer declared that "You have no idea how my prejudices with regard to Negro troops have been dispelled by the battle the other day. The brigade of Negroes behaved magnificently and fought splendidly; could not have done better. They are far superior in discipline to white troops and just as brave."[11] While it is difficult to assess conclusively the impact that Louisiana blacks had on the outcome of the war, it was no doubt substantial.

One largely untold story is that of the tens of thousands of black women from the South who crossed Rebel lines to serve as cooks, laundresses, nurses, and scouts for the Union army.[12] No specific accounts of Louisiana women are given, but in view of the widespread involvement of women from the South, it is likely that some were from Louisiana.

Unlike blacks anxious to join the Union army, free blacks who wished to join the Rebel cause were accepted early in the war. In Pointe Coupee and Natchitoches parishes, for instance, some free-Negro planters formed home guard companies soon after the war began; their motivation was to prevent slave uprisings. Free blacks of New Orleans, led by Jordan Noble, the drummer boy at the Battle of New Orleans, held several meetings and subsequently offered their

10. John Blassingame, *Black New Orleans* (Chicago: University of Chicago Press, 1973), 35, 38. See McPherson, *The Negro's Civil War* for a detailed discussion of the role black Americans played in the Civil War.

11. Blassingame, *Black New Orleans*, 41; McPherson, *The Negro's Civil War*, 185.

12. Lerone Bennett, Jr., "The Black Woman: A Historical Perspective," *Ebony* (August, 1977), 168.

services to the Confederacy in 1861. The governor of Louisiana, in response to this and other such black actions supportive of the Rebel cause, authorized the formation of a free-Negro regiment to guard New Orleans. By early 1862, more than three thousand free Louisiana blacks purchased uniforms and arms and enlisted in the Rebel army. However, by most reports, the black troops were rarely used, and the government refused to issue them arms and supplies.[13] It should, perhaps, be noted here that whatever prompted blacks to join the Confederate cause did not keep them from rejoicing when Union army occupation came.

In addition to their participation as soldiers among both Confederate and Union forces, blacks in Louisiana also directly influenced the political system in another way. When President Lincoln exempted certain parishes of the state from the provisions of the Emancipation Proclamation, articulate blacks began a concerted effort to make the Proclamation's coverage universal. To this end, they sent petitions to the state legislature, initiated and supported litigation, and presented supporting arguments in a bilingual newspaper, L'Union. Their efforts were rewarded when a state court ruled in October, 1863, that blacks could no longer be held in slavery in any part of Louisiana.[14]

The indirect influence of blacks on the state's political system continued as prewar codes were maintained and expanded by the Union army to control both free and enslaved blacks. For example, as late as April, 1863, rebellious slaves were still being legally imprisoned and flogged in New Orleans. As late as 1864, blacks, free and slave, were subject to a 7:30 P.M. curfew. Labor codes enforced by the Union army provided fixed rates of low wages, prompting the bilingual black newspaper, the New Orleans Tribune, to charge that "The condition of the slave is not materially altered." On the other hand, in March, 1864, the military commander also created a board of education for the Department of the Gulf, and by the fall of that year, more than half of the black children inside Union lines in Louisiana were in school.[15]

During the Civil War, black Louisianians were political beings both

13. Some Louisiana activities are reported in Capers, Occupied City, 214–19, Blassingame, Black New Orleans, 33–34, McPherson, The Negro's Civil War, 276–85. See also selections in Herbert Aptheker, A Documentary History of the Negro People in the United States.(2 vols.; New York: Citadel Press, 1951).

14. Blassingame, Black New Orleans, 33.

15. McPherson, The Negro's Civil War, 128–31.

as subjects of the law and as persons influencing the course of legal developments.

Reconstruction (1866–1890)

The first period in which large numbers of black Louisianians experienced any measure of traditional political involvement was immediately following the Civil War. During this period, newly enfranchised blacks participated in all of the traditional forms of political activities. They registered to vote, participated in partisan activities, contested for public offices, and developed political organizations.

C. Vann Woodward writes that the male population of voting age in Louisiana in 1860 was composed of 94,711 whites and 92,502 blacks. However, less than 50 percent of the eligible whites (45,218) were registered to vote, compared to 90 percent of the eligible blacks (84,436).[16] Almost all of the black registrants were Republicans, and this phenomenon was to continue until the 1930s.

Black Louisianians were very active in the state's Republican party during Reconstruction. They met in parish-based gatherings to discuss the problems facing black people and to explore resolutions consistent with the philosophy of the Republican party. In many instances, the resolutions growing out of these meetings were published bilingually in the New Orleans *Tribune*, the first black daily in Louisiana (published each day except Monday).[17]

The impact of the large number of black voters in Louisiana was manifested in the election of blacks to the Constitutional Convention of 1867 as well as to the Congress and to state and local offices. During the period after 1868, 3 blacks were elected to Congress, although only one actually served. Another 133 were elected to the state legislature (38 senators and 95 representatives), 3 served as lieutenant governor, 1 became superintendent of education, and 1 was state treasurer. Of the 98 delegates to the 1867 constitutional convention, exactly half were black. Pinckney Benton Stewart Pinchback, one of the black lieutenant governors, also served as governor of the state for a brief period.

16. C. Vann Woodward, *The Burden of Southern History* (New York: Vintage Books, 1961), 99.
17. Aptheker, *A Documentary History of the Negro People*, II, 559–60, 561–63.

At the local level, 19 blacks served as sheriffs between 1868 and 1877, 2 served as deputy sheriffs and 4 more sheriffs were elected after 1876. Blacks also held a number of local offices: 13 served as parish tax collectors, 12 as parish recorders, 12 as parish assessors, 13 as parish coroners, 2 as parish judges, 4 as mayors, and a large number of blacks served as constables, police jurors, and justices of the peace.[18]

It appears that blacks in Louisiana created their first political organizations during this period. Among these organizations were the Louisiana Equal Rights League, created in 1865, and the Union League. Black ministers and their congregations also functioned as political units. Within the Republican party, there were the Pinchback Republicans, who made up a relatively well defined intraparty faction with the lieutenant governor at its helm, and the Roudanez Radicals, under the leadership of Louis Roudanez, the editor of *L'Union*. Also significant was the Friends of Universal Suffrage, founded in May, 1865, which operated mostly under the presidency of Thomas Jefferson Durant.[19] These organizations existed over several years and exerted considerable influence in state politics.

A great deal of the direct impact the blacks had was through the black elected officials. These officials are credited by some historians with having played an important role in the liberalization of many of the practices of the state government. For example, at the constitutional convention blacks worked constantly to secure universal education and to improve educational facilities while exhibiting a willingness to forego enforcement of the integration clause if schools were established in black communities. They asked for laws to protect laborers and plantation workers and for what would now be considered social welfare legislation. Black legislators during Reconstruction were mainly interested in educational reform and civil rights. Other legislative priorities had to do with imprisonment of minors, regulation of insurance companies, relief provisions, protection from violence, labor conditions on plantations, and internal improvements.[20] It must be re-

18. Charles Vincent, *Black Legislators in Louisiana During Reconstruction* (Baton Rouge: Louisiana State University Press, 1976), 220–21.

19. McPherson, *The Negro's Civil War*, 130, 289; Joe Gray Taylor, "Louisiana Reconstructed," F. Wayne Binning, "Carpetbaggers' Triumph: The Louisiana State Election of 1868," both in Mark T. Carleton, Perry H. Howard, and Joseph D. Parker (eds.), *Readings in Louisiana Politics* (Baton Rouge: Claitor's, 1975), 286, 228–29.

20. Vincent, *Black Legislators in Louisiana*, 222, 152.

called that, while blacks represented a significant element in the state legislature, at no time was there a black majority. Therefore, blacks were in a position of influencing, but not dominating the legislature.

Particularly outstanding records of competency were achieved by black officials such as Robert Brown, superintendent of education, and Antoine Dubuclet, state treasurer. The official records of the latter were investigated after he left office and found to be devoid of any form of mismanagement, theft, or other violations. By some assessments, the performance of black legislators and public officials was less than exemplary. One Louisiana planter suggested that the forty-nine whites and forty-nine blacks of the 1867 Louisiana constitutional convention were "the lowest and most corrupt body of men ever assembled in the South." In their study of southern history, Hesseltine and Smiley contend that, with the possible exception of South Carolina, Louisiana was by far the worst governed state in the South during Reconstruction. However, the cast of characters in their account of the basis for this identification does not include blacks who held office at the state and local levels.[21]

It is probably true that many of the newly elected black officials were as corrupt and lacking in conviction as some of their white counterparts. However, it should be noted here, as John Hope Franklin has observed, that the graft and corruption attributed to the Reconstruction governments was neither new nor peculiar to the South. This position, in the case of Louisiana, is borne out when one examines the records and behavior of politicians in the state before Reconstruction. For example, the state constitutional convention of 1864 spent $9,400 on liquor and cigars, $4,237 for newspapers, $156,000 for printing, and $4,374 for carriage hire.[22]

The impact of the widespread participation of blacks on the politics of Louisiana during the period was significant. However, it was true in Louisiana, as in the rest of the reconstructed South, that blacks did not hold power equivalent to their voting strength. C. Vann Woodward makes this point regarding the entire South and theorizes that this

21. Nelson, "People of Color in Louisiana: Part II," 77; William Hesseltine and David Smiley, *The South in American History* (Englewood Cliffs, N.J.: Prentice-Hall, 1960), 328.

22. John Hope Franklin, *Reconstruction After the Civil War* (Chicago: University of Chicago Press, 1961), 46–48; Franklin, *From Slavery to Freedom*, 258–59.

was because the newly freed blacks were restrained in conduct and deferential in their political attitudes. Lerone Bennett, however, takes a somewhat different view. He asserts that Reconstruction was a revolution touching virtually every area of southern life, except the distribution of land. Black men moved in the highest social circles in New Orleans, attending official gatherings with their wives and sweethearts. He suggests that the worst thing that can be said about the black leaders of this period was that they did not seem to "know what time it was." That is, they failed to understand that a revolution can be accomplished only by "overwhelming force overwhelmingly applied." "Instead, the Black legislators, by placing too high an estimate on their respectability, let the crucial moment pass." [23]

One interesting dimension of the Reconstruction period is the political role that some reports attribute to black women. While black men were free to participate fully in political life, black women, like the white women of that day, were deprived of suffrage. Nevertheless, they had great impact on the political behavior of their husbands and other male relatives throughout the South and in Louisiana in particular. John H. Burch, white newspaperman and former Louisiana legislator, stated that black women followed their men from morning to night around the parishes demanding that they vote Republican and that women formed a large segment of those present at political assemblies and evinced a deep interest in all that pertained to politics. They were also said to have believed that voting Republican was the only means by which they could secure homes and education for their children. Burch also gave black women credit for masterminding some of the Louisiana emigration drives. According to Burch, in 1878 a committee of five hundred black women organized with Mary Garrett as president and published a document demanding that they be accorded every right and privilege guaranteed their race by the Constitution and vowing to use everything in their power to obtain these rights and privileges. [24]

23. Lerone Bennett, Jr., *Confrontation: Black and White* (Baltimore: Penguin Books, 1965), 68, 74–75; Lerone Bennett, Jr., *Black Power USA: The Human Side of Reconstruction, 1867–1877* (Baltimore: Penguin Books, 1965), especially "Black Governors, White Sugar, and Blood," 259–305.

24. Aptheker, *A Documentary History of the Negro People*, II, 721–22.

Post-Reconstruction and Early Twentieth Century
(1890–1943)

The Reconstruction experience was hardly motivated by philanthropy. Instead, the prime factors were the more pragmatic and materialistic concerns of party advantage and sectional economic interests. Thus, when sectional interests and party fortunes were better served in some other way, even in a way destructive of basic political rights of blacks, then the political interests of blacks would be sacrificed. This sacrifice was not long in coming. The Compromise of 1877, in which Louisiana played a critical role, and the resultant withdrawal of federal troops from the South marked the end of Reconstruction and the return of white domination in the South. Reconstruction did not come to an abrupt end as the result of any specific congressional or presidential action; it came to a gradual end with relaxed restraints and the repeal of legislation. Resistance to Reconstruction at home was aided by northern weariness with the crusade for the Negro. With the end of Reconstruction came the demise of Republican control in the region.[25]

In an interesting perspective on this era, Earl E. Thorpe suggests that "The Old South and the North long had been husband and wife: in Civil War the South lost a contested divorce action. Beginning in 1877 the reunited partners agreed not to argue any more over the black slave child: agreed that both regions would hold this child in adoption but that it was an error for either region to try to love him."[26]

The tone of black existence in the South was set by the northern desertion of the cause of black equality. The South took measures to rid its political elite of black men, and they were successful: the last black state senator left office in 1890, and the last black representatives departed in 1900. By 1900 only 5,320 blacks remained on voting rolls in Louisiana, compared to 130,344 in 1896. The extent of black disenfranchisement is further evidenced by the fact that black voters never exceeded 3.6 percent of the total Louisiana black voting-age population during the first forty years of the twentieth century.[27] Prin-

25. Woodward, *The Burden of Southern History*, 96–98; C. Vann Woodward, *The Strange Career of Jim Crow* (New York: Oxford University Press, 1966), 51–55.
26. Earl E. Thorpe, *The Old South: A Psychohistory* (Durham, N.C.: Seeman Printing, 1972), 224.
27. Vincent, *Black Legislators in Louisiana*, 220; Riley Baker, "Negro Voter Registra-

cipal among the techniques for disenfranchisement were the grandfather clause, poll taxes, literacy tests, intimidation, and purging of
registration rolls.

The grandfather clause provided the right to vote under a system of
permanent registration for all male persons whose fathers and grand-
fathers were qualified to vote on January 1, 1866, a time at which no
blacks were qualified to vote. Blacks wishing to vote had to pass literacy tests and morals tests and to overcome other impediments. The
registration figures provided in Table 8-2 attest to the effectiveness of
these and other disenfranchisement vehicles.

The violence against blacks in Louisiana deserves special attention.
One of the most violent techniques used was lynching. In most lynchings black males were the victims, but some black women were also
lynched, as were a few white men and women. Lynchings occurred
throughout the nation but were more common in the South. Between
1884 and 1900, there were over 2,500 lynchings, and between 1900
and World War I there were 1,100 more. There were 21 lynchings in
Louisiana in 1896, more than occurred in the entire United States
west of the Mississippi and over one-fifth of the nation's total for that
year. This record of violence and the use of the political process to keep
blacks in their place continued even into the 1950s in the South and in
Louisiana.[28]

Black participation in political processes of this era was minimal at
best, but blacks did protest against the loss of the political power they
had exerted during Reconstruction and against other devastating aspects of their lives. These protests began during the last years of the
Reconstruction period and included mass emigration, mostly to other
sections of the United States and the formation of antilynch, self-help,
and civil rights organizations.

Immediately before 1890 and throughout the remainder of the nine-

---

tion in Louisiana, 1879–1964," *Louisiana Studies*, IV (Winter, 1965), 332–50. For more
discussion of black suffrage in Louisiana, see Kirk H. Porter, *A History of Suffrage in the
United States* (New York: AMS Press, 1918), 212–13.

28. William Ivy Hair, "Rob Them! You Bet," in Mark T. Carleton, Perry H. Howard,
and Joseph D. Parker (eds.), *Readings in Louisiana Politics* (Baton Rouge: Claitor's,
1975) 370; Ralph Ginzburg, *100 Years of Lynching* (New York: Lancer Books, 1969),
262–63. See also Gunnar Myrdal, *An American Dilemma* (2 vols.; New York: McGraw-
Hill, 1964), II, 560–64.

Table 11-2
Black Voter Registration in Louisiana,
1910–1964

Dates	Black Registration	Estimated Black Adult Population (Most Recent Census)	Percentage of Black Adult Population Registered to Vote
1910	730	174,211 (Males)	.4
1920	3,533	359,251	.9
1928	2,054	359,251	.5
1932	1,591	415,047	.3
Oct., 1936	1,981	415,047	.4
Oct., 1940	886	473,562	.1
Oct., 1944	1,672	473,562	.3
Oct., 1948	28,177	473,562	5
Oct., 1952	107,844	481,284	22
July, 1954	112,789	481,284	23
Oct., 1956	152,578	481,284	31
Dec., 1960	158,765	514,589	30
Dec., 1962	150,878	514,589	29
Oct., 1964	164,717	514,589	32

Sources: Louisiana Voter Registration Statistics (Office of the Commissioner of Elections, Baton Rouge, 1979); U.S. Bureau of the Census, U.S. Census of Population: Characteristics of the Population, Louisiana for the years 1910, 1920, 1930, 1940, 1950, and 1960 (Washington, D.C.: U.S. Government Printing Office, various dates).

teenth century, blacks left Louisiana in large numbers. Emigration was principally in response to the gradual erosion of black legal rights and was organized through the Convention of Louisiana Negroes, which it appears, was based in Caddo Parish. As a result of the convention's activities thousands of blacks departed Louisiana for points North in 1879 and the following years. The group movements were also motivated by a bad crop, a devastating yellow fever epidemic, unsuccessful efforts by blacks to get a reduction in tenant rents, and abuse of Negro women. Most emigrants came from southern Louisiana.[29] World Wars I and II and the involvement of blacks in the

29. Aptheker, A Documentary History of the Negro People, II, 713–21.

armed forces and as workers in the defense industries in the North and West increased the pace of black movement from the South and from Louisiana.

Most Louisiana blacks remained in the state, however, and made some effort to salvage their waning political power. For example, faced with the adoption of the grandfather clause by the 1898 constitutional convention in the state, blacks asked Booker T. Washington for help. He conveyed a passionately drafted plea on behalf of black citizens. Convention delegates, undaunted by the plea, approved the addition of the clause.[30]

The antilynch activities of Louisiana blacks were another example of their nontraditional political activities. Spearheading the national antilynch movement were such national figures as W. E. B. DuBois and Ida Wells Barnett. A group of Louisiana blacks held mass meetings as early as 1888 to protest the fact that the state government afforded "no protection of the lives and property of the people against armed bodies of whites, who shed innocent blood and commit deeds of savagery unsurpassed in the dark ages of mankind." Much of the lynch activity in Louisiana was designed to curb black political activity, although it masqueraded as a response to the threat posed by black men to the safety of white women.[31]

Blacks engaged in political protest, but they did not affect the political system directly during post-Reconstruction period as they had during Reconstruction. However, it is obvious that their indirect impact was considerable. Whites, as in the periods prior to Reconstruction, devoted a substantial portion of their time and energy to devising and institutionalizing a variety of methods designed to strip blacks of their political power and to ensure that they remained powerless. It is probably true that white Louisianians spent more time on the negative acts characterizing this period than in any other since it was necessary not only to keep blacks in a subordinate posture but also first to deprive them of their power.

During the post-Reconstruction and early twentieth-century period, blacks made a deep impact on the mind of the South. Alexander Heard has written that southern concern over the Negro is the most deeply rooted source of political contention in American politics, while Gun-

30. *Ibid.*, 781–82.
31. *Ibid.*, 741–43; Hair, "Rob Them! You Bet," 370.

nar Myrdal observed that when we refer to a Negro problem in America, we mean that Americans are worried about it, that it is on their minds and their consciences. Lynchings, race-conscious laws and social customs, and the preeminence of racial themes in the works of southern writers and artists reflect the white southerners' preoccupation with the black presence.[32]

The Second Reconstruction (1944–Present)

Since 1900 blacks in the South have had an uphill struggle for full participation in traditional politics. The struggle was mostly in the South because the only record of meaningful traditional participation had been southern Reconstruction and because the bulk of the black population lived in the South. Initially, the strategy used by blacks or their adversaries in this struggle involved litigation in state and federal courts. However, protests and legislative lobbying were also used. The success of these strategies is evidenced by the outlawing of the grandfather clause in 1915 and the declaration that the white primary was unconstitutional in 1944. The latter decision, *Smith* v. *Allwright*, began the Second Reconstruction by opening the way for black entry into the Democratic party politics that dominated the political scene in Louisiana and throughout the one-party South. It also marked the beginning of increased federal intervention in traditional relations between blacks and whites in the South.[33]

Following *Smith* v. *Allwright*, there was a strong possibility that blacks would reenter the arena of traditional politics, and therefore, three dimensions of Louisiana's political culture—religion, racial distribution, and factionalism—came into play. Louisiana's French-Catholic/ Protestant regional dichotomy has been found to have a variety of influences on the state's politics. Studies of voter registration patterns, especially after 1944, indicate that markedly higher percentages of the

32. Alexander Heard, *A Two-Party South?* (Chapel Hill: University of North Carolina Press, 1952), 27; Myrdal, *An American Dilemma*, I, 26. See Wilbur J. Cash, *The Mind of the South* (New York: Knopf, 1941); Howard Zinn, *The Southern Mystique* (New York: Touchstone Books, 1972); Thorpe, *The Old South*; Lillian Smith, *Strange Fruit* (New York: Reynal and Hitchcock, 1944). See also the works of William Faulkner, Robert Penn Warren, and others.

33. *Guinn* v. *United States*, 238 U.S. 347 (1915); *Smith* v. *Allwright*, 321 U.S. 649 (1944).

black eligible voters registered in the French-Catholic region than in Protestant parishes.[34] What the political elites formulated and implemented in the way of regulations for black political life seems to have been affected by the religious tenets to which these elites conformed.

Several authors have cited the connection between the percentage of blacks in the population and formal and informal policies regarding black political participation.[35] Those Louisiana parishes in which blacks constituted 40 percent or more of the population were the ones in which the percentages of eligible blacks registered to vote were lowest between 1944 and passage of the Voting Rights Act of 1965. For example, in 1964 blacks made up 61.8 percent of the total population of West Feliciana Parish, but only 1.8 percent of these blacks were registered voters. This pattern had a tendency to aggravate even more the political disadvantage suffered by blacks in that the greater the potential for meaningful black impact on politics in the immediate geographic area the more rigid were the barriers to such impact. (See Table 11-3 for further evidence of this tendency.)

In addition to suppressing black voter registration, elites in parishes with heavy concentrations of blacks generally supported candidates dedicated to the racial status quo. Prime examples are the levels of support given to segregationist Willie Rainach's bid for governor in 1959, to the States Rights ticket in the 1960 presidential election and to the GOP Goldwater-Miller ticket in the 1964 presidential race. These trends are depicted in Table 11-3.

The bifactionalism in the Democratic party of Louisiana has influenced the elite's treatment of blacks. Huey Long interpreted the downtrodden as including blacks. He is quoted as saying "I have never been a party to any piece of legislation calculated to hurt the Negro. . . . I have always wanted to help them," and "you can't help white people without helping Negroes. It has to be that way." While blacks did not vote in any significant numbers in Huey Long's time, those who became heirs to his legacy have, for the most part, conformed to this tradition of refusing to capitalize on the race issue. For example, when segregationist legislators attempted to purge blacks from voter regis-

34. John Fenton and Kenneth Vines, "Negro Registration in Louisiana," *American Political Science Review*, LI (1957), 704–713.
35. See Donald R. Matthews and James W. Prothro, *Negroes and the New Southern Politics* (New York: Harcourt, Brace, and World, 1966), 115–20; Key, *Southern Politics in State and Nation*, 518.

Table 11-3

Black Percentage of Population as Related to Other Political Factors, 1959–1964

Lowest Quartile Vote for Johnson-Humphrey Ticket, 1964		Upper Quartile of Rainach Vote, 1959		Upper Quartile States Rights, 1960		Upper Quartile Concentration of Blacks		Lowest Quartile Black Registration, 1964		Upper Quartile Vote for Goldwater-Miller	
10.3	Tensas	78.9	Claiborne	65.0	Plaquemines	61.8	W. Feliciana	1.6	Tensas	89.6	Tensas
10.9	Claiborne	63.4	Bienville	59.1	E. Feliciana	60.8	Madison	1.8	W. Feliciana	89.0	Claiborne
11.5	W. Carroll	52.2	Madison	59.1	Red River	60.7	Tensas	1.9	Claiborne	88.4	W. Carroll
12.1	Franklin	51.3	Bossier	54.2	Madison	58.3	E. Carroll	2.9	E. Feliciana	87.8	Franklin
12.5	Morehouse	50.6	E. Carroll	52.6	Claiborne	50.7	DeSoto	3.2	E. Carroll	87.4	Morehouse
13.0	Red River	49.8	Red River	47.7	Bienville	46.8	St. Helena	3.3	Plaquemines	86.9	Red River
13.6	Plaquemines	49.0	Webster	47.5	W. Feliciana	46.8	W. Baton Rouge	4.4	Red River	86.3	Plaquemines
14.2	Richland	44.0	DeSoto	47.5	Winn	46.4	Pointe Coupee	5.4	W. Carroll	85.7	Richland
15.0	E. Carroll	42.4	Franklin	46.7	E. Carroll	46.3	E. Feliciana	5.6	Madison	84.9	E. Carroll
16.4	Bossier	39.6	Caddo	46.6	Concordia	46.1	St. John the Baptist	6.4	Franklin	83.5	Bossier
16.5	Ouachita	39.3	Lincoln	46.1	St. Helena	44.7	Iberville	6.8	Morehouse	83.4	Ouachita
16.6	LaSalle	39.2	Tensas	44.3	St. Bernard	44.7	St. James	6.3	Richland	83.3	LaSalle
16.7	Concordia	38.7	W. Feliciana	42.4	Webster	43.9	Claiborne	8.7	Bossier	83.2	Concordia
16.8	Madison	36.1	E. Feliciana	42.1	Livingston	43.4	Concordia	10.6	Ouachita	83.1	Madison
17.6	Webster	35.3	Concordia	38.6	Richland	42.0	Bienville	11.3	Webster	82.3	Webster
19.0	Catahoula	33.6	Richland	37.3	Tensas	41.1	Morehouse	11.8	Caddo	81.3	Bienville

Sources: Census Bureau, *1960 U.S. Census of Population*, I, Pt. 20, pp. 20–23, 20–26; election returns made available by the office of the Secretary of State, Baton Rouge.

tration rolls in the late 1950s, Huey Long's brother, Earl K. Long, then governor, emerged as defender of black voters.[36] His move to keep the black voters on the rolls is sufficient evidence of the loyalty of voting blacks to the Long faction. Again, a general feature of Louisiana politics is applied in a particularistic manner.

Blacks in Louisiana and the South since 1944 have mounted more challenges to discriminatory laws and practices and have increased their political participation. Litigation resulted in such victories as *Brown* v. *Board of Education* in 1954, and legislative lobbying was partly responsible for the passage of the Civil Rights Acts of 1957 and 1964 and the Voting Rights Act of 1965. The latter ushered in a period of black involvement in all of the traditional forms of political behavior on a large scale: registering and voting, seeking and holding public office, and developing political organizations. In addition, there was significant involvement of blacks in protest activities. In other words, blacks regained and used the political rights that they had enjoyed during Reconstruction and added others besides.

Black voter registration levels during this period consistently increased, but they have not yet reached the Reconstruction high of 90 percent of the eligible black population. Table 11-2 compares the percentages of blacks eligible during selected years of a large part of the post-Reconstruction period with the same figures for the early years of the Second Reconstruction. This comparison reveals that during the post-Reconstruction years the percentage of blacks eligible to vote declined steadily, but in the years of the Second Reconstruction it increased year by year. Beginning in 1944, black voter registration continued to increase until 1964. Passage of the Voting Rights Act of 1965, with its provisions for registration by federal officials in selected southern areas, including Louisiana, led to impressive increases in black registration. Table 11-4 reflects the increase in registration by Louisiana blacks.

As Table 11-5 shows, public-office holding by blacks in Louisiana increased as black voter registration increased. There were 36 blacks elected to office in Louisiana as of March 1, 1968. In December, 1968, the approximately 388 blacks elected to public office in the South, including 53 in Louisiana, were invited to a Southwide Conference of

36. A. J. Liebling, *The Earl of Louisiana* (Baton Rouge: Louisiana State University Press, 1970), 24–25.

Table 11-4
Black Voter Registration in Louisiana, 1965–1979

	Total Voter Registration	Black Registration (Louisiana Board of Registration)	Black Percentage of Registered Voters (Louisiana Board of Registration)	Total Black Voting Age Population (Most Recent Census)	Percentage of Black Voting Age Population Registered
March 31, 1965	1,190,122	163,414	13.7	514,589	31.7
October 8, 1966	1,281,919	238,356	18.6	514,589	46.3
June 30, 1967	1,285,933	245,275	19.1	514,589	47.6
August 31, 1968	1,411,071	279,468	19.8	514,589	54.3
September 30, 1969	1,422,900	291,547	20.5	540,470	56.6
October 3, 1970	1,438,727	298,054	20.7	613,401	55.1
October 6, 1971	1,633,181	347,098	21.3	613,401	56.5
October 7, 1972	1,704,890	397,158	22.3	613,401	64.7
August 31, 1973	1,712,850	380,490	22.2	613,401	62.0
October 5, 1974	1,726,693	391,666	22.7	613,401	63.8
October 1, 1975	1,798,032	408,696	22.7	613,401	66.6
October 2, 1976	1,866,117	420,697	22.5	613,401	68.5
September 30, 1977	1,787,031	413,178	23.2	613,401	67.3
October 7, 1978	1,821,026	429,231	23.6	613,401	69.9
June 30, 1979	1,831,507	431,196	23.5	613,401	70.2

Sources: Data provided by the Office of the Commissioner of Elections, Baton Rouge; Voter Education Project, Southern Regional Council, Atlanta; *U.S. Census of Population* (1970), I, Pt. 20, pp. 20–39, 20–40.

Table 11-5
Black Elected Officials, 1968–1979

Year	Number of Elected Officials
1968 (March)	36
1968 (December)	53
1969 (January)	53
1970 (February)	64
1971 (March)	74
1972 (February)	119
1973 (January)	127
1974 (January)	147
1975 (January)	194
1976 (January)	237
1977 (April)	276
1978 (April)	333
1979 (July)	334

Sources: Joint Center for Political Studies, Washington, D.C.; records at Public Affairs Service Center, Southern University, Baton Rouge, Louisiana.

Black Elected Officials in Atlanta, Georgia. By July, 1969, the number had risen to 473 for the South and 64 for Louisiana. As of 1978, Louisiana led the nation in the number of black elected officials (333) and in the percentage of state offices (5) held by blacks. Most of these officials served at the county and local levels. They included 74 parish governing board members, 11 mayors, 102 councilmen, 27 justices of the peace and constables, 93 school board members, 3 judges, 9 police chiefs and marshals, 2 members of state governing boards of education, and 1 clerk of court. In 1979 Louisiana had 334 black officials, including 75 parish governing board members, 11 mayors, 110 municipal governing board members, 26 justices of the peace and constables, 88 school board members, 3 judges, 9 police chiefs and marshals, 1 other judicial official, 1 member of a special county board, 10 legislators (1 state senator and 9 state representatives).[37]

The first black to serve in the Louisiana legislature since Reconstruction was Ernest "Dutch" Morial, who was elected from New Or-

37. *National Roster of Black Elected Officials, 1978* and *1979* (Washington, D.C.: Joint Center for Political Studies, 1979), 94–106.

leans in 1967. After he resigned to accept a judgeship, he was replaced in 1971 by Dorothy Mae Taylor, the first black woman ever to serve in the Louisiana legislature. She was joined by seven other black representatives in 1972. Sidney Barthelemy became the first black ever elected to the state senate in 1974. When the 1980 session opened there were twelve black members—ten in the house and two in the senate. Also of particular interest was the election in 1977 of Ernest Morial as New Orleans' first black mayor. Since 1972 blacks have also been appointed to offices and positions on boards and commissions by governors. In an unprecedented development, Jesse N. Stone, Jr., a lawyer and president of Southern University, was appointed to an interim term of several weeks on the Louisiana State Supreme Court. Only one other southern state has had a black on its court of last resort.

In addition to the increase in black officeholders, the impact of black voters can be seen in the elections of nonblack officials at the local, parish, state, and national levels since 1965. When Moon Landrieu, a city councilman in New Orleans, won the Democratic nomination for mayor, the Baton Rouge *Morning Advocate* carried a story entitled "Negro Voters Figure Heavily in Landrieu's Upset for Mayor." Black voters were said to be well represented among his campaign workers. The loser in the race "cited the black vote as the reason for his defeat." Landrieu had a reputation as a liberal and a defender of the downtrodden during his tenure in the legislature, including making a one-man stand against an attempt to ramrod a complement of segregation bills through that body in 1960. Similarly, the elevation of Edwin W. Edwards, a United States congressman from southwest Louisiana, to the governorship was followed by numerous election analyses, almost all of which attributed his 1971 victory over state senator J. Bennett Johnston in the Democratic primary to support from black voters. Even the losing primary candidate acknowledged the black vote as the major contributing factor in his defeat. Following Edwards' victory over the Republican in the general election, the Shreveport *Times* stated in an editorial: "The black voters of Louisiana, and not the Cajuns, elected Edwin Edwards governor, and it is they who deserve a cheer from the congressman." Utilizing a formula based on an analysis of predominantly black voting precincts in its local parish, the newspaper estimated that Edwards had received 202,055 black votes statewide, as compared to only 10,709 for his opponent. Since Edwards' statewide victory margin was about 160,000 votes, clearly the strong black vote was a factor in it. If the *Times* analysis is correct, about 95 percent of the black vote went to Edwards or about 190,000 more black votes than went to Treen in that election. Treen actually received about 30,000 more white votes than did the victorious Edwards.[38]

State senator J. Bennett Johnston, who had been defeated by Edwards in the 1971 Democratic gubernatorial primary, won the black vote in his bid for a United States Senate seat in November, 1972, and defeated former governor John McKeithen. Analysis of the vote in seventy-two sample precincts in the general election reveals that, while only one white precinct gave him 70 percent of the vote, twenty black precincts did so.[39]

The 1976 gubernatorial election and the 1978 election for the United States Senate resulted in reelection of incumbents Edwards and Johnston by very comfortable margins, each buttressed by almost solid black support. However, the 1979 gubernatorial election was an extremely close one. Governor Edwards was ineligible to run again under the constitutional provision limiting a governor to two consecutive terms. This was also the first gubernatorial election conducted under the state's new primary election law. A field of nine candidates entered the race and the controversial primary resulted in a runoff between Republican Congressman Dave Treen and Democratic Public Utilities Commissioner Louis Lambert. The impact of black votes was easily discernible in the tabulations and analyses of the vote. Comparisons were made of voter choices in seventy-four selected precincts, thirty-seven of which were all or predominantly black and thirty-seven of which were all or predominantly white. Black precincts gave solid support to the Democratic candidate; eighteen of the thirty-seven precincts gave him 90 percent or more of the vote. In the thirty-seven white precincts Republican winner Treen fared better than Lambert, capturing over 50 percent of the vote in twenty-four of them. The other thirteen precincts supported Lambert.[40] For the first time since the Reconstruction era, Louisiana elected a Republican governor. Ironically,

38. Baton Rouge *Morning Advocate*, December 15, 1969, Sec. A, p. 10; Shreveport *Times*, February 3, 1972, Sec. A, p. 8.

39. Public Affairs Research Council, "General Election," *Analysis* (November, 1972), 12.

40. Public Affairs Research Council, "General Election," *Analysis* (December, 1979), 10.

the Republican party had been solidly supported by Louisiana blacks during Reconstruction. While Treen won without black support, he did make a limited appeal for such support. As of June 30, 1979, according to official figures, there were 438,878 black Democrats registered and 8,570 black Republicans. The Republican figure represents an increase of almost 100 percent since 1975. The future of the Republican party in Louisiana and the role of blacks within the party promise to be important topics in Louisiana politics.

White Louisiana Democrats have been somewhat inconsistent in their support for the Democratic ticket in presidential elections since 1948. Emergence of civil rights as a major Democratic convention issue is largely responsible for the deterioration of the solid white support which the party had received since Reconstruction. In 1948 the Dixiecrats carried Louisiana with 204,290 votes as opposed to 136,344 votes for the Truman-Barkley Democratic ticket. The state supported the Stevenson-Sparkman Democratic ticket in 1952. Republicans carried the state in 1956, 1964, and 1972, and George Wallace's American party swept the state in 1968. Only in 1960 and 1976 did the national Democratic presidential nominees gain electoral endorsement in Louisiana.

Despite the declining support among white Louisiana Democrats, black Democrats have been remarkably loyal to Democratic presidential and vice-presidential nominees, even in the face of opposition from Democratic leaders in the state. For example, it is estimated that the Johnson-Humphrey ticket in 1964 received virtually all of the votes cast by blacks. Analysis of votes in thirty-seven predominantly black precincts in Orleans Parish and in nine similar precincts in East Baton Rouge Parish revealed Democratic support at the 95 percent level. In the Fifth Congressional District (northeast Louisiana) the ticket received a majority in only one precinct, a virtually all-black precinct.[41] Analysis of the returns in the 1972 presidential election reveals a similar pattern of black support for the Democratic McGovern-Shriver ticket even though Nixon carried sixty-three of the sixty-four parishes. West Feliciana, the only parish carried by the Democratic ticket, had the state's highest percentage of blacks—50 percent of the parish's registered voters were black. Greatest support for the Democratic

41. Jewel L. Prestage, "The 1964 Presidential Election in Louisiana" (paper presented at the Southwestern Political Science Association, Dallas, Texas, April 17, 1965).

ticket in other parishes came where blacks made up significant proportions of the population. Succinctly put, Louisiana blacks have supported the national Democratic party ticket independently of white Democrats in the state.

In 1976 Jimmy Carter benefited from the inclination of Louisiana blacks to support Democrats as he carried the state with 51.45 percent of the votes cast. At the time, the state's registered voters included 1,445,420 whites and 420,697 blacks. Blacks then constituted 22.5 percent of the total registrants but approximately 26.4 percent of the estimated voting age population. Participation in the election was relatively high, with 68.8 percent of the registered voters and over half of the projected voting-age populace voting. A total of 660,338 votes went to the victor and 591,057 were cast for President Gerald Ford. Excluding the Kennedy win in 1960, this marked the narrowest margin of victory for any candidate carrying the state by a majority in the twentieth century. Almost all analyses of the election attributed this victory, in large measure, to the solid support given the Democratic ticket by blacks. No predominantly black precinct gave Carter less than a majority and in forty-two sample-ballot precincts chosen by the Public Affairs Research Council, the margin was over 60 percent; twenty-six of them directed over 80 percent of their ballots to the Carter-Mondale ticket. The Republican incumbent was unable to acquire a majority in any black precinct.[42]

Blacks continue to be heavily involved in partisan activities at every level. Since 1965 they have served on the state central committee, on parish executive committees, and as delegates to national party conventions. They have also served on the Democratic National Committee and on special committees and units at the national level. As of April, 1980, Louisiana's representation on the Democratic National Committee consisted of 4 whites and 1 black, and 18 blacks served on the 203-member state central committee.

Participation by blacks in Republican partisan activity has increased somewhat in the past decade. Several blacks were involved in Republican Governor David Treen's candidacy in 1979. In his victory over Democrat Louis Lambert, however, he had only minimal black sup-

42. Public Affairs Research Council, "Presidential Election, November, 1976," *Analysis* (November, 1976).

port. Even so, he has appointed three blacks to major state offices and has claimed he will be responsive to black needs.

It was indicated earlier that blacks had developed political organizations during Reconstruction. During the Second Reconstruction, black political organizations have become quite numerous and visible. These organizations developed in response to two factors. First, increased black voter registration in Louisiana created a pool of new voters that was bound to attract the attention of office seekers and of aspirants for leadership roles in the black community. Second, the absence of a strong, competitive two-party system led to the development of alternative competitive structures through which these new political resources could be mobilized. This second factor also undoubtedly led to the development of white political organizations.

In 1978 and early 1979, we conducted a survey of seventeen of these black organizations, using our own interview schedule of twenty-seven items. Each schedule was completed in an interview with either the head of the organization or another officer identified by the head, and the survey was conducted in the organizations' hometown locations in three of the state's urban areas. Organizations were selected for the survey through contacts with political officeholders and others knowledgeable about politics in the areas and through newspaper and other media coverage of political events, especially elections. Of the seventeen organizations, five were located in East Baton Rouge Parish (east central Louisiana), five were in Rapides Parish (central Louisiana), and seven were located in Orleans Parish (southern Louisiana). In both East Baton Rouge and Rapides parishes, all of the organizations chosen for study on the basis of contact with informational sources participated in the survey. In Orleans an interview could not be arranged with one organization that undoubtedly plays a significant role in the political life of the parish. With this single exception, the group of organizations studied seems comprehensive enough to provide defensible conclusions about black political organizations.

All of the political organizations were of rather recent origin. Of the seventeen organizations, only four had been founded prior to 1963. The oldest of these was established in 1943 and the others in 1945, 1950, and 1951. Incorporated status has been acquired by all but one of these early groups. In that case, a technicality—the inclusion of the name of the parish in the official name of the organization—prevents

Table 11-6

Voter Registration in Urban Areas

Parish	Total Voting Age Population of Parish (1970 Census)		Total Registered Voters in Parish, October, 1976	
	Black	*White*	*Black*	*White*
East Baton Rouge	48,107	131,692	33,226	118,026
Orleans	152,660	236,597	86,678	129,545
Rapides	18,758	54,693	10,132	47,597

Source: *U.S. Census of Population* (1970), I, Pt. 20, pp. 20–58, 20–66; Report of the Commissioner of Elections, October, 1976 (Office of the Commissioner of Elections, Baton Rouge).

incorporation. The older organizations are distributed among the three areas, one in Orleans, two in East Baton Rouge, and one in Rapides. All indicated that some persons involved in the founding of the organization were still active members.

The real upsurge in organizational effort seems to have come mostly in the 1960s and especially after the passage of the Voting Rights Act of 1965. Organizations were established in 1963, 1964, 1966, 1971, and 1975; two organizations were started in 1969 and in 1972, and three new organizations appeared in 1968. Three of the groups were initially formed as factions of older groups. The organizations' structures followed a rather traditional pattern. All were headed by a president or chairman and had a number of vice-presidents (ranging from one to three), a secretary, and a treasurer. Only three reported the office of sergeant-at-arms, only five had a parliamentarian, and only four had chaplains. All but one reported the existence of a supervisory body called a board of directors, executive committee, or similar title. The sizes of these committees ranged from five to thirty, and the average committee consisted of fifteen or sixteen members. No unusual organizational structures were described in the interviews.

In a pattern of secrecy reminiscent of an earlier historical epoch, slightly less than one-third of the organizations had policies that prohibited them from releasing the names of officers and members without prior express permission of the board of directors or executive committee. Fear of economic or physical reprisal, avoidance of candidate solicitation of support from individual officers outside the organization's official procedures and structure, and tradition were the three major justifications for these policies. One organization could not reveal the number of its members. Although most of the groups were of recent origin, this pattern of secrecy has its roots in very real fears.[43]

Reported organizational size ranged from a low of ten members to a high of three thousand. With the exception of one group, which claimed a leadership orientation rather than a membership orientation, the groups were all kindly disposed toward growth through the affiliation of new members. Oddly enough, the leadership-oriented group exceeded some of the mass-based groups in actual members. Nine organizations reported current memberships of less than 100 persons, none indicated between 100 and 200 members, three had between 200 and 300, one had 365 members, one was uncertain, and another reported 3,000 members. Methods of determining membership status were not specifically probed by the survey instrument. However, several interviewees indicated an open admissions policy "to those who would cooperate" or to "any registered voter in the area." None indicated a specific dues-paying requirement for membership.

Like political parties, these organizations include substantial numbers of women in their ranks. Nine organizations indicated that women constituted over half of their membership, and seven stipulated that women represented "a significant number but less than half" of the membership. One offered no response to the item. As to the role women play in the organizations—two respondents described women's role in modest terms, fifteen respondents attributed a significant role to women members. One stated that "women damn near run the organization. They plan the activities, execute the plans and have a major role in decision-making. They take care of most fund-raisers." Another responded that of twenty-one precinct captains, only four were men. That women perform a disproportionate amount of the actual work seems clear from the responses. However, the role played by women can be discounted somewhat since responses on other items suggested that the officeholders were overwhelmingly male. In this respect, the pattern characteristic of traditional political parties tends to prevail in the black political groups in our study.

The two major support sources reported for organizational activities

43. Matthews and Prothro, *Negroes and the New Southern Politics*, 166.

were contributions from candidates for office and fund-raisers. Six respondents identified the former source as dominant and five indicated the latter. Among the others, individual dues was the prime source for three, contributions from members for three, and contributions from citizens for one. Some spokespersons offered expanded commentary on sources of financial support. These comments were directed mostly toward clarification of the use made of contributions from candidates for office. Funds so solicited were apparently spent on the activities in which the groups engaged in the interest of the election of the contributing candidates. This practice seems reasonably well established in Louisiana politics.

Black political organizations seem to have a more positive relationship with the state and local Democratic organizations than with Republican units at these two levels, but no formal ties exist with either. Most heads of the involved organizations are Democrats, however, and there is some overlap of officeholding in organizations and Democratic party units. Responses about relations with the Republican party were "non-existent," "non-cooperative," "none," "foreign." In the main, Republican candidates apparently have resisted the temptation to compete seriously for the new black vote.

Two very significant aspects of these political organizations were not investigated: their ability to mobilize and turn out the vote on election day and their ability to command rewards for the membership group once the candidates supported have won office. Earlier studies suggest that the mobilization and turnout have been effectively handled in the New Orleans area.[44]

Blacks have not limited themselves to traditional political actions since 1944. In addition to legal action aimed at changing their status, blacks conducted an extralegal protest—the Civil Rights Movement—across the South and, to a more limited extent, across the nation from the late 1950s through the late 1960s. Louisiana witnessed a significant amount of this activity. Student sit-ins and demonstrations, as well as citizen marches and sit-ins in the interest of desegregating

44. Wilbur Scott, "An Assessment of Political Organization Effectiveness in New Orleans" (paper presented at the Annual Meeting of the Southwestern Sociological Society, New Orleans, March 29–April 1, 1978); Murphy Sanchez, "An Analysis of Black Political Participation in the 1969–70 New Orleans Mayoralty Election" (M.A. thesis, Southern University, 1972).

public facilities and acquiring the ballot, occurred in all parts of the state. Students at Southern University in Baton Rouge played a leading role in these developments. The 1959–1960 academic year and the three years that followed were marked by a high level of student activity designed to end segregation in public places. For example, on December 14, 1961, twenty-three blacks were arrested in sit-ins at lunch counters. The next day over fifteen hundred blacks demonstrated in protest of their arrests. The traumatic effects of involvement on these students, the faculty, and the administration have been reported in a number of studies. The severity of sanctions leveled against those arrested in these cases and the impact of such sanctions can be discerned from comments by Harvard Law School graduate Weldon Rougeau after his first arrest as a Southern University student protestor in 1961. "I and about 20 other people were arrested for disturbing the peace and illegal picketing. We spent 21 days in jail. . . . I had never been in jail. We were thrown in with people who had committed violent crimes. We were freshmen and sophomores in college." Of a second arrest only hours after release from his first jail experience, Rougeau writes: "two of us were in a solitary cell. . . . We spent 58 days in a solitary cell! A 7 by 7 cubicle. There was only one bed."[45]

Louisiana devoted considerable resources to opposing the Civil Rights Movement, and the names of protestors and law enforcement officers became household words. Two major decisions of the United States Supreme Court grew out of the Louisiana student demonstrations.[46]

Blacks have had substantial direct impact on the politics of Louisiana during the Second Reconstruction. In addition, blacks have indirectly influenced state politics, particularly the tenor of campaigns. Racial epithets and slurs, a trademark of state politics, began to disappear from candidates' vocabularies as more and more blacks registered to vote. Styles of dealing with blacks became open as opposed to clan-

45. C. Vann Woodward, "The Unreported Crisis in the Southern Colleges," *Harper's* (October, 1962), 86; Adolph Reed, "Crisis on the Negro Campus," *Nation* (February 10, 1962), 111–13; Melinda Bartley, "Southern University Student Activists: 1960–63 Revisited" (M.A. thesis, Southern University, 1973); "OFCCP: New Directions; Forum Interviews Weldon Rougeau, Director OFCCP," *Forum Affirmative Action Monthly* (August, 1977), 3, 18–22.

46. *Cox* v. *Louisiana*, 379 U.S. 536 (1965); *Garner* v. *Louisiana*, 368 U.S. 167 (1961).

destine, and black campaign officials became more visible. It appears that certain legislative reforms, especially those having to do with the banning of nonmembers from the floors of the two legislative chambers, have been attributed by some to the increased black membership. Blacks have secured positions on the staffs of legislative and executive units and appointment to various boards and commissions at all levels of government. Louisiana's United States senators, for example, have supported the appointment of a black federal district judge and blacks for other federal positions.

Summary and Conclusions

Black participation in Louisiana's politics has been reflective of the black politics of the nation at large and of the southern region. Thus, the nature of black political involvement can best be understood within the context of national and regional politics. As the political fortunes or misfortunes of blacks changed nationally, they changed in Louisiana. Historically, Louisiana's political environment has been hostile to the aspirations of blacks for equal political participation. Any alteration in this basic environment has been largely the result of "outside interference" in the form of federal intervention. The Emancipation Proclamation, Reconstruction legislation, certain United States Supreme Court decisions, the 1964 Civil Rights Act, and the 1965 Voting Rights Act constitute prime examples of actions taken by federal units to enhance black political fortunes in the state and region. When these actions have been rescinded or deemphasized at the federal level, state conditions have returned to "normal."

Blacks have twice exercised substantial political power in the state as a direct consequence of black activism. However, they have also influenced the politics of the state indirectly as political elites have centered their concern around stripping blacks of their political power and then keeping them politically powerless. The patterns that have evolved indicate black vacillation between traditional electoral politics and nontraditional protest politics. Whenever feasible, blacks seem to opt for the more traditional types of political involvement, but they actively embrace nontraditional means when traditional modes are inaccessible. The political conduct of blacks during the Reconstruction and post-Reconstruction periods would seem to attest to their willingness to participate in the democratic process, in large numbers, when such participation does not pose extraordinary hazards to their physical well-being. Physical, psychological, and economic threats have been used by white authorities in Louisiana to deter black political participation; blacks are justifiably concerned as they ponder the advisability of adopting a "participant" orientation.

Several projections are relevant to the future of black politics in Louisiana. Principal among these is the impending expiration of the 1965 Voting Rights Act in 1981. Its expiration could mean doom for the Second Reconstruction period as did the Compromise of 1877 for the first Reconstruction. Experience strongly indicates the need for continued federal monitoring of states like Louisiana, which have been willing in the past to make black political impotency a part of their fundamental law. A second concern is the problem of translating political gains (increased black voter registration and officeholding) into real gains in the quality of life for the bulk of black citizens of the state. Failure to meet these challenges could result in the withdrawal of blacks from participant roles in the system or, alternatively, the reappearance of black anger and militancy characteristic of the 1960s.

Finally, some concern exists with regard to the maturation of black politics in the state. Specifically, how can black political actors, individually and collectively, enter the bargaining process, the give and take of the allocation of resources, without assuming some of the shockingly negative characteristics that have come to characterize that process in Louisiana?

12.

Voting Behavior
in Gubernatorial Elections

JOHN WILDGEN

Given the fact that it is only one of fifty states, an extraordinary amount is known about Louisiana. It has been written about and discussed out of proportion to its size or population. Scholarly, journalistic, and just plain vulgar monographs on Louisiana politics find a ready market. Moreover, of the hundreds of state governors who did not become president of the United States, few have had Pulitzer Prize–winning biographies written about them.[1]

Several factors come readily to mind to explain the vast literature of Louisiana politics: flamboyant politicians, a tradition of political corruption, a high level of citizen interest in state politics, and a complex institutional political structure. The coexistence of these characteristics makes Louisiana a political paradox. Adding to the paradox is the fact that the state shares many attributes with third-world nations whose economies are based on agriculture and/or the extraction of minerals. These countries frequently have political systems with divisions of labor as simple as that found in their economies. Some have no division of political labor at all—they are out and out dictatorships.

Louisiana also went through a period of near dictatorship. That, at least, was the view of V. O. Key, who observed that "Huey P. Long's control of Louisiana more nearly matched the power of a South American dictator than of any other American State boss."[2] But in the fifty

---

1. T. Harry Williams, *Huey Long* (New York: Knopf, 1969).
2. V. O. Key, Jr., *Southern Politics in State and Nation* (New York: Vintage Books, 1949), 156.

years since Long wielded power Louisiana has undergone remarkable political change. Far from resembling a dictatorship, the state seems to possess many of the attributes of modern and sophisticated political systems. There are a complex division of political labor with effective separation of powers and checks and balances, a high degree of competition for leadership positions, a high degree of political participation, an excellent system of political communication, a capacity for self-generated change, and autonomy from the outside environment.

A full analysis of all these attributes would require a lengthy volume. Therefore in this essay, I will concentrate on the last two items: political change and political autonomy, both at the level of the mass electorate. The other attributes are, of course, also important parts of the total picture of Louisiana politics and are, indeed, prerequisites for self-generated change and autonomy. I will discuss these two factors in light of the state's socioeconomic structure—a structure that would hardly suggest the presence of such a sophisticated, state-of-the-art political system. In part, it is necessary to mix economics and sociology with politics in order to underscore the Louisiana paradox: modern politics practiced in the context of a premodern socioeconomic base. I will attempt to illustrate the connections between Louisiana's politics and other aspects of the state's collective life—aspects that have been the engines of political change.

In developing the theme of modern political change and autonomy in the light of socioeconomic concerns, I will examine several major political developments of the past half-century, the Longite alignment, the nature of bifactionalism, the nature of ticketing, the realignment of the 1960s, the demise of ticketing, and Louisiana's insulation from national politics. As with all aspects of political development, we can separate these elements analytically, but it is important to remind ourselves that they are all part of the fabric of Louisiana politics.

Much of the evidence presented in this chapter is derived from parish-level election returns and census reports. These data are an important reflection of Louisiana's history, society, and politics. But numbers in isolation, or even in tables, can be impossibly tedious; it is an arduous task to separate trivial detail from overall patterns. To assist in finding overall patterns, where they exist, use has been made throughout this chapter of three-dimensional maps generated by computer. In a technical sense the maps are mathematical models of statistical distributions. For our purposes, however, they are visual representations of social, economic, and political information. For any topic under discussion the value for each particular parish is represented by the apparent height of the parish on the map. High values elevate parishes; low values depress them. When a parish is isolated it will stand out quite clearly (as do the heavily populated urban parishes); when parishes cluster together to form a region (the parishes with a high proportion of Roman Catholics in their population) individual parish boundaries will appear to merge on the surface of a plateau. At times the pattern that emerges will be quite striking; in other cases the map will look quite confusing. In either event the reader has an opportunity to check the author's findings or substitute his or her alternative judgment. In that sense the maps are not measurement devices (the original data do that), but summaries that serve to illustrate a point or provoke thought.

Map 12-1
Percentage Voting for Huey Long, 1928

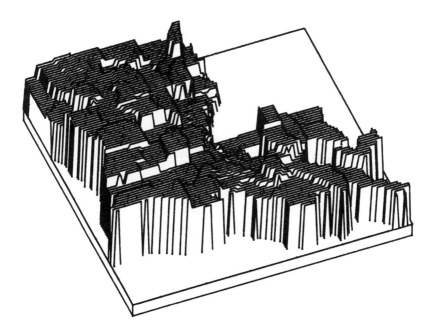

Map 12-2
Population Distribution, 1970

The Longite Alignment

Huey P. Long is one of the legendary figures of twentieth-century politics, and his political rivalry with President Franklin D. Roosevelt was of major national significance. Key's comparison of Long to a dictator was apt, although something of an exaggeration. One of the ironies of Long's rule was that his dictatorial style set in motion the elements of change that led to fully modern political institutions in Louisiana. His removal of the poll tax in the early 1930s, for example, created a notable increase in the state's level of political participation.

Long's support was strongest in areas of the state known for dirt farming, sharecropping, and a heritage of nineteenth-century populism. Conversely, his political enemies were concentrated in plantation and commercial areas. Maps 12-1 through 12-3, which show, in turn,

Map 12-3
Percentage of Blacks in the Population, 1970

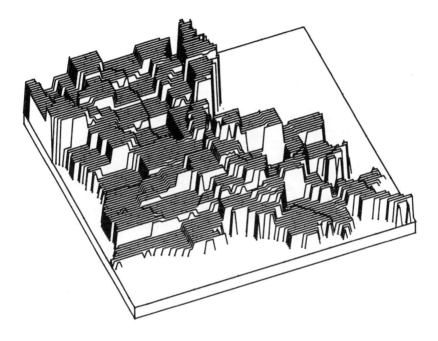

the vote for Long, the state's population concentrations, and the state's black areas, tell much of the story. Although drawn from different data bases and different years, the three maps strongly suggest Long's strength in predominantly white, rural areas. For example, in 1928 he did rather badly in Caddo Parish in the extreme northwest part of the state. Then, as now, it was one of the state's more urbanized areas. He fared just as badly, or worse, in the plantation parishes along the Mississippi River and in northeastern Louisiana. Those who might have voted for him, the disadvantaged black citizens in these areas, were still disenfranchised, and Long's style had little appeal for planters and businessmen.

The geographical pattern of Longism remained intact over an extended period. Map 12-4 shows the 1956 vote for Huey Long's younger brother, Earl. The rough equivalence of the maps understates the

Map 12-4
Percentage Voting for Earl Long, 1956

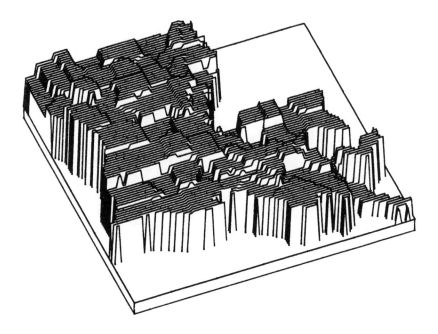

strength of association between the elections of the two brothers. In both instances the results were from first-primary victories. If runoffs had been necessary, parishes would have fallen in line more regularly. Yet, in any case the basic pattern of a north-south bridge across the state stands out. Equally clear is Longite weakness in urban-commercial areas.

Bifactionalism

The Longs were a faction, and by their existence, they created an Anti-Long faction that was content with that name. Although all important elections were held under the umbrella of the Democratic party, Louisiana's factions were, in effect, two distinct parties. In contemporary terms, we would think of the Longs as liberals and the Anti-Longs as conservatives. Furthermore, we would think of the Longs as more inclined to political corruption than the Anti-Longs.

Modern political parties tend to develop and keep relatively stable partisan bases in part because of economic conditions and in part because of deliberate patterns of political socialization over generations. Both forces were at work in the Long/Anti-Long antagonism. The regular pattern of election results and the alternation of the faction in office during the Long era were ultramodern. The two factions had rather clearly defined programs and the power to carry them out. Every four years a faction selected a new leader and submittted the faction's record to the electorate. It was a much more intelligible situation than existed at the national level in the United States at that time.

Figure 12-1
Bifactionalism, 1944–1948: Davis and Long

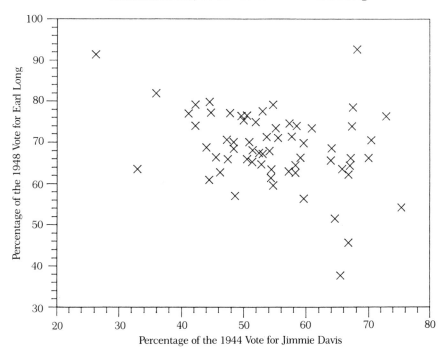

Figure 12-2

Bifactionalism, 1948–1952: Long and Kennon

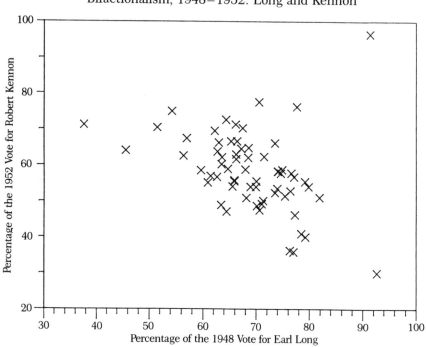

Louisiana had, essentially, a responsible two-party system along British lines, or at least on imagined British lines.[3]

Vote totals clearly show a healthy alternation in office. The Long faction held office from 1928 through 1940, winning three elections; from 1940 through 1948 the Anti-Longs were in power. Earl Long became governor in 1948, four years later Anti-Long Robert Kennon replaced him, and Earl Long was elected once again in 1956. Out of eight gubernatorial elections, the Longs won five and the Anti-Longs won three. It was a sound record for any modern democratic political system, and particularly significant because from Reconstruction until Huey Long's first gubernatorial win, the Bourbon Democrats had completely dominated state politics.

3. See "Toward a More Responsible Two-Party System," *American Political Science Review*, XLIV (September, 1950), Supplement.

Figure 12-3

Bifactionalism, 1952–1956: Kennon and Long

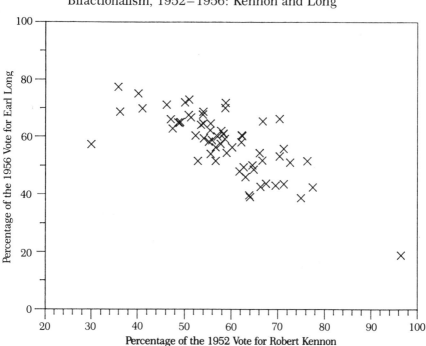

Figures 12-1 through 12-3 show the factional voting of Louisiana's sixty-four parishes in gubernatorial elections at the height of the bifactional era. Fitted lines of regression would indicate that, in each case, we are dealing with an alternation in factions: Davis to Long, Long to Kennon, Kennon to Long. There is enough scatter of parishes around the slopes to suggest that the elections were not instant replays. There was some flexibility in the alignment pattern, but it is, nevertheless, a distinctive pattern. With few exceptions, parish points follow the line of regression closely. In the upper right of Figure 12-2, showing the Long-Kennon succession, there is one stray parish. This would seem to be an error, but in fact, the parish in question, Plaquemines, had been solidly Longite in 1948. In the next gubernatorial election, however, the Plaquemines voters followed the lead of Leander Perez into the Anti-Longite camp. They were outraged by Earl Long's support of the Democratic party's civil rights plank in the 1948 party platform.

This evidence is generally consistent with the notion of a modern, disciplined party system at the mass level.[4]

Ticketing

Discussions of ticketing systems are often subsumed into discussions of bifactionalism because ticketing is a prerequisite of bifactionalism. The study of bifactionalism can be reduced to the analysis of correlations between elections across time while ticketing studies concentrate on correlations among candidates in a given election. In Louisiana, ticketing is especially important because of the multiplicity of elective executive state offices. Voters elect a governor, lieutenant governor, attorney general, secretary of state, commissioner of agriculture, treasurer, commissioner of elections, commissioner of insurance, and a Public Service Commission. Ticketing presupposes that candidates for various offices mutually support one another. The idea of ticketing did not originate in the bifactional era, but its scope and effectiveness were clearly evident during the period.

Figure 12-4 depicts a remarkable example of effective ticketing. The scattergram shows the correlation between the vote for Kennon and his ticket-mate for registrar of state lands, Ellen Bryan Moore. In this particular instance the fit between votes for Kennon and votes for Moore was tight. The correlation coefficient was 0.92. In the next election, the fit between Earl Long and his candidate for registrar of state lands, Lucille May Grace, was 0.83. In the 1960 election, the correlation between Jimmie Davis' vote and the vote for custodian of voting machines candidate Douglas Fowler was 0.93. These examples are merely suggestive of an overall pattern that prevailed throughout the period. Factor analytic studies covering all candidates have been performed for the period 1952–1964. The results indicate unambiguously the existence of a superbly efficient ticket system.[5]

4. Perry Howard, *Political Tendencies in Louisiana* (Rev. ed.; Baton Rouge: Louisiana State University Press, 1971), expressed some reservations. Significantly, his chapter on this topic was entitled "The Long Era, 1928–56; Bifactional Politics?" Howard did not dispense with the notion, however. He did document much of the slope in the year-to-year correlations.

5. John K. Wildgen, "The Detection of Critical Elections in the Absence of Two-Party Competition," *Journal of Politics*, XXXVI (May, 1974), 465–79.

Figure 12-4
Ticketing in 1952: Kennon and Moore

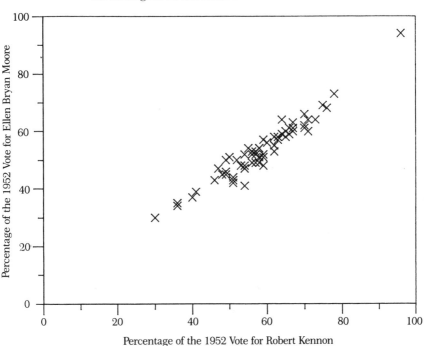

In practice, ticketing was a difficult technique in Louisiana. Meaningful elections in the state during this period were Democratic primaries and runoffs. Candidates were listed and numbered on the ballots, but the ballots gave no indication of factional loyalties. That is, voters could not pull a Long or Anti-Long master lever to vote a straight ticket. Instead, voters had to scrutinize the ballot to find co-factionalists. Nevertheless, the available evidence supports the view that ticketing was successful in spite of this obstacle.

Two points may be made in interpreting the relationship of ticketing to our ideas of political modernization. First, ticketing was essential to the workings of bifactionalism—it made possible entire slates of executive candidates who formed a kind of elected cabinet. If they did not function like a cabinet in the full sense of the word, they were, for the most part, collectively responsible to the electorate. In the entire period only one official, Wade O. Martin, managed to raise himself above the ticket system and gain reelection independently, but even Martin started out on the Long ticket.

Second, ticketing was possible only through an efficient system of political communication. It was necessary to inform the electorate about who was on the ticket. To be sure, newspapers and, later, radio and television played roles. At certain times factions even published their own newspapers. But the bulk of the work of political communication was done by knocking on doors and by passing out ticket leaflets to voters at the polls. Numbers were used in addition to names on the ballots to aid illiterate voters. This was clearly an efficient system that required good campaign organization and the recruitment of numerous workers at the precinct level. That is, ticketing in this era required effective political communication that depended upon extensive personal participation. These elements—participation, communication, ticketing, and bifactionalism—were all essential to a highly competitive political system with an extensive division of labor.

Realignment

The Longite alignment, with the modernization it brought to Louisiana politics, had considerable potential for self-perpetuation. Voters divided themselves into rival camps largely on the basis of class or economic differences. Despite the imposing edifice of government and politics built by the Longs and their rivals, little was done to eradicate socioeconomic differences. Map 12-5 shows the 1970 distribution of illiteracy in Louisiana. It was a pattern that had persisted for generations. Map 12-6, which shows median family income, is almost a reverse image of the illiteracy map. Whether one considers illiteracy or income, however, Louisiana has had (and continues to have) a poor record of socioeconomic reform. In 1960 the state's per capita personal income ranked forty-first in the nation, and in the same year Louisiana ranked forty-seventh in U.S. Selective Service mental requirements.[6] Figure 12-5, which compares white and black median family income across parishes, shows that poverty and illiteracy were worse among blacks than among whites—even though whites were not doing well themselves.

6. David R. Morgan, *Handbook of State Policy Indicators* (Norman: University of Oklahoma, Bureau of Government Research, 1978).

Figure 12-5
Income Disparity in Louisiana, 1970

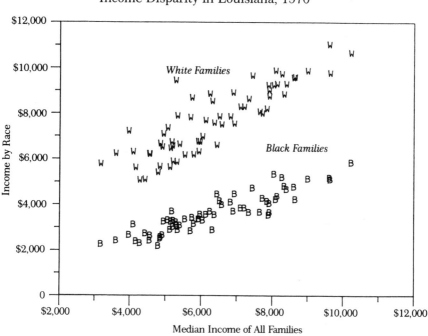

Nonetheless, it was impossible for Louisiana not to benefit some-what from postwar prosperity. Insofar as Longism depended upon the poor for a base, new poor had to be found. In early 1956 black regis-tration had grown from 7.5 percent to just under 15 percent. Some growth in black registration was due to national pressures, but some of it was due to indigenous political considerations. A major considera-tion was the necessity to increase the electoral basis of Longism. The Longs assumed, correctly, that blacks would support them rather than the Anti-Longs, and Earl Long courted what black vote there was. This change in the suffrage, along with the stirrings of the Civil Rights Movement, set the stage for an end to Longite bifactionalism in the state. Although it was premised on class conflict, the axiomatic basis of the conflict was that it was for whites only. As blacks began to enter the system, racism became more important than class issues. Conse-quently, the election of 1959–1960 saw the beginning of the end of

Map 12-5
Percentage of Population Illiterate, 1970

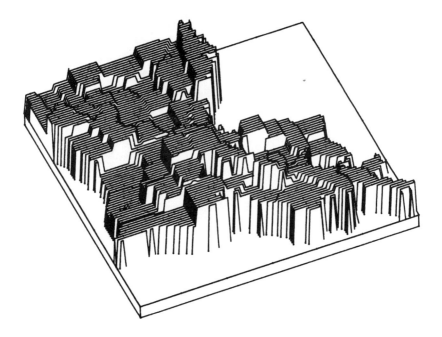

bifactional politics in Louisiana. That electoral period created as much acrimony and drama as any in Louisiana history, and included the kidnapping of Governor Earl Long and his involuntary commitment to a mental institution.[7] The victor in the election was an old Anti-Long leader and former governor, Jimmie Davis.

Map 12-7 shows the distribution of the vote for Davis. It looks like no political map out of the Long era, but it does bear a striking reverse similarity to Map 12-8, which depicts estimates of the state's Roman Catholic population. Catholic-Protestant tensions had not surfaced in

7. Howard, *Political Tendencies*, 422; John S. Fenton and Kenneth N. Vines, "Negro Registration in Louisiana," *American Political Science Review*, LI (September, 1957), 711; New York *Times*, June 3, 1959, p. 1, June 16, 1959, p. 1, June 19, 1959, p. 1, June 27, 1959, p. 1.

Map 12-6
Median Family Income, 1970

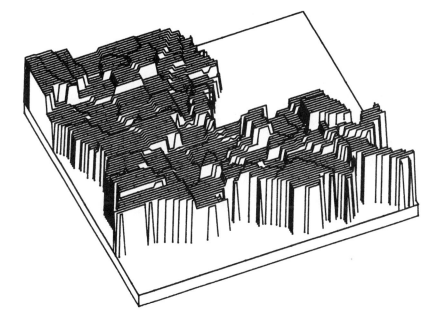

public life since the Klan's heyday in the 1920s. But among the whites in North Louisiana, there was a feeling that predominantly Catholic South Louisiana was "soft on race."

Religious tensions were crystallized by the prominence of New Orleans mayor deLesseps Morrison. Neither the Longs nor the Anti-Longs cared for him—his urban Catholicism was in sharp contrast to the style of rural Protestantism that pervaded Louisiana politics. Despite some common political views, Earl Long utterly detested Morrison, and the feeling was mutual. Thus, in the 1959–1960 primary series, Earl Long endorsed his old Anti-Long foe Jimmie Davis rather than Morrison in the runoff.

Morrison lost to Davis but returned four years later to face John McKeithen. The pattern of votes in the 1964 contest was nearly identi-

cal to that of the 1960 contest. Curiously, McKeithen, who was a life-
long Longite, picked up votes in the same parishes as did Davis, a dedicated Anti-Longite. (See Figure 12-7.) The state's voters were now
split along new lines. The Davis-McKeithen electorate was antiblack,
anti-Catholic, much like the Bourbon Democrats of the nineteenth
century. These Neo-Bourbons, based in North Louisiana, won both
elections because of the weakness of the Catholic and black alliance.
But by 1971–1972, the balance had shifted. Edwin Edwards' theme of
"Cajun Power" kept alive the idea of a Catholic governor (despite uncertainty in many quarters about Edwards' religious devotion) with appeal to blacks. Map 12-9 shows his bases of support. The map looks
very much like a map of the strength of Roman Catholicism in the
state—with some dipping into North Louisiana's portion of the black
belt. Thus, for three contested elections (in 1967 McKeithen handily

Map 12-7
Percentage Voting for Davis, 1959

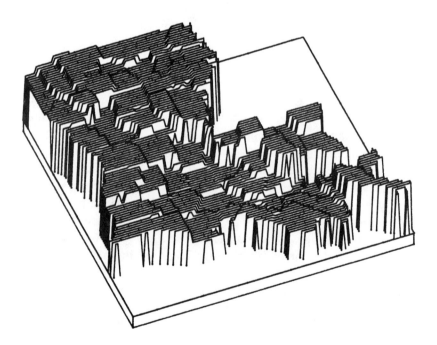

Map 12-8
Percentage of the Population Roman Catholic, 1970

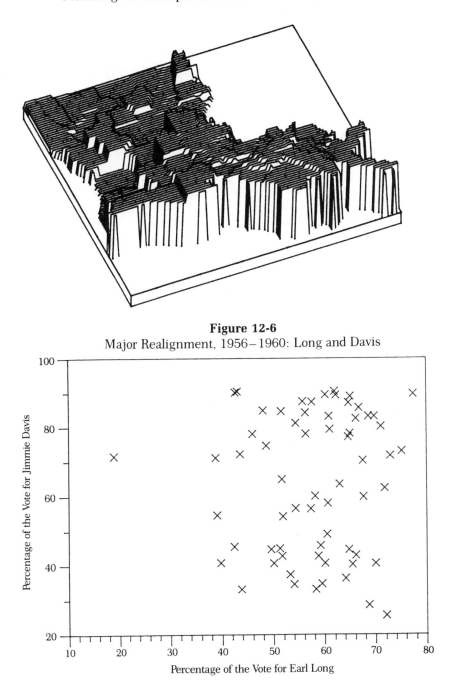

Figure 12-6
Major Realignment, 1956–1960: Long and Davis

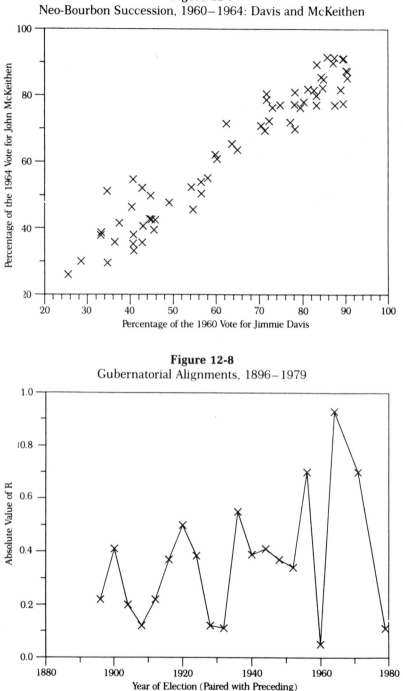

Figure 12-7
Neo-Bourbon Succession, 1960–1964: Davis and McKeithen

Figure 12-8
Gubernatorial Alignments, 1896–1979

Map 12-9
Percentage Voting for Edwards, 1971

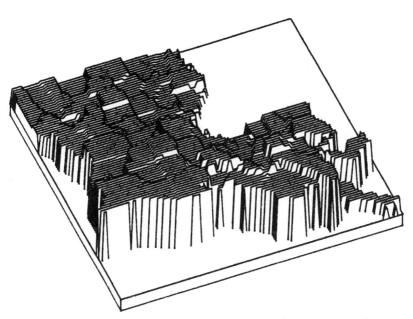

succeeded himself after a constitutional amendment permitting second terms was passed), Louisiana demonstrated a north-south split completely uncharacteristic of the Long era. It was a major realignment of factions, but not without precedent, for as Figure 12-8 shows, similar shifts took place in 1904 and 1928. Thus, about once a generation the state has shifted its bases for selecting governors.

It is not completely clear whether the election of 1960 was what political scientists call a critical election.[8] Louisiana has not entirely replaced the class basis of Longism with a racial, religious, and regional alignment, but it has lost the political practices that enabled the Longs and Anti-Longs to come to grips with the issues dividing the state. The first piece of evidence we have to support this notion is the outcome of the 1979 statewide elections. These elections were markedly irregular even by Louisiana standards. It may take years to sort out the numerous charges of vote buying and voting-machine tampering. The winner of the governor's seat, David Treen, has not been involved in those

8. V. O. Key, "A Theory of Critical Elections," *Journal of Politics*, XVII (February, 1955), 3.

disputes, an interesting fact, considering the history of Louisiana politics. Another important point to consider is that Treen is Louisiana's
first Republican governor since the Reconstruction era. His election
attests to the growing strength of Republicanism in the South. More to
the point, however, is the nature of the vote that elected him. Map
12-10, which shows the percentage of the vote that Treen won, bears
no resemblance to the map of Edwards' 1972 victory—nor even to
Treen's own vote against Edwards in 1972. If anything, Treen's basis of
support is correlated with that of the old Anti-Longs (an r of 0.52 with
Kennon), Nixon's 1968 vote (r = 0.64), and negatively with that of
Carter's 1976 vote (r = 0.61). Thus, the statistical evidence suggests a
return to the politics that existed before the north-south split of the
sixties and seventies.

The campaign rhetoric was also reminiscent of the Long era. Treen
presented himself as a conservative, good-government candidate. His

Map 12-10
Percentage Voting for Treen, 1979

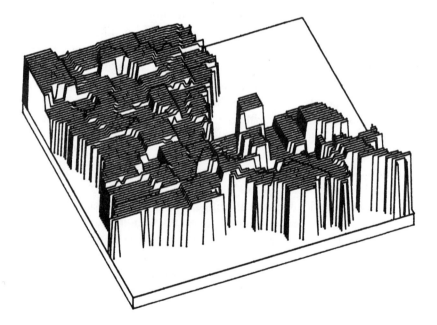

opponent, Louis Lambert (like Huey Long, recruited from the Public Service Commission) presented himself as a populist opposed to OPEC, Wall Street, and nuclear hazards. The return to a Longite alignment, at least geographically, raises the question of whether the realignment of the sixties was an aberration. It would be tempting to conclude that it was, but it is important to realize that the election of 1979 was conducted in the shadow of Edwin Edwards, who retained great popularity after eight years in office and who promised to return in 1983. If this comes about, it may be the 1979 election that will be viewed as an aberration. Still, the return to a long-term geographical alignment and class-based political rhetoric certainly confuses discussion of a state-level critical election.

Deticketing

A second set of evidence pertinent to political change since Longism is the demise of the ticketing system. Even after the great shift of 1959–1960 to regional voting, candidates like Davis and McKeithen kept the notion of ticketing alive. No doubt it was part of their own set of political instincts, schooled as they were by the Longs and the Anti-Longs. But in 1971 ticketing for statewide offices became extinct. Figure 12-9 shows this graphically by plotting the vote for Sherman Bernard, commissioner of insurance, against that for Edwards. The value of the correlation here is simply zero. While other candidates in this campaign, Lieutenant Governor James Fitzmorris and Attorney General William Guste, were not as dramatically uncorrelated with Edwards, they remained fundamentally statistically independent of Edwards' vote. They were, in fact, all mutually independent. More formally stated, a factor analysis of the vote for these four yielded four factors. In effect, Louisiana returned in 1971 to pre-Longite multifactionalism—a pattern that continued in 1979. Candidates no longer belong to statewide factions as in the past—each candidate is his or her own faction. Deticketing completes the abandonment of the political practices of the bifactional era.

The explanation for the abandonment of ticketing is relatively simple. A politician like Edwin Edwards was able to forge, as did deLesseps Morrison, a Catholic-black coalition. Other candidates seek-

Figure 12-9
Ticketing in 1971: Edwards and Bernard

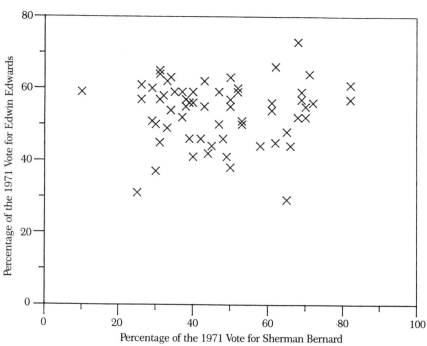

ing the governorship or other offices could not, or would not, imitate Edwards. They were constrained to use other forms of electoral calculus to find voter bases that could win them a majority in a state electorate that was 70 percent white and 30 percent black. None of the several candidates wanted to reject black votes, yet overt courting of black votes risked alienation of white voters. Finding the right approach and combination is one of the most challenging tasks for the statewide office seeker in Louisiana.

Insulation

Presidential and gubernatorial voting in Louisiana have traditionally been insulated from each other. As a state of the Solid South, the state's electoral votes, from readmission to the Union until Eisen-

spite their reputation for what V. O. Key called "boodling," the state's politicians appear to be remarkably popular. Those who have run afoul of federal standards of probity in office, such as Congressmen Otto Passman and Richard "Buddy" Leach, find sympathetic jurors, and many a convicted politician has won reelection from his jail cell.

Not only are politicians popular; there is evidence that politics itself is increasingly popular. Some form of elections are held every year in Louisiana. Voter turnout is comparable or superior to that at the national level in current presidential elections. For a contested gubernatorial primary and runoff the rate of turnout is commonly close to 70 percent.

Of course, voting is a minimal political act. What of some of the other indicators of participation such as joining organizations? In most political contexts, interest groups and political organizations will assess their members and contribute to a candidate's war chest. In Louisiana the process is reversed. It is more common for candidates to offer financial support to political action groups in return for their promise of support. It is very much a form of vote-buying, but in Louisiana it is not only legal but it is a standard operating procedure from governors down to constables. Understandably this practice has encouraged a proliferation of organizations at the grassroots level.

Political communication is also highly developed in the state. It has been since the time of Huey Long. Radio and television consume about half of a typical candidate's budget, the other half going to vote-gathering organizations. An idea of the joint importance of media and organizational work can be gathered by keeping in mind that in 1979 the six major gubernatorial candidates spent a combined total of $20 million on 2.0 million votes or $10 per voter. In 1976 the two major presidential candidates spent only $112.8 million (in the primaries and the general election) for 81.5 million votes, or $1.38 per voter.

Thus, signs of alienation, withdrawal from organizational life, and breakdown of communication symptomatic of political decay are lacking. The state's authorities and institutions enjoy a good deal of support. But if the case for political decline is not persuasive, it still helps to account for the fact that in the loss of bifactionalism Louisiana has lost a certain neatness or crispness in the structure of its politics.

It can be argued that the current complexity of state voting patterns, rather than being a sign of decay, is a sign of adaptive change. Bifactionalism was suited to an age of rich-versus-poor conflict among whites. The political agenda of the bifactional era has been changed by an expanded electorate that now includes blacks who, despite increasing diversity, tend to vote as a bloc. This means that the electorate has become more complex. Blacks, Catholics, Protestants, city dwellers, suburbanites, and rural folk have criss-crossing views of economics, taxation, energy, the environment, and the role of government. It is impractical to try to fit this electorate into a bifactional mold. Thus, the advent of multifactionalism in Louisiana should be viewed as a form of political development.

Prospects for the Future

In its political history Louisiana has developed a record of adaptability to changing circumstances. The challenge to change was frequently a crisis of legitimacy fought over the issue of participation. During the Civil War and Reconstruction, major barriers to mass participation were removed for adult males; the Bourbon Democrats disenfranchised blacks and poor whites; Longism and bifactionalism came about when poor whites regained the franchise; the multifactionalism of the late 1970s came about when blacks also retrieved the franchise. Essentially Louisiana's political practices have changed with the participants.

How well is the new multifactionalism going to work? Its most obvious advantage is its flexibility and freedom from centralization. No one in Louisiana can wield the near dictatorial powers of a Huey Long, despite the still considerable powers of the governorship. On the other hand, it is ironic that the multifactionalism that was created by the participation of blacks at the polls rules out their winning statewide office. There is no sign that any black politician in the state can independently put together a statewide majority of voters. This creates a problem of legitimacy as serious as the lack of enfranchisement once did. Early in the 1980s this problem of legitimacy is not yet widely felt, but as the decade progresses the growing class of skilled and ambitious black elected officials at the municipal and parochial levels will likely chafe under the restrictions of the current system. This fact promises to keep alive the element of drama that Louisianians take for granted in their politics.

Appendix
Louisiana Statistical Data

Table 1
Louisiana Parish Population and Social Statistics, 1970

Parish	Population 1970	Percentage Urban	Percentage Nonwhite	Median Income	Median School Years Completed
Acadia	52,109	56.8	19.9	$ 5,550	8.3
Allen	20,794	56.8	24.7	5,931	9.0
Ascension	37,086	32.0	27.1	7,894	10.3
Assumption	19,654	0.0	37.4	6,135	7.5
Avoyelles	37,751	26.3	27.7	4,435	8.6
Beauregard	22,888	35.1	18.9	6,940	11.1
Bienville	16,024	18.5	46.9	5,187	9.5
Bossier	65,877	64.9	20.2	7,927	12.1
Caddo	230,184	85.5	36.9	8,103	12.0
Calcasieu	145,415	74.8	21.8	8,404	11.7
Caldwell	9,354	0.0	23.7	5,224	9.7
Cameron	8,194	0.0	6.9	7,726	9.4
Catahoula	11,769	23.5	29.3	4,850	9.3
Claiborne	17,024	44.3	50.1	5,347	9.3
Concordia	22,578	47.7	39.0	6,321	9.9
DeSoto	22,764	28.3	53.4	5,074	8.9
East Baton Rouge	285,167	86.9	29.0	9,627	12.3
East Carroll	12,884	48.0	59.2	3,612	8.1
East Feliciana	17,657	26.6	53.9	5,755	8.4
Evangeline	31,932	40.6	27.2	4,289	7.6
Franklin	23,946	22.3	35.8	4,171	8.9
Grant	13,671	0.0	22.9	5,329	9.6
Iberia	57,397	63.5	28.0	7,109	9.4
Iberville	30,746	33.3	47.6	6,251	8.7
Jackson	15,963	31.8	32.1	6,608	10.0
Jefferson	338,229	95.8	12.8	10,235	12.1
Jefferson Davis	29,554	62.7	20.5	6,049	9.2
Lafayette	111,643	71.6	21.9	7,916	11.7
Lafourche	68,941	38.8	11.5	7,855	8.5
LaSalle	13,295	0.0	11.4	5,799	10.2
Lincoln	33,800	64.4	40.2	6,535	12.0
Livingston	36,511	18.5	11.3	7,652	10.5
Madison	15,065	64.0	61.1	3,981	8.5
Morehouse	32,463	45.3	42.5	5,708	9.5
Natchitoches	35,219	45.4	37.6	4,598	9.4

Table 1 (*Continued*)

Parish	Population 1970	Percentage Urban	Percentage Nonwhite	Median Income	Median School Years Completed
Orleans	593,471	99.7	45.5	$7,445	10.8
Ouachita	115,387	78.5	27.4	7,354	11.7
Plaquemines	25,225	28.3	25.3	8,601	9.8
Pointe Coupee	22,002	17.9	50.3	4,957	8.2
Rapides	118,078	52.2	28.1	6,831	11.1
Red River	9,226	0.0	42.2	4,563	9.2
Richland	21,774	31.5	40.7	4,868	8.9
Sabine	18,638	16.9	19.8	5,146	9.3
St. Bernard	51,185	91.3	5.5	9,638	11.0
St. Charles	29,550	27.2	26.4	9,004	10.9
St. Helena	9,937	0.0	55.8	4,107	9.2
St. James	19,733	32.8	45.3	8,049	9.6
St. John the Baptist	23,813	51.8	46.5	8,275	9.9
St. Landry	80,364	39.1	41.4	4,919	7.8
St. Martin	32,453	37.3	35.0	5,157	7.5
St. Mary	60,752	65.2	28.6	8,146	9.9
St. Tammany	63,585	36.6	19.0	8,655	11.9
Tangipahoa	65,875	35.5	31.5	5,208	9.6
Tensas	9,732	0.0	59.4	3,173	7.9
Terrebonne	76,049	52.6	18.1	8,338	9.6
Union	18,447	18.5	33.4	5,976	9.7
Vermilion	43,071	38.4	13.6	5,946	8.3
Vernon	53,794	60.4	11.5	6,450	11.8
Washington	41,987	52.3	32.3	6,377	10.3
Webster	39,939	51.3	31.4	7,215	10.6
West Baton Rouge	16,864	38.9	43.1	6,920	10.1
West Carroll	13,028	0.0	19.1	4,802	9.2
West Feliciana	10,761	0.0	67.2	5,355	9.1
Winn	16,369	43.6	30.5	5,405	9.7

SOURCES: James R. Bobo and Harris S. Segal (eds.), *Statistical Abstract of Louisiana* (New Orleans: Division of Business and Economic Research, University of New Orleans, 1977), 25–27; U.S. Bureau of the Census, *Census of Population, 1970: General Social and Economic Characteristics Final Report* (Washington, D.C.: U.S. Government Printing Office, 1970), I, Pt. 20, pp. 152–53.

Table 2

Louisiana Standard Metropolitan Statistical Area Population and
Social Statistics, 1970

SMSA	1970 Population	Percentage Nonwhite	Median Income	Median School Years Completed
Alexandria*	131,749	43.5	$6,452	11.5
Grant	13,671			
Rapides	118,078			
Baton Rouge	375,628	29.0	9,627	12.3
Ascension	37,086			
East Baton Rouge	385,167			
Livingston	36,511			
West Baton Rouge	16,864			
Lafayette	109,716	21.9	7,916	11.7
Lake Charles	145,415	21.8	8,404	11.7
Monroe	115,387	27.4	7,354	11.7
New Orleans	1,045,809	31.4	8,670	11.4
Jefferson	337,568			
Orleans	593,471			
St. Bernard	51,185			
St. Tammany	63,585			
Shreveport	334,642	33.2	8,061	12.0
Bossier	64,519			
Caddo	230,184			
Webster	39,939			

SOURCES: Bobo and Segal (eds.), *Statistical Abstract of Louisiana*, 50; Census Bureau, *Census of Population*, 1970, I, Pt. 20, pp. 39, 149, 150.

*Alexandria was not an SMSA in the 1970 census. These data are for the city of Alexandria only.

Table 3

1975 and 1976 Louisiana Parish Election Data

(In Percentages)

| Parish | 1975 Gubernatorial Election | | | | 1976 Presidential Election | | |
	Edwards	Jones	Martin	All Others	Democratic	Republican	Other
Acadia	82.7	11.6	5.1	0.6	61.2	35.6	3.1
Allen	61.5	26.4	16.2	0.9	69.0	27.1	3.1
Ascension	61.5	19.8	18.1	0.6	65.0	3.17	3.3
Assumption	66.3	23.2	8.9	1.6	57.0	40.4	2.6
Avoyelles	61.8	21.3	15.4	1.5	60.8	34.3	4.8
Beauregard	48.7	39.0	11.3	0.9	60.5	36.3	3.2
Bienville	63.8	27.0	7.6	1.7	56.4	41.4	2.1
Bossier	59.5	35.1	4.6	0.8	39.2	59.0	1.8
Caddo	57.3	37.5	4.3	0.9	41.1	57.3	1.6
Calcasieu	55.2	37.6	6.3	0.8	64.6	33.2	2.2
Caldwell	33.8	35.6	28.2	2.4	48.0	49.6	2.5
Cameron	63.4	27.1	8.4	1.1	72.4	24.4	3.2
Catahoula	46.5	30.8	20.6	2.1	53.3	43.7	3.0
Claiborne	64.0	26.9	8.2	0.9	48.1	49.8	2.0
Concordia	50.8	32.2	15.8	1.2	47.7	49.7	2.6
DeSoto	67.5	25.3	6.2	1.1	55.4	43.1	1.6
East Baton Rouge	51.9	26.4	20.9	0.8	47.8	19.8	2.4
East Carroll	65.7	20.4	12.3	1.7	56.9	40.4	2.7
East Feliciana	49.9	20.7	28.5	0.9	65.2	31.2	3.5
Evangeline	66.1	21.2	11.6	1.1	64.8	31.8	3.4
Franklin	38.2	37.1	22.5	2.3	47.8	49.4	2.8
Grant	38.9	40.3	18.8	2.1	59.7	37.1	3.2

Table 3 (*Continued*)

Parish	1975 Gubernatorial Election				1976 Presidential Election		
	Edwards	Jones	Martin	All Others	Democratic	Republican	Other
Iberia	67.7	18.0	13.0	1.3	48.1	50.1	1.9
Iberville	65.4	15.0	18.7	0.9	63.6	33.5	2.8
Jackson	55.6	28.6	13.7	2.1	51.1	46.9	2.1
Jefferson	70.9	19.4	8.8	1.0	41.1	56.8	2.1
Jefferson Davis	63.3	29.8	6.4	0.5	62.0	35.0	3.0
Lafayette	69.8	18.0	11.2	1.0	45.5	52.1	2.3
Lafourche	72.5	15.5	11.1	1.0	53.8	43.5	2.7
LaSalle	39.0	38.1	21.0	1.9	46.8	50.0	1.5
Lincoln	48.6	37.3	12.7	1.4	41.5	57.0	1.5
Livingston	44.9	25.4	28.3	1.5	62.1	34.9	3.0
Madison	68.3	19.1	10.8	1.8	69.1	29.4	1.5
Morehouse	51.2	36.1	10.6	2.1	42.4	54.9	2.8
Natchitoches	57.9	29.1	11.3	1.7	53.8	42.2	4.0
Orleans	72.5	17.6	8.5	1.4	54.7	42.6	2.7
Ouachita	53.4	30.0	15.0	1.6	38.9	59.5	1.6
Plaquemines	86.2	9.7	3.5	0.6	29.4	68.1	2.5
Pointe Coupee	70.0	13.8	15.5	0.6	65.3	32.6	2.1
Rapides	49.6	34.1	14.7	1.6	53.1	45.2	1.7
Red River	64.3	26.9	7.7	1.1	51.4	46.6	2.0
Richland	45.8	34.3	17.9	2.0	47.9	49.8	2.3
Sabine	62.8	26.3	9.2	1.7	54.2	42.0	3.9
St. Bernard	75.1	17.0	6.7	1.2	47.3	49.4	2.3
St. Charles	69.4	19.3	9.8	1.4	58.9	37.3	3.8
St. Helena	54.6	25.0	18.5	1.9	69.0	27.5	3.5
St. James	71.4	16.5	10.9	1.1	60.7	36.8	2.5

Table 3 (*Continued*)

Parish	1975 Gubernatorial Election				1976 Presidential Election		
	Edwards	Jones	Martin	All Others	Democratic	Republican	Other
St. John the Baptist	73.1	16.4	9.2	1.2	59.2	37.4	3.4
St. Landry	69.8	15.4	13.9	0.8	59.5	37.9	2.6
St. Martin	61.0	9.1	28.8	1.1	64.2	33.0	2.8
St. Mary	70.1	19.2	9.3	1.4	50.2	47.6	2.2
St. Tammany	57.8	27.2	13.6	1.3	46.4	50.4	3.2
Tangipahoa	56.4	29.6	12.9	1.1	59.3	38.0	2.7
Tensas	64.2	20.3	14.1	1.3	56.5	42.2	1.3
Terrebonne	68.0	18.5	12.4	1.1	53.6	53.0	3.4
Union	46.7	33.3	17.7	2.3	45.4	52.3	2.2
Vermilion	74.4	15.3	9.3	1.0	62.9	34.3	2.7
Vernon	51.3	31.7	14.9	2.1	59.2	37.9	3.0
Washington	55.1	30.3	13.7	1.0	62.0	35.2	2.7
Webster	59.8	32.8	6.6	0.8	48.3	50.0	1.7
West Baton Rouge	67.0	15.0	17.2	0.8	64.6	32.5	2.9
West Carroll	48.3	28.2	21.5	2.0	50.7	47.0	2.3
West Feliciana	61.0	20.0	18.2	0.7	64.4	38.8	1.8
Winn	41.2	37.9	18.7	2.2	51.3	46.5	2.2
TOTAL	62.4	24.3	12.2	1.2	51.45	46.06	2.49

SOURCES: Public Affairs Research Council, "Presidential Election, November, 1976," *Analysis* (November, 1976), 7; Public Affairs Research Council, "Primary Election, November 1, 1975," *Analysis* (December, 1975), 5.

Table 4

1975 and 1976 Louisiana Standard Metropolitan Statistical Area Election Data

(In Percentages)

| SMSA | 1975 Gubernatorial Election | | | | 1976 Presidential Election | | |
	Edwards	Jones	Martin	All Others	Democratic	Republican	Other
Alexandria	47.8	35.1	15.4	1.7	54.0	44.1	1.9
Grant	38.9	40.3	18.8	2.1	59.7	37.1	3.2
Rapides	49.6	34.1	14.7	1.6	53.1	45.2	1.7
Baton Rouge	52.8	24.9	21.4	0.9	51.9	45.6	2.5
Ascension	61.5	19.8	18.1	0.6	65.0	31.7	3.3
East Baton Rouge	51.9	26.4	20.9	0.8	47.8	49.8	2.4
Livingston	44.9	25.4	28.3	1.5	62.1	34.9	3.0
West Baton Rouge	67.0	15.0	17.2	0.8	64.6	32.5	2.9
Lafayette (Lafayette)	69.8	18.0	11.2	1.1	45.5	52.1	2.3
Lake Charles							
Calcasieu	55.2	37.6	6.3	0.8	64.6	33.2	2.2
Monroe							
Ouachita	53.4	30.0	15.0	1.6	38.9	59.5	1.6
New Orleans	70.9	19.0	8.9	1.2	48.5	48.9	2.6
Jefferson	70.9	19.4	8.8	1.0	41.1	56.8	2.1
Orleans	72.5	19.4	8.5	1.4	54.7	42.6	1.7
St. Bernard	75.1	17.0	6.7	1.2	47.3	49.4	3.3
St. Tammany	57.8	27.2	13.6	1.3	46.4	50.4	3.2
Shreveport	58.1	36.2	4.7	0.9	41.7	56.6	1.7
Bossier	59.5	35.1	4.6	0.8	39.2	59.0	1.8
Caddo	57.3	37.5	4.3	0.9	41.1	57.3	1.6
Webster	59.8	32.8	6.6	0.8	48.3	50.0	1.7
TOTAL SMSAs	62.2	25.2	11.4	1.1	48.9	48.8	2.3

SOURCES: Public Affairs Research Council, "Presidential Election, November, 1976," 10; Public Affairs Research Council, "Primary Election, November 1, 1975," 9.

Table 5
1979 Louisiana Parish Gubernatorial and Lieutenant Gubernatorial
Election Data
(In Percentages)

	Gubernatorial Election		Lieutenant Gubernatorial Election	
Parish	Louis Lambert	Dave Treen	Jim Donlon	Bobby Freeman
Acadia	49.6	50.4	53.0	47.0
Allen	66.5	33.5	35.3	64.7
Ascension	84.9	15.1	17.7	82.3
Assumption	61.8	38.2	27.0	73.0
Avoyelles	58.1	41.9	41.0	59.0
Beauregard	47.9	52.1	49.9	50.1
Bienville	56.4	43.6	47.5	52.5
Bossier	40.6	59.4	55.2	44.8
Caddo	41.2	58.8	56.1	43.9
Calcasieu	52.4	47.6	46.3	57.7
Caldwell	53.7	46.3	45.4	54.6
Cameron	51.0	49.0	47.0	53.0
Catahoula	58.0	42.0	44.2	35.8
Claiborne	51.1	48.9	53.2	46.8
Concordia	53.1	46.9	45.1	54.9
DeSoto	59.0	41.0	51.2	48.8
East Baton Rouge	48.5	51.5	43.2	56.8
East Carroll	55.8	44.2	43.3	56.7
East Feliciana	71.9	29.1	26.4	73.6
Evangeline	55.9	44.1	46.1	53.9
Franklin	52.6	47.4	46.7	53.8
Grant	58.5	41.5	46.7	53.3
Iberia	33.9	66.1	49.0	51.0
Iberville	75.9	24.1	17.5	82.5
Jackson	61.8	38.2	38.4	61.6
Jefferson	35.7	64.3	63.3	36.7
Jefferson Davis	45.6	54.4	54.7	45.3
Lafayette	30.9	69.1	60.4	39.6
Lafourche	40.2	59.8	48.2	51.8
LaSalle	47.6	52.4	51.1	48.9
Lincoln	39.6	60.4	55.5	44.5
Livingston	74.2	25.8	23.5	76.5

Table 5 (*Continued*)

Parish	Gubernatorial Election		Lieutenant Gubernatorial Election	
	Louis Lambert	*Dave Treen*	*Jim Donlon*	*Bobby Freeman*
Madison	59.8	40.2	35.8	64.2
Morehouse	51.0	49.0	54.5	45.5
Natchitoches	52.6	47.4	43.0	57.0
Orleans	51.4	48.6	52.6	47.4
Ouachita	43.1	57.0	55.4	27.3
Plaquemines	28.3	71.7	72.7	27.3
Pointe Coupee	72.8	27.2	21.3	78.7
Rapides	50.1	49.9	46.7	53.3
Red River	61.8	38.2	45.0	55.0
Richland	49.5	50.5	53.9	46.1
Sabine	56.3	43.7	42.1	57.9
St. Bernard	49.2	50.8	46.3	53.7
St. Charles	55.4	44.6	46.8	53.2
St. Helena	73.8	26.3	28.0	72.0
St. James	78.6	21.4	24.9	75.1
St. John the Baptist	69.1	30.9	42.2	57.8
St. Landry	56.3	43.8	44.5	55.5
St. Martin	49.0	51.0	44.1	55.9
St. Mary	41.9	58.1	42.4	57.6
St. Tammany	40.0	60.0	57.6	42.4
Tangipahoa	61.7	38.3	38.1	61.9
Tensas	57.6	42.4	39.8	60.2
Terrebonne	34.7	65.3	51.6	48.4
Union	49.4	50.6	48.3	51.7
Vermilion	45.4	54.6	49.3	50.7
Vernon	57.7	42.3	44.9	55.1
Washington	63.5	36.5	43.6	55.4
Webster	54.7	45.3	47.7	52.3
West Baton Rouge	72.1	27.9	21.1	78.9
West Carroll	52.1	47.9	49.5	50.5
West Feliciana	71.6	28.4	24.7	75.3
Winn	56.0	44.0	47.6	52.4
TOTAL	49.7	50.3	48.3	51.7

SOURCE: Public Affairs Research Council, "Vote for Governor by Parish," *Analysis* (December, 1979), 7; Public Affairs Research Council, "Vote for Lieutenant Governor by Parish," *Analysis* (December, 1979), 9.

Table 6
1980 Louisiana Parish Presidential Election Data
(In Percentages)

Parish	Carter	Reagan	Anderson	Other
Acadia	45.0	52.2	1.9	0.9
Allen	63.3	34.8	1.2	0.7
Ascension	61.3	35.8	1.4	1.5
Assumption	51.6	44.1	1.7	2.7
Avoyelles	44.6	51.1	1.2	3.1
Beauregard	50.2	47.5	1.5	0.8
Bienville	53.1	45.2	0.7	1.1
Bossier	35.6	62.7	1.2	0.5
Caddo	40.8	57.4	1.3	0.5
Calcasieu	54.7	42.6	1.9	0.9
Caldwell	39.0	57.9	0.9	2.2
Cameron	58.5	38.2	2.2	1.2
Catahoula	43.6	53.2	0.7	2.5
Claiborne	48.7	50.0	0.8	0.6
Concordia	43.5	54.2	0.6	1.8
DeSoto	56.8	42.1	0.5	0.7
East Baton Rouge	43.1	53.4	2.5	1.0
East Carroll	54.0	44.1	0.6	1.4
East Feliciana	58.7	38.6	0.8	2.0
Evangeline	46.5	51.3	1.1	1.2
Franklin	42.9	54.4	0.7	2.1
Grant	46.0	50.5	1.1	2.4
Iberia	38.7	57.0	1.6	2.7
Iberville	66.2	31.6	1.2	1.0
Jackson	46.7	50.8	0.7	1.8
Jefferson	32.8	64.1	2.3	0.8
Jefferson Davis	50.6	46.7	1.7	1.0
Lafayette	36.8	58.7	2.4	2.1
Lafourche	46.2	48.5	2.2	3.2
LaSalle	40.2	57.2	0.9	1.8
Lincoln	41.6	55.8	1.3	1.3
Livingston	50.1	47.2	1.3	1.5
Madison	55.1	42.7	0.3	2.0
Morehouse	39.2	58.5	0.5	1.8
Natchitoches	50.1	47.0	1.1	1.8
Orleans	56.9	39.5	2.3	1.3

Table 6 (*Continued*)

Parish	Carter	Reagan	Anderson	Other
Ouachita	34.5	63.0	1.1	1.5
Plaquemines	42.8	54.5	1.5	1.2
Pointe Coupee	62.3	35.7	1.0	0.9
Rapides	42.0	55.2	1.1	1.6
Red River	55.7	43.1	0.6	0.7
Richland	42.8	54.6	0.6	2.1
Sabine	53.2	44.5	0.8	1.5
St. Bernard	35.5	60.5	1.9	2.1
St. Charles	52.2	44.8	1.9	1.1
St. Helena	65.6	31.6	0.9	2.0
St. James	63.2	34.9	1.2	0.8
St. John the Baptist	55.2	42.0	1.9	1.0
St. Landry	52.4	45.7	1.0	0.9
St. Martin	51.6	44.6	1.9	2.0
St. Mary	48.6	48.0	1.6	1.8
St. Tammany	33.2	63.7	2.0	1.1
Tangipahoa	48.7	48.5	1.6	1.3
Tensas	54.1	43.5	0.7	1.8
Terrebonne	37.7	58.0	2.0	2.4
Union	41.8	55.8	0.7	1.8
Vermilion	45.5	49.0	2.2	3.3
Vernon	53.6	43.7	1.2	1.5
Washington	53.5	44.6	0.9	1.1
Webster	48.6	50.2	0.7	0.5
West Baton Rouge	61.1	36.5	1.5	0.9
West Carroll	37.1	60.1	0.7	2.2
West Feliciana	62.9	33.2	1.1	2.8
Winn	45.2	52.3	0.8	1.8
TOTAL	45.8	51.2	1.7	1.4

SOURCE: Public Affairs Research Council, "Presidential Election, November, 1980," *Analysis* (November, 1980), 80.

Table 7

1980 Louisiana Standard Metropolitan Statistical Area Presidential
Election Data
(In Percentages)

SMSA	Carter	Reagan	Anderson	Other
Alexandria	42.5	54.6	1.1	1.7
Grant	46.0	50.5	1.1	2.4
Rapides	42.0	55.2	1.1	1.6
Baton Rouge	46.7	50.0	2.2	1.1
Ascension	61.3	35.8	1.4	1.5
East Baton Rouge	43.1	53.4	2.5	1.0
Livingston	50.1	47.2	1.3	1.5
West Baton Rouge	61.1	36.5	1.5	0.9
Lafayette				
Lafayette	36.8	58.7	2.4	2.1
Lake Charles				
Calcasieu	54.7	42.6	1.9	0.9
Monroe				
Ouachita	34.5	63.0	1.1	1.5
New Orleans	43.9	52.7	2.2	1.2
Jefferson	32.8	64.1	2.3	0.8
Orleans	56.9	39.5	2.3	1.3
St. Bernard	35.5	60.5	1.9	2.1
St. Tammany	33.2	63.7	2.0	1.1
Shreveport	40.8	57.5	1.2	0.5
Bossier	35.6	62.7	1.2	0.5
Caddo	40.8	57.4	1.3	0.5
Webster	48.6	50.2	0.7	0.5
TOTAL FOR SMSAs	43.8	53.1	1.9	1.1

SOURCE: Public Affairs Research Council, "Presidential Election, November, 1980,"
p. 11.

Table 8

1980 Louisiana Population by Race and Spanish Origin and Housing Counts

Parish	Persons								Housing Units	
		Percent Change, 1970 to 1980	RACE							Percent Change, 1970 to 1980
	1980		White	Black	Am. Indian, Eskimo, and Aleut	Asian and Pacific Islander	Other	Spanish Origin	1980	
Acadia	56,427	8.3	46,403	9,902	23	43	56	663	19,265	20.4
Allen	21,390	2.9	16,720	4,383	234	20	33	198	7,843	21.0
Ascension	50,068	35.0	38,542	11,262	76	82	106	1,094	16,622	48.0
Assumption	22,084	12.4	15,031	6,995	21	24	13	517	7,554	41.3
Avoyelles	41,393	9.6	30,720	10,542	46	18	67	572	14,724	22.3
Beauregard	29,692	29.7	24,755	4,756	27	82	72	314	11,429	44.6
Bienville	16,387	2.3	9,390	6,939	21	25	12	176	6,955	23.4
Bossier	80,721	22.5	64,229	15,236	188	416	652	1,710	28,884	44.5
Caddo	252,294	9.6	155,127	95,242	387	840	698	3,378	97,584	24.0
Calcasieu	167,048	14.9	129,764	36,284	263	403	334	2,228	60,781	33.5
Caldwell	10,761	15.0	8,731	1,969	1	13	47	161	4,624	40.8
Cameron	9,336	13.9	8,782	524	7	3	20	177	4,487	35.8
Catahoula	12,287	4.4	9,092	3,175	17	3	—	69	4,880	28.7
Claiborne	17,095	0.4	9,063	8,002	2	10	18	187	7,043	19.3
Concordia	22,981	1.8	14,854	8,056	23	17	31	164	8,919	24.5
DeSoto	25,664	12.7	14,093	11,494	27	21	29	371	9,910	25.7
East Baton Rouge	366,164	28.4	246,375	114,680	516	2,422	2,171	6,305	133,626	50.2
East Carroll	11,772	-8.6	4,460	7,201	1	40	70	275	4,108	6.2
East Feliciana	19,015	7.7	9,689	9,240	20	52	14	265	5,860	42.7
Evangeline	33,343	4.4	25,201	8,027	19	41	55	550	12,315	18.8
Franklin	24,141	0.8	16,347	7,735	6	31	22	158	8,884	18.1
Grant	16,703	22.2	13,802	2,840	24	26	11	152	6,781	32.0
Iberia	63,752	11.1	45,770	17,640	100	97	145	2,331	21,282	28.2

Table 8 (*Continued*)

Parish	Persons								Housing Units	
			RACE							
	1980	Percent Change, 1970 to 1980	White	Black	Am. Indian, Eskimo, and Aleut	Asian and Pacific Islander	Other	Spanish Origin	1980	Percent Change, 1970 to 1980
Iberville	32,159	4.6	16,606	15,414	24	55	60	789	10,980	20.0
Jackson	17,321	8.5	11,751	5,522	18	19	11	119	6,886	24.0
Jefferson	454,592	34.4	380,645	63,001	1,391	5,681	3,874	21,772	166,124	63.6
Jefferson Davis	32,168	8.8	25,933	6,146	34	25	30	483	11,041	18.7
Lafayette	150,017	34.4	117,867	30,334	214	681	921	3,721	53,136	63.3
Lafourche	82,483	19.6	72,039	9,127	831	319	167	1,644	27,033	40.8
LaSalle	17,004	27.9	15,227	1,585	143	21	28	80	6,611	38.3
Lincoln	39,763	17.6	24,661	14,590	36	173	303	444	13,354	36.8
Livingston	58,655	60.7	54,489	3,952	71	78	65	670	21,134	76.4
Madison	14,733	−2.2	6,098	8,527	5	11	92	279	5,513	13.7
Morehouse	34,803	7.2	20,731	13,980	17	36	39	333	12,826	22.8
Natchitoches	39,863	13.2	24,953	14,450	124	90	246	755	14,895	32.4
Orleans	557,482	−6.1	236,967	308,136	524	7,332	4,523	19,219	226,452	8.6
Ouachita	139,241	20.7	97,843	40,582	108	385	323	1,276	51,477	39.6
Plaquemines	26,049	3.3	19,918	5,540	283	108	200	715	9,550	39.7
Pointe Coupee	24,045	9.3	13,984	10,001	10	22	28	412	8,750	25.2
Rapides	135,282	14.6	97,459	36,308	429	554	532	1,629	48,264	29.7
Red River	10,433	13.1	6,609	3,797	13	3	11	137	4,045	27.5
Richland	22,187	1.9	14,250	7,851	11	21	54	246	7,892	8.9
Sabine	25,280	35.6	19,691	4,694	774	25	96	2,028	12,105	82.6
St. Bernard	64,097	25.2	60,868	2,411	290	335	193	5,162	21,592	51.8
St. Charles	37,259	26.1	27,437	9,479	68	73	202	823	12,409	50.4
St. Helena	9,827	−1.1	4,758	5,059	4	5	1	110	3,582	27.2

Table 8 (Continued)

Parish	Persons		RACE						Housing Units	
	1980	Percent Change, 1970 to 1980	White	Black	Am. Indian, Eskimo, and Aleut	Asian and Pacific Islander	Other	Spanish Origin	1980	Percent Change, 1970 to 1980
St. James	21,495	8.9	11,299	10,156	2	25	13	330	6,452	34.0
St. John the Baptist	31,924	34.1	19,595	12,175	36	53	65	678	10,522	62.6
St. Landry	84,128	4.7	51,827	31,965	35	156	145	1,212	29,481	21.8
St. Martin	40,214	23.9	26,810	13,185	26	131	62	631	13,702	40.8
St. Mary	64,395	6.0	44,746	18,516	388	528	217	1,579	21,611	25.1
St. Tammany	110,554	73.9	95,624	13,845	304	346	435	2,254	41,130	91.3
Tangipahoa	80,698	22.5	55,990	24,295	84	141	188	1,054	29,263	41.2
Tensas	8,525	-12.4	3,856	4,659	—	8	2	83	3,892	18.0
Terrebonne	94,393	24.1	76,058	14,598	3,274	282	181	1,606	30,831	47.8
Union	21,167	14.7	14,931	6,166	18	14	38	164	8,625	32.5
Vermilion	48,458	12.5	41,720	6,425	35	216	62	826	17,869	30.0
Vernon	53,475	-0.6	41,181	9,764	238	893	1,399	2,239	18,141	73.3
Washington	44,207	5.3	30,753	13,308	29	87	30	433	16,758	18.3
Webster	43,631	9.2	29,555	13,937	53	41	45	419	17,820	26.0
West Baton Rouge	19,086	13.2	11,384	7,626	18	21	37	354	6,434	33.7
West Carroll	12,922	-0.8	10,780	2,099	16	8	19	78	5,073	19.5
West Feliciana	12,186	13.2	5,079	7,061	17	20	9	196	2,898	33.1
Winn Parish	17,253	5.4	12,331	4,873	20	20	9	108	7,081	19.4
TOTAL	4,203,972	15.3	2,911,243	1,237,263	12,064	23,771	19,631	99,105	1,547,594	34.5

SOURCE: U.S. Department of Commerce, Bureau of the Census, *1980 Census of Population and Housing* (Washington, D.C.: n.p., March, 1981).

NOTE: A dash "—" represents zero. A minus sign preceding a figure denotes decrease.

Notes on Contributors

Riley Baker is associate professor of political science at Louisiana Tech University, Ruston, Louisiana. He is the author of one of the chief works on Louisiana politics, *The History and Government of Louisiana*, revised edition, and of articles in the *Southwestern Social Sciences Quarterly*, *Louisiana Studies*, and *Social Studies*. He has served as president of the Louisiana Political Science Association.

Mark T. Carleton, who earned a Ph.D. in history from Stanford, is associate professor of history at Louisiana State University and a leading authority on Louisiana political history. He is the author of *Politics and Punishment: The History of the Louisiana State Penal System* (LSU Press).

Richard L. Engstrom is professor of political science and chairman of the Department of Political Science at the University of New Orleans. He earned his doctorate from the University of Kentucky and has published widely on municipal government and redistricting in such journals as the *Journal of Politics*, the *Journal of Public Law*, *American Political Science Review*, *American Journal of Political Science*, and *Polity*. During the 1981–1982 academic year he has been a Fulbright lecturer at National Taiwan University and National Chen Chi University in Taipei, Taiwan.

Paul Grosser, assistant professor of political science at Louisiana State University, is a graduate of Pennsylvania State University. He is the co-author, with Edwin G. Halperin, of *The Causes and Effects of Anti-Semitism: The Dimensions of a Prejudice.*

Charles Holbrook is a member of the staff of the Government Services Institute of Louisiana State University. He holds the M.A. degree in economics from the University of Southern Mississippi.

Ronald M. Labbé, professor of political science and chairman of the Political Science Department at the University of Southwestern Louisiana, holds an LL.B. from Loyola University, New Orleans, and a Ph.D. from Tulane University. He has contributed to the *Louisiana Bar Association Journal* and *Criminal Law and Criminology.* He is currently researching the *Slaughter House Cases.*

David M. Landry, chairman of the Department of Government and professor of government at Nicholls State University, is a graduate of Tulane University. He is the co-author of *Mississippi Government and Politics in Transition* and has contributed to various journals, including *World Affairs.*

Patrick F. O'Connor is a research analyst with the Department of Health and Human Resources of the State of Louisiana. Formerly assistant professor of political science at Louisiana State University, he holds a Ph.D. degree from Indiana University. He has contributed to a number of journals, including the *Journal of Politics, Western Political Quarterly,* and *Polity.* He is also the co-author of *Voting in Indiana: A Century of Persistence and Change.*

Joseph Parker holds a Ph.D. degree from Tulane University. He is professor of political science at the University of Southern Mississippi.

Jewel L. Prestage, professor and chairwoman of political science at Southern University, received her Ph.D. degree from the University of Iowa. She has served as officer of a number of national and regional professional organizations. She is the co-author of *A Portrait of Marginality: The Political Behavior of the American Woman.*

Ed Renwick, who holds the Ph.D. degree from the University of Arizona, is associate professor of political science at Loyola University, New Orleans. He also directs Loyola's Institute of Politics, which conducts educational programs for persons seeking public office and for the press and other persons working in political campaigns.

June Savoy Rowell holds the Ph.D. degree in political science from Louisiana State University. She is a former director of the Government Services Institute of Louisiana State University. She has written frequently on problems of state and local politics.

John Wildgen, who received his Ph.D. degree from Duke University, is professor of political science at the University of New Orleans. With Ronald Feld, he wrote *Domestic Political Realities and European Unification*, and he has published articles in a number of journals.

Carolyn Sue Williams, executive vice-president of TANYA, a private research firm in Washington, D.C., holds the Ph.D. degree from the University of Oregon. She is a former deputy assistant secretary of the U.S. Department of Housing and Urban Development.

Index

Abortion, 2
Acadiana, 1–5. *See also* Cajuns; Catholics; South Louisiana
Actual cash value, 36
Administrative Procedure Act, 141
Ad valorem taxes: on federal property, 230; mentioned, 33, 160, 161. *See also* Property tax
Advisory Commission on Intergovernmental Relations, 243, 247
AFL-CIO, 3, 12, 39
AFSCME (American Federation of State, County, and Municipal Employees), 132
Allen, O. K., 169, 171
Annexation, 213
Anti-Long faction: and Neo-Bourbons, 8; as Democratic faction, 17; mentioned, 50, 57. *See also* Bifactionalism
Assessed value, 33, 35, 37
Assessment ratio, 33, 34, 36
Assessors: and property tax administration, 34; and Louisiana Tax Commission, 34–37, 173; and CC-73, 37–38, 39–40; powers and duties of, 159–61
Attorney General, 172
Automobile licenses, 239

Baker v. *Carr*, 45, 229
Barthlemy, Sidney, 307
Baton Rouge, 217
Bauer, R. Norman, 57
Bifactionalism: as substitute for two-party competition, 11; of Long era, 17, 262–64 *passim*, 324–28, 331–34, 337–38; and legislative elections, 50; and class politics, 264; demise of, 266,

266–67, 329–30; and race issue, 267–68, 301–302, 304
Bill of Rights, 225
Black caucus, 59
Black political organizations: during Reconstruction, 294; origins of, 311; structure of, 312; financial support for, 313–14; mentioned, 5
Blacks: as liberal force, 4, 5–6; and Voting Rights Act of 1965, 304; and disenfranchisement, 5, 16–17, 263; and reapportionment, 5, 47; voting power of, 5, 195–97; in blue-collar coalition, 7; and constitutional convention of 1973, 25; and political officeholding, 47, 149, 292–95, 304, 306–308; 340; in legislature, 47, 54, 305–306; and legal profession, 98; in classified service, 126; as police jurors, 149; political role of, 286–87, 288–90, 293–94, 297–98, 307, 310, 323; free, during slavery, 289–90, 291; in Union army, 290–91; women, 291, 296; during Reconstruction, 293–96; in constitutional convention of 1867, 295; and Compromise of 1877, 297; and post-Reconstruction period, 297–301 *passim*; and emigration to North, 296; and Second Reconstruction, 301–302, 304, 306–307; and New Orleans mayoral election of 1971, 307; and service on Democratic party committees, 310; and support of Huey P. Long, 323; poverty and illiteracy of, 330; and political realignment, 331–32; in coalition with Catholics, 334; and demise of ticketing, 339; and multifactionalism, 344

Block grants, 236, 237
Boards and commissions, 80–81
Boards of aldermen, 190. *See also*
   Mayor–board of aldermen governments; Municipalities
Bourbons: philosophy of, 7; as governors,
   7–8; as element in Democratic party,
   262; challenged by Progressives,
   263–64; and domination of state politics, 326. *See also* Neo-Bourbons
Brown v. *Board of Education*, 229, 304
Bureaucracy: political nature of, 123–24;
   increase in number of agencies,
   124–25; increase in size of, 134; and
   parish government, 173; and centralization, 252–54
Bussie v. *Long*, 36

Cajuns, 7, 334
Campaign techniques: after bifactional
   period, 274–75; and erosion of power
   of Democratic leadership, 278
Carter, Jimmy: and black–blue-collar
   coalition, 5, 6; and black vote, 310
Categorical grants: and parish finances,
   158; and federal aid to municipalities,
   236, 237
Catholics: in New Orleans, 1; and Consti-
   tution of 1974, 3; in the legislature, 54;
   and black voting, 301–302; voting pat-
   terns of, 331–32, 334, 339; and demise
   of ticketing, 339; mentioned, 4, 321.
   See also Acadiana; Cajuns; South
   Louisiana
CC-73. *See* Constitutional conventions
Centralization: as trend in federal-state
   relations, 252–54; conservative and
   liberal views of, 253–54
CETA (Comprehensive Employment and
   Training Act), 158
Charters. *See* Municipalities
Chehardy, Lawrence A., 36–37, 39–40
City courts. *See* Courts
Civil Code system, 90–92
Civil Service. *See* State employees
Civil Service Commission, 31, 125, 130
Constitution, U.S., 223–25
Constitutional conventions: in eighteenth
   century, 16–17; of 1845, 94
—of 1973: delegate selection procedures,
   20; representation of special interests
   in, 20–21; media coverage of, 22; pub-
   lic indifference to, 22–23, 25; educa-
   tional level of delegates, 23–24;

occupational profile of delegates, 24;
   Committee on Revenue, Finance, and
   Taxation of, 24
Constitutional revision: and political
   elite, 15; in 1852–96 period, 16; in
   1896–1972 period, 16–20; by commission, 20; and federal-state relationships, 225–27
Consulting contracts, 81
Coordinating and Development Council
   of Northwest Louisiana, 237–38
Coordination and Development Agencies:
   and securing federal funds, 237–38
Coroner, 162–63
Corporations, 240
Corruption: public attitude toward,
   10–11, 86–88; history of, 86–88; con-
   nection with low taxes and high
   spending, 84; during Reconstruction,
   295; and decline of political structures,
   343
Council for a Better Louisiana, 22
Council-manager plan: and decline of
   commission plan, 197–99. *See also*
   Municipalities
Council of State Governments, 243
Councils, parish. *See* Parish councils
Councils of Government, 237
Counties, 144. *See also* Parishes
Courts: under Constitution of 1974, 30;
   courts of limited jurisdiction, 101–103;
   juvenile and family, 103; small claims,
   106–107; case load of, 113–14; and Judicial Council, 118–19; proposals for
   reform of, 117, 119–20; and legal services, 122. *See also* Judges; Judicial reform; Lawyers
—appeal: circuits and judges of, 107;
   election districts of, 107; organization,
   jurisdiction, and role of, 109–110, 114,
   121–22; since 1906, 108–109; and
   1980 constitutional amendment, 114;
   under Constitution of 1921, 108
—city: city and parish, 103–104; location
   and jurisdiction of, 103–104; and jury
   trials, 103; and traffic cases, 104
—district: under 1980 legislation,
   100–101; jurisdiction, 100; review role,
   105; mentioned, 164–65
—justice of the peace, 105–106
—Louisiana Supreme: supervisory jurisdiction and rule-making authority of,
   110–12; organization and jurisdiction
   of, 110–17 *passim*; mandatory jurisdic-

tion of, 113–14; case load of, 113–14; and criminal appeals, 113–17; decision-making procedures of, 114–15; analysis of cases reviewed in 1976 by, 115–17; and claims of individual rights, 116; and judicial reform, 117–22; selection of chief justice, 121
—mayors': number and jurisdiction of, 105; and municipal government, 189–90; procedures in, 190; review of decisions of, 190
—United States Supreme, 116

Davis, Jimmie: as governor, 29; scandals during administration of, 86–87; as political entertainer, 85; and ticketing, 328; as Anti-Longite, 334; mentioned, 57, 76
DeBlieux, J. D., 36
Democratic Parish Executive Committees, 281
Democratic party: and neo-Bourbons, 8; role in election of Republican governor, 12; and factions, 17; and police juries, 149; profile of, 150; performance of, since Long era, 258–61; and farmer-worker coalition, 261; in antebellum period, 261, 262; and post-Reconstruction propertied class, 262; and modern campaign techniques, 276; and open-primary strategy, 276–77; state convention in 1980, 278; as recognized party under state law, 278; and National Democratic Committee, 281, 310; auxiliary organizations of, 281–82; and women, 281–82; and blacks, 310–11; and black political organizations, 314; mentioned, 50
Democratic State Central Committee, 281, 310
Democratic Women, 281–82
DemoPAC (Democratic Political Action Committee), 281
Desegregation and federal grants-in-aid, 233
Deticketing, 339–40
Dillon's Rule, 19, 182–83, 184, 218
Disenfranchisement: in post-Reconstruction period, 262–63, 297–98; of blacks and poor whites, 297–98
District Attorney: powers and duties of, 163; selection and term of office, 163; and other state officials, 172
District courts. See Courts

Division of Administration: and appropriations process, 69; and unclassified workers, 130; mentioned, 77

East Baton Rouge Parish, 151–52
East Baton Rouge Republican Executive Committee, 282
Education: level of in Louisiana, 10, 19; under Constitution of 1974, 31–32, 171–72; state aid for, 156; and parish government, 166–68 passim; and conflict between governing bodies, 171–72; and federal grants-in-aid, 232–33
Edwards, Edwin W.: and constitutional convention of 1973, 3–4, 20, 21, 26, 40; and black vote, 5, 307–308; as political entertainer, 11, 85–86; reelection of, 29; and executive-branch reorganization, 29, 135–36, 139–40; on property taxes, 32; on role of governor, 75; on pardoning power, 82; on severance taxes, 84; and political corruption, 85–86; and press, 86; and productivity of state employees, 134; and gas allocation policies, 233; and federal-state cooperation, 233; and Louisiana Commission on Intergovernmental Relations, 238; and Cajun-Catholic vote, 334; and Catholic-black coalition, 339; popularity of, 339; mentioned, 55
Election Code of Louisiana, 279–81
Elections: of 1975, 47, 49–50, 52; of legislators, 49–52; of judges, 94–95, 96–98; and clerks of court, 165; and racial discrimination, 195–97; and poll tax, 226; and political parties, 256; of Parker, 268; for mayor of New Orleans, 306–307; of 1976 and black vote, 307–308, 309–310; of 1964, 309; of 1960, and ticketing, 328; of 1959–60, and racism, 331–32; gubernatorial and presidential, insulation of, 340–42. See also Reapportionment; Slating; Ticketing
—of 1971: legislative, 49–50; and blacks, 308; and deticketing, 339–40
—of 1972: turnout for, 19; and black vote, 309–310; mentioned, 47
—of 1978: and Republicans, 259; and black vote, 308
—of 1979: and runoff, 8; expenditures during, 75; and Republican Politica Action Council, 282; and black vote,

308–309; and political realignment, 337–340 *passim*; mentioned, 47, 49–50, 52
Electoral trends, 342–44
Eleventh Amendment, 226
Elitism: and constitutional revision, 15, 18, 20; and constitutional convention of 1973, 23–24; and Constitution of 1974, 40–41; in post-Reconstruction period, 262
Emigration of blacks, post-Reconstruction, 296
Entertainment, political uses of, 85, 255
Equal protection of the laws, 27–28
Executive branch, 28–29. *See also* Bureaucracy
Executive budget, 69, 70
Executive clemency, 82
Executive reorganization: in 1975 and 1976, 135–36; under Act 83 of 1977, 135–36, 139–40 *passim*; and consolidation of agencies, 139
Extradition, 241

Federal aid: to parishes, 158–59, 234–35; for education, 168; to municipalities, 202, 235–36; increase in, 231; as percentage of state revenues, 231–32; purpose of, 231–32; coordinating agencies for obtaining, 237–38
Federalism: and Articles of Confederation, 222; and division of powers, 224; and voluntary cooperation, 233
Federal power, growth of, 226, 231–32
Floor leaders. *See* Governor; Legislature
Ford, Gerald, 8
Foster, Murphy J., 29
Fourteenth Amendment, 226
Fry v. *United States*, 228

Gambling: extent of, 2; and public officials, 11; and Constitution of 1974, 30
Governmental units, number of, 220
Governor: and succession rule, 29, 77; legislative powers of under Constitution of 1974, 56; and legislative leadership, 57–58, 79; floor leaders for, 58; and selection of legislative committee members, 63; and budget process, 69, 79–80; and Legislative Budget Committee, 70; influence over legislature of, 73; and campaign contributions, 75; and perquisites of office, 76; and veto powers, 79; and other elected officials,

79–81; and public employees, 79–81; and retirement programs, 82; and power to parole and pardon, 82; and support for home rule, 83; as chief executive, 83; and state police, 83; as entertainer, 85–86; and executive reorganization, 139–40; and district courts, 165; and local affairs, 169, 171; as focus of attention, 319; role of in ticketing, 328–30 *passim*
Grandfather clause, 298, 301
Grants-in-aid: to parishes, 158; and federal control, 225–233 *passim*. *See also* Federal aid
Great Society, 7

Henry, E. L "Bubba," 25, 58
Highways: and federal grants-in-aid, 231–33; and state and local governments, 247–48
Home rule: under Constitution of 1974, 30; for parishes, 152, 154; after 1960, 152, 155; for New Orleans, 152; and police juries, 155–56; and American political thought, 181–82; and Dillon's Rule, 182–84, 203, 206; and autonomy and initiative, 202–203, 212; defined, 202; history of, 202–203; and responsive government, 204–205; and amendments to Constitution of 1921, 205; and charter adoptions, 206–208, 212; mentioned, 83, 171, 218
Homestead exemption, 9, 35, 38
Hospitals, 249–50
House Appropriations Committee, 57, 69, 70
House Legislative Services Agency, 71–72
House of Representatives, 44

Illiteracy: and constitutional amendment process, 19–20; in Louisiana, 330
Implied powers, 228
Income taxes, federal, 226–27
Independent Legislative Study Group, 59
Inferior courts. *See* Courts
Inheritance taxes, 231
Initiative and referendum, 194
Insulation in presidential and gubernatorial elections, 340–42
Intergovernmental relations, 173–76, 221–54. *See also* Courts; Governor; Municipalities; Parishes
Interstate compacts, 241–42

Interstate cooperation: and extradition of fugitives, 241; associations to foster, 242–43
Item veto, 79

Johnston, J. Bennett, 308
Joint Legislative Committee on Reorganization of the Executive Branch, 135
Joint Legislative Committee on the Budget, 70, 80
Jones, Sam: ridiculed by Earl K. Long, 86; and executive reorganization, 134; mentioned, 57
Judges: retirement benefits of, 30; method of selection, 94–99; terms of office of, 95; salaries of, 95–96; and electoral competition, 96; appointed, 96; qualifications of, 97–99; number of, 97–98; removal of, 99; of city court, 103–104; of courts of appeal, 107; case load of, 113–14; of district courts, 164–65; lay magistrates, 189; and interpretation of home rule charters, 212
Judicial districts, establishment of, 97–98, 164–65
Judicial interpretation and federal-state relations, 229
Judicial power under civil code, 91–92
Judicial reform: and election of judges, 96–97; and Institute of Judicial Administration, 119–20; current issues in, 119–22 passim
Judiciary. See Courts; Judges
Justices of the peace. See Courts

Kennon, Robert F., 326–27
Kentucky v. Dennison, 241
Ku Klux Klan: in South Louisiana, 2; and Constitution of 1974, 39; and civil rights movement, 268

LABI (Louisiana Association of Business and Industry), 8, 12, 247
Labor. See Unions
Lafayette, 217–18
Lambert, Louis: and black–blue-collar coalition, 6; and black vote, 308–309; and election of 1979, 339
Land leases, 84
Law enforcement: and sheriffs, 161–62; and parish-state conflicts, 172; and parish-municipal cooperation, 250–51, 255
Lawrason Act, 187–88, 199

Lawyers: and constitutional convention of 1973, 24; and legislature, 54–55; and integrated bar, 92; political power of, 92; and judicial system, 92–96, 122; and legal education, 93–94; number of, 94
Leach, Claude "Buddy," 259
League of Women Voters, xv, 22, 39
Legislative Auditor, Office of, 73, 174
Legislative Budget Committee: and appropriations process, 69; reform of, 69–70; mentioned, 79
Legislative committees: assignment of bills to, 59, 60; hearings of, 59; powers of, 59–60; work load of, 60; standing, 60, 67–68; leadership of, 63–65; membership of, 63, 65–66; and seniority, 65; reform of, 66, 68
Legislative Council: composition and work of, 70–71; altered status of, 71–72; mentioned, 63
Legislative Fiscal Office, 70, 72–73
Legislative sessions, 28
Legislators: and constitutional convention of 1973, 24; profile of, 54–55; and previous service in parish and local government, 180
Legislature: membership, 52–54; organization, 56; constitutional powers, 56–57; leadership, 57–59; and speaker of the house, 57; committees of, 59–70 passim; seniority in, 65; reform of, 73–74; and policy-making, 140–41; and parish affairs, 171;and police juries, 173–74
Liberals: blacks as, 4, 5–6; and centralization, 253–54
Lieutenant governor, 28
Livingston, Edward, 90
Lobbying: in constitutional convention of 1973, 23; by local officials, 175
Local government. See Municipalities; Parishes
Long, Earl K.: and call for constitutional convention, 17; and two-thirds rule on new taxes, 28; as governor, 29; and political corruption, 78; as political entertainer, 85–86; and blacks, 304, 327; support of, 323–24; and ticketing, 328; kidnapping and commitment of, 332; mentioned, 43, 50
Long faction. See Bifactionalism
Long, Huey P.: and populism, 7, 8; and centralized government, 85; as political

entertainer, 85; and *Louisiana Progress*, 86; and parish affairs, 169–70,
171; and farmer-worker coalition,
265–66; and social reforms, 266–67;
and demise of bifactionalism, 267; and
blacks, 302, 304; and political dictatorship, 319–20; and political participation, 322; support of, 322–24; mentioned, 41, 43, 58
Louisiana: as French and Spanish colony,
89; as subject of political writing, 319
Louisiana Association of Manufacturers,
3
Louisiana Commission on Intergovernmental Relations, 238
Louisiana Education Association, 39
Louisiana Native Guards, 291
Louisiana Political Science Association,
xv
Louisiana Purchase, 89, 143
Louisiana Register, 141
Louisiana State Bar Association, 93
Louisiana State University, 31–32
Louisiana Supreme Court. *See* Courts
Louisiana Tax Commission: role in tax
administration, 34–36, 38; and rela-
tions with assessors, 173; and property
taxes, 201
Louisiana Teachers' Association, 38–39
Lynching, 298, 300, 31

McCulloch v. *Maryland*, 224
McKeithen, John J.: as governor, 29; as
political entertainer, 85; and *Life* maga-
zine, 86–87; and Commission on In-
tergovernmental Relations, 238; as
Longite, 333–34; mentioned, 76
Mafia, 87
Mayor–board of aldermen governments,
187–88
Mayor-commission governments, 151
Mayor-council governments, 187–88
Mayors' courts. *See* Courts
Morial, Ernest "Dutch," 306–307
Morrison, deLesseps, 86, 339–40
Multifactionalism: political consequences
of, 11–12; as form of political development, 343–44
Municipalities: incorporation of, 181,
185–86; number and populations of,
181; services provided by, 181, 244; de-
fined, 182; and Dillon's Rule, 182–83;
fragmentation of, 251–52
—charters: special legislative, 186; under

Lawrason Act, 187–88; and commission plan, 190–97
—commission plan: history of, 190–94;
decline of, 190–91; in Louisiana,
191–94; and general-law commission
form, 194
—council-manager plan: and general legislative charters, 197–99; history of,
197–99; in DeRidder, 198; in Bogalusa,
198–99; in Louisiana, 198–99
—revenue: from municipal taxes,
200–202 *passim*; from property taxes,
200–201; sources of, 200–202; and
borrowing power, 202; from federal aid,
235–36; from state aid, 245–47

NAACP (National Association for the Ad-
vancement of Colored People), 38
Napoleonic Code, 90
National Governors' Conference, 243
National League of Cities v. *Usery*,
228–29
National Legislative Conference, 243
Neo-Bourbons: philosophy and political
base of, 8; and multifactionalism,
11–12. *See also* Anti-Long faction;
Bifactionalism
New Deal, 7
New Orleans: ethnic background of, 1;
black population of, 5; constitutional
amendments relating to, 18–19; and
Constitution of 1974, 40; and 1966 reapportionment, 45; police strike in,
133; and consolidated parish government, 151; and mayor-commission government, 151; home rule for, 152, 205;
and metropolitan fragmentation, 215,
217; and political cleavage, 269
New Orleans City Park, 18–19
New Orleans Sewage and Water Board,
18
North Louisiana: defined, 2; and conservatism, 2; and Constitution of 1974, 3,
40; relative decline in population and
economic power of, 4; and South Louisiana, 269; and neo-Bourbons, 334

Occupational taxes, 201
Oil, political role of, 9, 11, 13, 83–85
O'Keefe, Michael, 58
Orleans Parish: court system of, 100, 101,
103; criminal cases in, 118; assessor of,
159; sheriffs in, 161. *See also* New
Orleans

Pardoning power. *See* Executive clemency
Parish councils, 151
Parish courts, 107–108. *See also* Courts
Parish executive committees, 280
Parishes: early history of, 143–45; defined, 144; and state government, 145, 169, 171–76 *passim*; governing bodies in, 145, 148–52, 155–56; and district courts, 164–65; reorganization of, 171; audits of, 174; prospects for change in governance of, 179; services performed by, 244; and municipalities, 250–51; and Republican parish executive committees, 282–83
—officials: coroner, 162–63; clerk of court, 165–66. *See also* Police juries; Sheriffs
—revenues: and state aid, 156–58, 244–47; and federal aid, 158–59, 234–35. *See also* Property tax
Parker, John M., 264
Parochial schools, 2, 3
Patronage, 80, 156, 275
Per capita income, 10
Petrochemical industries, 4
Police juries: history of, 144, 145, 148; as parish governing body, 145, 148–52 *passim*; composition of, 148; turnover in membership of, 148–49; operating procedures of, 149–50; powers of, 150; services provided by, 150; employees and officers of, 150–51; and home rule, 155–56; and state officials, 173–74
Political culture: defined, 1; ethnic origins of in Louisiana, 1–2; and economic differences, 7; and political corruption, 10–11; and attitudes toward waste and inefficiency, 11; and politics as entertainment, 11, 85–86; and constitutional revision, 15; elements of, 301
Political parties: decline of, 11–12; and interest articulation, 256; defined, 256, 279; and two-party system, 258; and neofeudal political style, 259; periods of development of, 260; in pre-Jacksonian era, 260–61; following demise of bifactionalism, 267–69, 272, 274–79 *passim*; and modernization, 271–72; organization of, 279–83 *passim*; auxiliary organizations of, 281–82; and black political organizations, 314. *See also* Democratic party; Parish executive committees; Republican party

Politics: in life of Louisianians, 10–11, 254–55; definitions of, 285–86
Polls, 274
Poll tax, 322
Poor whites and the role of blacks, 288–89
Populism: philosophy of, 7; and property taxes, 9; and multifactionalism, 11–12; and disenfranchisement movement, 16–17; in post-Reconstruction period, 263; mentioned, 4. *See also* Bifactionalism; Bourbons; Long, Earl K.; Long, Huey P.
Poverty, 10
Primary elections. *See* Elections
Progressives, 264–65
Property tax: and Bourbon-Populist conflict, 8–9; exemptions, 8–9, 30, 31, 32–40 *passim*; administration of, 33–34; under Constitution of 1921, 34; amounts paid in, 35–36; as parish revenue, 157–58; collection of, 161–62; and education, 167; and municipal revenues, 200–201; and federal reimbursements, 230; mentioned, 173
Protestants: and Cajun life-style, 2; in legislature, 54; and Catholics, 269; and black voting, 301–302; mentioned, 5
Public Affairs Research Council: and constitutional convention of 1973, 22, 39; and property tax administration, 34–35; and local government revenues, 247; mentioned, xv, 9
Public Service Commission, 39
Purchasing contracts, 81–82

Race: and Democratic party after Reconstruction, 263; and demise of bifactionalism, 267–68; and political culture, 301; as political issue, 331–32
Racing: and funding of Legislative Council, 71; mentioned, 30
Rayburn, B. B. "Sixty," 80
Realignment in Louisiana politics, 330–34, 337–39
Reapportionment: and South Louisiana, 4; prior to 1963, 43; and "one person, one vote," 44; after 1960, 44–45; of 1921, 44–45; of 1966, 45; of 1971, 45–47, 52; and black political power, 47; and Republican party, 47–48; and Constitution of 1974, 48–49; mentioned, 229

Referenda, constitutional revision, 16, 18, 19
Referendum and initiative, 194
Religion and political culture, 4, 301
Reorganization. *See* Executive reorganization
Republican Parish Executive Committee, 282–83
Republican party: and neo-Bourbons, 8; disenfranchisement of, 16–17; and constitutional convention of 1973, 25; and election of 1979, 47–48; and reapportionment of 1971, 47–48; and police juries, 149; role of since Reconstruction, 257–60; and Louisiana congressmen, 257–58, 259, 276; as alternative to Democrats, 258; registered voters, 258, 283; and race, 275; and educational and demographic changes, 275; organizational efforts of, 276; officeholders of, 276; under Louisiana law, 282; auxiliary organizations of, 283; and blacks, 293, 308–311; and black political organizations, 314
Republican Political Action Council, 282
Republican State Central Committee, 2, 39, 282
Republican Women, 283
Retirement programs: for public officials, 82; for judges, 30, 96
Revenue-sharing: and aid to parishes, 159; and sheriffs, 162; state-local, 202, 245; federal-parish, 235; federal-municipal, 235–36
Right-to-work law, 132
Roemer, Charles, 9
Royalty taxes, 41. *See also* Severance tax

Sales tax: as part of state budget, 9; exemption for food and prescription drugs, 9; regressive nature of, 9; and parish revenues, 160–61; and funding for education, 167; and municipal revenues, 201
School boards, 166–68
Secretary of state, 172–73
Senate Finance Committee, 69
Separation of powers: under Constitution of 1974, 56–57; at parish level, 145
Severance tax: as part of state budget, 9; impact on tax policy, 9; income from, 9–10; eventual depletion of, 10; under Constitution of 1974, 30; mentioned, 13, 41, 84

Sheriffs: and law enforcement, 161; as tax collectors, 161–62; sources of revenue for, 161–62; and relations with state officials, 172
Shreveport, 205, 269
Slating: in legislative elections, 50; as evidence of bifactionalism, 266
Slavery: extent of, 286–87; and uprising of 1811, 287–88
Small-claims courts. *See* Courts
Smith v. *Allwright*, 301
Socialists, 263
Social services: level of expenditure for, 10; expected by populace, 13
SOUL (Southern Organization for Unified Leadership), 5
Southern University, 31–32
South Louisiana: alcohol, gambling, and race in, 2; economic and political changes in, 4; and reapportionment, 4; and constitutional convention of 1973, 24–25
Southwide Conference of Black Elected Officials, 304, 306
Speaker of the house: powers, 57–58; and selection of legislative committee members, 63
Speaker's Study Group, 59
Special districts: and parish government, 168–69; and intergovernmental cooperation, 251
Spoils system, 126
Standard Metropolitan Statistical Areas, 213, 251–52
State agencies, powers of, 141. *See also* Bureaucracy
State aid: to municipalities, 235–36, 244–45; to local governments, 244–45; to parishes, 247
State Bond Commission, 202
State central committees, 280–83
State Civil Service Commission. *See* Civil Service Commission
State employees: and supplemental pay, 81; number of, 124; turnover rate of, 128; productivity of, 133–34; and federal wage-and-hour regulations, 228–29
Steimel, Edward J., 37, 46
Succession, gubernatorial. *See* Governor
Suffrage: constitutional protection of, 226; in post-Reconstruction period, 262; before 1845, 261; under Longism, 265; of free blacks, 290; of blacks dur-

ing Reconstruction, 293; of blacks since 1960, 304
Superintendent of Education, 31
Supreme Court. *See* Courts

Tauzin, Billy, 259
Taxes: income, 7, 30, 133; corporation, 11–12; and social services, 13; and Constitution of 1974, 28, 30; and assessors' discretion, 159–60; federal inheritance, 231. *See also* Property tax; Royalty taxes; Sales tax; Severance tax
Tax offset, 230–31
Taylor, Dorothy Mae, 307
Television in political campaigns, 274
Tenure of teachers, 131
Ticketing: and number of elective state offices, 328; in 1960 election, 330; and political communication, 330; mentioned, 26, 171. *See also* Slating
Tobacco tax, 202, 245
Traffic Violations Compact, 242
Treaty of Paris, 89
Treen, David: as Republican governor, 75–76; and black vote, 308–309; significance of election as governor, 337–38; and political insulation, 342; mentioned, 75, 259
Two-party system. *See* Bifactionalism; Democratic party; Political parties; Republican party

Unclassified service: status of employees in, 131; advantages of, 131–32; political nature of, 131–32; mentioned, 128, 130
Unemployment compensation program, 230
Uniform Real Estate Trust Act of 1962, 243
Uniform state laws movement, 242–43

Unions: and reapportionment, 48; in public sector, 132–33; mentioned, 81
Urbanization: and centralization, 252–53; and support of Huey P. Long, 323

Veterans: and property tax exemption, 35, 38; and Civil Service preference, 125
Veto: gubernatorial, 58, 79; mayoral, 188. *See also* Item veto
Voting: of blacks during Reconstruction, 293; and black women during Reconstruction, 296; and disenfranchisement of blacks after 1896, 297–98; and election of 1979, 337; turnout, 340–41; changes in, 342–44
Voting discrimination. *See* Disenfranchisement; Election; Suffrage; Voting
Voting Rights Act of 1965, 2, 302

Wards, 148
Welfare: and federal grants-in-aid, 231–32; and interstate travel, 240; and state and local governments, 248
West, E. Gordon, 46
Whig party, 261, 262
White Citizens' Councils, 268
White primary, 301
Wilson, Jimmy, 259
Win or Lose Oil Co., 84
Women: as delegates to constitutional convention of 1973, 25; in legislature, 54; in legal profession, 94, 98; as police jurors, 149; black, 296; political organizations, 281–82, 313

"You Are My Sunshine," 85
Young Democrats, 281–82
Young Republicans, 283